P9-CKX-081

## DATE DUE

| | | | |
|---|---|---|---|
| | | | |
| | | | |
| | | | |
| | | | |
| | | | |
| | | | |
| | | | |
| | | | |
| | | | |
| | | | |
| | | | |
| | | | |
| | | | |
| | | | |
| | | | |
| | | | |
| | | | |
| | | | |
| | | | |

# Kakungulu

## &

### the creation of
### Uganda

# EASTERN AFRICAN STUDIES

\* *forthcoming*

# Kakungulu
# &

## the creation of
## Uganda
### 1868–1928

## Michael Twaddle

*James Currey*
LONDON

*E·A·E·P*
NAIROBI

*Ohio University Press*
ATHENS

*Fountain Publishers*
KAMPALA

James Currey Ltd
54b Thornhill Square
London N1 1BE

Fountain Publishers
P.O. Box 488
Kampala

Ohio University Press
Scott Quadrangle
Athens, Ohio 45701, USA

E·A·E·P
Kijabe Street, P.O. Box 45314
Nairobi, Kenya

**British Library Cataloguing in Publication Data**
Twaddle, Michael.
  Kakungulu and the creation of Uganda,
  1868–1928. – (East African Studies)
  I. Title II. Series
  967.61

        ISBN 0-85255-710-8 (James Currey Cloth)
        ISBN 0-85255-702-7 (James Currey Paper)

**Library of Congress Cataloging-in-Publication Data**
Twaddle. Michael.
  Kakungulu and the creation of Uganda, 1868-1928 / Michael
  Twaddle
      p.   cm. -- (Eastern African studies)
  Includes bibliographical references and index.
  ISBN 0-8214-1058-X, -- ISBN 0-8214-1059-8 (pbk)
  1. Uganda--History--1890-1962.   2. Kakungulu, Semei, 1868-1928.
  3. Soga, Gisu, etc (African peoples)--Kings and rulers--Biography.   I. Title
  II. Series: Eastern African studies (London, England)
  DT433.27.T87   1993
  967.61--dc20                                                    92-47361
                                                                      CIP

*The contribution of Danchurchaid*
*in helping to make copies of this book available in Uganda*
*is acknowledged with thanks*

Typeset in 10/11pt Baskerville
by Opus 43, Cumbria
Printed in Great Britain
by Villiers Publications, London N6

# Contents

# List of Illustrations

# List of Maps & Figures

# Note on Orthography

During the late nineteenth and early twentieth centuries the spelling of African names in Uganda varied considerably. Quotations from original written sources aside, I have simplified spellings (e.g., *Pokino* is used instead of *Ppookino*).

The name 'Uganda' itself was originally the Swahili version of 'Buganda' – just one of Uganda's pre-colonial kingdoms – but after 1894 it came to be used for the whole area of the wider British protectorate.

# Foreword

This study began in 1963 in a bicycle shed in eastern Uganda, where a local government official showed me a plaque prepared for erection at Budaka by British colonial administrators but rejected by the local people as no longer appropriate. The plaque ran thus:

> At this spot in the year 1901 the British flag was first hoisted by Semei Kakunguru, emissary and loyal servant of His Majesty the King. He built here a *boma* which was for a short time the headquarters of the district. From this beginning came the establishment of peace and the development of orderly progress in this part of Uganda.

These words were then repeated on the plaque in the Luganda language.

'That man', commented the official, 'created the Uganda which we Ugandans are fighting for today.'

I had heard similar claims made on behalf of several white men involved with the area of Africa now called Uganda during the British colonial takeover in the late nineteenth and early twentieth centuries, but none on behalf of any black African. I decided to investigate.

In completing my investigations I have amassed a mountain of obligations. Most of these debts are listed in detail in the endnotes attached to each chapter. But here I must thank my wife Margaret for her love and support throughout the whole period of research and composition; Ibrahim Ndaula for facilitating access to the Kakungulu papers; Professors John Hargreaves, Noel King, M.S.M. Kiwanuka, D.A. Low, Shula Marks, Ali Mazrui, W.H. Morris-Jones, Phares Mutibwa, Merrick Posnansky, G.N. Sanderson, G. Shepperson, Bertin Webster, and other colleagues and students at Makerere and London Universities for their stimulation; the British Academy and the Hayter and Central Research Funds of London University for supporting several visits to Rome and Uganda during the 1980s; staff at the Entebbe Secretariat Archives, Church Missionary Society, Institute of Commonwealth Studies, the Mill Hill Fathers, Rhodes

## Foreword

House, the Royal Commonwealth Society, SOAS, and the White Fathers for facilitating access to records in their care; Professors Holger Bernt Hansen and John Rowe for multifaceted support and help over many years; Professor John Iliffe for his encouragement at a crucial moment; James and Clare Currey, Mike Kirkwood, Keith Sambrook, Lynn Taylor, and anonymous referee for their expert help and advice; Professor Kenneth Robinson for reading an earlier draft; J. Bamuta, G.W. Kiggundu, S. Mudoba, D. Muloni, G. Nangudi-Gubi, the Hon. S.K. Njuba and C. Sentongo for help with questions of language; Professor Roland Oliver for supervising the London doctoral thesis, parts of which reappear in revised form in Chapters 5, 6 and 7; Ronald Snoxall for teaching me the elements of Luganda at SOAS; Professor Ronald Robinson for earlier educating me about Africa more generally at St John's College, Cambridge, and for his subsequent encouragement; and, last but not least, Ray Clarke, sixth form teacher at Battersea Grammar School, for still earlier arousing an interest in all 'past politics'.

Ray asked a question when I first told him of my plan to compose a biography of one of the leading African figures in what is now Uganda during the late nineteenth and early twentieth centuries. 'Will it be as complicated as some of the stories Maurice Cowling tells of British politics at that time?', he enquired. Cowling had been one of Ray's earlier pupils at BGS and he was currently reading one of his books. Alas, Ray is now no longer with us; so we will never know what he would have thought of the following account. But his question about complexity has been constantly in my mind as this work has progressed, as too has the comment by the official in the bicycle shed in eastern Uganda.

This, then, is the story of an important African political figure. It is both more and less than a study of one particular human being. From one perspective it is a study of how the circumstances commonly called 'imperialism', originating outside Africa but quickly becoming entwined with developments within it, created Uganda. This is not therefore just one person's story but concerns the dilemmas of a whole generation of East Africans. In other respects it is a somewhat extraordinary tale of a person whom one British colonial official considered 'in point of general intelligence, progressive ideas, and charm of manner ... far above all other natives in the Protectorate';[1] whom another dismissed, along with his companions, as 'no better than Masai or Nandi cattle lifters';[2] and whom yet another viewed as 'undoubtedly ... a partial religious maniac'.[3] It is a tale which has taken some considerable time to research into, both before and after Idi Amin's period of power in Uganda, and which must now be told.

# Notes

1. A.G. Boyle, 4 November 1908, SMP 1760/08, Entebbe Secretariat Archives (ESA), Uganda.
2. F. Jackson, 30 August 1900, A11/1, ESA.
3. Guy Eden, 1 May 1923, SMP 1760/08, ESA.

Plate 1. *Semei Kakungulu as a leading chief in the still independent kingdom of Buganda. Pictured together with his wife, Princess Nakalema.* (Reproduced by courtesy of Dr Theodora Crabtree, daughter of the CMS missionary: Crabtree collection)

# One

# The Road from Rakai
# 1868–88

## 1

Kakungulu was born in 1868,[1] most probably in the East African kingdom of Koki.

Koki was then a small state, no larger than one of the smallest counties in its eastern neighbour, Buganda. It was a kingdom in which leading positions of power were reserved for members of cattle-keeping clans whose traditions of origin linked them with Bunyoro, another large kingdom in the lakes region of East Africa. By the nineteenth century, however, most material ties had been broken between Koki and Bunyoro. Koki was now an independent state, but only just. Its herds of cattle, before the great rinderpest epidemic of the late nineteenth century, made it a constant prey to plundering expeditions by more powerful neighbours, as too did the iron implements for which it was renowned in the region. Its survival as an independent entity depended upon playing off one powerful neighbour against another, while keeping its own agricultural clans and slaves under careful control. Increasingly it depended, too, upon controlling an appropriate percentage of the manufactures imported into the East African interior during the second half of the nineteenth century, firearms especially.[2]

These firearms were mostly muzzleloading guns first rendered obsolete in Europe by the invention of the breechloader, then doubly so by the manufacture of the repeating rifle. They were brought to the lakes region of East and Central Africa by traders in search of ivory and slaves – ivory to exchange with agents of foreign firms for more guns, machine-spun cloth and beads; slaves, as far as the traders themselves were concerned, in order to service their trading centres, to present as gifts to local notables, and to carry their ivory back to Khartoum or to one or other of the Indian ocean ports. By the 1860s there were several such trading centres in Karagwe, then one of the very largest interlacustrine states. One was at

Kafuro, close to the royal capital of Karagwe (see Map 1, p. 3). Another was at Kyaka Kitangule, near the northern border of Karagwe with Koki, Kiziba and Buganda (see same map).[3]

Kitahimbwa II was the first king of Koki recorded in oral tradition to have exchanged ivory and slaves with coastal traders. His reign was remembered as having been 'a time of plenty; cultivation was extensive; millet, sorghum, bananas, and beer were plentiful; cattle thrived; people could move to and fro with greater ease than previously. Unexplained arrests, hurried sentences, the daily routine of previous rulers ceased'.[4] Though there is a large element of nostalgia in this account, control of coastal trade undoubtedly contributed towards a more relaxed style of royal rule in Koki.

Other external changes helped too. The political hegemony exercised over Koki by the kingdom of Bunyoro had ended by the early nineteenth century, and dominance by Buganda was only just beginning. Ganda power on the eastern frontier was considerable following conquest of the Buddu chiefdoms during the eighteenth century. From the reign of Kitahimbwa II onwards, Koki was expected to provide an annual levy of cowrie shells and iron products for the Ganda king. But neither development yet threatened Koki's autonomous stance too seriously. Indeed, for a time they strengthened it markedly. For while it was in the Ganda interest to retain Koki as an independent kingdom, friendly, deferential, and small, it was also in the Ganda interest to assist Koki against its enemies. Strengthened by this support, people from Koki raided more frequently into Nkore, another large kingdom on Koki's western side. According to one tradition, Kitahimbwa's son Isansa even poked fun in public at the king of Nkore's teeth; they protruded excessively, he was reported as having said. For that insult Isansa was slaughtered in a retaliatory raid, in accordance with the values of honour then dominant. But for reasons of regional interest as well as honour, Ganda warriors were soon induced by Bakoki to counter by killing the Nkore king himself in yet another raid.[5]

Isansa's son tried to play the same game, balancing this big neighbour against that one while at the same time amassing muskets and machine-spun cloth to redistribute to favoured followers. Like other East African leaders in the third quarter of the nineteenth century, Lubambula, too, tried to increase his power by creating a special corps of musketeers. That, as far as the Buganda kingdom was concerned, was going too far. From being a useful pawn in East African politics, Koki appeared to be consolidating an independent position that might jeopardize Ganda access to supplies of European firearms at a time of spiralling regional tumult. For while trade routes from Zanzibar still ran overland to Buganda through Karagwe and Kiziba rather than directly across Lake Victoria – the lake traffic in guns and slaves did not really develop substantially until the 1880s[6] – that was a serious possibility. When Buganda's most serious rival, the kingdom of Bunyoro, was thrusting southwards (as well as westwards and northwards) in order to gain a still greater share of the slaves and

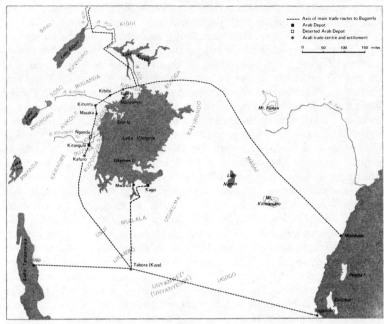

Map 1 (above). *Trade routes to Buganda and Arab trade centres.* (From Arye Oded, *Islam in Uganda* (Wiley NY 1974), p. 24)

Map 2 (below). *The kingdom of Buganda.* (From Oded, *Islam*, p. 2)

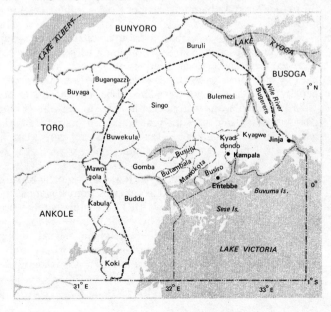

firearms available, that was a doubly serious possibility. Clearly the tiny kingdom of Koki had to be brought to heel.[7]

This was done through a plundering expedition. By the nineteenth century the power of the Ganda king depended largely upon two things: management of the chiefs by whom Buganda was then governed, and control of the scarce resources with which chiefs in turn attracted free followers and purchased chattel slaves, seized them in war or were given them by the king. In the third quarter of the nineteenth century, these in turn depended upon plundering expeditions taking place at frequent intervals: the resultant loot provided rewards for Ganda chiefs as well as the items of exchange which the Ganda king himself needed in order to acquire firearms and other scarce commodities from coastal traders. Elsewhere in East and Central Africa coastal traders had to consolidate fresh positions of power before they could obtain substantial supplies of ivory and slaves. Here they simply fitted into the existing pattern of competition and plunder, and stepped it up. In 1875 *Kabaka* Mutesa I gave one of his plundering expeditions the additional task of bringing Lubambula of Koki to heel. Its commander was Tebukoza, a Ganda county chief.[8] The expedition did not acquire very much booty: only 4,000 cows and an unspecified number of women and children as slaves – usually many more cows were seized.[9] Nonetheless, the numbers were high enough by Koki standards to drive the point of the expedition home to Lubambula. Within months he presented himself at the Ganda court, 'to make submission and to recognise the sovereignty of the powerful monarch of Uganda praying him not to invade his country in the future'.[10] There a European visitor found him three years later, again paying his respects to the Ganda king: 'Lubambula, king of Koki, Muhima chief under Mutesa's lordship'.[11]

Koki was now more than a tributary state. Besides supplying iron implements and cowrie shells to Buganda as before, the Koki king was expected to attend council meetings at the royal capital of Buganda just like any other first-grade Ganda chief. But if there was now an additional penalty to be paid, there were also additional benefits to be enjoyed. In 1875 Lubambula was seen paying homage to the Ganda king by a European visitor.[12] Later the same year Ganda chroniclers record that he himself was given command of a Ganda plundering expedition.[13] So, if at one moment Koki was treated as a tributary state, at another it was dealt with like part of Buganda itself.

Kakungulu's father benefitted both ways. Originally Kakungulu's family appear to have settled in Koki as refugees from Buganda, most probably during the reign of Kitahimbwa II.[14] Unfortunately, the precise reasons for this flight are now clouded by a clan dispute. What is clear, though, is that as Ganda aggression intensified against Koki during the 1870s, Semuwemba acquired a powerful position at the Koki court both as a diplomatic intermediary with Buganda and as a war leader in his own right.

How this happened was related by Semuwemba's last surviving son in the 1960s.[15] By this account, immediately after Tebukoza's campaign,

Lubambula sent a Bakoki delegation to intercede with Pokino Mukasa, the county chief of Buddu:

> The Pokino said he would take the delegation with him to the Kabaka. The delegates were now afraid that they would be killed. They decided to send Semuwemba, the only Muganda in their delegation, to see the Kabaka; if he died, it would not be serious. Semuwemba therefore went alone as the delegate of the king of Koki to the king of Buganda. Mukabya [Mutesa I] said that he was disappointed to hear that his obedient subjects had been suffering and robbed of their things, and he gave Kakungulu's father a drum called *Buganda mirembe* to take back to the king of Koki. When he arrived back in Koki, Lubambula was so pleased with Kakungulu's father that he made him his katikiro.

The story accords with the facts known about Semuwemba from other sources. But whether *katikiro* was the actual word used in Koki at the time to describe Semuwemba's new status is open to doubt.

*Katikiro* was the word used in the Luganda language for the chief minister of Buganda, both during the nineteenth century and at the time the interview with Semuwemba's last surviving son took place. It was then a natural word for somebody in Buganda to use of high non-royal power in a neighbouring kingdom, in a general rather than a precise sense. For there were crucial differences in structure as well as scale between Koki and Buganda during the second half of the nineteenth century. Semuwemba's new status in the Koki political system also seems to have been more diplomatic and less judicial than the role played by a *katikiro* in the Ganda one. The word *katikiro* is probably best understood in Semuwemba's case, therefore, as a general description of power rather than a precise delimitation of status.

Power Semuwemba certainly had now. When Lubambula died of small-pox in 1883 or 1884,[16] Semuwemba had a considerable say in the choice of a successor. The choice fell upon Lubambula's younger brother, Ndawula. 'The Bakoki became very angry when this happened', related another informant who was living near the Koki/Buganda border at the time. '"This young child who had no strength, how can he become the successor of Lubambula ?", they asked'. Only through the intervention of the Muganda Semuwemba, implied this particular informant.[17] Semuwemba appears to have been one beneficiary of Koki's changed position during the 1870s and 1880s. Kakungulu was another.

Whether Kakungulu was the natural son of Semuwemba was doubted by some Baganda subsequently,[18] but during the nineteenth century few such doubts appear to have been very widely expressed. Socially Kakungulu was accepted as Semuwemba's son, and would appear to have spent much of his childhood living in Semuwemba's enclosure near the *Omukama* of Koki's palace at Rakai. While staying there Kakungulu was presented to Lubambula by Semuwemba for service at court and, by one account, quickly became one of Lubambula's favourites; the mixture of parental influence with personal behaviour described by the Ganda chronicler as 'obedient' (*muulize*) and 'intelligent' (*omutegevu*) as well as 'manly and brave' (*musaja owamanyi era omuzira*) proving an irresistible combination.[19] The same combination eased access to the European muskets then coming into Koki. 'King Kamuswaga [Lubambula] liked him very much and gave him guns', relates the same chronicler, 'since at that time guns were still scarce and they were only given to favourites'.[20] However, Kakungulu's younger brother remarked that, as the son of one of Lubambula's favourites, Kakungulu would have had privileged access to muzzle-loading guns in Koki anyway.[21]

With firearms, Kakungulu was soon established in a minor chieftaincy at Rakai (see Map 1, p. 3). There, according to his brother Sedulaka Kyesirikidde, 'he did some profitable elephant-hunting for the king'.[22] There he also took part in several Ganda plundering expeditions as well as smaller Koki ones commanded by his father Semuwemba. Gayo Kagwa, another of Kakungulu's early contemporaries to be interviewed for this study, literally on his death-bed, remembered fighting with Kakungulu in three Ganda campaigns during the reign of Lubambula – the ones commanded by *Mutatya* Bunyaga in 1879, *Kajerero* Ngobya in 1882, and *Mukomazi* Ndalike in 1884.[23] Besides his share in the plunder obtained through these campaigns, Kakungulu was allowed by Lubambula to seize goats wherever he wished as a reward for his elephant-hunting activities.[24] Comparatively wealthy and powerful though this made him locally, Kakungulu nonetheless suddenly left Koki, probably early in 1884, in order to take service at the Ganda court.

In surviving fragments of what is virtually his autobiography, Kakungulu relates a story to explain this sudden transfer of allegiance. One day at the Koki court, Lubambula took away a gun from his younger brother Ndawula and gave it to Kakungulu, ordering him to apprehend a rebellious subject called Kazana. Kakungulu caught Kazana after shooting him in the legs. Unfortunately, after a few days the wounds turned septic and Kazana died. When Ndawula succeeded Lubambula as king of Koki, Kazana's death provided a convenient pretext for liquidating the man who had been the principal actor in his earlier humiliation at court. There had been a blood-brotherhood relationship between Kazana and Lubambula, and local people now said that Lubambula died because Kakungulu had broken that relationship. To put matters right, the same people asserted that Kakungulu also should now die. Ndawula did not disagree. Semuwemba therefore advised his son to transfer his allegiance from the king of Koki to the king of Buganda – advice that Kakungulu acted upon with suitable speed. When Kakungulu presented himself at the Ganda court, Kabaka Mutesa I created a fresh chieftaincy for him to continue his elephant-hunting in Buddu county.[25]

Symbolically, the Kazana story may retain some significance. According to some accounts, Kazana was a diviner (*omulaguzi*), according to others a spirit medium (*emmandwa*).[26] Elsewhere in the African interior at this time, new centres of power were developing to satisfy the additional demands for slaves and ivory created by traders from Khartoum and the East

African coast. In Buganda, these demands were met by increased specialization within the existing pattern of predation. Nonetheless, wherever
ivory and slaves were in increasing demand, traditional religious authorities
were under threat from new economic and military specialists. All over
the East African interior, the Kazanas were being challenged by the
Kakungulus.[27]

As an actual explanation of Kakungulu's personal motivation at this
time, however, the Kazana story must be considered suspect upon internal
grounds alone. For, however ill-disposed towards him the new king of
Koki may have been, Kakungulu would have been in no particular danger
when Ndawula succeeded Lubambula if his father remained powerful
enough – as he did – to protect him from the new ruler's wrath. Kakungulu
would only have been in real danger if he had also offended his father
Semuwemba, and this possibility is pre-empted by the story itself. This,
however, appears to have been what actually happened.

Gayo Kagwa and Paulo Kibi were two of Kakungulu's contemporaries
at the time. We have already noted that Gayo accompanied Kakungulu
on several plundering expeditions before Kakungulu's departure for
Buganda; Kibi became one of his followers shortly afterwards. According
to Kibi, Kakungulu left Koki after quarrelling with Semuwemba over
alleged cowardice on Kakungulu's part during a Koki raid into Nkore.[28]
Gayo did not mention this quarrel specifically, but considered that
Kakungulu's defection to Buganda with ten of the Koki king's firearms
was explicable in terms of his 'rebellious instinct' alone.[29] Both suggestions
ring truer than the careful fabrications of the Kazana story.

These fabrications we shall consider more fully elsewhere. But here we
should note that Gayo's testimony also half-makes a further point.
Kakungulu did not leave for Buganda at this time merely because he did
not want to work in Koki any longer. He also left because Buganda offered
better future prospects. This point was made more plainly by Sedulaka
Kyesirikidde:

Why did Kakungulu leave Koki ?

The Bakoki did not like him because he was a Muganda and because
he was becoming too powerful.

Did Kakungulu hold any important offices under Lubambula ?

He did not hold any important offices until he came to Buganda,
though he did do some profitable elephant-hunting for the king while
he was still in Koki.[30]

Too powerful, not powerful enough: purely personal reasons aside,
Kakungulu most probably left Koki for Buganda in order to enlarge his
room for manoeuvre.

## 2

Buganda stretches crescent-like for almost 200 miles along the northern
littoral of Lake Victoria. It is a well-watered region for the most part,

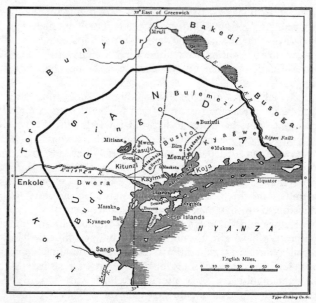

Map 3. *Sketch map of Buganda.* (From R.H. Walker, 'Notes on Uganda' in *Church Missionary Intelligencer*, March 1893, p. 199)

supporting banana groves which supply food throughout the year. Population was dense in the 1880s, but food supply was only rarely a major problem for Buganda's rulers. 'Food production was so sure and easy', asserts one authority, 'that it could be relegated to the background of life and left entirely to the women of the tribe'. By the nineteenth century, the male energies thereby released were devoted to the service of a centralized state. Because Buganda was banana rather than cattle country, those energies were devoted to a state in which a pastoral caste played no very prominent part, and in which cattle were obtained through plundering neighbouring countries as much as through local breeding.[31]

In the early 1880s Buganda was also an African kingdom where royal authority did not depend markedly upon any one crucially important royal cult. The reverse, in many respects, seems to have been the case. 'Ganda myth', asserts another authority, 'reverses the usual order; the gods (*balubaale*) came into being after men and, more importantly, after the king and kingship. It does not go quite so far as to claim that the Kabaka created the gods; but it does imply that the status of the gods, as of other important subordinates in Buganda, derives from service to the monarchy'.[32] Traditional religious authorities were not wholly unimportant in Ganda politics, as we shall shortly see; and at least one Christian missionary to Buganda in the 1880s considered the dominant possession cults not to be without spiritual attractions. 'Lubare is not a cold, bare, unmeaning system

8

of devil worship, as some have represented it to be but rather an attractive service calculated to fill the heart of the simple-hearted with awe and wonder and to captivate him with charms ... It is a mixture of Alexandrian Gnosticism and ancient Egyptianism'.[33] One does not have to accept the condescension (and evolutionism) implicit in this description to acknowledge its essential respect for an earlier African spiritual tradition. Nonetheless, the overall influence of traditional religious authorities upon public affairs in Buganda was decreasing in the nineteenth century; undoubtedly one of the reasons was the arrival at the royal court of Muslims from the East African coast and Christians from still further afield.

Ganda royal power had developed from small beginnings around modern Kampala, during the sixteenth century, to lordship by the mid-nineteenth century of probably half its ultimately largest extent. Besides expanding territorially, Ganda kings increased their powers pragmatically by displacing local leaders and replacing them with royal appointees. Sometimes these appointees were, or quickly became, leaders of clans. But, unlike their predecessors, these notables owed their positions to the Ganda king. With the territorial conquests of the eighteenth century and the plundering expeditions of the nineteenth, these men became the dominant influence in the Ganda political system. The king's power now depended essentially upon the king's men.[34]

Ganda royal power was managerial power. Elderly Baganda have sometimes exaggerated the sheer physical power enjoyed by nineteenth century Ganda kings. Ideologically, it is not difficult to see why they have done this – not only because it was a glory that had departed by the twentieth century, but because during the nineteenth century that power had itself constituted one of the main bases of Ganda royal authority. To be sure, granted the still pre-industrial level that Ganda technology had reached by that time, it is difficult to see how Ganda kings could possibly have been the absolute despots in practice that they have been assumed to be in theory. For, even in the 1880s, literacy was still limited, the wheel was still a recent introduction by coastal traders, and guns were still used as much for psychological effect as for actual destruction throughout the old kingdom. The authority of Mutesa I and his son Mwanga II did largely depend upon their effective power, and that power was considerable in comparison with the neighbouring kingdoms of the time. But its essence was managerial as much as technological. Externally, it depended upon the effective management of frequent plundering expeditions. Internally, it depended upon skilfully managing an intricately interlocking network of appointive chiefs together with the associated structures of clientage and chattel slavery.

The chiefs were essentially of three types. First were the *bakungu*. These were the territorial chiefs administering the ten counties into which Buganda was then divided (see previous page). One was the Pokino, who ruled the most westerly county of Buddu. Immediately under him were were sub-chiefs Katabalwa, Kagolo, Kajerero and Bugala; and under each of these came further successions of lesser dignitaries. Each dispensed

SEKEBOBO, CHIEF OF CHAGWÉ.        MTESA, THE EMPEROR OF UGANDA        CHAMBARANGO, THE CHIEF.
POKINO, THE PRIME MINISTER.
OTHER CHIEFS.
(*From a photograph by the Author.*)

Plate 2. *Kabaka Mutesa and his leading chiefs.* (From H.M. Stanley, *Through the Dark Continent* (1899 ed.), i. p. 152)

justice in the king's name, helped to collect taxes on his behalf, and assembled soldiers for his plundering expeditions. This pattern was repeated in the nine other administrative divisions of the old kingdom.

Scattered throughout the realm were also clan chiefs belonging to about 40 patrilineal descent groups. These were the *bataka*. Some descent groups had estates in five or six counties, others only in one. The Mutima clan, for example only possessed land in Buddu, while the Mamba clan had estates in Bulemezi, Busiro, Kyaggwe, Butambala and Mawokota counties, and on the Sesse islands in Lake Victoria. Each clan was distinguished by a totemic avoidance (*mamba* translates into English as 'lungfish', *mutima* as 'heart'), and each acted as a friendly society for its members. According to one ethnography of the old kingdom, 'the totemic system ... bound the members of a clan together for mutual assistance and defence, and it regulated the social life of the community, especially in the matter of marriage restrictions'.[35]

In Buganda there was no royal clan as such, the kings taking their mothers' clans as their own. Since theoretically every son of a Ganda king had a chance of becoming the next monarch, Ganda clans competed with one another in supplying wives for the royal harem in the hope of also

10

supplying the eventual king's mother. They also performed other services for Buganda commensurate with their size. Thus the Mamba clan, being a very large descent group, was responsible for canoe construction and water transport generally in the kingdom while the smaller Mutima clan supplied the court with certain fish and baskets on demand.[36]

Services of other kinds were performed for the Ganda king by a third set of chiefs, the *batongole*. Many of these catered for the immediate needs of the court, but some served more long-term needs as additional territorial chiefs, elephant hunters and border guards (such as *Mutatya* Bunyaga, with whom Kakungulu had fought in 1879 and in whose enclosure he would seek refuge ten years' later). Like the *bataka*, these chiefs, too, possessed estates scattered through the ten administrative counties of the old kingdom.

Possessing estates in each county were the four great chiefs of Buganda: the *Katikiro* and *Kimbugwe*, the king's first and second ministers; and his *Namasole* and *Lubuga*, the queen mother and queen sister. Being great chiefs, their estates were all exempt from royal taxes. Their subordinates, too, carried titles paralleling those of the king's *bakungu*. Individually, these four great chiefs also enjoyed the title *kabaka omuto*, 'the lesser king'.

It was an intricate political structure, and by the 1880s a highly centralized one. Not only were its constituent segments spatially overlapping rather than separate (as in many other African states), but each chief in each segment held office at the king's pleasure. Among nineteenth-century African kingdoms, Buganda appears to have been paralleled only by Dahomey in the extent to which the king was said to control the appointment of subordinate personnel.[37]

Plate 3. *The royal capital of Buganda.* (From H.M. Stanley, *Through the Dark Continent* (1899 ed.), p. 308)

At the centre of the kingdom lay the royal capital. Here were the king's palace, the residences of his great chiefs and the huts of the many pages and slaves who served them. Here also were the enclosures of the other leading chiefs, neatly divided off from one another by reed fences and banana plantations. It was here that domestic tax collections were started. It was here that major law cases were heard and that plundering expeditions were commissioned. It was here that visitors from abroad were kept, where they could be watched. It was here that the king held council with his leading chiefs, again as much to watch them as to benefit from their advice. It was here that many of the features of an advanced urban society developed: transient, neurotic, and competitive.[38]

It was transient because the royal capital never stayed in any one place for any substantial period, largely for sanitary reasons. In the reign of Mutesa I (1856–84) the capital shunted several times between Banda, Nakawa, Nabulagala and Rubaga, all sites in or extremely close to modern Kampala. It was also transient because the population of the capital was constantly changing as chiefs were replaced by younger men, sometimes palace pages in their early twenties, at other times youths in late adolescence. It was neurotic and competitive because few people knew when they might be promoted to high office or be executed for some seemingly trivial offence. All ultimately depended upon the royal favour and, military service aside, the most effective way of securing that favour lay through denouncing one's rivals at the same time as flattering the king.[39]

In retrospect it appears in many ways an odious political system. But during the 1880s it was tolerated by more than a million Baganda,[40] because their king was the source of patronage as well as punishment, and because by comparison with other East African kingdoms both advancement and justice were relatively open-ended. For slaves, to be sure, life-chances were much more limited. The subjection of most women too was severe. Nonetheless, however much the British missionary Alexander Mackay might condemn Mutesa I for being 'guilty of every form of uncleanness and robbery, and tyranny, and murder, and fratricide', he admitted to finding

> a strange anomaly in his character, viz. a seeming affection for some of his younger children, to which may be added a real sense of justice without respect of persons, in giving judgement in cases of appeal to him e.g. a sub-chief bringing a complaint that he had been plundered of his all by some superior and stronger officer.
>
> Strange to say, in this most lawless land, there is a never-ending amount of *musango* [legal disputation] going on.[41]

That Mutesa I's immediate successor as Ganda king, Mwanga II (1884–8, 1889–97), was similarly not entirely unjust in this sphere doubtless also lies behind Mackay's later remark to a fellow missionary that 'Buganda in spite of everything is better governed than Ireland'.[42] It was the 'genius of successive kabakas' to enhance their power 'by undermining the strength of localized clans and by keeping chiefs entirely subordinate and dependent on themselves', writes Martin Southwold. 'In such a system, where royal jealousy curbs the power of subordinate groups in the nation, the individual becomes relatively free. In Buganda the individual valued this freedom and used it to seek his own advantage by changing his allegiance from village to village and from chief to chief.'[43]

Relatively free, yes, provided one was not a chattel slave nor an ordinary woman – princesses of the drum were, by definition, extraordinary women – but only relatively. The strength of localized clans had been reduced by successive Ganda kings. But taking away offices from particular clans did not necessarily reduce the political importance of clanship itself. Indeed, in certain respects it enhanced it, by increasing the power of larger descent groups at the expense of smaller ones. As M.S.M. Kiwanuka points out, there was a clan establishment during the nineteenth century consisting of the Manis, Lungfish, Monkey and Grasshopper clans, which took a lion's share of all offices.[44] Kings Mutesa I and Mwanga II might change the balance of this predominantly masculine establishment by favouring particular clans and persecuting others, but an establishment it remained. To gain promotion in Buganda during these reigns, sometimes it was as important to change clans as to exchange chiefs.

As important as both was an apprenticeship as a palace page. That was the main avenue to chiefly office in nineteenth-century Buganda. But it was an avenue only walked by pages who distinguished themselves in bravery as well as in flattery. Gallantry during plundering expeditions was as important a qualification for future chiefship as deferential behaviour at court. Indeed, the successful acquisition of honour – what Baganda called *ekitibwa* [*ekitiibwa* in the modern orthography] – required both qualities to be cultivated assiduously.

By the 1880s, Ganda plundering expeditions had acquired formalized procedures. First the king, *Katikiro* and *Kimbugwe* would decide upon the enemy. The royal drums would be sounded and the leading chiefs gathered. Then an expedition commander, or *omugabe*, and a suitable second-in-command would be selected from the many aspiring generals at the Ganda court. The person nominated as *omugabe* would then brandish his spear before the king and swear that his leadership would be utterly fearless. 'My name is Kimoga. I was born at Kungu. My clan is Mpewo [Oribi Antelope]. Whoever meets me in battle, I will fight until I die: I will fight until I snap like a needle'. Those, according to Apolo Kagwa, were the sorts of words a Ganda *omugabe* would use.[45] They symbolized the values cherished in the hand-to-hand fighting honoured in Buganda before the onset of European imperialism and its seemingly unstoppable maxim guns: reckless bravery in personal combat.

After swearing allegiance to the Ganda king, the *omugabe* would daub himself with ashes from the sacred fire that blazed before the royal enclosure. Then more drums would be sounded in order to summon soldiers from the provinces, and within ten days the whole army would be on the frontier. There the *omugabe* would confer with his leading chiefs. There he would consult a spirit medium of the appropriate deity: Nende if the expedition was marching eastwards, Kibuka if northwards or westwards. There, too, the *omugabe* would review his troops. Then spies would be sent on ahead to locate supplies of food and to discover where cattle, women and other booty were located. Shortly afterwards, fighting would begin.

The disposition of troops during battle closely reflected the political structure of the Buganda kingdom. To the left of the *omugabe* stood the warriors of Buddu, Butambala, Gomba and Singo, each commanded by their respective county chief. Also on the left were the personal warriors of the queen sister. On the right stood the men of Kyaggwe and Bulemezi counties together with the clients of the Kimbugwe and the Queen Mother. In front fought the men of Mawokota, the clients of the *Katikiro* and the military commander's own men. Behind him stood the men of Kyadondo, Busiro and Busuju counties. The *omugabe* himself marched in the middle of the army, together with a growing number of royal musketeers.[46]

By the 1880s the distribution of booty had become as formalized as the disposition of troops. In his ethnography of the old kingdom, Apolo Kagwa gives sample figures for the shares of loot that Ganda chiefs might expect to obtain from plundering expeditions. The figures are only rough ones, but they show clearly enough what substantial rewards in slaves, wives and livestock chiefs could acquire both for themselves and for redistribution to their followers. Only the ivory tusks appear to have been retained officially by the Ganda king himself for redistribution and trade.[47]

Frequent warfare was now crucial for the maintenance of the Ganda economic system as well as the political one. But that did not prevent milder forms of exchange and procurement persisting, especially where ivory tusks and additional varieties of food were concerned. To be sure, Apolo Kagwa tells us that plundering expeditions were by now so productive that they deterred Ganda completely from trading with their neighbours.[48] He exaggerates. Concerning slaves, cattle and ivory tusks he is only partly correct, and concerning a wide range of other commodities completely incorrect. On the borders of Busoga, Bukedi, Bunyoro and Karagwe there were markets during the 1880s where a wide variety of goods could be obtained; while all over Lake Victoria Ganda traders acquired 'goods of less importance ... mats, skin rugs, other skins, pipes of baked clay, pots and drinking vessels and good carrying nets, baskets and similar items' in exchange for different sorts of fresh food, tobacco and coloured stuffs'.[49] Tributary relationships, such as Mutesa I's with the tiny kingdom of Koki, falling midway between plunder and trade, were also increasingly entered into as Ganda royal power reached its apogee in the late-nineteenth century. 'Ivory is imported into Uganda from Usoga and the Wakidi (Lango) district', reported another European visitor in 1883. 'Wasoga and Wakidi chiefs, bearing rich presents of ivory, are frequently to be seen at Mutesa's court.'[50]

Ivory was such an important item of exchange with the wider world that Mutesa I now encouraged a fourth mode of acquisition: improved cropping of elephants through specialized chieftaincies using firearms. It was to one of these posts that Kakungulu was appointed soon after being presented at the Ganda court.

# 3

Why Kakungulu gained promotion so quickly at the Ganda court is not difficult to explain. How he was presented there is far harder to ascertain.

By his own account, Kakungulu presented himself at Nabulagala with the minimum of preliminary introduction.[51] According to Salimu Mbogo, immediately after leaving Koki, Kakungulu took refuge with relatives at Lusalira in Buddu county who introduced him to *Katabalwa* Muguluma, who introduced him to *Katikiro* Mukasa, who introduced him to the Ganda king.[52] According to Paulo Kibi, it was *Pokino* Kamanyiro who introduced Kakungulu to the Ganda court, but nobody introduced him to Kamanyiro. Upon reaching Nabulagala, Kibi also said that Kakungulu presented one ivory tusk to *Katikiro* Mukasa before donating another to King Mutesa I.[53]

On the surface this is simply a confusion of evidence typical of any largely preliterate time. Old men forget, and when they lack early letters and diaries to jog their memories, their recollections of the past have to be treated with caution. When they also exhibit varying degrees of intimacy with the subject under discussion, their testimony has to be treated with additional caution. But here the problem is more than one of oral transmission and social distance. There is also a clan dispute, the historical echoes of which still reverberate in Uganda in the 1990s.

In 1918 Kakungulu renounced his membership of the Mamba clan of Buganda and stated that he was really a member of the royal Bito clan of Koki. His real father, he now revealed, was not Semuwemba but one Matambagala who visited his mother during one of Semuwemba's absences abroad.[54] The exact circumstances of this declaration we shall examine in a subsequent chapter, but here we should note that it caused an immediate rift among Kakungulu's relatives. During the 1940s, further complications arose when Kakungulu's principal heir decided to return to the Mamba clan.[55] Ten years later, the matter was taken to court. Publicly the Mamba clan of Buganda disputed with the Bito of Koki over which of them was entitled to perform the ceremony of presenting the death of a distinguished man's heir to the Ganda king.[56] The Ganda king of the day decided the case in favour of the Mamba clan, but the arguments deployed by the contestants continue among their descendants.

Biographically, this dispute has been disastrous for the dispassionate study of Kakungulu's earliest years. Today there are traditions defending the claims of four ladies to be his mother as well as those of two gentlemen to be his father: Nakibuka,[57] Kabutu,[58] Kyangwa,[59] and Kabejja.[60] The fourth lady may be illusory, but the first three are real fighters. Kabutu and Kyangwa are both Bakoki, Nakibuka is a member of the Mamba clan, and Kabejja is of indeterminate descent. Nakibuka is supported by the most extreme advocates of the Mamba clan – '*Mamba* marries *Mamba*', the only Ganda descent group, indeed, to allow this; Kabutu and Kyangwa by the more realistic ones who wanted to account for Kakungulu's Koki-like face. That problem did not arise for Bito supporters, of course, so Kabejja is good enough for them: it was the official name given to one of any leading Ganda chief's first four wives.[61]

Nonetheless, the struggle for motherhood pales into insignificance when compared with the confusions caused by the fight for fatherhood. Judged simply by the persuasiveness of their arguments, the Bito of Koki and the Mamba clan of Buganda come out roughly equal.[62]

On Matambagala's side there are two principal arguments. One concerns Ganda custom, the other political advantage in pre-colonial Buganda. The first argument is straightforward. It is not uncommon for a Ganda child whose actual father differs from the official one to conceal this fact – if known to the child – until late in life for reasons of physical safety as well as personal pride.[63] The second argument is more complicated. To start with, members of the Bito clan point out that several of Kakungulu's contemporaries are known to have renounced membership of large descent groups after acquiring high office in Buganda, thus strengthening their suspicion that Kakungulu himself originally joined the Mamba clan for political advancement before the British period. One contemporary whom we shall encounter later in this study is Alexis Sebowa. He became a Ganda county chief in 1889 and leader of the Roman Catholic politico-religious party in the old kingdom. Then he was a member of the Civet Cat (*Fumbe*) clan, but shortly before his death he admitted that really he belonged to the much smaller Reedbuck (*Njaza*) clan.[64] Bito clan members also say that it would have been politically unwise for Kakungulu to admit that he was 'a prince' – for that is what *bito* means literally in Luganda – during the 1880s. At the start of the decade, it would have been an obstacle to appointive office of most kinds in the old kingdom, while at its close it would have been dangerous for personal survival, too, in the succession war that had just commenced.[65] Finally, they point out that whereas Kakungulu's attachment to the Mamba clan had definite political advantages, it is difficult to attach any convincing motive to his subsequent renunciation of that enormous Ganda descent group in favour of the much smaller Koki-based Bito one.[66]

It is difficult in a purely Ganda political arena, to be sure; but not so within the wider setting of the Uganda Protectorate established by British colonial officials at the end of the nineteenth and the start of the twentieth centuries. For, as we shall see in the middle sections of this study, during the 1900s Kakungulu almost succeeded in making himself king of an area of the Uganda Protectorate in which previous political allegiances had been decentralized. One of the reasons he failed was possibly his lack of traditional legitimacy in British colonial eyes. His declaration of 1918 may be interpreted in part, therefore, as a belated attempt to acquire that legitimacy, though doing so in that year does raise a further question about why he did not decide to make his declaration 15 or more years before.

That, however, is not one of the Mamba clan's main arguments. Their supporters make two main points. One is that Kakungulu repudiated his membership of the Mamba clan shortly after a close relative in the clan seduced his principal wife.[67] Their other argument concerns Amani, a prince from Koki who became one of Kakungulu's leading followers soon after Kakungulu repudiated his membership of the Mamba clan. That, supporters of the Mamba clan allege, was no coincidence: Amani poisoned Kakungulu's mind in order to acquire a lucrative post in his service, and he only succeeded because Kakungulu was already disenchanted with the Mamba clan because of the seduction of his principal wife by a close relative in that clan.[68]

The two cases are as persuasive as each other. They are equally as unanswerable. This is not just because any biological evidence is now clearly irrecoverable, but because the two clan cases are as much a product of the honour Kakungulu acquired during his lifetime as of any antenatal activity by his parents. That honour explains why both Ganda clans have been so anxious to number Semei Kakungulu amongst their members. This in turn explains the extraordinarily imaginative lengths to which both descent groups go to tailor traditions relating to Kakungulu's earliest years to suit their subsequent social standing. So intricate, indeed, are the resultant patterns of evidence that it is now difficult to reconstruct with credibility even the barest outline of Kakungulu's career in Koki. That is all that is attempted in this chapter. Unfortunately, the clan dispute also distorts sources for his subsequent career in Buganda too.

His transfer to Buganda is one example. As a diehard Mamba supporter, Salimu Mbogo not only supplies him with a mother as well as a father from that clan, but also asserts that Kakungulu obtained his first office in Buganda through the help of Mamba clansmen. The relatives Kakungulu contacted at Lusalira belonged to the Mamba clan, and it was they who obtained the first crucial introduction to the chief Katabalwa in Buddu county.[69] Kakungulu's own account of the transfer was composed after his repudiation of Mamba affiliations, so this introduction is naturally ignored; instead he stresses that he acquired office largely on his own efforts.[70]

Paulo Kibi gives the most convincing account, but even his testimony is not untainted by clanship considerations. In fact, his evidence here supports the pretensions of the small Heart (Mutima) clan to which Kibi's mother's father was attached. Supporters of this descent group assert that Semuwemba was one of their members who took refuge in the larger Mamba clan during a period of persecution. Like the Bito of Koki, they believe that Kakungulu obtained his first chieftaincy in Buganda largely on his own merits as an elephant hunter, but say that he later changed to the Mamba clan in order to obtain further promotion. Unlike Bito supporters, they say Kakungulu joined the Bito in 1918 only in order to acquire the royal blood that was such an important ingredient of African rulership under British colonial overrule. He may have been unhappy because somebody seduced his wife, but that did not make him the victim of Amani. Rather it was Kakungulu who manipulated Amani when he considered it politically advantageous again to change his clan. In reality, however, Kakungulu remained a member of the small Mutima clan. 'It was a time of bad customs', commented a Mutima informant concerning the late nineteenth and early twentieth centuries in Buganda.[71]

It is certainly a confusing one for students of Kakungulu. The evidence for Kakungulu's earliest years is seriously contaminated by three clan claims, not to mention less persuasive gossiping by members of one or two other Ganda descent groups.[72] Simply supplementing the written sources for those years with oral ones does little to assist analysis. Rather it makes it still more difficult by drawing attention to additional areas of pollution which otherwise would not be taken especially seriously, as with the oral testimony of Paulo Kibi.

Admittedly, Kibi provides the most likely story, both regarding reasons for Kakungulu's departure from Koki and the political calculations underlying his subsequent changes in clan affiliation. His allegation of personal cowardice by Kakungulu also provides a tempting key to the excessive emphasis upon personal bravery in what amounts to Kakungulu's autobiography as well as in other Kakungulu chronicles. That emphasis now becomes explicable in terms of a man always trying to prove himself brave because of an earlier act of cowardice. Unfortunately for analysis, it is an imperfect key. The emphasis upon personal bravery in the Kakungulu chronicles is also explicable in terms of the dominant value system of the time which stressed the merits of such behaviour in small-scale hand-to-hand fighting; indeed, it would be difficult to make sense of Kakungulu's career at all without this continuous preoccupation with heroism and honour. Kibi's other remarks on Kakungulu's family background are also open to objection upon the same ground as those made by Bito and Mamba supporters: they are unverifiable.

A biography of Semei Kakungulu upon the usual Western lines is therefore not a serious proposition. In 'Biography and the debate about imperialism', John Hargreaves suggested that studies of 'the motives and social backgrounds of the prime movers of European expansion should help to define the problem more clearly', provided such studies 'stay close enough to their sources to relate any general theory which they may suggest to the complex historical reality'.[73] That may be a possible explanatory equation for Lord Lugard[74] or Sir Harry Johnston,[75] or even Sir Samuel Lewis,[76] but not for Semei Kakungulu. Reconstructing family background and early motivation may be practicable for leading British actors (or British-educated African actors) in the partition of Africa between European powers at the close of the last century, but it is impracticable for the main Ganda ones. Clanship was far too important a political matter for them to leave entirely unambiguous evidence about their family lives behind them. With Kakungulu's early years, all that we may seriously hope to do is to establish the main rules of the political game. On his actual parentage, or his actual motivation at this time, the evidence necessitates that we remain agnostic.

However, once this restricted analytical focus is conceded, the very confusions caused by conflicting clan cases may assume an explanatory significance. For, though these claims were a feature of British-controlled

Buganda and Uganda, in order to present convincing cases each clan concerned had to present a convincing picture of how the Ganda political system worked in the last years of pre-colonial independence, at a time when this period was still within living memory. Through their very confusions, therefore, these clan claims provide keys to the political and economic background of Kakungulu's early career that they remove from its foreground.

To begin with, they reveal a political context in which recruitment to chiefly office in the old kingdom remained relatively open, but where clanship was also an important consideration. On both the Bito and the Mutima views, Kakungulu simply presented himself at the court of Mutesa I and obtained employment largely on his own merits. On the Mamba view, he first obtained office through clan introductions. In the circumstances of Mutesa's last years, both were possible. Kakungulu's previous experience as an elephant hunter would have been valuable in itself, and alien origin no necessary bar to employment in the old kingdom. Nevertheless, clan affiliation was not unimportant and it would undoubtedly have assisted promotion to belong to a large descent group like the Mamba clan. In Buganda as elsewhere, it was no disadvantage to have powerful relatives.

The second thing each clan case reveals about Kakungulu's early career is the despotic character of the surrounding political culture. This, too, adds to the credibility of the various stories propounded about his parentage. In a despotic atmosphere, promotion is by favour. Character assassination flourishes, and in pre-colonial Buganda one of the chief forms this took was suggesting that so-and-so was not really the son of the man he said he was. So risky was life at the Ganda court that sometimes a chief would send some subordinate's son there as one of his own sons. So common in fact was this practice that Kakungulu's actual father may well have been neither Semuwemba nor Matambagala, but some recently captured or purchased slave, as an earlier writer has actually suggested.[77] In pre-colonial Buganda the despotic power of the Ganda king was linked to social and political mobility in an intricate manner, through substitutions of sons and changes in clan affiliations as well as through ultimate royal control over chiefly appointments and external resources.

Thirdly, each clan case emphasizes the associated political values of deference. Disagreeing over much else, each agrees that to succeed in traditional politics Kakungulu would have had to master what Ganda called *okufugibwa*, the art of being deferential to a superior, and each of their accounts of his early career betrays this basic value assumption. That art would have been taught to Kakungulu, along with the virtues of valour and the demands of honour, regardless of who his actual parents were, through proverbs if nothing else. *Omuddu awulira: y'atabaaza engule ya Mukama ye*: 'the obedient [slave or] servant is the one who carries his master's crown into battle'. *Sifugibwa: afa agera*: 'the man who says "I will not be ruled" dies without a roof over his head'.[78] This was something as useful to remember subsequently upon British colonial verandahs as for the moment at the Ganda royal capital.

These, then, were some rules of the political game in Buganda during Kakungulu's earliest years there. To succeed as a political actor, Kakungulu could no more afford to ignore them than anyone else could in the last years of Mutesa I and the first months of Mwanga II. But as an elephant hunter he had the additional advantage of economic utility to assist him as incoming British imperialism cast its first shadows across the East African interior. As a former member of an agriculturalist's family in a predominantly pastoralist enclave like Koki, with what a modern scholar rightly describes as 'the ability of pioneering groups or individuals to contract and manipulate effectively a wide range of kinship and other ties in order to mobilize the social and political resources necessary for colonization' in such situations,[79] Kakungulu was also well equipped to beat a hasty retreat should his fortunes in Buganda suddenly deteriorate. But, for the moment, that must have seemed very unlikely. 'Kakungulu was a crafty man [*mukujjukujju*] and *Kabaka* Mwanga wanted ivory', commented one informant from the Mutima clan.[80] The same point is made more circumspectly by Kakungulu's personal chronicler. 'Omulumba Kakungulu continued hunting elephants and participating in plundering expeditions with the leading men of the land up to the time that Kabaka Mwanga first lost his throne'.[81]

## 4

Upon presenting himself at the Ganda court, Kakungulu acquired 'many guns, gun caps and bullets'.[82] He also acquired land at Kyanyi in Buddu county as his base for elephant hunting expeditions.[83] Previously Kyanyi had been attached to another chieftaincy, but since Buddu was an area where elephants were still numerous it was a logical place to reallocate to an office specializing in ivory collection. The new chieftaincy was known as *Ekirumba njovu*, 'for hunting elephants', and Kakungulu himself was addressed as *Omulumba njovu*, 'Hunter of elephants'.[84]

Kyanyi was not a large place. According to a follower of Kakungulu at the time, the land attached to it was 'merely a *mutalla*' – a single ridge of land separating two swamps. About 500 people were living there when Kakungulu gave up his position in 1888.[85] Considering this figure included wives and children as well as male followers and slaves, it was not a very large number. Compared with a powerful office of the royal *batongole* in Buddu like that held by *Mutatya* Bunyaga, the chieftaincy guarding the southern border with Koki, Kiziba and Karagwe, it was small beer. But compared with Kakungulu's previous position in Koki, it represented a considerable promotion.

To satisfy the Ganda king's increasing demand for ivory, the chieftaincy was a specialized one. Mutesa I gave Kakungulu 100 guns as well as confirming possession of the ten he had brought with him from Koki. Special parties of hunters were soon working regular shifts under Kakungulu and sharing a common pool of muzzleloading guns. According to one participant, there were usually 30 men in each party and more than one shift each day. 'Sedulaka said he remembered it vividly as one of the elephants had only one tusk, so that the total number of ivories was 49. They took these ivories to the *Kabaka*, who said this was the first time so many had been brought to him as the result of one expedition. Kakungulu was made overlord of Ekirumba by the *Kabaka* and Kakungulu went to hunt in Bulemezi'.[86] In other words, so successful was Kakungulu's chieftaincy that its activities were extended beyond Buddu county during its very first year.

That year was also the last one of Mutesa I. In October 1884 Mutesa died and was buried at Nabulagala. Unlike many other chiefs, Kakungulu did not lose office in the general reshuffle of posts which followed the enthronement of a successor. Instead, as his personal chronicler puts it, 'he carried the personal favour of *Kabaka* Mwanga'.[87] This we may attribute to his economic utility; the story about a boyhood friendship between Kakungulu and Mwanga seems much less likely, and may just be another chronicler's way of explaining his subsequent devotion to the new king.[88] When Mwanga II first acquired the Ganda throne, eight muskets could be obtained from coastal merchants for one average-sized ivory tusk, compared with two or three guns for a female slave.[89] Given this exchange value of ivory, Kakungulu was far too valuable a servant to be ousted from office simply because he owed his post to Mwanga's predecessor. Furthermore, instead of supplying one tusk for every elephant killed like other Ganda chiefs, Mutesa I had arranged that Kakungulu should give him both tusks from every elephant killed by Kakungulu's followers.[90]

In return for this very special service, Kakungulu was granted certain very special privileges. To start with, he and his followers were exempted from the general ban on smoking hemp in Buganda. 'When he was *Omulumba njovu*', related one of Kakungulu's neighbours at the time, 'he was allowed to smoke Indian hemp as a narcotic with his followers; he did not have to cut his hair, and he looked very wild and brave indeed !'[91] Besides looking the most modern ruffian imaginable, Kakungulu also built up his personal following by raiding neighbouring kingdoms. Kakungulu was 'a crafty man', stressed another contemporary. 'During his time the young men of Buddu appreciated eating meat and dressing themselves with foreign cloth. Because of his craftiness, Kakungulu used to go and plunder cattle from Nkore with these young men and also to seize young boys and women as slaves. Then they would go to Kiziba with this booty. There he bought guns and gathered [an additional] group of youths with guns around him, about 40 of them'.[92] Muskets were as important an attraction to younger followers during the 1880s as hemp-smoking, foreign cloth and a full stomach. 'Kakungulu smoked Indian hemp a lot, and his young men did too. He had a drum with the beat "I eat what I choose: I eat what I find: I eat whatever does not belong to me".'[93] Without guns, that drumbeat would doubtless have been less extravagant.

Compared with the followings of the leading chiefs of Buddu, Kakungulu's personal clientage was small. But the growing scale of his activities and the increasing number of guns under his personal command made him more unpopular with the county chief of Buddu than many men with larger followings. Tebukoza had replaced Kamanyiro as county chief upon Mwanga's accession to power.[94] Kamanyiro had been *Pokino* when Kakungulu first acquired his post. Kakungulu was therefore not indebted to Tebukoza in any way, nor Tebukoza to Kakungulu: all the ivory that Kakungulu acquired in the king's name went straight to the king without Tebukoza himself getting any share. Irritation rather than interest arose from Kakungulu's growing power as far as the new county chief was concerned. What survives of Kakungulu's autobiography summarizes the situation succinctly: 'Omulumba Kakungulu and Pokino Tebukoza were not on good terms'.[95]

In 1886 Kakungulu seems to have improved relations somewhat by performing a special service for Tebukoza. A large plundering expedition was sent by Mwanga II against Bunyoro. Command of it was given to Kibirango, the new county chief of Bulemezi who also happened to be a member of Tebukoza's clan. For Kakungulu the expedition started badly. Some of Kakungulu's men were caught looting before the frontier was reached, something that was traditionally frowned upon. As usual too, the men of Buddu were all immediately answerable to their county chief. It was therefore Pokino Tebukoza who reprimanded Kakungulu for the looting by his followers. If Kakungulu himself displayed any trace of personal cowardice during subsequent fighting he would have to clear out of Buddu completely, warned Tebukoza. It was a serious warning, and Kakungulu took it seriously. Throughout hostilities he was careful to keep close to Tebukoza so that his personal recklessness in combat could be witnessed personally by his county chief. 'Kakungulu remained at Pokino's side even when the whole of Buddu had been defeated', boasts his personal chronicler.[96] Kakungulu also acted as one of Tebukoza's envoys to Kibirango to advise delaying the final assault upon the king of Bunyoro's forces until the following day, subsequently returning to Tebukoza with news both of Kibirango's death and of his own valour at the dead commander's side. After this Tebukoza evidently concluded a blood-pact with Kakungulu, and thereafter their personal relations were considerably less strained.[97]

More serious tension for Kakungulu arose from stress his new chiefship caused the Ganda king's chief minister, *Katikiro* Mukasa. Three stories survive in chronicle sources about this tension. In one of them Kakungulu's followers plunder Mukasa's cows by mistake during an elephant-hunting expedition. The chief minister brings Kakungulu before the *Kabaka*; Kakungulu is found guilty and placed in the stocks; but he is released through the personal intervention of Pokino Tebukoza, who journeys through the night to intercede with the Ganda king on his behalf.[98] Kakungulu is thus saved by a chief who is not only a more powerful one in the Ganda political system, but one of a different type. He is also saved by a chief who might have been ill-disposed towards him but for his personal bravery and the debt of honour implicit in the blood-brotherhood relationship.

In the second story, the structural opposition between *Katikiro* Mukasa and *Omulumba* Kakungulu is made more explicit. Tebukoza again acts as Kakungulu's saviour, but the *Kabaka*'s attitude towards the whole affair is made more ambiguous, and Mukasa's hatred of Kakungulu is ascribed to irritation at not getting his customary share of all ivory brought to the Ganda court, rather than to the personal cruelty stressed in the first story. The plundering of Mukasa's cows now appears as merely the pretext for Kakungulu's arrest. The real reason is shown to be structural opposition between the overlord of county administration in Buganda and a minor but annoying new functionary within the royal household arm of government.[99]

This point is also made in the third chronicle account of Kakungulu's confrontation with *Katikiro* Mukasa. Again Mukasa imprisons Kakungulu for plundering his cattle, but this time Tebukoza is not mentioned at all. It is Mwanga who orders Kakungulu's release.

> Then the Kabaka sent Lutaya to the Katikiro to tell him 'You seized my man Lwakirenzi [Kakungulu]; you beat him; and now I hear you want to kill him. Well, do not kill all of him. Just cut off one side of him and kill that: leave the other side alive for me'. Then the Katikiro ordered Kakungulu to be brought before him, and he asked the executioner 'Why didn't you strangle him and say he committed suicide?' After this the Katikiro ordered Kakungulu to be released.

There was clearly little else that he could now do.[100]

Besides illustrating oppositions between differing types of chief in the old kingdom, these stories illustrate further the surrounding political culture. At the old Ganda court, life was frequently both brutal and short. It was one of the attractions of Islam and Christianity in Buganda in the 1880s that both faiths offered assurance of a future life free from the insecurities of the earthly one. That point was implicit in our third story of Kakungulu's imprisonment by Mukasa. For, continues the same chronicler, 'After his release Lwakirenzi returned to Buddu and continued hunting elephants. At the same time he started to study the Protestant religion'.[101] The chronicler's account does violence to chronology – Kakungulu was already studying Protestant Christianity at this time, according to Sedulaka Kyesirikidde[102] – but the causal connection between Kakungulu's public insecurity and his private interest in Protestant Christianity is well taken.

European missionaries first arrived at the Ganda court in 1877, several decades after Swahili-speaking coastal traders from the Indian ocean littoral had introduced Islam. Islamic evangelization was a two-pronged process. First an accommodating version of the faith was brought to Buganda by the coastmen along with firearms and foreign cloth. Mutesa I assisted this sort of evangelization by making Islamic observance compulsory throughout the kingdom for a time. The popularity of Islam among artisans, courtiers and palace pages was further enhanced during Mutesa's middle years by the honour accorded to Muslim expatriates working at the royal capital, like Toli the Malagasy handyman and Idi the Zanzibari

Plate 4. *Alexander Mackay, early Anglican missionary in Uganda.* (From *Mackay,* by his sister (1890), frontispiece)

scribe. But then a rather stricter form of Islam was introduced in the 1870s by Sudanese teachers from Khartoum. This brought division amongst Ganda Muslims, when one northern *shaykh* sharply criticized mosques which were built facing westwards. When this stricter type of Islamic teaching also took root among palace pages, it brought the first known persecution of Muslim palace personnel for following their religion in Buganda.[103]

How Islam took such a hold upon young Ganda at court is not known with any certainty.[104] But, to begin with, it would seem to have attracted adherents within the kingdom because of its association with the tech-nological superiority of the coastal traders, its initally syncretistic character (and consequently the ease of adopting its rituals without immediate threat to existing religious practices), and royal support, especially during the middle years of Mutesa I's reign. Subsequently the association of Islam with technological superiority still appears to have been important for conversions. But by the 1870s it was the doctrinal distinctivenes of Islam, in its Sudanese form especially, which now appears particularly to have attracted Ganda palace pages. Given the competitive, neurotic and frequently harsh nature of life at court, this is not difficult to understand.

The ambiguous attitude towards Islam now adopted by the Ganda king is also understandable. Previously encouragement of Muslim devotion by Mutesa I had contained no obvious threat to his own position, but now palace pages were developing a separate loyalty which challenged amongst other things his right to lead Islamic prayer. In the mid-1870s scores of Ganda pages appear to have been slaughtered on the king's orders for this reason alone. Nonetheless, Mutesa I did not enforce a total ban upon Islamic observance throughout Buganda, and the Sudanese *shaykh* who had proselytized palace pages into a more fervent devotion appears to have been allowed to stay at the royal capital.

In 1877 the situation was further complicated by the arrival of Christian missionaries sent by the Church Misionary Society of London. Two years later, they were joined by White Fathers from Algiers. In December 1879 there was a religious reaction in Buganda against all foreign book-based religions, closely associated with the search for a cure to Mutesa's now extremely serious illness. However, when the expected cure was not forthcoming, traditionalist religious authorities were further discredited at the Ganda court and Christianity as well as Islam made further progress among the palace pages.

The reception of Christianity in Buganda has been studied by a number of modern scholars. With Islam it shared the prestige of association with technologically more advanced cultures as well as the initial favour of the Ganda king. With Islam, too, it shared the attraction to Ganda at the royal court of otherworldly dogma: 'heaven' seems to have been especially attractive to the adherents of all foreign religions in Buganda during the 1870s and 1880s. As John Peel points out, there are 'various ways in which a religion may be satisfying: it may bring its adherents material benefit; it may associate them with the prestigious; it may justify their good fortune or console them for their bad; and so forth. But the most essential element of religion, because the most inseparable from its definition and identification, is its world-view, its presentation of the relations of man, God and nature'.[105] However, Christianity in both its Protestant Anglican and Roman Catholic formulations in Buganda appears to have been accepted initially, even among palace pages, as 'a supplement rather than a substitute for the traditional obligations and moral code'.[106] 'Possession of a reading sheet or a rosary became a new sign of progress', John Waliggo remarks; and 'from this rather materialistic competition in acquiring the new religious beliefs, several pages gradually came to a personal belief in the saving power of Christianity, but always in addition to the new skills'.[107]

The enforced confinement of foreign visitors to the Ganda capital made both Protestant and Catholic missionaries more accessible to the strategic category of artisans, courtiers and pages. Paradoxically, public disputations between two brash young representatives of Protestantism and Catholicism at the Ganda court, Alexander Mackay and Simeon Lourdel, served to deepen rather than undermine the attractions of both denominations for this strategic category. For, as Waliggo also remarks,

Among the young pages two competitive allegiances sprang up. The courage, enthusiasm, eloquence, conviction and clarity of the two missionaries had greatly appealed to them. The battle of words had been conducted in the fashion admired by Ganda ... of pleading one's case or defending one's position. Unknowingly Lourdel and Mackay had distinguished themselves as the rival founders and advisers of the two allegiances – a position they were to maintain until their deaths in 1890. Their oversimplified and often incorrect summary of each other's faith was to remain the distinguishing symbol of their respective converts.[108]

Furthermore, because they and other Christian missionaries tended to stay at the Ganda capital for longer periods than Muslim traders, they also tended to be treated more like chiefs. Soon some Ganda were even asking 'to join' (*kusenga*) Christian missionaries on the usual clientage terms.

Kakungulu was not one of these. As we have already seen, he was established in a specialized chieftaincy in Buganda when he first expressed interest in the Christian faith. According to his last surviving brother, 'it was in Mukabya's [Mutesa I's] reign when he decided to stop the Arabs teaching any more' that Kakungulu first studied Christianity seriously:

When exactly did Kakungulu become a Christian ?

When they were still hunting at Ekirumba. At that time they were just beginning to read.

Who taught them how to read ?

Bwana Mackay.

Where?

Kakungulu went secretly to Natete at night and Bwana Mackay taught them how to read.

Was there any other teacher besides Mackay ?

None. Kakungulu visited Mackay when he was at the Kabaka's palace between his hunting trips.

When did Kakungulu first read the Bible ?

He first read Matthew, Mark, Luke and John, and Acts, in private before the death of Mutesa. They were in Swahili.[109]

In the light of these answers we may speculate upon at least some of the early attractions of Christianity to Kakungulu. As an elephant hunter with experience of dealing with coastal traders on the borders of Buddu, Koki and Kiziba, Kakungulu would have been conversant with the first language of Christian evangelism in Buganda – Swahili. As an ambitious young chief, he would have been aware of the high status already accorded to literate expatriates there like Idi the Zanzibari scribe or Mafta, his Christian Nyasa counterpart. As a periodical visitor to the Ganda court, he would have known that at the very end of his life Mutesa I's attitude towards Christianity was at best ambivalent. However, as possibly still a teenager when he first came to Buganda as well as an individual now involved in the highly hazardous occupation of elephant hunting, he would have been as vulnerable to its otherworldly attractions as any palace page, and as eager as any of them to fulfil the demands of the new religion.[110] Yet, whatever his precise motivations may have been, Kakungulu was careful to follow his new faith unostentatiously.

Indeed, so unostentatious to start with was Kakungulu's practice of Christianity that Christian palace pages did not even consider him to be a Christian – after all, he still smoked hemp and he did not cut his hair.[111] As a result, Kakungulu nearly got the worst of both religious worlds, the traditionalist Ganda one as well as the incoming Christian order.

In 1886, his personal chronicler considers, his life was at risk during the anti-Christian persecution. The persecution was probably sparked off by the refusal of Christian pages to take part in homosexual practices at the Ganda court, and by more general suspicions about their loyalty to the king.[112] Most of the Ganda Christians who died in the persecution were palace pages. The European scramble for colonial territory was now affecting the East African coast, and Arab and Swahili traders at the Ganda court warned that Buganda would be annexed in the very near future should European missionaries be allowed to become too influential at the palace.[113] A person who was one of Kakungulu's followers at the time says that Kakungulu himself was not in notable danger. He was away from the capital when Mwanga's anti-Christian persecution started; he was not a palace page; and he was careful not to go near the court until the persecution subsided.[114] In these senses, the follower is undoubtedly correct. The real danger to Kakungulu at this time arose from another quarter. It came from one of his chiefly rivals within the royal *batongole*.

When the anti-Christian persecution actually broke out, Mujasi Kapalaga was still quarrelling with Pokino Tebukoza over land belonging to the chieftaincy out of which Kakungulu's elephant-hunting office had been originally taken. To secure that land, Kapalaga tried to liquidate Kakungulu during this persecution.[115] He failed, largely because throughout the persecution Kakungulu was protected by Tebukoza. It is tempting to associate this assistance with the blood pact entered into with Tebukoza around this time, but this is unnecessary. Tebukoza's distaste for Kapalaga is sufficient explanation for Kakungulu's survival at this time. Such quarrels between chiefs were a constant feature of life at the Ganda court, and indeed one of the principal means whereby successive Ganda kings – and their subsequent British overlords – kept their leading officials under control. At a later date Kakungulu himself would suffer bitterly from another long-term quarrel with a rival official in Buganda. On this occasion, however, he was clearly a beneficiary from inter-chiefly tensions involving other high officials.

Nevertheless, in order to make his personal survival doubly sure, Kakungulu sent two extra ivory tusks to Mwanga II to remind the Ganda king of his economic utility. Upon receiving four more, Mwanga gave

Kakungulu a formal pardon.[116] From Mwanga's point of view, Kakungulu was doubtless too valuable a servant to be destroyed in a religious purge.

In 1886 Kakungulu may well have thought that he might die for being too Christian. Two years later, he must have realized that he had probably lost his first substantial position in Buganda for not being Christian enough. This was when Mwanga II was toppled from power in September 1888 by a palace coup.

## 5

When the coup took place, Kakungulu was otherwise occupied in the Buddu countryside. Upon hearing of Mwanga's deposition he went immediately to the capital. There he discovered that he had been ousted from his chieftaincy by the new regime, 'because you are a man of Kabaka Mwanga'.[117] His Christian allegiance was considered insufficiently pronounced to warrant him a place in the coalition of Muslim and Christian chiefs now ruling Buganda, and anyway Christian chiefs were less prominent in the new government than Muslim ones. Besides this, Kakungulu may well have been regarded now as a foreigner, and an unpolished one at that. His Ekirumba chieftaincy had also grown into a modest political prize during his five-year tenure of it, and now Muslim Ganda warriors seized it along with most other *batongole* offices in the old kingdom.

Ekirumba was given to Wakisonko, and Kakungulu himself ordered to hand over his guns to Kikoyo, one of the new county chiefs. Before collection of these was complete, 70 of Kakungulu's slaves abandoned him in order to join the following of Honorat Nyonyintono, the new chief minister of the Buganda kingdom.[118] In order, no doubt, to retain some sort of control over them, as the start of a new Ganda king's reign was a time when slaves might emancipate themselves if their former owner fell completely from political favour, Kakungulu too joined Nyonyintono at this time. His first attempt to form a substantial following of his own within the Ganda political system had however clearly ended.

Kakungulu's future attempts would be shaped by the Ganda succession war which now commenced. Not everything would change immediately. The material basis of the Ganda political system would not change overnight, nor would its associated value system of valour, honour and deference be transformed very suddenly. But during the armed struggle which now commenced, new communal ties of a politico-religious sort would emerge as well as new leaders brought to power. Much would depend upon which particular leaders Kakungulu supported. Much would depend upon how he responded to the politico-religious parties which would soon be formed. Much would also depend upon how he reacted to the British colonial entry into the Uganda region just when the succession war between Mwanga and his principal Muslim rival reached apparent stalemate.

# Notes

1. S. Kakungulu, 'Ekitabo kyakuzalibwa kwa B.S. Kakungulu', unpublished MS (written 1918) in Kakungulu papers (KP) in Ibrahim Ndaula's possession at Mbale, gives 'during the reign of Kabaka Mukabya Mutesa, when he was staying at Nakawa, in the year 1868'. The entry in Kakungulu's diary for 24 October 1905 states he was then 37 years old. We know from other evidence that Mutesa I's palace was at Nakawa between about 1864 and 1869.

2. E.C. Lanning, 'Notes on the history of Koki', *Uganda Journal* 23 (1959), pp. 162-72; J. Roscoe, *Twenty-five Years in East Africa* (Cambridge 1921), pp. 215-22. Regional setting is provided by D.A. Low, 'The northern interior, 1840-1884' in eds R. Oliver and G. Mathew, *History of East Africa*, Vol. 1 (Oxford 1963); J. Iliffe, *A Modern History of Tanganyika* (Cambridge 1979); and J. Koponen, *People and Production in Late Precolonial Tanzania* (Finnish Anthropological Society 1988).

3. J. Ford and R. de Z. Hall, 'The history of Karagwe', *Tanganyika Notes and Records* 24 (1947), pp. 16-17; R.W. Beachey, 'The arms trade in East Africa in the late nineteenth century', *Journal of African History* 3 (1962), pp. 451-4; A.D. Roberts, 'Nyamwezi trade' in eds R. Gray and D. Birmingham, *Pre-colonial African Trade* (London 1970), pp. 59-61.

4. Lanning, 'Notes', p. 165.

5. H.F. Morris, *A History of Ankole* (Kampala 1962), pp. 12-13; Lanning, 'Notes', p. 166; B.M. Zimbe, *Buganda ne Kabaka* (Mengo 1939), p. 177; S.Karugire. 'The emergence ... of Nkore', Ph.D., London University, 1969, pp. 400-3; S.Lwanga-Lunyiigo, 'The foundation of the Babiito kingdom in Kkooki', *Makerere Historical Journal* 2, 1 (1976), pp. 90-1.

6. G.W. Hartwig, 'The Victoria Nyanza as a trade route in the nineteenth century', *Journal of African History* 11 (1970), pp. 535-52; Lanning, 'Notes', p. 166; Low, 'The northern interior', pp. 332-45.

7. A. Kagwa, *Ekitabo kya Basekabaka be Buganda* (Kampala 1952), p. 129.

8. E. Linant de Bellefonds, 'Itinéraire et notes', entry for 18 May 1875 in *Bulletin de la société khedivale de geographie du Caire*, 1876-7, p. 77; Lanning, 'Notes', p. 171.

9. A. Kagwa, *Ekitabo kye Mpisa za Baganda* (Kampala 1952), Chapter 14, describes these plundering expeditions.

10. de Bellefonds, 'Itinéraire', 18 May 1875.

11. Ed. and trans. Sir J. Gray, 'The diaries of Emin Pasha', *Uganda Journal* 26 (1962), p. 88, entry for 11 March 1878.

12. *Ibid* .

13. A. Kagwa, *Basekabaka* , p. 132; J.S. Kasirye, *Abateregga ku Nnamulondo ya Buganda* (London 1959), p. 60.

14. E.M. Buligwanga, *Ekitabo kye Kika kye Mamba* (Mengo 1916), p. 111.

15. Interview with Sedulaka Kyesirikidde, Kasawo, Buganda, 27 March 1964.

16. Lubambula is reported in oral sources to have died a few months before Mutesa I of Buganda. Mutesa died in October 1884. In *Two Kings of Uganda* (London 1889), p. 57, R.P. Ashe reports seeing Lubambula paying homage to Mutesa soon after his arrival in Buganda. As Ashe only arrived in 1883, this would make early 1884 the most likely time that Lubambula died.

17. Paulo Kibi, oral testimony recorded at Namanve, Buganda, 1969.

18. M.S.M. Kiwanuka, 'Semei Kakungulu – was he a Mubiito of Kooki or a Muganda of the Mamba clan?', unpublished typescript, 1960. I am indebted to Ron Clarke for drawing my attention to this paper.

19. Paulo Kagwa, 'Kakungulu Omuzira wa Uganda', unpublished MS in Makerere University Library (MUL), p. 2.

20. *Ibid* .

21. Gayo Kagwa, oral testimony recorded at Kako, Buganda, 1968.

22. S. Kyesirikidde, interview, 26 August 1964.

23. Gayo Kagwa, oral testimony.

24. Temuteo Kagwa, 'Kakungulu Omuzira Omuwanguzi', unpublished MS in MUL, p. 3.

25. Solomon Wamala, 'Obulamu bwa Semei Kakungulu', unpublished MS in MUL, pp. 16-8.

26. Paulo Kagwa, 'Omukwano gwa Kabaka Mwanga', unpublished MS in MUL, pp. 1–3; Yona Wajja, interview, 10 August 1964.

27. A.D. Roberts, ed., *Tanzania before 1900* (Nairobi 1968), Chapter 15, and 'Political change in the nineteenth century', in eds I.N. Kimambo and A.J. Temu, *A History of Tanzania* (Nairobi 1969), p. 58.

28. P. Kibi, interviews, 1968 and 1969.

29. Gayo Kagwa, testimony, 1968.

30. S. Kyesirikidde, interview, 26 August 1964.

31. C.C. Wrigley, 'Buganda: an outline economic history', *Economic History Review*, 2nd series, 10 (1957), p. 71; M. Southwold, 'The Ganda of Uganda' in ed. J.L. Gibbs, *Peoples of Africa* (New York 1965), p. 100.

32. M. Southwold, 'Was the kingdom sacred?', *Mawazo* (December 1967), p.19. For further discussion, see B.C. Ray, *Myth, Ritual and Kingship in Buganda* (New York 1991).

33. *Church Missionary Intelligencer* (*CMI*), April 1884, p. 224; quoting O'Flaherty, 1 June 1983.

34. A.H. Cox, 'The growth and expansion of Buganda', *Uganda Journal* 14 (1950), pp. 153–9; M.S.M. Kiwanuka, 'The evolution of chieftaincy in Buganda', *Journal of Asian and African Studies* 4 (1969), pp. 172–85.

35. J. Roscoe, *The Baganda* (London 1911), p. 135, pp. 133–85. Nowadays, 50 separate clans are acknowledged: 'The Ssaabataka's Electoral Commission yesterday confirmed that there were 50 Buganda clans and not 52', *New Vision*, 19 June 1992.

36. Roscoe, *Baganda*, pp. 150, 169.

37. See L.A. Fallers in ed. L.A. Fallers, *The King's Men* (London 1964), p. 99.

38. For the nineteenth-century court, see P.C.W. Gutkind, *The Royal Capital of Buganda* (The Hague 1963).

39. The political culture of nineteenth-century Buganda is discussed in L.A. Fallers, *King's Men*; J.A. Rowe, 'Revolution in Buganda 1856–1900: part one, The reign of Kabaka Mukabya Mutesa, 1856–1884', Ph.D. dissertation, University of Wisconsin, 1966; M.S.M. Kiwanuka, *Muteesa of Uganda* (Kampala 1968); W. Rusch, *Klassen und Staat in Buganda vor der Kolonialzeit* (Berlin 1975); and M. Twaddle, 'The ending of slavery in Buganda' in eds S. Miers and R. Roberts, *The End of Slavery in Africa*, (Madison 1988).

40. Rowe, 'Revolution in Buganda', p. 6.

41. *A.M. Mackay*, by his sister (London 1890), p. 187.

42. Robert Walker to family, 7 June 1888, CMS Walker Papers (WP); now at Birmingham University Library.

43. Southwold, 'Ganda', p. 100.

44. Kiwanuka, 'Evolution of chieftaincy', p. 182.

45. Kagwa, *Mpisa*, p. 153; Roscoe, *Baganda*, pp. 348–64.

46. *Ibid.*

47. Kagwa, *Mpisa*, pp. 157–60.

48. *Ibid.*, p. 160; cited by E.M. Chilver in ' "Feudalism" in the Interlacustrine Kingdoms' in ed. A.I Richards, *East African Chiefs* (London 1960), p. 387.

49. P. Killmann, trans. H.A. Nesbitt, *The Victoria Nyanza* (London 1899), p. 40. See also Paulo Kagwa, 'Kakungulu Omuzira', p. 10; W. Grant, 13 November 1895, 8 January 1896 in A4/3 and 4/4, Entebbe Secretariat Archives (ESA); Roscoe, *Baganda*, p. 456; and J. Tosh, Chapter 5 in eds Gray and Birmingham, *Pre-colonial African Trade* (London 1970).

50. Emin Pasha, 'On trade and commerce among the Waganda and Wanyoro', 1883; repr. in G. Schweinfurth *et al.*, eds, *Emin Pasha in Central Africa* (London 1888), pp. 117–18.

51. Wamala, 'Obulamu' p. 18.

52. S. Mbogo, oral testimony recorded at Kachumbala, Teso, 1968.

53. P. Kibi, testimony, 1968 and 1969.

54. S. Kakungulu, 'Ekitabo kyakuzalibwa', p. 1; also his will reprinted in *Ebifa mu Buganda* (1929), p. 68.

55. I. Kakungulu to Mengo, 12 September 1957, concerning case No. 12/57: Gabunga v Ssaababiito', copy in KP.

56. *Ibid.*

57. Salimu Mbogo, many times.

58. I.B.M. Nsubuga, 'Obuwandike oluzala bwa S.M.N. Kakungulu' (KP, 1958), p. 1.

59. J.M. Gray. 'Kakunguru in Bukedi', *Uganda Journal* 27 (1963), p. 31; Yona Wajja, interview at my home at Mbale, 10 August 1964.
60. Enoka Maleza, interview at his home at Siroko, Bugisu, 4 July 1964.
61. Le Veux, *Premier essai de vocabulaire Luganda* (Algiers 1917), p. 274; Salimu Mbogo, interview, 11 July 1964.
62. Consideration here must start with an unpublished paper by M.S.M. Kiwanuka cited in note 18, 'Semei Kakungulu – was he a Mubiito of Koki or a Muganda of the Mamba Clan?' This was composed in association with the late Erisa Kironde in 1960, and analyses litigation between these two clans in 1957 and 1958. My account is indebted to it, but draws upon further interviews with supporters of both clans and also takes account of the Mutima clan which was not considered by Kiwanuka and Kironde.
63. M.S.M. Kiwanuka, 'Semei Kakungulu', also stresses this point.
64. Noted in Ssaababiito to Kabaka, 5 May 1958, copy in KP; Kagwa, *Basekabaka*, p. 273, gives Sebowa as a member of the Fumbe clan, just as Kagwa, *Mpisa*, p. 83, attaches Kakungulu to the Mamba clan.
65. This is discussed further in Chapter 2.
66. That was the burden of Ssaababiito's arguments in the 1950s.
67. See below, p. 287.
68. Kiwanuka, 'Semei Kakungulu', gives the best account.
69. Salimu Mbogo, several interviews.
70. Wamala, 'Obulamu', p. 18. The relevant section of S. Kakungulu, 'Ekitabo kyakuzalibwa', is missing.
71. Paulo Kibi, testimony, 1969.
72. I have heard other Ganda state that Kakungulu's clan was another one, but their contenders were less plausible than the three considered here.
73. J.D. Hargreaves, 'Biography and the debate about imperialism', *Journal of Modern African Studies* 2 (1964), pp. 279–85.
74. M. Perham, *Lugard, The Years of Adventure, 1858–1898* (London 1956).
75. R. Oliver, *Sir Harry Johnston and the Scramble for Africa* (London 1959).
76. J.D. Hargreaves, *Life of Sir Samuel Lewis* (London 1959).
77. H.B. Thomas, 'Capax Imperii – the story of Semei Kakungulu', *Uganda Journal* 6 (1939), p. 125.
78. F.Walzer, *Luganda Proverbs* (Berlin 1982).
79. R.Waller, 'Ecology, migration and expansion in East Africa', *African Affairs* 84 (1985), p. 349.
80. Danieri Kato, oral testimony recorded at Kako, Buganda, 1968.
81. Wamala, 'Obulamu', p. 21.
82. *Ibid.*, p. 18.
83. *Ibid.*
84. *Ibid.*
85. Paulo Kibi, testimony, 1969.
86. S.Kyesirikidde, interview, 27 March1964.
87. Wamala, 'Obulamu', p. 19.
88. Paulo Kagwa, 'Omukwano', p. 1.
89. Testimony of Paulo Kibi's father, related by Kibi.
90. S.Kyesirikidde, interview, 26 August 1964.
91. S.Tekiwagala, interview at his home at Nakaloke, Mbale, 17 August 1965.
92. Paulo Kibi, testimony, 1969.
93. *Ibid.*
94. Kagwa, *Basekabaka*, p. 145.
95. Wamala, 'Obulamu', p. 19; identical here to account in S. Kakungulu, 'Ekitabo kyakuzalibwa'.
96. Wamala, 'Obulamu', p. 21.
97. Wamala, 'Obulamu', pp. 19–21; Paulo Kagwa, 'Omukwano', pp. 3–4; Paulo Kibi, testimony, 1969; Yona Wajja, interview, 10 August 1964.
98. Paulo Kagwa, 'Omukwano', pp. 5–6.
99. Temuteo Kagwa, 'Kakungulu', pp. 5–6.
100. Paulo Kagwa, 'Kakungulu Omuzira', pp. 2–3.

101. *Ibid.*
102. Interviewed in 1964.
103. A. Katumba and F.B. Welbourn, 'Muslim martyrs of Buganda', *Uganda Journal* 28 (1964), pp. 151–63; Ham Mukasa, *Simuda Nyuma* (London 1938), pp. 18–23.
104. Rowe, 'Revolution in Buganda', pp. 46–94; A. Oded, *Islam in Uganda* (Jerusalem 1974); A.B.K. Kasozi, *The Spread of Islam in Uganda* (Nairobi 1986).
105. J.D.Y. Peel, 'Conversion and tradition in two African societies: Ijebu and Buganda', *Past & Present*, 77 (1977), pp. 121–2. Other studies include J.V. Taylor, *The Growth of the Church in Buganda* (London 1958); D.A. Low, 'Converts and martyrs in Buganda' in G.C. Baeta, ed., *Christianity in Tropical Africa* (London 1968); A. Hastings, 'From mission to church in Buganda', *Zeitschrift für Missionswissenschaft und Religionswissenschaft* 53 (1969), pp. 206–28; J. Waliggo, 'The religio-political context of the Uganda martyrs', *African Christian Studies* 2, 1 (Nairobi 1986), pp. 3–40; L. Pirouet, 'Traditional religion and the response to Christianity . . . Uganda', *Geographia Religionen* 6 (Berlin 1989), pp. 191–200.
106. J. Waliggo, 'The religio-political context', p. 25.
107. *Ibid.*
108. Waliggo, 'The religio-political context', pp. 12–13.
109. S.Kyesirikidde, interview, 27 March 1964.
110. On elephant hunters, see White Fathers, *Rubaga Diary* [RD], 9 September 1986 and below, p. 80.
111. Paulo Kibi, testimony, 1968 and 1969.
112. Aspects are discussed in Waliggo, 'The religio-political context'; R. Kassimir, 'Uganda martyrs: Catholic or Christian ?', *New Vision*, 22–23 January 1992; J.F. Faupel, *African Holocaust* (London 1965); J.A. Rowe, 'The purge of Christians at Mwanga's court', *Journal of African History* 5 (1964), pp. 55–72; and L. Pirouet, *Strong in the Faith* (Mukono 1969).
113. N.R. Bennett, *Arab versus European: Diplomacy and War in Nineteenth-century East Central Africa* (New York 1986), Chapter 13.
114. Paulo Kibi, testimony, 1969.
115. Wamala, 'Obulamu', p. 21.
116. *Ibid.*
117. *Ibid.*
118. Wamala, 'Obulamu', p. 22.

# Two

# Conflict in Buganda
# 1888–90

## 1

This was not the first succession war in the history of Buganda, nor would it be the last.[1]

Ganda kingship was a considerable political prize, and by the nineteenth century the only substantial one to which princes of the drum might aspire. As such, it was a prize open to many competitors. The royal harem was by now enormous and, as we have noted, theoretically any son or brother of a Ganda king could become his successor. Because the roles played in the traditional political system by the Queen Mother and her relatives were so prominent, any princely contender for the Ganda throne could depend for at least part of his support upon his mother's brothers. But, to stand any real chance of success, he would also have to build further alliances with other *bataka* dignitaries as well as with *bakungu* and *batongole* chiefs disenchanted with the current regime or linked personally to his kinsmen through marriage or the special attachment of blood-brotherhood. Since the stakes were so high, such alliances were being constructed continuously. In the old Buganda kingdom, princely rebellion was endemic.

Strife was especially strong at the start of a reign, when the rivals of a new king's supporters were likely to fight for another prince before those supporters had had time to establish themselves in power. Strife was also stronger when the system of royal succession tended to be fraternal rather than father-to-son. This appears to have been the case during the middle period of Ganda kingship, in the seventeenth and eighteenth centuries, when the kingdom was under pressure from Bunyoro and in constant need of mature military leadership. One particularly acute crisis occurred at the end of this period, when *Kabaka* Junju was murdered by supporters of his successor, Semakokiro. Junju and Semakokiro were full brothers; that is to say, they shared a mother as well as a father, and this murder not only violated Ganda customary values for that reason, but threw Buganda off balance by interrupting the circulation of the kingship among different descent groups.[2]

This particular crisis was resolved, partly by Semakokiro himself slaughtering most surviving princes of the drum shortly after ascending the Ganda throne, and then killing off the clansmen of one of the few princes who remained; partly also by nominating a successor clearly attached to another descent-group. 'You will eat Buganda as an orphan', Semakokiro is reputed to have told Kamanya, the son he wished to succeed him.[3] Semakokiro also constructed prisons for princes and continued the earlier exclusion of persons of royal descent from *bakungu* and *batongole* offices. But excluding princes of the drum from lower and middle-grade administrative positions in the kingdom further enhanced the attractiveness of the top royal one, while murdering possible rivals to the kingship increased seditiousness among the survivors.

Kamanya's reign is remembered in Ganda tradition as one 'marked by constant rebellions and disturbances'.[4] He had to do battle with another son of Semakokiro even before completing his installation rituals, while a third caused trouble on the frontier when these rituals were complete. That brother was pardoned by Semakokiro, one chronicler tells us, 'because he was a father of twins and because the oracles had given a warning that should he be executed the king would die. But he was banished to Bunyoro all the same'.[5] There that particular brother acquired armed support, with which he returned to plunder Buganda. But memorable though the resultant raids were in their daring – so much so that subsequently Semei Kakungulu took his principal surname from this very chief – Prince Kakungulu nonetheless failed to replace Kamanya as king of Buganda and instead later died obscurely in Busoga.[6] When Kamanya himself died his place was taken by his son Suna, then only about 12 years old.

In arranging this succession, a crucial role was played by Kamanya's chief minister, Sebuko. A similarly strategic role was played subsequently by Suna's chief minister, Kayira, when Suna himself died and was replaced by another young prince, Mutesa – and by *Katikiro* Mukasa when Mutesa in turn died and was replaced by his son Mwanga in 1884. The shift back to a father-to-son system of succession clearly increased the power of a Ganda chief minister, both during the very first years of a king's reign and at its close. The status of a *katikiro* was further enhanced by the increasingly prominent legal and economic roles played by this functionary in the system of gift exchange in slaves, firearms, ivory, cattle and cloth which developed so much more intensively at the Ganda court with the growing importance of the caravan trade with the East African coast.[7]

Raiding for slaves in surrounding areas was of course ancient, but it much increased as a result of the caravan trade. Slaves traditionally provided the royal capital with food, and chiefs with administrative orderlies as well as workmen and workwomen. Most free persons in Buganda also employed slaves as labourers on their farms. Chiefs with sizeable numbers of slaves found it easier to attract and retain the services of freemen as followers, and easier therefore to respond competently to royal demands for road-building and the provision of warriors for plundering expeditions against neighbouring countries. Slavery was also crucial in providing the poorest followers of a Ganda chief with wives, and chiefs themselves with additional women.[8] However, when the caravan trade with the East African coast led to a significant outflow of slaves as well as ivory, Mutesa I confessed privately to a British missionary that if the outflow continued unabated he feared for the future stability of his kingdom.[9] Mutesa died peacefully in his bed, nonetheless, and it was his son Mwanga who inherited the whirlwind – suppressing several abortive princely rebellions before succumbing to a successful one in September 1888.

Nonetheless, from the longer-term perspective, this particular change of regime appears both less and more distinctive than is sometimes thought. Less distinctive, because like earlier princely rebellions in Buganda it was much more a *coup d'état* than a massive social dislocation, and one organized by a coalition of Ganda chiefs mobilized in the traditional manner.[10] More distinctive, because with the possible exception of the deposition of King Kagulu during the middle period of Ganda kingship,[11] the rebellion against Mwanga II in September 1888 was ultimately to involve the populace of Buganda as intimately as the palace in its final resolution.

But here we must be careful. Popular involvement in the ensuing succession war was a result of the deposition of Mwanga II, not (as apparently in the case of Kagulu) its cause. In Ganda tradition as analysed by a modern scholar, Kagulu appears as an impossibly arbitrary and tyrannical king in comparison with whom Mutesa I seems to have been both sage and benevolent.[12] Yet, barely a year before his deposition, elderly Ganda were telling European missionaries that, despite his massacring of Christian palace pages, Mwanga struck them as being kinder and gentler than Mutesa had been while a youth.[13] For sheer tyranny, Mwanga II was easily outclassed by his father, grandfather and great-grandfather, each of whom was remembered in Ganda tradition at the time of the British colonial takeover as having 'become uncontrollable' at some stage during their respective reigns.[14] This is something that Mwanga himself never became. The massacring of Christian Ganda during his reign was largely confined to the palace compound. Mwanga's deposition in September 1888 was also organized by chiefs living close to the palace. The Ganda populace only came in when the ensuing succession war turned into something approaching a revolution.

The use of firearms and the influence of foreign religions are also said to distinguish this particular succession war from earlier ones in Buganda.[15] As will be shown, guns were important, but not overwhelmingly so, in deciding issues as hostilities widened from a palace coup into a wider war – or at least not until such time as British colonial intruders into the Uganda region demonstrated how devastating their more advanced rifles and machine guns could be when supported by more effective military organization. For a palace coup in the immediate pre-British period, to be sure, muzzleloading guns were of immense importance, and Mwanga II's concentration of so many of them into especially favoured *batongole* chieftaincies close to his capital made his replacement by Kiwewa as Ganda king through the agency of these very same musketeers especially easy to effect. But for a war of attrition, in which food supplies, intelligence about enemy positions, and sheer weight of numbers were to prove on occasion as important as anything else, muzzleloading guns would prove a decidedly mixed blessing in the hands of rival African armies still fighting one another with tactics inherited from the pre-muzzleloading era.

Islam and Christianity, on the other hand, were to play increasingly important roles as hostilities widened to include the populace as well as the palace. This was not inevitable. To be sure, the deposition of Mwanga II had been prompted by fears that followers of foreign religions in Buganda might all be stranded on some deserted island in Lake Victoria and left there to starve. Also, as the principal rebels in September 1888 were Muslim and Christian Ganda, many of the new chiefs, not unnaturally, were Muslim and Christian.[16] But these new chiefs were still linked to their countrymen by clanship and marriage as well as divided off from most of them by religion; Ganda society, after all, was (and is) polygynous and criss-crossed by extended families. By manipulating each criss-crossing tie as occasion allowed, and by exploiting the inevitable inter-personal tensions which would arise among the new chiefs, the new king should have been able to build himself up very quickly to the position enjoyed by his immediate predecessor a few months before his overthrow. But what Mwanga's first successor, Kiwewa, undoubtedly did not expect, was that foreign religious allegiances would within weeks be given further significance in Ganda politics by unforeseen events, and that soon he himself would be replaced upon the Ganda throne by yet another prince.

There is also a related point here. Insofar as there was a Christian grouping in Ganda politics as opposed to a Muslim one immediately after the deposition of Mwanga II, it was a relatively undifferentiated one politically. While European missionaries at the Ganda court quarrelled publicly over doctrinal differences, Ganda converts privately agreed over sociological similarities. We have already noted that earlier in the decade Alexander Mackay had denounced Roman Catholic theology before the Ganda king and Simeon Lourdel had countered with insinuations about Anglican Christianity. Both Mackay and Lourdel built up intensely loyal and competing personal followings of converts as a direct consequence of those public debates.[17] Mackay went further and advised his Protestant converts not to consort with Catholics at all, advice that he continued to bombard them with from his new base at the southern end of Lake Victoria at the end of the 1880s; but, as Ham Mukasa wrote subsequently, and without conscious irony, 'we were too foolish to listen to him'.[18] John Waliggo also tells us that the leading Catholic Ganda converts 'continued long after joining the Catholic mission to get lessons from Mackay and to read his books'.[19] The first Protestant converts visited Lourdel too for lessons in gun-repairing. Indeed, in Nyonyintono's enclosure at this time, a Ganda Protestant tells us that 'nobody could tell whether one was a Catholic or a Protestant since we all behaved in a similar way – the Christian way'.[20] Had the situation been otherwise, it is hardly conceivable that Semei Kakungulu would have fought as energetically as he now did on the side of Honorat Nyonyintono, slaves or no slaves. For while in European missionary parlance Nyonyintono was clearly Roman Catholic, Kakungulu (or 'Wakilenzi' as he was still known at this time) was 'a Protestant'.[21]

## 2

The opportunity for Semei Kakungulu to display reckless bravery on Nyonyintono's side came about six weeks after the establishment of the new government in Buganda, when the new ruling coalition of Muslim and Christian chiefs was disrupted and Nyonyintono and other Christians were suddenly forced to flee from the capital.

It was Dungu's fault, said the Muslims. Dungu, a Christian firebrand, had just returned from a tribute-collecting trip to the Bahaya chiefdoms beyond Buddu county, whence he had been sent by the previous Ganda monarch. Upon Mwanga's deposition a middle-grade office in Kyagwe county had been reserved for him by the new government. But now he demanded something better: the headship of the royal cooks. This was one of the palace offices initially allocated to the Muslims and of symbolic significance for them as well as of strategic importance. It was in Dungu's demand for this particular office that Muslim Ganda would subsequently explain the sudden and bitter confrontation that now took place with Honorat Nyonyintono.[22]

Subsequent Christian chroniclers report matters differently. To them the events of 12 October 1888 were the result of a Muslim plot to remove Nyonyintono as chief minister of the Buganda kindom and to replace him with a Muslim dignitary.[23] In retrospect, both interpretations appear to be more symptoms of the sudden strife which erupted on that day than convincing explanations of it. Structurally, several other matters would seem to have been more important.

Because the anti-Mwanga coup had been sparked off by a religious scare – the rumour that leading Muslim and Christian chiefs were to be stranded on a deserted island in Lake Victoria in yet another persecution of foreign religions – religion had been an important factor in allocating posts after Mwanga's overthrow. Because of their earlier numerical preponderance over Christians, and their prominence in organizing the coup, Muslims had taken the cream of chieftaincies: not only the kingship itself – for the new monarch was expected to declare allegiance to Islam very shortly – but many offices amongst the royal *batongole* scattered throughout the ten counties of the old kingdom. One of these was Kakungulu's chieftaincy in Buddu, whence so many of the coastal-supplied firearms were imported through the Bahaya chiefdoms at that time. Muslims had also taken the post of *Kimbugwe*, which was second only in importance to the chief ministership under the king, and a pride of *bakungu* appointments too. Christians had taken the chief ministership and several county chieftaincies as well as retaining control over two of the four strategic *batongole* offices in which so many muskets had been mustered by Mwanga II. These were the chieftaincies earlier administered by Honorat Nyonyintono, the Roman Catholic convert who had suffered castration during Mwanga's anti-Christian persecution and was now Kiwewa's chief minister, and Apolo Kagwa, who had closer ties with CMS missionaries and had been assaulted less grievously during the persecution and was now county chief of Singo. Christian Ganda did not therefore do so badly out of the post-coup settlement. Nonetheless they feared Muslim superiority in firepower because of the Muslims' confessional links with Zanzibari traders.[24]

The Muslim Ganda coup leaders were troubled by other things. Once Christianity as well as Islam became respectable at the Ganda court, and no longer something to be followed with danger of persecution, many previously secret adherents of both traditions declared themselves openly. Muslims were surprised by the proportionately greater numbers of Christians who came forward once Kiwewa became king. Distribution of offices also favoured Christians more than the Muslims had originally envisaged and – to add irritation to unease – the new king hesitated about becoming a Muslim.[25] It was therefore not surprising, in view of the importance of the Muslim contribution to Mwanga II's downfall, that a demand arose now that the chief ministership should go to a Muslim. However, before 12 October 1888 Muslim Ganda evidently felt unable to press this particular demand home because of the growth in clientage support for the Christians which had resulted from the increasing numbers of Ganda now declaring their preference for Christianity publicly. If anything, Nyonyintono's position as chief minister of the Buganda kingdom was probably stronger as dawn broke over the Ganda capital on 12 October 1888 than it had been six weeks before.

Here Kakungulu's chieftaincy was probably typical. Muslim Ganda might seize it on the morrow of Mwanga's downfall for one of their own people, but they had no effective means of preventing 70 of Kakungulu's slaves from defecting to Nyonyintono – and probably taking a comparable number of muzzleloaders to their new master too. Under the previous regime the attitude of the king would have been decisive, and a complaint doubtless lodged before him about this. But now there was a change of regime, and Kiwewa had not yet managed to build up an independent power base against the chiefs initially installing him in power. With the benefit of hindsight, what seems extraordinary is not so much the Muslim concern at growing Christian numbers, but rather Christian concern about Muslim superiority in firearms at a time when Muslims themselves did not consider this gave them any unconditional advantage, guns being so closely tied to clientage connections. Nonetheless, fears on both sides were symptomatic of a precariously balanced political situation that might collapse into armed conflict at any time.

Here Dungu's demands were clearly critical. But even more critical on

12 October 1888 was a breakdown in communication between Muslims and Christians, and a failure of nerve at a vital moment by Nyonyintono.

According to an eyewitness source, at breakfast Nyonyintono heard a rumour that this was to be the day upon which Kiwewa would give his post as chief minister to the current Muslim chief of Buddu county.[26] He also learnt that an unknown number of Muslim soldiers had been moved to the capital during the night. Nyonyintono's followers were divided. Some favoured immediate fighting. Others wanted to find out first whether the rumour was true. Nyonyintono decided to go to the palace to size things up for himself. There he found many Muslim soldiers present. Nyonyintono asked the new king whether he wanted any of Nyonyintono's men killed. Kiwewa said no, but Nyonyintono was uncertain what to make of this answer. At the palace gate, Muslim soldiers increased Nyonyintono's unease by first pointing their guns at him and then withdrawing them in order to salute him.

Meanwhile, at his enclosure at the capital, Nyonyintono's followers had increased considerably in number. A further decision was taken to request Kiwewa to send four Muslim chiefs to discuss peace terms, but this request was refused by the Muslims; they preferred a Christian party to visit them. Nyonyintono again went to the palace, this time taking 60 armed followers with him. These were asked to leave their firearms at the palace gate, a request to which Nyonyintono agreed. However, Nyonyintono himself was kept waiting by Kiwewa for some time and, since such delay was not customary for a king's chief minister seeking a royal audience, Nyonyintono left suddenly without actually seeing the king.

The crisis deepened. Another Christian chief went to the palace with armed followers to see whether there was any real danger, while the Muslims sent their man Lubanga to visit Nyonyintono's enclosure for the same purpose. The Christian chief was stopped at the palace gate and asked to order his companions to leave their guns there but, unlike Nyonyintono earlier, he refused. Instead he advanced into the palace with his companions still carrying their guns. Several shots were fired, and he fell. The shots were heard at Nyonyintono's enclosure; Lubanga tried to seize Nyonyintono but was himself killed by one of Nyonyintono's entourage. Things now got completely out of hand. Most of Nyonyintono's followers abandoned his enclosure in the belief that the Muslims were about to attack them immediately. Nyonyinytono himself, relates an eyewitness source, then 'became confused and could see nowhere to go'.[27]

Kakungulu was in another part of the capital when the crucial shots were fired. Nonetheless, when he heard them, he was one of the Christian firebrands who immediately 'chased their enemies up Rubaga hill'. There, his chronicler relates, he could see Nyonyintono's enclosure on fire.[28] He had very little ammunition. To acquire bullets and powder he ran to the enclosure of Samwili Mukasa. There Kakungulu obtained ammunition, but saw that the situation had deteriorated further: Nyonyintono was now visibly in flight. Kakungulu and his immediate company paused to consider their next step. Some favoured withdrawal from hostilities. But Kakungulu was not one of these. Instead he was one of those 'saying we should pray God in continuing the battle'.[29] Having so recently lost his chieftaincy, Kakungulu had little to lose from continued fighting apart from his own life and those of his dependents still fighting with him.

Kakungulu now ran towards the road from Natete, where many Ganda Muslims were to be seen; shot his way through them; and made his way with others to the prison of the princes, then situated just below the southerly slopes of Rubaga hill.[30] The prison appeared unattended, but Kakungulu's party did not storm it; possibly because they did not feel sufficiently aware of what had caused Nyonyintono's flight to know whether an attack upon it was necessary or, if it was, whether they had allies in sufficient strength and spirit to back up effectively any attack upon it. Kakungulu's chronicler notes anyway that it was 'here that some of their companions who were timid disappeared'.[31] He also reports that gunfire could still be heard from where Nyonyintono had last been seen, further along the Nakulongo swamp, and it was in that direction that Kakungulu now made his way quickly.[32]

Initially Nyonyintono's companions thought that Kakungulu's party were Muslims and fired at them – unsuccessfully it would seem, as the next part of the chronicler's account describes what Kakungulu did at Nyonyintono's side. For Kakungulu was one of about 5,000 supporters who joined Nyonyintono to discuss future tactics at Kabowa market just south of the Nakulongo swamp. That so many were able to assemble at this point, says much for the confusion still reigning amongst Muslims at the capital. Apolo Kagwa was for mediation with the other side. Roman Catholic missionary advice was for flight to Bunyoro. Kakungulu was one of those advocating another break-in at the royal prison in order to enthrone yet another prince of the drum. However, discussion at Kabowa was cut short by the appearance of a hostile force under the command of Tebukoza (the former county chief of Buddu during Kakungulu's tenure of the Ekirumba chieftaincy there). Solomon Wamala reports that Kakungulu now distinguished himself by fighting a vigorous rearguard action against this force. 'Kakungulu had of late been disliked by his colleagues, even being expelled from his *kitongole* office; but now he was very popular because he had fought hard'.[33]

So too had Tebukoza, who had also lost office upon the deposition of Mwanga. Wamala reports that, as a reward for Tebukoza's bravery on this occasion, Kiwewa awarded him the county chieftaincy of Kyagwe which Nyonyintono had held along with his position as *Katikiro*.[34] There was to be no similar immediate reward for Kakungulu: he had chosen the losing side in this particular confrontation.

However, there was no particular necessity for Kakungulu to leave Buganda altogether now because he was a Christian convert. To be sure, subsequent Ganda Christian tradition would glorify the flight of Nyonyintono and Kagwa from Buganda at this time in terms comparable to the Jewish exodus from Egypt recorded in the Old Testament. But, as one Muslim Ganda chronicler remarks, in fact on this occasion 'they did not fight for religion but for chieftainship'.[35] We also know from other sources that a number of other Christian firebrands like Gabrieli Kintu, whose subsequent career in the Buganda kingdom was to parallel Kakungulu's in so many respects, stayed on to try their luck under Kiwewa after Nyonyintono and Kagwa's departure.[36] Kakungulu could have stayed on to try his luck like Kintu. He could also have eased any change of sides by taking advantage of his earlier blood-pact with Tebukoza. Instead, Kakungulu decided to leave Buganda altogether at this juncture, and he appears to have so decided because of the rival attractions of life in Bunyoro.

Earlier Bunyoro had provided sanctuary to a number of Christian refugees from Mwanga's first period of rule in Buganda, and it was not until a later stage of the Ganda succession war that the Nyoro king, too, would acquire the reputation of being the murderer of followers of foreign religions. Like other rulers in the East African interior, Kabalega was concerned to obtain ivory as well as slaves to exchange with foreign merchants for firearms and other scarce goods. As an elephant hunter with experience of firearms in both Koki and Buganda, Kakungulu could have acquired comparable employment under King Kabalega with reasonable ease. There were markets in Bunyoro attracting traders from a very wide swathe of eastern Africa. The Nyoro armed forces were known at this time not to bar even the highest posts to foreigners. It was therefore not surprising that Kakungulu was one of those arguing for flight to Bunyoro.[37]

However, some way beyond Kabowa the retreating Christians encountered Nicodemo Sebwato. Sebwato was a leading convert of the CMS connection in Buganda and he was returning from an errand on behalf of his master, the former chief minister Mukasa.[38] Sebwato now persuaded the defeated Christians accompanying Nyonyintono and Kagwa to go to Nkore instead of Bunyoro.[39]

Sebwato is said to have persuaded the exiles to change direction with two arguments. One was that Ntare, king of Nkore, was a gentler ruler than Kabalega;[40] but this suggestion, as just remarked, would appear to be product of later Christian Ganda tradition. The other argument seems to have been the more likely and persuasive one at the time. As Sebwato and other Christian Ganda had friends amongst the cattle-keeping aristocracy of Nkore, the exiles were more likely to play an important role there than in Bunyoro.[41] And indeed Nyonyintono and company were very shortly established in a specialized chieftaincy at Kabula, on the Nkore side of the Nkore/Buganda frontier. There they busied themselves in plundering cattle for the Nkore king from their native Buganda, and in building a bridge to facilitate plunder by Nkore of smaller states to the south.[42]

All these developments created fresh anxieties for Kakungulu. By the time of the exiles' meeting with Sebwato, his fortunes were tied up far too closely with Nyonyintono and company for him to be able to disengage himself from them easily or quickly. The switch to Nkore is said by his principal chronicler to have appeared particularly dangerous for him because of his earlier raids there for slaves and cattle while working as an elephant hunter in Buddu county.[43] The bridge constructed by the Christian exiles furthermore turned Koki into a potentially still more dangerous refuge in future for any Christian such as himself.

## 3

The kingdom of Nkore, bigger than Koki but smaller than Buganda and Bunyoro, was now approaching its peak of pre-colonial power. It had survived for much of the eighteenth and nineteenth centuries as an unstable polity with frequent succession wars. But in the third quarter of the nineteenth century the situation changed. Under two capable kings, Mutambuka and Ntare V, sway was extended over pastoralist Hima and agriculturalist Bairu alike through the agency of newly created warbands.[44] The success of these seems to have been based, not so much upon control of the new firearms or upon refinements in spear warfare (as in the case of Zulu power in southern Africa),[45] as upon more effective organization of existing weaponry and warriors by more competent leaders. Needless to say, agriculturalist acceptance of pastoralist superiority was doubtless also assisted by that 'combination of fear and reciprocity in social and economic matters tempered by the geographical and social separation of the two classes',[46] typical of many kingdoms in the East African interlacustrine region.

Spatially, the Christian exiles settled at some distance from the Nkore royal capital at Lulembo. Socially, the drawbacks of their status in Kabula as *bairu* or 'grain-eaters' (*balyabulo*, in Luganda) were moderated not just by their utility to Ntare V as bridge builders and cattle raiders, but also by favourable memories of earlier Ganda assistance during his own installation in power.[47] Nonetheless, the Christian exiles were aware that Ganda intervention in Nkore had not always been positive; Apolo Kagwa in particular was careful to call himself 'Mityana' rather than 'Mukwenda' at this time in order not to remind the rulers of Nkore of one of the less creditable earlier Ganda interventions.[48] Kakungulu, too, appears to have decided fairly soon after the exiles' arrival in Nkore that it would be sensible for him to return to Koki, because during his chieftaincy in Buddu he had been unwise enough to kill an Nkore prince during one of his private raids. Kakungulu's chroniclers provide several descriptions of his bravery at Ntare's court shortly after his arrival with the Christian exiles, but unfortunately it is not possible to be sure that these accounts are not chroniclers' conceits. There was no independent confirmation in interviews for these supposed exploits, and Kakungulu was still a comparatively unimportant figure within the exile community in Nkore.[49]

Koki was still ruled by Ndawula when Kakungulu returned there at the end of 1888. There is no suggestion in any of the sources relating to his life at this time that there was any great opposition to Kakungulu's return to Koki. Serwanga, a close relative, gave Kakungulu land at Kitente, his father Semuwemba having died during his time as a Ganda chief in Buddu county. From incidental details in his principal chronicle, it seems clear that Kakungulu also resumed elephant-hunting for the ruler of Koki and continued in this occupation for several months.[50] What brought this period to an abrupt close was an attack upon Kakungulu's family by Ndawula's retainers. The reasons for this attack are not clear: possibly fear that the study of Christianity now spreading amongst Kakungulu's relatives and others in Koki, if uncurbed, might cause Ndawula also to lose his throne.[51] But the attack upon Kakungulu's family could as easily have been caused by some quite different motive, prompted by Serwanga's rather than Kakungulu's behaviour.[52] However, the attack itself was real enough, as eyewitness evidence makes clear: those of his family who were not enslaved or, like Kakungulu himself, managed to escape, were killed.[53]

Kakungulu was away hunting when this brutal attack was launched, and he took refuge a few miles away in the enclosure of the border chief of southern Buddu, *Mutatya* Bunyaga, to whom he was already allied by marriage and tied by trade.[54] Bunyaga advised Kakungulu to join Kalema, who had replaced Kiwewa as Ganda king within a month of Nyonyintono and Kagwa's departure from Buganda. Bunyaga also offered to lend him three elephant tusks for this purpose. Kakungulu's chronicler reports that he declined the offer;[55] but it is unlikely that the matter would have been mentioned at all in the chronicle if Kakungulu had not in fact considered the offer seriously.

However, by this time the Christian exiles in Kabula had grown from initially just over a hundred people to over a thousand, and many of them were known to be in favour of returning to Buganda to instal yet another prince upon the Ganda throne.[56] Kakungulu would have been aware of this. He would also have known about the envoys sent recently by the exiles to the Christian missionaries who had earlier ministered to them in Buganda and were now settled in separate stations at the southern end of Lake Victoria together with a now apparently repentant ex-king Mwanga – the envoys were journeying there to discover whether a restoration bid by Christian Ganda suppporting Mwanga II might be practicable.[57] There was an alternative to joining Kalema. After a period of reflection in Bunyaga's enclosure, Kakungulu decided to rejoin the Christian exiles at Kabula.

Less than a week after his return, news arrived that a plundering expedition had been despatched by Kalema against the principality just south of Koki which had earlier provided the Christian envoys to Mwanga with their canoes.[58] Kakungulu was again one of the firebrands favouring immediate retaliation against the expedition before it had a chance to commence its work of devastation.[59] Honorat Nyonyintono and Apolo Kagwa were away at the Nkore court when news of the expedition's approach arrived at Kabula. In their absence, a decision was taken to attack it (the veteran Protestant leader Nicodemo Sebwato, was amongst those arguing for non-retaliation). To everybody's surprise, the attack proved successful; Wamala, Kalema's expedition commander, hardly put up any fight at the first engagement at Matale in Buddu county; and then, instead of pressing on after Matale, he retreated. Inevitably, firebrands like

Kakungulu agitated for further action while Kalema's forces were in retreat. Powerful support for this policy now came from non-Christian forces within Buganda itself. For at the chief Katabalwa's headquarters still further into Buddu county, notables and chiefs from western Buganda urged further attack upon Kalema's regime. Their only concern was that the anti-Kalema coalition needed to be spearheaded by a prince of the drum.[60]

Such leadership was crucial, remarks another chronicler, because without a prince no rebellion could succeed in pre-colonial Buganda.[61] Grievances there were already aplenty because of Kalema's Islamizing policy. That was already proving much more thorough going than Mutesa I's efforts in this direction before the CMS missionaries and White Fathers had arrived in the kingdom: Kalema's order that all male Ganda should be circumcised was proving especially unpopular.[62] Soon there would be further popular revulsion against Islam, when most princes and princesses of the drum would be rounded up and killed – princesses as well as princes, because of the fear that the Christian exiles might otherwise make one of them Queen of Buganda, after the example of Queen Victoria in Britain.[63] Arousing suppport for resistance against Kalema's regime within Buganda did not therefore pose major problems for the Christian exiles campaigning during the first half of 1889. Providing legitimate leadership for the anti-Kalema revolt, on the other hand, did pose acute problems, at least until such time as Mwanga II publicly attached himself to the Ganda Christians' cause.

The battle of Mawuki proved an indecisive follow-up to Matale. The Christians started the battle from a much smaller numerical base than the Muslims and therefore suffered proportionately more from their casualties; in themselves, by no means excessive ones. However, one casualty on the Christian side was catastrophic: Honorat Nyonyintono. The battles of Ndese and Bajja, which followed Mawuki within days, proved still greater military disasters for the Christians – Ndese, because the Roman Catholics refused to fight so soon after Nyonyintono's death ('they were not cowardly but were distraught and did not see why they should fight just for Protestants', relates Solomon Wamala);[64] Bajja, basically because Mwanga II lost his nerve. Charles Stokes, an Irish trader and former CMS missionary, ferried Mwanga across Lake Victoria to aid the anti-Kalema rebellion as well as to obtain additional supplies of ivory for himself.[65] But Mwanga simply ran away when the Christian Ganda forces were taken by surprise at Bajja by a large Muslim Ganda army. Bajja was an igno-minious defeat for the Christian exiles and their Ganda traditionalist allies. After it, most of the surviving Christians in Mwanga's army struggled to return to Kabula as quickly as possible.[66]

Kakungulu was not among them. He had distinguished himself in personal valour at Mawuki. According to his fellow Christian, James Miti, it was

Serwano Mazinga and Lwakirenzi Kakungulu, whose bravery inspired and urged their followers to desperate fighting ... It was in this engagement that Lwakirenzi Kakungulu began to distinguish himself as a brave man; he not only fought more heroically in the heat of battle but he even captured one of the enemy in the act of loading his gun.[67]

These battles also confirmed Apolo Kagwa as one of the leading commanders on the exiles' side. Nyonyintono had died at Mawuki, along with Dungu on the exiles' side and Tebukoza on Kalema's. Nyonyintono's place as the principal Roman Catholic commander had been taken first by Lule Muwemba, who died at Bajja; then by Alexis Sebowa, who survived that battle; and subsequently by Stanislas Mugwanya.[68] On the Protestant side, Sebwato was still active, but unpopular because of his initial unwillingness to fight at Matale and his continuing preference for a permanent home for Ganda Christians outside rather than inside Buganda; leadership of the exile Protestant party in Kabula was therefore taken by the more warlike Apolo Kagwa.[69]

Kakungulu was too unimportant in the Ganda Protestant politico-religious grouping that emerged in the wake of Kalema's attempt to transform Buganda into an Islamic state, to be considered a serious rival to Kagwa for headship of the new party. At this time, relates his principal chronicler,[70] Kakungulu forsook areas along the northern and westerly shores of Lake Victoria for life on an island in the lake itself.

4

Mwanga II was not the bravest of Ganda kings in battle. Faced with the prospect of personal combat, his instinct almost always was to turn and run. From the battle of Bajja, he ran away very fast indeed; 'the king really loved his navy', comments one chronicler.[71] Another defends Mwanga's speedy exit on the ground that, thereby, he prevented still greater slaughter taking place.[72] Strategically, there is a still better defence. By running away Mwanga may have helped to lose a battle, but in so doing he helped his followers to win the subsequent war.

After Bajja Mwanga wanted to build fresh headquarters safely amongst the Sesse islands in Lake Victoria. But it so happened that Sesse chiefs were encamped temporarily on Bulingugwe island at the very northernmost end of the lake, and so it was there too that Mwanga settled initially.[73] 'This is only quite a small island & is covered with little huts', reported Robert Walker to his family in September 1889. 'The people are so crowded in places, that the plague has broken out. All seem to have sores or skin diseases.'[74] As a consequence there was a considerable demand for medicines from the various Christian missionaries who had just returned to Buganda from the southern end of Lake Victoria.[75]

Because Bulingugwe island was a small outcrop devoid of substantial banana plantations, frequent trips had to be made to the mainland in order to obtain food. However, though Bulingugwe was only separated from the mainland by a channel varying in width between 400 and 1,000 yards of clear water, the 50 or so miles of surrounding countryside was comparatively easy to slip across to unnoticed because it was deeply

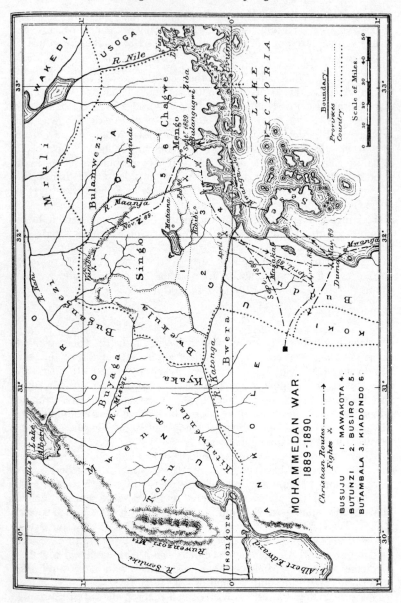

Map 4. *Macdonald's map of the 'Mohammedan war'.* (From J.R.L. Macdonald, *Soldiering and Surveying in British East Africa* (1897), p. 186)

indented and swampy. For the same reasons, it was difficult for Kalema's followers to know precisely where the occupants of Bulingugwe island would land at any one time. The Sesse islanders declared for Mwanga II shortly after his return from the southern end of Lake Victoria in mid-1889. Mwanga thereafter had many canoes at his disposal. Kalema had comparatively few.

Another strategic advantage of Bulingugwe island, at least according to Ham Mukasa who was one of Mwanga's fighters there, was that it was 'in the middle of the countryside between Kyagwe and Kyadondo where we could hear news, and reliable news at that, from both sides'.[76] Some rumours reported that Kalema was currently fomenting traditionalist discontent against Islamization on the Ganda mainland. Now that he had killed off nearly every rival for his throne from amongst the princesses of the drum as well as the princes, Kalema appeared to be in an ideologically strong position to put the Muslim revolution in Buganda into reverse gear, so to speak. He would then be able, if this happened, to build up royal power again, much as his immediate predecessors had done, by playing off one group of Ganda chiefs and notables against another within the constraints imposed upon the wider society by hoe agriculture and a slave mode of production requiring frequent plundering expeditions to replenish slaves dying or freed by their owners. Several chroniclers confirm the vitality of traditional resistance to Islamization in Buganda at this time;[77] others that Kalema was indeed now making secret overtures to non-Muslim notables on the mainland;[78] while from missionary evidence of informers' reports we know in addition that Kalema's principal chiefs were 'much divided'.[79] Strategically it soon became apparent that if Mwanga left Bulingugwe island for a royal capital upon a more distant island in Lake Victoria, he might lose the traditionalist initiative to Kalema. By staying on Bulingugwe island, on the other hand, not only would he be able to keep in touch much more effectively with anti-Islamic sentiment on the Ganda mainland: his followers would be able to fight a much more effective war too against Kalema's regime.

It was on Bulingugwe that Mwanga's followers first heard that Kalema's regime had been attacked not only by the Christian-led army operating out of Nkore in the west, but by another associated with 'pagans' (*bakafiri*) in the east, and that Kalema had had secret contacts with these people. Ham Mukasa reports that these traditionalists were not strong militarily, but they controlled food supplies in both Kyagwe and Bulemezi counties.[80] For this reason alone, their friendship appeared critical to the Christians on Bulingugwe island. Mwanga therefore remained upon Bulingugwe island. But how would the wider anti-Kalema coalition on the mainland actually supplant the Kalema regime there?

Previous battles in this particular succession war had been fought within tactics bequeathed by earlier Ganda plundering expeditions. Insofar as these tactics had meant more than raiding for scarce resources outside Buganda – and subsequent Christian chroniclers stress that the Christians operating out of Nkore were conscious of the need not to alienate popular support in Buganda by too obviously living off the land through which they had to fight [81] – the earlier battles had involved hand-to-hand fighting in which reckless bravery was not only cherished symbolically but of the greatest importance in deciding outcomes. Muzzleloading guns might be important in keeping subordinate populations under control, and in protecting strategic positions close to the royal capital of Buganda during peacetime. But, to be fully effective elsewhere, particularly during wartime, muskets needed to be assimilated to tactics designed for their use rather than for campaigning with spears. For, as a British officer was to remark just a few years later, Ganda warriors

> still acted as if armed with the spear alone, and, rushing to close quarters, fired at short range, but with little idea of aim. The now empty musket had to be recharged, and for this purpose the foremost warriors retired, and thus the impetuosity of the attack was lost. Had they retained a stabbing spear, and after the fusillade at close quarters pressed home with it, the attack would have been much more formidable ... The Waganda in battle bore some resemblance to the formation adopted by the Highlanders of Scotland. They were drawn up in a number of parallel columns, each headed by its chief, and the front rank of which contained the best armed men, while behind them followed spearmen. The attack was most impetuous, but, as they did not understand the use of supports or reserves [as employed by post-Napoleonic European armies], anything more than a temporary check was likely to involve the retreat of the whole force ... [82]

Firearms added fresh force and hazard to such fighting rather than fresh strategy.

The element of surprise was especially important in this kind of warfare. By surprise, the Christian exiles had won the battle at Matale and been defeated at Bajja, while at Mawuki the tangled deployment of opposing columns in dense mist had created opportunities for reckless bravery by young bloods like Mazinga and Kakungulu as well as contributing to the calamitous loss of morale that occurred amongst Roman Catholic warriors once Honorat Nyonyintono's severed head had been found. By staying on Bulingugwe island in Lake Victoria, not much more than ten miles from Kalema's capital itself, however, two changes in strategy simultaneously became possible within the existing, essentially transitional tactics. First, Kalema's Muslim supporters could be divided operationally – one army being kept across the Katonga river in Buddu county in order to keep an eye on Christian incursions from Nkore, another much closer to the capital in order to deal with attacks from Bulingugwe island. Secondly, rapid strikes could be made upon the mainland from Bulingugwe at the expense of Kalema's supporters and at very low cost to Mwanga's followers. Needless to say, when the resultant string of low-cost victories turned the traditionalist backlash against the Kalema regime's Islamizing policies into widespread positive support for Mwanga's reinstatement in power, everybody on Mwanga's side started taking credit for the new strategy, Kakungulu and his chroniclers included.[83]

As far as Kalema was concerned, once Mwanga had cut off his traditionalist escape route by winning over the 'pagans' of Kyagwe, canoes were his next priority. Or so they appeared to be, after his expedition to tackle the traditionalists militarily in Kyagwe after the clear failure of his covert overtures towards them, itself came to grief at the hands of a special force sent to intercept it by Mwanga. This force was commanded by Gabrieli Kintu. Kintu was one of several young army commanders who first came to prominence on Bulingugwe island, and whose success in this and other engagements was to be rewarded by a marriage alliance with one of Mwanga's sisters.[84] Kakungulu, too, distinguished himself by killing an important Muslim chief, Kubeba, at this time; a lucky achievement, implies James Miti in his account of the war, but a notable one nonetheless.[85] Shortly afterwards Kalema sent another expedition to collect canoes from Busoga, with which doubtlessly he hoped to counter any future raids from Bulingugwe island. But this expedition, too, was defeated by another of Mwanga's forces despatched from the island, this time commanded by another new general: Abusolomu Mudiima.[86] After this reverse, Kalema sent one of his leading chiefs belonging to the Mamba clan, Gabunga Sendikwanawa, to arrange for the construction of canoes on the Entebbe peninsula, at Buwaya close to the modern Kampala–Entebbe road.[87] A force with Nicodemo Sebwato as commander, and Semei Kakungulu as deputy commander, managed not only to disrupt this enterprise but also to kill the Muslim Gabunga. As a consequence, 'Peasants of that side got to know we were lucky for the battles we fought there were in our favour', reported Ham Mukasa. 'Then they began to come on our side and they told us about their [the Muslims'] plans. They told us true things'.[88]

Some of the 'true things' concerned the whereabouts of some Arab boats which now arrived to replenish Kalema's stores of ammunition from the southern end of Lake Victoria. Symbolically, the subsequent burning of these dhows and the capture of their surviving cargo was to have considerable significance for morale amongst Mwanga's followers throughout Buganda.[89]

Also helpful here was the success attending Kakungulu's first independent command of a force commissioned by Mwanga. This was to intercept yet another army sent out by Kalema to rescue Muslim warriors scattered while attempting earlier to obtain canoes from Busoga. As Ham Mukasa again relates,

> we were told that Kalema had sent general Wakigadya to go for Kyayambade where he had been driven to. Our Kabaka also sent Simeyi Lwakirenzi Kakungulu [who ...] attacked Wakigadya. They met at Senyi and they fought very hard. Simeyi Lwakirenzi the general on our side defeated [the] Moslems and killed many including general Wakigadya.[90]

To reward Kakungulu, Mwanga concluded a marriage alliance between him and another of his sisters, the Princess Nawati.[91] Kakungulu now became one of Mwanga's closest associates on Bulingugwe island. As Kakungulu still smoked Indian hemp (*njaye*) and Mwanga too was a smoker of it, he had this additional tie to his king.

Nonetheless, according to one of Kakungulu's personal retainers, Kakungulu considered himself to be as good a Christian as any on Bulingugwe island. 'I noticed that when we set off to fight Wakigadya, Kakungulu said "Kneel down and let us see how God will protect us" ... and in every battle Kakungulu would still be praying when the guns started firing.'[92] Such spirituality reinforced disrespect for Ganda traditional specialists at the very time that Mwanga II himself was courting their support on the mainland. Kakungulu's drum on Bulingugwe island at this time frequently rang out to the beat:

I eat whatever I find;
I eat whatever belongs to *emmandwa*[93]

and *emmandwa*, as we have seen, meant spirit medium. However, Christianity of any sort coexisted less easily with other songs sung by Kakungulu's followers at this time, such as the one with the impudent refrain:

Whoever does not smoke Indian hemp is a frog;
don't you know the frog ?

– at least in the opinion of the older Christians also resident on the island.[94] Kakungulu's former retainer testified that hemp-smoking was merely 'a fashion' (*mutindo*) amongst the younger Christian commanders closest to *Kabaka* Mwanga on Bulingugwe. But he admitted that the older Christians there 'did not smoke it'[95] – and it was to be those older Christian no-smokers who were to have by far the greatest say in deciding who would get what in the immediate aftermath of what otherwise was to prove Kakungulu's most spectacular success during Mwanga II's residence on Bulingugwe island: the storming of Kalema's capital at Lunguja.

## 5

Lunguja was stormed shortly after Mwanga's supporters suffered their first major defeat following establishment of their king's headquarters upon Bulingugwe island. This happened when the Christian exiles in Nkore combined with Ndawula of Koki and other traditionalist allies on the Buganda mainland to confront Kalema's forces at Nasenyi, and suffered a serious reverse.

This was in September 1889. Mwanga sent reinforcements to the mainland under the command of Sepiriya Mutagwanya. Mutagwanya caught his foot upon a splinter while climbing out of a canoe at Jungo. The foot soon swelled to an uncomfortable degree. Mutagwanya stayed at Jungo for several days in the hope that the swelling would subside, but it grew worse and he therefore had to abandon command of the large army by now assembling. It was a critical moment. Not only was Mwanga's army at Jungo without its commissioned leader, but the muskets at its disposal were outnumbered probably by at least four to one,[96] by its opponents' firearms.

Besides weaker firepower, Mwanga's army at Jungo was deeply divided along factional and confessional lines. Roman Catholics now grouped themselves separately from Protestants, with supporters of Ganda traditional religious cults apparently organized independently as a third group. Further fragmenting Mwanga's warriors at Jungo were factional differences between the so-called 'grain-eaters' (*balyabulo*), representing the older Christian leadership amongst Mwanga's mainland forces, and the younger *balyangege* or 'fish-eaters' who had only become prominent militarily after Mwanga's move to Bulingugwe island. It was therefore important for Mwanga that the overall command of his divided and out-gunned army should be decided as quickly as possible.

Traditionally, there had been an inbuilt safeguard against leadership emergencies in Ganda military expeditions. Whenever a commander (*omugabe*) was selected for any campaign, the Ganda king selected a suitable second-in-command called the *kalabalaba* who took control when the commander became indisposed.[97] On this occasion the *kalabalaba* was another young commander from Bulingugwe island like Sepiriya Mutagwanya, and one whose leadership was fortunately acceptable to overwhelming majorities of both the *abalyabulo* and *abalyangege* factions because of the successes attending his most recent raids upon the mainland. But this was no normal emergency, and this no ordinary campaign. Besides the sheer size of the opposition, there was also the politico-religious problem. For while Mutagwanya was classified within Mwanga's army as a Roman Catholic, his deputy was considered to be a Protestant. Special envoys were therefore despatched to Bulingugwe in order to obtain sanction from *Kabaka* Mwanga himself for the replacement of Mutagwanya by Kakungulu.

When sanction was obtained, morale revived immediately within Mwanga's army at Jungo. As one of the grain-eating faction later commented in one of the vernacular chronicles composed in commemoration of the war: 'All of us Christians became very glad after seeing our general who was well experienced in commanding an army to fight [and who] knew how to confer cleverly and unflappably with the army – that is why the whole army rejoiced for being given Semei Lwakirenzi'.[98]

Semei Lwakirenzi lived up to his reputation. After conferring with other army leaders, he led Mwanga's forces northwards from Jungo on the morning of 3 October 1889, the opposing forces being assembled under Kalema's commander, Mulowoza, a few miles away. The first night was spent at Bunkabira, on a ridge just south of the present Kampala–Masaka road. There Kakungulu is reported by one chronicler to have tried to unite the two Christian politico-religious groupings in Mwanga's army by emphasizing the common Muslim danger and his army's dependence upon the single Christian God. 'Never will any of you Christians turn his back to a Muslim – I call it obscene, for as our God Isa Messiah

[Jesus Christ] is living we shall win'. Those are the words Batolomayo Zimbe puts into Kakungulu's mouth on this occasion. 'Then fearlessly all of us Christians shouted loudly and repeated the statement of the general and said "God is the owner of power, He is the conqueror of our enemies" '.[99] Temuteo Kagwa tells us that the assembled Christians spent the remainder of that first night in prayer.[100]

The following day was occupied with rather less spiritual concerns. 'Do you people know how to fight ?', yet another chronicler remembers the fish-eating faction taunting members of the grain-consuming one once daylight appeared. 'No, you do not know how to fight. That is why you were defeated by the Muslims the other day, because you do not know how to fight. But we fish-eaters, we are quite used to dealing with our Muslim opponents because we are always fighting with them.'[101]

Just after lunch this taunting was cut short by the appearance upon the opposing ridge of the Muslim army. Promptly the Christians at Bunkabira appear to have divided into separate regiments mobilized upon factional rather than denominational lines, if Kakungulu's principal chronicler is to be believed. Kakungulu is also reported to have ordered his drummers to sound out beats indicating 'that his people were the fish-eaters and that we fought with the Muslims every day'.[102] The Muslim general retorted by ordering his drummer Batuma to sound out again the beat which had so demoralized the Christian warriors who had fought earlier at Nasenyi.[103] Then his entourage converged upon Kakungulu's forces.

Meanwhile most of the grain-consuming faction seem to have been grouped under the command of Apolo Kagwa, the leading Protestant general from the Christian exiles in Nkore. These were confronted by a weaker Muslim regiment on Nkungulutale hill; not only was this regiment less numerous than the one converging upon Kakungulu's forces, relates Kakungulu's principal chronicler, but it was 'a regiment of despised people, commanded by Mukwenda Wamala'[104] – the Muslim general who had been so easily defeated at the battle of Matale earlier in the year. Seeing that most fighting was taking place on Kakungulu's side of the battlefield, Apolo Kagwa offered him support from the grain-eaters. The offer was declined. 'Only when you see that they have completely defeated us, only then send help to us' being the gist of Kakungulu's reported reply.[105]

Anyway Kagwa's offer would probably not have been of decisive help. Early in the engagement at Bunkabira the fish-eating faction amongst Mwanga's forces killed the principal Muslim drummer and then there was great confusion throughout Kakungulu's side of the battlefield, musketeers on both sides using their guns as cudgels in close combat as well as firing them whenever they got the chance. 'Every man seized his enemy by the collar', reported Solomon Wamala. 'Then one person would strike his enemy with the barrel of his musket while the next one would strike his opponent with the butt. Really the mode of fighting was quite extra-ordinary. So many people died that in order to get any idea of their number you must revisit the scene of battle today. If you do that, you will still find that skulls are as numerous there as mushrooms'.[106]

Out of this confusion Kakungulu's forces emerged victorious, albeit with many casualties. 'God thus blessed Mwanga's commander and he defeated Kalema's general', relates Kakungulu's principal chronicler.[107]

Soon Kakungulu had cause for even greater thankfulness. While pursuing Mulowoza's forces on towards Kalema's capital, Kakungulu's fish-eaters encountered another Muslim force at the Wakaliga river. This they also managed to rout. Again there were many deaths. As one Muslim participant later remembered it, 'The battle of Bunkabira was notable for the number of people slaughtered; of 400 of Kalema's bravest young warriors, only 70 returned home'.[108] According to Kakungulu's own chronicler, there were at least 600 casualties and 200 Christian ones amongst them, Kakungulu's personal line of 300 musketeers alone losing 96 men.[109] But, whatever the precise casualties on both sides, the day had been a clear victory for Mwanga's men. Kalema's forces had been pushed back almost to the gates of his royal enclosure at Lunguja, a distance of eleven miles.[110] And for this enforced retreat Kakungulu and the fish-eating faction amongst Mwanga's followers happily took the principal credit.

Not surprisingly, the warriors who fought with the grain-eating grouping were somewhat sore at this. It was not their fault that they had been involved in less combat than their fish-eating allies. Furthermore, by the time the day's hostilities were over, they were in a much more exposed position. Just a mile away from Lunguja, their progress had been halted by a large party of Arabs from Natete and now they were encamped around Mutundwe and Kitebe hills, hemmed in not only by those Arabs to the west but by Kalema's royal enclosure to the north. Meanwhile Kakungulu and the fish-eaters were settled more safely further south at Kabowa. 'It was not a good place to stay', wrote Ham Mukasa of the grain-consuming group subsequently; 'it was only one mile away from Lunguja and within sound of the *entamivu* drums'.[111] The sound of those drums informed Mwanga's followers that Kalema himself was still in residence, since they would not have been sounded there during his absence. For another thing, their sound indicated that Kalema was already preparing his followers for still further combat.[112]

Further south at Kabowa, Kakungulu was reportedly in a much happier frame of mind. Besides the greater security created by distance, he knew that Kalema had suffered considerable losses at Bunkabira in both men and ammunition. 'If God wills', his principal chronicler remembers him commanding an envoy to tell Mwanga on Bulingugwe island, 'tomorrow your general Kakungulu will inform you how your kingdom is to be restored to you.'[113] If Christian religious commitment, together with knowledge of Muslim losses, left Kakungulu with confidence of a positive result, prudence nonetheless dictated the advisability of making certain additional arrangements. Kakungulu therefore ordered the same envoy to ask Mwanga to send him further supplies of gunpowder, caps and bullets.[114]

Throughout the night, the *entamivu* drums continued to sound out from Lunguja. For Christians in the grain-eating grouping, they were far too close for comfort. Once during the night they were actually attacked by a force sent out specifically against them under the command of the ill-famed Muslim Mukwenda Wamala, which they only managed to repulse by sustaining serious casualties themselves.[115] When additional supplies of ammunition arrived from Bulingugwe island around 2 a.m., Kakungulu quickly shared the ammunition out between the two Christian groupings.[116] But even this did not completely reassure the grain-eaters. When news reached them around 4.30 a.m. that Muslims were again advancing, Apolo Kagwa suggested to Kakungulu that the fish-eating regiment should replace the grain-eating one on Kitebe hill in order to enable the grain-eaters to assume a more westerly position closer to the Arabs at Natete.[117] Kakungulu rejected the suggestion out of hand. 'There is no reason why you should go to Natete', Kakungulu's principal chronicler records him as replying. 'Let us fight here together. If we win here, we shall also have defeated the Natete people at the same time. If they defeat us here, they would also have defeated us at Natete'.[118]

Around the same time Kakungulu was also petitioned by representatives of warriors wounded on the previous day to arrange transport for them away from the immediate scene of hostilities. This request Kakungulu also rejected, records the same chronicler. 'I cannot detail men who should be fighting to take you to the lake. It is better for you simply to trust God. If we win, given time, you will recover from your wounds. If the Muslims defeat us, they will get you as well as us wherever you may be'.[119]

At dawn came the final confrontation. Kakungulu's drummers were sounding out warbeats and Kalema's drummers were replying in kind. The Muslims attacked Kakungulu's side first, initially causing the front line of the fish-eaters to fall back. 'Then our commander Kakungulu was face-to-face with Mulowoza, Kalema's other commander', relates Kakungulu's personal chronicler. 'But he did not leave that spot; he died where Stanislas Mugwanya's house now stands on Rubaga hill. Kakungulu climbed to the top of Rubaga. From there he could see right into the royal enclosure itself and could see *Kabaka* Kalema himself actually leaving it.' The same chronicler also tells us that the Muslims then set fire to Kalema's enclosure; and when the generality of Muslim fighters saw Kalema's palace ablaze, they too turned round and fled. 'Meanwhile', continues the chronicler, 'guns were still sounding from Apolo Kagwa's line of soldiers at Nakulongo.'[120]

Christian chroniclers more sympathetic to the grain-eaters amongst Mwanga's forces tell a different story. One such chronicler relates that, upon seeing the defeat of Kakungulu's front line, Apolo Kagwa recklessly abandoned the cover of the banana plantations on his side of the battlefield and led his followers quickly towards Lunguja along an open road.[121] This diverted Muslim attention from the fish-eaters for a time, thus enabling them to rally for a counter-attack. Meanwhile, other Christian fighters from the grain-eating grouping gained further time for them by racing across the bridge at the foot of Kalema's enclosure and firing upon the Muslims there at close range. It was only then, comments this chronicler, that the people from Bulingugwe 'defeated those who had previously defeated them'.[122]

Doubtless these discrepancies reflect confusion in the fighting at Lunguja as well as factionalism amongst the fighters. But factionalism there certainly was, both at the time and subsequently, and this makes any exact reconstruction of the storming of Lunguja difficult. Probably the chroniclers favouring Kagwa were more accurate over this latest engagement than those supporting Kakungulu. Probably, it was during Kagwa's diversion of Muslim attention that Kakungulu's men managed to kill the Muslim general, Mulowoza. But, whatever the precise circumstances, it was that act which above all others turned the retreat from Lunguja into a rout. There were many Muslim casualties as a consequence. Over 600 Muslims are thought to have been slaughtered by the Christians while the battle lasted, not counting deaths on the previous day.[123] Kalema himself just escaped with his life. 'What saved Kalema was our poverty', confessed one Christian participant subsequently. 'Just when our victory was almost complete, everybody went to the place of the coastal traders in order to plunder the cloth'.[124]

Nonetheless, retreating Muslims were pursued by other Christian fighters northwards through almost the entire length of Buganda. Very few Muslims left behind at Lunguja escaped with their lives. The Arabs at Natete were not only robbed of their cloth but locked in their houses by the victorious Christians and burnt alive. Many Muslim Ganda elsewhere in Buganda were put to the spear, women and children as well as men. Unlike Ganda Christians earlier in the year, Muslims were not protected by their relatives, and this inevitably left a legacy of great bitterness amongst the Muslim Ganda who did survive.[125]

Upon reaching the Mayanja swamp in northern Bulemezi on the day after the storming of Lunguja, Christian fighters pursuing the fleeing Muslims paused to discuss subsequent strategy. Factional differences now reappeared. But, instead of polarizing around the differing fighting records of the respective mainland and island contingents of warriors, or coalescing again along denominational lines, this time differences solidified around the policy positions of the Christian commanders, Semei Kakungulu and Apolo Kagwa. Kagwa favoured continued pursuit of the retreating Muslims in order to gain maximum military advantage from the capture of Lunguja. Kakungulu favoured a temporary cessation of hostilities in order to reinstate Mwanga immediately as king on the mainland, thus legitimizing the Christian victory in the minds of most ordinary people. Strategically, there were arguments for both approaches but, as the formally agreed commander of the combined Christian army, Kakungulu necessarily had the last word on this particular occasion.[126]

This did not please Apolo Kagwa. As a more established Christian leader, he was not accustomed to taking orders from a comparatively junior member of the Ganda Protestant politico-religious grouping. But what appears to have irked Kagwa still more were the public taunts of Kakungulu's personal followers. At the capture of Lunguja, Kagwa's followers had extolled their master's bravery by shouting that 'Kagwa's chest is full of battle scars'.[127] Now Kakungulu's followers taunted: 'Who are you anyway? We picked you up at Buwaya, where you were hiding in the forest [immediately after the battle of Nasenyi]. How can you now oppose the proposals of our general?' Kakungulu's personal chronicler reports that there followed 'an exchange of words'.[128]

Afterwards, Kakungulu sent a formal letter to *Kabaka* Mwanga on Bulingugwe island. According to Batolomayo Zimbe, it was phrased extravagantly. 'There is no danger. I have conquered Kalema, Come in pomp and reascend the throne as we already told you when we promised to fight and return you to your kingdom of Buganda. Come and sit on your throne Namulondo and enjoy the privileges thereto in peace.'[129]

These were extravagant words. Apolo Kagwa and the Christians of the grain-eating grouping had helped to conquer Kalema as much as Semei Kakungulu and the fish-eaters. Even with this help, the capture of Lunguja had been a very close-run thing: the battle could so easily have gone the other way. But, close or not, Mwanga's forces had won and Kakungulu had been their commander. Along with other young commanders from Bulingugwe island who had staged such startlingly successful raids upon Kalema's supporters in recent months, Kakungulu was one of the restored king's most favoured supporters. Upon reascending his throne on the Ganda mainland, Mwanga II ordered *mujaguzo* drums to be played in Kakungulu's honour for seven days.[130] Apolo Kagwa, however, became the new chief minister of the Buganda kingdom.

## 6

In the distribution of offices following the capture of Lunguja, *Kabaka* Mwanga is reported by Kakungulu's chroniclers to have wanted him to become principal chief of Buddu county, but instead he became *Mulondo*, a second-grade official in the eastern county of Kyagwe.[131] Basically, this was because the now dominant chiefs of Buganda distrusted Mwanga and, insofar as any particular internal alignment of social forces influenced the distribution of chieftaincies at this time, it was the Protestant–Catholic politico-religious divide.[132]

It had not been so even a year previously. Then there had been just two politico-religious groupings in Buganda. One was Muslim, the other Christian. Then differences between European missionaries had been no greater in Ganda eyes than ones distinguishing the differing types of Islam brought by Khartoumers and Swahili-speaking traders.[133] Before the toppling of Mwanga II in 1888, the politico-religious situation in Buganda had been even more fluid. In the Rubaga Diary for September 1887, for example, there is a report of a dozen of 'our Christians' wanting to abandon the following of Honorat Nyonyintono for the service of a king who by no stretch of the imagination could yet be considered pro-Christian. The White Fathers' converts had expected better treatment from a Christian chief, the Christian chief himself greater devotion from followers who were Christians. Both sides had been disappointed in these expectations – and the White Fathers stepped in smartly before their converts acted upon their intention of deserting Nyonyintono for the still unrepentent Mwanga.[134] It was surely because Christianity in Buganda at that time was *not* easily convertible into political loyalty that *Kabaka* Mwanga made what otherwise appears in retrospect to have been an absurd political decision – appointing somebody like Honorat Nyonyintono, mutilated on Mwanga's orders during the anti-Christian persecution just a year or so before, to one of the most powerful chieftaincies in his kingdom.

On that occasion the White Fathers succeeded in keeping their converts politically together. Like Mackay, doubtless they also urged them to beware of the rival Christian denomination. However, after their initial public debates at the close of the 1870s, both Catholic and Protestant missionaries in Buganda adopted a similarly low profile and indirect method of evangelization. To be sure, Lourdel and Mackay continued to act as poles of attraction for competing collectivities of converts in succeeding years; but they were unable to prevent even their most enthusiastic followers from taking instruction from the rival mission as the spirit moved them.[135] When Mwanga fell from power in September 1888, there were as a consequence basically only two religious groupings in Ganda politics – one Muslim, the other a still undifferentiated Christian one. It was only as the ensuing succession war developed into a wider and more protracted conflict that two Christian parties sprouted out of the woodwork; 'like barkcloth trees out of a newly-cut fence' built with logs from more than one kind of tree, as one Muslim chronicler later described it.[136]

How did that happen? Subsequent Christian tradition would stress the importance of the day we have described earlier in this chapter,[137] on which both Honorat Nyonyintono and Apolo Kagwa fled from Buganda with their respective followings, as the crucial moment for the formation within eastern Nkore of an exile community which would eventually overthrow the Muslim *Kabaka* Kalema and replace him with a Christian oligarchy of chiefs. Because Apolo Kagwa was to remain chief minister of the Buganda kingdom until the 1920s and to spend much of his spare time composing the first histories to be published in the Luganda language, this tradition is dominant in most subsequent accounts, including the fullest description of the period in English in Michael Wright's *Buganda in the Heroic Age*.[138] But in several respects the tradition retrospectively Christian-izes events which were much more ambiguous and open at the time. Furthermore, as may be clear from this chapter, insofar as there was any specifically religious transformation taking place now in Ganda politics, initially it was a Muslim rather than a Christian one – and a Muslim one, moreover, to which Christian exiles at first responded opportunistically rather than denominationally.[139]

After Nyonyintono, Kagwa, and smaller fry like Kakungulu had left the capital on 12 October 1888, a substantial number of native Christians continued to live in Buganda. They continued to live there, too, after the European missionaries attached to the CMS and White Fathers were expelled to the southern end of Lake Victoria. An unpublished chronicle by Tefiro Kisosonkole makes clear that before Kalema was made king and became a vigorous propagator of Islam, Mwanga's immediate successor, Kiwewa, attempted to assassinate the three most senior Muslim chiefs in his kingdom. Two were killed, but the third (Muguluma, who by now was Buganda's chief minister) was kept in cords until freed during the subsequent battle that replaced Kiwewa with Kalema as Ganda king. When this battle took place, Kisosonkole reports that there was a large Christian regiment fighting on Kiwewa's side along with Ganda traditionalists like Kamanyiro and Madwambi.[140] It was only after this battle that Ganda Christians abandoned Buganda en masse and their numbers in Nkore increased sufficiently to make feasible an armed attack against Kalema by Christians as such.

The first attempts in this direction were, as we saw earlier, worrying to Kalema but essentially unsuccessful. It was only when Mwanga II established himself on Bulingugwe island in Lake Victoria that a new strategy – and new commanders – came to the fore and decisively contributed to Mwanga's first restoration in 1889. This restoration – and the one effected early in the following year, after Apolo Kagwa had been wounded while leading a further campaign against Kalema and Mwanga had been forced back to Bulingugwe again – were both made possible by two things: further forays launched by Mwanga's commanders from Bulingugwe, and the broad coalition of interests still opposed to Kalema's Islamizing policies:

> what helped them, the pagans, and those who practised divination, and the hemp-smokers joined together, they joined with the Europeans [meaning the Christian Ganda supporters of Mwanga] and we went to Kijungute.
> Then we, the Muslims, joined together and God gave us strength and we defeated them. We got rid of Mwanga again, returned to Buganda and Kalema became king again.
> Then they joined together, all of them, the pagans, the readers [of Christianity] and the hunters, and they defeated us, so we were pushed back into Bunyoro.[141]

In Muslim eyes, Ganda Christians behaved opportunistically throughout this period, allying with hemp-smokers and unreconstructed traditionalists alike. Whatever covert dealings Kalema may have had earlier with non-Muslim groups, by late 1889 and until his death in 1890, he was 'a Muslim completely' (*Omusiramu ddala*).[142]

Major political differences between Catholic and Protestant Christians first became serious in Nkore. Nicodemo Sebwato told the CMS that the Christian Ganda exiles there had arrived 'in two crowds',[143] and when emissaries were sent to contact the repentent Mwanga at the southern tip of Lake Victoria in 1889 to see whether he would be willing to put himself at the head of an invasion of his former kingdom, it was agreed to send separate representatives for each denomination.[144] James Miti reports that there was further bad blood in Nkore over land allocations, but 'happily it did not end in bloodshed as subsequent differences of opinion did'.[145]

Tefiro Kisosonkole additionally describes a hothouse kind of Christianity in Nkore, in which between 6 and 10 young men would sleep in a hut and there would be few women and slaves to minister to their material needs.[146] In such circumstances, it was not surprising that political clientage should have coalesced much more closely with denominational loyalty, particularly when the Kalema regime in Buganda itself was attempting to build upon another such coalescence an Islamic state.

Indeed, it appears to have been the prospect of replacing the Muslims in power in Buganda that proved the strongest precipitant to denominational rivalry between Catholics and Protestants. In the immediate run-up to the battle of Bajja, Charles Stokes reported that the exiles' differences reminded him of Orangemen and Ribbonmen in his native Ireland.[147] When CMS missionaries and White Fathers arrived on Bulingugwe island in September 1889, they discovered that their most difficult tasks included not only curing sickness but stopping their respective converts from fighting one another.[148] Providentially for Mwanga's immediate political future, the Christian missionaries proved successful in this endeavour, right up to the time that Captain Lugard marched into Buganda with his maxim gun at the end of 1890. Thereafter, however, the oath which Catholic and Protestant chiefs swore at the start of that year – immediately before defeating Kalema's forces for a second time on the mainland – was to prove doubly defective: too wide in scope ('we shall not betray or kill our friends'), and with a penalty for non-observance ('eternal damnation') which was far too long-term in character to have much immediate effect.[149]

Also underlying the conflict in Buganda was a hidden class struggle associated with the intensification of slavery during the later years of Mutesa I and the initial ones of Mwanga II, which merged with wider tensions encompassing both chiefs and followers, slave and free. For Buganda was still a slave-based state. Continuous enslavement was still considered essential, along with ivory acquired by specialist freemen and by other means, to pay for firearms and machine-spun cloth acquired from Swahili-speaking traders hailing ultimately from the East African coast. It was also considered essential in a kingdom where social relations between chiefs and free followers were eased by the worst jobs continuing to be done by slaves. For their eventual emancipation, slaves still usually depended, if they were men, upon finding replacements for themselves through plundering expeditions; or, if they were women married to a freeman rather than to another slave, upon success in pressuring their husbands into providing addditional domestic help in the shape of concubines who themselves were also often acquired through plundering expeditions.[150] In the period immediately preceding Mwanga II's downfall in September 1888, warfare against neighbouring countries seems to have been stepped up considerably and many muskets concentrated in particular *batongole* chieftaincies in order to safeguard the chief beneficiary of this distinctive social structure, namely the Ganda king. In September 1888 the structure was briefly disrupted when Mwanga himself was overthrown. But, as both Mwanga and British protectorate officials were to discover subsequently, slavery would prove difficult to suppress as a social system, and even more difficult to replace.

In the years immediately preceding Mwanga's overthrow in 1888, even pawns and palace pages had been seized sometimes for export from Buganda by unscrupulous middlemen. But during the succeeding succession war social relations became even more arbitrary. Slaves who ran away might become free persons under some rival regime, but this did not mean that people who stayed behind were treated less harshly. Under Kalema, many free persons (*bakopi*) living within Buganda were raided and exported as slaves and, as a Nyoro chronicler remarks, 'there is reason to believe that the people of Kitara [Bunyoro] increased in population as a result'.[151] Because of the protracted character of this particular succession war, Buganda almost became not one kingdom but two in the year preceding the British colonial entry – one presided over by Mwanga II in the south, another administered by Muslims in the north. Christian missionaries with Mwanga at this time reported that many *bakopi* moved completely out of Buganda into neighbouring areas because of the devastation caused by the war and its two inevitable companions, famine and disease.[152] *Bakopi* who stayed, they reported, played a waiting game while missionaries themselves wrote less frequently of 'revolution' now and more about the war being a game of 'tip and run',[153] as both White Fathers and CMS missionaries waited to see which particular European power would take over the territory as part of its respective 'sphere of influence' in the now greatly increased European scramble for territorial acquisitions in Africa.

Politically, this was a very uncertain time for both Ganda and Christian missionaries. It was indeed a time of 'bad customs', as Paulo Kibi has reminded us – and not only because slaves who escaped with their lives from one interlacustrine kingdom in East Africa might become clansmen in another. Within Buganda, Wright correctly stresses the importance of clanship in the immediate aftermath of this troubled time, as Ganda freemen tried to reestablish social relationships with one another. For, as elderly Ganda were to state frequently in subsequent years, there were good clan members in each of the three politico-religious groupings in Buganda, Catholic and Protestant now as well as Muslim.[154] It was to be with these groupings, however, and with the continuing quest by Ganda chiefs like Semei Kakungulu within them for honour, as well as with struggles by their dependants, slave and 'free', for a better life, that the immediate political future of Buganda would also lie – as the first Europeans claiming to represent either Britain or Germany marched into, or quickly past, this very divided kingdom.

# *Notes*

1. See M. Southwold, 'Succession to the throne in Buganda' in ed. J. Goody, *Succession to High Office* (Cambridge 1966), pp. 82–126.
2. *Ibid.*, pp. 112–14.
3. *Ibid.*, p. 113.
4. J. Roscoe, *The Baganda* (London 1911), p. 226.
5. A. Kagwa, *Ekitabo kya Basekabaka be Buganda* (Kampala, 1952), p. 71, quoted in translation in M.S.M. Kiwanuka, *The Kings of Buganda* (Nairobi 1971), p. 335.
6. A. Kagwa, *Basekabaka*, p. 81.
7. Roscoe, *Baganda*, pp. 234–5, for the 1880s. Previously the Queen Mother had been 'a person of more consideration and honour than the Katikiro', testimony of S. Mugwanya to John Roscoe in MS Af. s.17 at Rhodes House Library, Oxford.
8. See further M. Twaddle, 'Slaves and peasants in Buganda' in ed. L. Archer, *Slavery and Other Forms of Unfree Labour* (London 1988) and 'The ending of slavery in Buganda' in eds S. Miers and R. Roberts, *The End of Slavery in Africa* (Madison 1988).
9. O'Flaherty to CMS, 28 February 1883, G3AG/0, CMS archives, Birmingham University Library.
10. For earlier rebellions, see Southwold, 'Succession', and J. A. Rowe, 'Revolution in Buganda 1856–1900: part one, The reign of Kabaka Mukabya Mutesa, 1856–1884', Ph.D. dissertation, University of Wisconsin, 1966. B.M. Zimbe, *Buganda ne Kabaka* (Mengo 1939), p. 130, for an earlier chiefly conspiracy against Mwanga II.
11. M. Southwold, *Bureaucracy and Chiefship in Buganda* (Kampala 1961), p. 17.
12. M.S.M. Kiwanuka, *A History of Buganda* (London 1971), *passim*.
13. Father Denoit, 20 July 1887, *Les Missions catholiques*, 39, (1888); R. Walker, 3 June 1888, Walker Papers, CMS collection, Birmingham University Library (WP).
14. Translating the phrase *yeesala akajegere*.
15. J.M. Gray, 'The year of the three kings of Buganda', *Uganda Journal* 14, 24 (1950), p. 38; D.A. Low, *Buganda in Modern History* (London 1971), pp. 27–35; A. Luck, *Charles Stokes in Africa* (Nairobi 1972), p. 76; T. Pakenham, *The Scramble for Africa* (London 1991), p. 415.
16. A. Kagwa, *Basekabaka*, pp. 144, 148.
17. *A.M. Mackay* by his sister (London 1890), pp. 116–36; A. Nicq, *La Vie du vénérable Père Siméon Lourdel* (Algiers 1906), pp. 135–42; J. Waliggo, 'The religio-political context of the Uganda martyrs', *African Christian Studies*, 2, 1 (Nairobi 1986), pp. 11–13.
18. 'The life of Ham Mukasa . . . ' in J.D. Mullins, *The Wonderful Story of Uganda* (London 1904), p. 197.
19. Waliggo, 'The religio-political context', p. 25.
20. B.M. Zimbe, *Buganda ne Kabaka* (Mengo 1939), p. 146.
21. Solomon Wamala, 'Obulamu bwa Semei Kakungulu', unpublished MS in Makerere University Library, pp. 22–3.
22. Bakale Mukasa bin Mayanja, *Akatabo ke Byafayo byentalo za Kabaka Mwanga, Kiwewa ne Kalema* (Kampala *c*.1940), pp. 5–7; English translation to be published by John Rowe and myself in *War, Religion and Revolution in Buganda: Six Dissident Discourses* (Michigan State University Press, in preparation). Zimbe, *Buganda ne Kabaka*, and sections of A. Kagwa, *Basekabaka*, dealing with the reign of Mwanga II, have been translated by Frank Kamoga and Simon Musoke respectively and copies are available at Makerere University Library and the Seeley Library at Cambridge University. Copies of G. Rock's translation of Miti's *History of Buganda* are at SOAS and Makerere. John Rowe has a translation of Ham Mukasa, *Simuda Nyuma*, Vol. 3, unpub. ms in MUL, which he hopes to publish shortly. Unless indicated, all quotations will be from these translations.
23. This rests on J. Ddiba, *Eddini mu Uganda*, Vol. 2 (Masaka 1967), pp. 29–34, which is based on the eyewitness testimony of Matayo Kirevu; A. Lugolobi, *Mbulire* (Lugala 1933), pp. 6–9.

24. See my 'Muslim revolution in Buganda', *African Affairs* 71 (1972), pp. 59–61, for a fuller discussion of these events; also Abdu Kasozi, *The Spread of Islam in Uganda* (Nairobi 1988), pp. 45–9.

25. Bakale Mukasa, *Byafayo*, pp. 4–7.

26. Ddiba, *Eddini*.

27. *Ibid.*

28. Wamala, 'Obulamu', p. 23.

29. *Ibid.*

30. *Ibid.*

31. Wamala, 'Obulamu', p. 24.

32. *Ibid.*

33. *Ibid.*, p. 26. See also Zimbe, *Buganda ne Kabaka*, Chapter 24.

34. Wamala, 'Obulamu', p. 26.

35. Bakale Mukasa, *Byafayo*, p. 15: *tebalwanira dini wabula balwanira bwami.*

36. Lugolobi, *Mbulire*, pp. 8–9.

37. Wamala, 'Obulamu', p.26; Zimbe, *Buganda ne Kabaka*, p. 163.

38. Sebwato was one of the wealthiest Christians in Buganda, closely associated with the former *Katikiro* Mukasa; baptized in 1883 by the CMS mission, and a member of the first Anglican church council: L. Pirouet, *A Dictionary of Christianity in Uganda* (Department of Religious Studies, Makerere, 1969), p. 69.

39. Zimbe, *Buganda ne Kabaka*, p. 166.

40. *Ibid* .

41. Wamala, 'Obulamu', p. 27.

42. A. Kagwa, *Basekabaka*, p. 149.

43. Wamala, 'Obulamu', pp. 26–7.

44. S.K. Karugire, *A History of the Kingdom of Nkore to 1896* (Oxford 1971), pp. 200–50.

45. R. Oliver and A. Atmore, *Africa since 1800* (Cambridge 1967), pp. 55–6; L. Mair, *African Kingdoms* (Oxford 1977), pp. 68–9.

46. E.I. Steinhart, *Conflict and Collaboration in the Kingdoms of Western Uganda* (Princeton 1977), p. 9.

47. Karugire, *A History*, has the best discussion.

48. M. Wright, *Buganda in the Heroic Age* (Nairobi 1971), pp. 69–73, for a good summary.

49. Wamala, 'Obulamu', the first part of which appears to be based upon Kakungulu's own 'Ekitabo kyakuzalibwa', is the principal source for these stories; see especially pp. 27–8.

50. Wamala, 'Obulamu'; A. Kagwa, *Basekabaka*, p. 150.

51. The ruler of Koki was one of the severest opponents of Christianity in the lakes region of East Africa at this time.

52. Wamala, 'Obulamu', p. 28, hints at other reasons.

53. Paulo Kibi, personal testimony (Kibi was an eyewitness of this massacre); Kakungulu, 'Ekitabo kyakuzalibwa', p. 11; Wamala, 'Obulamu', p. 6.

54. Wamala, 'Obulamu', p. 29.

55. *Ibid.*

56. *Ibid.*

57. Lugolobi, *Mbulire*, p. 10; *Church Missionary Intelligencer (CMI)*, January 1890, pp. 35–7.

58. Wamala, 'Obulamu', p. 30; Bakale Mukasa, *Byafayo*, p. 8, among many references in Ganda sources.

59. *Ibid.*

60. Wamala, 'Obulamu', p. 31.

61. Tefiro Kisosonkole, 'Obulamu bwange', unpublished MS in Makerere University Library, p. 45.

62. Abdu Nyanzi, *Ebyafayo bye Ntalo eze Ddini mu Buganda* (Katwe, n.d.), divides supporters and opponents of Kalema into those favouring circumcision and those opposing it. This division appears in both Muslim and non-Muslim accounts. See also on this issue Kasozi, *The Spread of Islam*, p. 28.

63. J.R.L. Macdonald, *Soldiering and Surveying in British East Africa* (London 1897), p. 187; A. Kagwa, *Basekabaka*, p. 151.
64. Wamala, 'Obulamu', p. 34.
65. Lugolobi, *Mbulire*, p. 15; A. Luck, *Charles Stokes*, pp. 72–5; N. Harman, *Bwana Stokesi* (London 1986), Chapter 7, for another account.
66. Lugolobi, *Mbulire*, pp. 13–17; A. Kagwa, *Basekabaka*, pp. 150–2; Wamala, 'Obulamu', pp. 37–9.
67. Miti (trans. Rock), *History of Buganda*, p. 340.
68. J.S. Kasirye, *Obulamu bwa Stanislaus Mugwanya* (Dublin 1963), Chapter 6; Miti (trans. Rock), *History of Buganda*, p. 335.
69. Lugolobi, *Mbulire*, p. 17; Kisosonkole, 'Obulamu bwange', pp. 84–92.
70. Wamala, 'Obulamu', pp. 40–1.
71. Lugolobi, *Mbulire*, p. 16: *kabaka yali ayagala nnyo empingu ye.*
72. Ham Mukasa, *Simuda Nyuma*, Vol. 3, p. 378–9.
73. Wamala, 'Obulamu', p. 41.
74. R. Walker, 20 September 1889, WP, Birmingham University Library.
75. Luck, *Charles Stokes*, p. 73.
76. Ham Mukasa, *Simuda Nyuma*, pp. 382–3: *wakati wensi kyagwe ni kyadondo nga tuinza okuulira ebifa eruyi ne luyi.*
77. *Ibid.*
78. *Ibid.*, p. 381; Miti (trans. Rock), *History of Buganda*, p. 346.
79. R. Walker, 20 September 1889, WP.
80. Ham Mukasa, *Simuda Nyuma*, p. 383.
81. This is especially stressed by Solomon Wamala.
82. Macdonald, *Soldiering and Surveying*, pp. 141–3.
83. C. Stokes, 3 March 1890 in FO 84/2060, PRO; Wamala, 'Obulamu', p. 41; Zimbe, *Buganda ne Kabaka*, p. 203.
84. Miti (trans. Rock), *History of Buganda*, pp. 347–8.
85. *Ibid.*, p. 348.
85. Ham Mukasa, *Simuda Nyuma*, p. 384.
87. A. Kagwa, *Basekabaka*, p. 152; Wamala, 'Obulamu', p. 47–9.
88. Ham Mukasa, *Simuda Nyuma*, p. 385.
89. A. Kagwa, *Basekabaka*, p. 152.
90. Ham Mukasa, *Simuda Nyuma*, p. 389.
91. Paulo Kibi, oral testimony.
92. *Ibid.*
93. *Ibid.*
94. *Ibid.*
95. *Ibid.*
96. A. Kagwa, *Basekabaka*, p. 154; Zimbe, *Buganda ne Kabaka*, p. 212.
97. Ganda military practice is described by Apolo Kagwa, *Ekitabo kye Mpisa za Baganda* (Kampala 1952), Chapter 14, and Roscoe, *Baganda*, pp. 346–64.
98. Zimbe, *Buganda ne Kabaka*, p. 213, quoted in English translation by F.Kamoga in Makerere University Library, p. 288. However, I have translated *nga talina kabugujo* here as 'unflappably' rather than 'quickly'.
99. Zimbe, *Buganda ne Kabaka*, p. 213.
100. Temuteo Kagwa, 'Kakungulu Omuzira Omuwanguzi', unpublished MS in Makerere University Library, p. 11.
101. Wamala, 'Obulamu', p. 59.
102. *Ibid.*, p. 60.
103. *Ibid.*; Kisonsonkole, 'Obulamu bwange', p. 96.
104. Wamala, 'Obulamu', p. 60.
105. *Ibid.*
106. Wamala, 'Obulamu', p. 61; Kasozi, *The Spread of Islam*, pp. 49–50, stresses the catastrophic effect of Batuma's death.

107. Wamala, 'Obulamu', p. 61.
108. Salimini Damulira, 14 August 1965, and taped testimony to be published in *War, Religion and Revolution* (see note 22 above). Damulira fought on Kalema's side at the battle of Lunguja.
109. Wamala, 'Obulamu', p. 61.
110. Ham Mukasa, *Simuda Nyuma*, p. 390.
111. *Ibid.*
112. *Ibid.*
113. Wamala, 'Obulamu', p. 62.
114. *Ibid.*
115. Wamala, 'Obulamu', p. 63; Ham Mukasa, *Simuda Nyuma*, p. 390.
116. Wamala, 'Obulamu', p. 63.
117. *Ibid.*
118. *Ibid.*
119. *Ibid.*
120. Wamala, 'Obulamu', pp. 64–5.
121. Kisosonkole, 'Obulamu bwange', p. 98.
122. *Ibid.*, p. 99.
123. S.Damulira, oral testimony.
124. Paulo Kibi, oral testimony.
125. WP, 16 October 1889; Bakale Mukasa, *Byafayo*, pp. 10–12. Bakale Mukasa remarks that even one's brother-in-law, grandfather or father would have killed one at this time if one admitted to being a Muslim. See also Kasozi, *The Spread of Islam*, pp. 51–2.
126. Wamala, 'Obulamu', pp. 70–3.
127. *Ekifuba kya Kagwa kyajula mizinga misa.*
128. Paulo Kagwa, 'Omukwano gwa Kabaka Mwanga', unpublished MS at Makerere Univrersity Library, p. 9; Wamala, 'Obulamu'.
129. Zimbe, *Buganda ne Kabaka*, p. 218.
130. T. Kagwa, 'Kakungulu', pp. 10–12.
131. E. Kibuga, unpublished MS in the Kakungulu Papers, Mbale, p. 3; P. Kagwa, 'Omukwano', pp. 11–12; Miti (trans. Rock), *History of Buganda*, p. 355 and unpublished MS in box 1, notebook 2, Miti papers, Makerere University Library, p. 109.
132. Miti (trans. Rock), *History of Buganda*, p. 355; E.C. Gordon to Mackay, 21 October 1889, reproduced *CMI*, June 1890, pp. 356–7.
133. Bakale Mukasa, *Byafayo*, p. 15. See further my 'The emergence of politico–religious groupings in late-nineteenth-century Buganda', *Journal of African History* 29 (1988), pp. 81–92.
134. Rubaga Diary of the White Fathers, Rome Archives (RD), 1 September 1887.
135. J. Waliggo, 'The religio-political context', p. 25.
136. Bakale Mukasa, *Byafayo*, p. 1: *olukomera luzala mituba..*
137. See above, p. 37.
138. Michael Wright, *Buganda in the Heroic Age* (Nairobi 1971).
139. See my 'Muslim revolution in Buganda', *African Affairs* 71 (1972), pp. 54–72.
140. Kisosonkole, 'Obulamu bwange', p. 56.
141. Hamuli Suku, oral tesimony, 1969, quoted from English translation at Department of Religious Studies, Makerere University, by Abdu Kasozi.
142. S. Damulira's words (see note 108).
143. *CMI* (1890), pp. 25–6, repr. Sebwato to Mackay, 4 March 1889.
144. Lugolobi, *Mbulire*, p. 10.
145. Miti (trans.Rock), *History of Buganda*, p. 327.
146. Kisosonkole, 'Obulamu bwange', p. 74.
147. Stokes, 6 October 1889 in FO 84/2060, PRO; Wright, *Buganda in the Heroic Age*, pp. 80–1; Luck, *Charles Stokes*, pp. 73–4.
148. R. Walker, 20 September 1889, 24 October 1889, WP.
149. Kasirye, 'Obulamu', pp. 36–7.

150. M. Twaddle, 'The ending of slavery', pp. 119–38.
151. J.Nyakature, *Anatomy of an African Kingdom* (English translation by T. Mugwanwa, ed. G.N. Uzoigwe, New York 1973), p. 144.
152. R.Walker, 4 January 1890, 5 March 1890, WP.
153. *Ibid.*
154. This is one of Wright's principal themes in *Buganda in the Heroic Age.*

# Three

# The British Colonial Entry
# 1890–3

1

European interest in Buganda was a comparatively late development. Even in the 1880s, this part of Africa was one with the fewest contacts with the wider world; so few, indeed, that Norman Leys would later describe it as resembling somewhere on another planet altogether.[1] That was an exaggeration. Pre-colonial Buganda resembled a number of African kingdoms at the time in being essentially an aristocracy of honour whose internal economy and society depended upon large numbers of slaves doing the meanest jobs.[2] In its relative isolation from earlier contacts with Europe, however, Buganda was most unlike West African kingdoms like Asante or Benin. It was also somewhat unusual in eastern and southern Africa in the degree to which the Europeans who opened it up to the forces of imperialism in the late nineteenth century were neither traders nor farmers, but missionaries of just two Christian denominations.

The first Europeans to visit Buganda in the nineteenth century had been unofficial travellers such as Speke and Stanley, to whom we owe the first printed descriptions of the kingdom.[3] These accounts are picaresque, distorted by racial stereotypes, and need to be compared with the vernacular chronicles of the period produced by the first generation of literates taught by Christian missionaries,[4] alongside whatever other evidence survives of an archival or an oral nature. For obvious reasons Speke was not 'remembered' by most of the elderly Ganda first interviewed for this study – he had visited Buganda during the early 1860s – but Stanley was still a vague memory. It had been Stanley whose famous letter to the *Daily Telegraph* in 1875 stimulated British Anglican missionaries to go to Buganda, to be followed so very quickly by Cardinal Lavigerie's White Fathers from Algiers. Stanley was also visiting the East African interior again in 1888–9, as Buganda slid into its extended succession war.

Stanley's objective was what is today the southern Sudan. There Eduard

Plate 5. *Bishop Tucker (Top left), George Pilkington (Top right), Captain Lugard (Centre), Frederick Jackson (Bottom right), and Captain Macdonald (Bottom left).* (From J.D. Mullins, *The Wonderful Story of Uganda* (1904), frontispiece; Margery Perham, *Lugard: The Years of Adventure* (1956), frontispiece; F. Jackson, *Early Days in East Africa* (1930), frontispiece; H.H. Austen, *With Macdonald in Uganda* (1903), frontispiece)

Schnitzer, better known to posterity as Emin Pasha, was believed to be still alive and running a skeleton administration with the remnants of an earlier Egyptian army. During the earlier nineteenth century Emin had been one of a small number of European and North American expatriates whom the Khedive of Egypt had employed during his push to enlarge the Turko-Egyptian empire southwards. But by the later 1880s this experiment in imperialism by proxy had come to grief. The British bombardment of Alexandria early in the 1880s had provoked what Ronald Robinson and Jack Gallagher later called a 'recognisably modern nationalist movement'[5] against outside infidel interests – familiar today in its mixture of modern and pre-modern characteristics, but then far less familiar. The British Government's subsequent 'bondage in Egypt', together with the Madhist revolt in the Sudan, cut off the most southerly tip of the Khedive's empire, and with it Emin Pasha, from Cairo.

Emin, however, was less interested in being rescued than in being reprovisioned and rearmed. In June 1886, to be sure, he had written to the CMS mission in Buganda vaguely suggesting a British protectorate in Equatoria. This suggestion Mackay supported enthusiastically.[6] But the British Government preferred to support a private expedition led by Stanley via the Congo, to get Emin out of the area. Unfortunately, by the time the expedition reached Emin in 1888, it was scarcely in a condition to rescue anybody. But it could still cause trouble. Emin was respected by his Sudanese subordinates, Professor Sanderson has remarked, 'for his impartiality and administrative skill, and for his personal qualities of tact and patience'. Nonetheless, he was 'trusted and obeyed so long, and only so long, as no suspicion arose that his policy was in conflict with the deeper loyalties of his "people". A man less fitted than H.M. Stanley to understand the subtleties of such a relationship would have been hard to find'.[7] When eventually Emin was released by his now rebellious troops, he was in no position to form the basis of any administration, British or otherwise. After rapidly walking round Buganda, Stanley took Emin to the newly established German imperialist toehold opposite Zanzibar.

Before leaving the lakes region, Stanley had been approached by Christian exiles in Nkore to support their campaign to reinstate the now repentent Mwanga II in power. Stanley refused to help them.[8] He also advised William Mackinnon that Buganda would prove extremely expensive to administer, even under the economical British chartered company that the British Government was now prepared to support in view of the rival campaigns for colonies currently being undertaken on behalf of Leopold of the Belgians and other European powers. Stanley told Mackinnon that 'to assure control of Buganda a formidable expedition would be required involving not less that 500 white men with 2,000 porters, and an expenditure of not less than £100,000'. Furthermore, 'such an undertaking was not desirable until a railway was constructed'.[9] It was hardly surprising that Mackinnon and his colleagues therefore appealed to the British Government for more support for their chartered company than it was prepared to provide.

The IBEAC was granted its charter in 1888. Initially the British prime minister, Lord Salisbury, had been unwilling to commit his countrymen to any British imperialist presence on the East African mainland. But when the Anglo-German Agreement of October 1886 partitioned the mainland up to Lake Victoria, and the Germans made clear the seriousness of *their* designs upon the more southerly sphere, Salisbury hoped that a British chartered company might yet again prove useful in meeting the British Government's theoretical responsibilities to their sphere at minimum cost.[10] In June 1888 Mackinnon wrote to Emin, offering to take over Equatoria as a going concern, and at the start of 1889 the Imperial British East Africa Company despatched an expedition from Mombasa under the command of Frederick Jackson. Jackson was instructed to join forces with Stanley and Emin.[11] However, when Stanley and Emin, by now no longer pro-British, arrived at the coast and received a special telegram of congratulation from the German emperor, the situation had changed. Jackson was nowhere near his objective in the interior. Carl Peters was.

Peters was the founder of the *Gesellschaft für Deutsche Kolonisation*. Disguised as a mechanic, and travelling third-class to Zanzibar by William Mackinnon's British India steamship line, he concluded a number of 'treaties' with chiefs on the mainland through various subterfuges. In February 1885, he handed these treaties to Bismarck in Berlin.[12] In March 1885, just a day after delegates to the Berlin Conference on Africa had dispersed, the Kaiser's *Schutzbrief* was published taking the territories covered by Peters's treaties under German protection. Later that year, a German naval squadron was sent to Zanzibar to back up the new German chartered company which Peters had by now established.[13] German metropolitan reasons for this sudden imperialist coup are still a matter of some uncertainty.[14] But clearly Bismarck himself did not wish to push things too far. In October 1886 he agreed to a 'rounding-up' treaty whereby the East African mainland up to, but not beyond, Lake Victoria was partitioned on paper into respective German and British 'spheres of influence'.[15]

Nonetheless, what Carl Peters had done successfully once in deception of British officials, he might well do again. During 1888–9 Britain collaborated with Germany over a naval blockade of the East African coast in order to quell the Abushiri rebellion which had just erupted against the German chartered company. Bismarck publicly rebuked the German company; obtained the equivalent of £100,000 from the Reichstag; and put in Wissmann as commissioner with full powers. But, even while the blockade was continuing, Peters landed at Witu and led another expedition up the Tana river and across what is nowadays Kenya in order to himself 'rescue' Emin Pasha, thus breaking the spirit if not the letter of the Anglo-German Agreement of 1886.[16] This was in June 1889. Peters caught up with Jackson's expedition at Mumias, opened its mail while its members were away climbing Mount Elgon, and read amongst other things *Kabaka* Mwanga's appeal at the close of 1889 for the IBEAC's help after being driven back to Bulingugwe again. Peters immediately hurried on to Buganda. There he concluded a treaty of friendship with Mwanga. He was greatly assisted in this by the White Fathers. Mwanga's camp prompted Peters to think of Attila the Hun.[17] But any resemblance to Attila would have been surely more applicable to Peters himself, with his seemingly endless capacity for concluding unequal treaties in the heart of Africa – that is, had Peters not upon being informed of the impending arrival of Jackson's caravan made an exit from Buganda, according to the White Fathers' superior at the southern end of Lake Victoria, 'unique in the history of travel in Uganda' in its rapidity.[18] Later Peters was disgusted to discover that his further treaties in the East African interior had been overtaken by the second Anglo-German Agreement of July 1890. 'We have bartered three kingdoms for a bathtub in the North Sea', he complained bitterly.[19]

Meanwhile Emin too was planning to enlarge the German sphere of influence in East Africa. In April 1890 he had left the coast in order to establish Germany's 'natural hinterland' in what is now eastern Zaire and western Uganda.[20] But, in addition to the complications caused by Emin's activities, the scramble for territorial concessions in Africa was now threatening to become uncontrollable in Europe. Both British and German governments now felt it necessary to act quickly. Hitherto both governments had relied upon Bismarck to keep German imperialism within bounds. But in March 1890 Bismarck fell from power. Stanley as well as Peters had been making treaties with East Africans, or at least saying he had been making treaties, and agitation for colonial annexation was increasing in Britain as well as in Germany so long as there were areas beyond Lake Victoria remaining unpartitioned on paper. Lord Salisbury dealt with this rising tide of 'social imperialism', associated with the onset of industrialism and new democratic electorates in Europe,[21] in three ways: partly by simply omitting to tell Germany of the IBEAC's most contentious demands; partly by accepting the German desire for a common boundary with King Leopold's Congo (and thus sabotaging Mackinnon's own plan for a 'Cape-to-Cairo' link-up with Cecil Rhodes's chartered company in Southern Africa, through retention of a corridor of territory between Uganda and Lake Tanganyika); but mainly by offering the island of Heligoland in the North Sea as a sop to German naval ambitions nearer home.[22]

In Bismarck's view, acquiring Heligoland in exchange for concessions in East Africa showed 'more imagination than sound calculation' on the German side. 'In the event of war it would be better for us that it should be in the hands of a neutral power. It is difficult and most expensive to fortify'.[23] To Salisbury's mind there was a similar problem with the British 'sphere of influence' in the East African interior: without a railway the 'sphere' would remain largely a diplomatic fiction. Direct government money for a railway was 'of course unthinkable', but 'private enterprise, which had failed to protect the Upper Nile from foreign encroachment, might yet succeed in this purely technical task if given some public assistance'.[24] This was where the IBEAC came in and was to prove, economically as well as politically, an embarrassment to Britain and a disaster for Uganda.

To Lord Salisbury the basic trouble with the Imperial British East Africa Company was its lack of commercial drive.[25] To the IBEAC's historian, it was more a matter of commercial drive being unduly subordinated to imperialist sentiment: 'the directors believed that in investing their money they were acting not primarily as businessmen but as imperialists and that the greatest dividends would not be in personal profit'. Furthermore, William Mackinnon especially manifested towards the end of his life 'all the attributes of a convert to the religion of imperialism'.[26] Both views underestimate the extent to which Mackinnon's idiosyncrasies, including his tendency to act on occasion 'as if the Company were his personal property by making commitments without consultation with the directors', [27] have been idiosyncrasies shared by successful as well as unsuccessful tycoons throughout capitalist history. The views also underestimated the fluidity of a situation 'which, with the absence of internal strife in this part of East Africa, and a different British electoral result there, could conceivably have produced a very different result'.[28] Thirdly, the views overestimated the degree to which British governments would act as generously as their German counterparts within their 'sphere of influence' after the Abushiri rebellion.[29]

Captain Lugard, who commanded the second IBEAC expedition to Buganda towards the end of 1890, in fact had nothing like the back-up enjoyed by his nearest counterpart in German East Africa, *Reichskommissar* Wissmann. Lugard had just under 300 porters – a third of them good men, a third indifferent, and a third useless, according to his biographer. He also had about 50 Somali and Sudanese soldiers, with whom he could only communicate through an interpreter; about eleven rounds of ammunition per man; the Maxim gun which Stanley's Emin Pasha Relief Expedition had dragged across Africa and was now showing signs of wear; extremely little food by the time Buganda was reached; and an ornate pair of pyjamas which doubled up as his dress uniform.[30]

## 2

Lugard figures prominently in all histories of Uganda.[31] Just months after reaching this particular section of the East African interior, he set off on a further long march to the western part of it. During this march he recruited remnants of Emin Pasha's earlier forces to form a much bigger colonial army than he would have been able to finance with British chartered company suppport alone.[32] These 'Nubians' (*banubi*), as they quickly became known locally, were to have considerable importance for Uganda as late as the 1970s; when the dictator Idi Amin would call their descendants the most important tribe in the whole of East Africa and base his own regime principally upon their administrative manpower.[33] In 1897, too, there was a major army mutiny in which these Nubians would act as the principal rebels.[34] And, in Lugard's own time, his recruitment of

Sudanese troops and slaves from Kavalli's for service within the new and more southerly British 'sphere', necessitated a far more tolerant attitude towards Islam than Christian missionaries of both denominations wished for, as well as further strengthening Lugard's preference for uniting local Christians and Muslims within a single reconstituted Ganda kingdom, as opposed to dividing it up into a number of smaller, weaker units as was British policy further south, for instance, towards the Zulu kingdom. But by far Lugard's most controversial decision during his period as IBEAC representative in Uganda, was his issuing in January 1892 of precision firearms to Ganda Protestants only.

That led to armed conflict between Catholics and Protestants at the Ganda capital. 'Every RC house & garden is a mass of ashes & charred bananas & some Protestant places too', noted one CMS missionary. Such was the devastation that only the worst example of industrialization in Britain seemed comparable. 'The place reminds one of entering Birmingham from Wolverhampton by night'.[35] Elsewhere in Europe, the battle of Mengo brought Lugard instant obloquy amongst Roman Catholics in general, and in France the full force of government propaganda because Cardinal Lavigerie, the White Fathers' founder, had been of enormous importance only recently in the rallying of Roman Catholic support to the Third French Republic through his symbolic toast at a dinner for officers of the French Mediterranean fleet in November 1890.[36] Lugard wrote a massive defence of his actions, characteristically entitled *The Rise of our East African Empire*.[37] Margery Perham, too, in her biography, defends at length the honourableness of Lugard's behaviour in issuing guns only to Protestants in January 1892.[38] But, as has been remarked elsewhere,[39] so much of this apologia is beside the point. Lugard's real problem at this time was that he was a captive of circumstance in the closing stages of a bitterly contested succession war with very limited independent power of his own. Even after he had recruited his additional Sudanese soldiery, he had very limited independent power to deploy against the massed ranks of the various Ganda factions which he felt obliged to play off, one against another, as effectively as he could from his very first day in Buganda; for there was just no possibility of Lugard conquering them all in one go.

The White Fathers were naturally indignant when their converts lost at the battle of Mengo. They made as much trouble as possible in Europe about the atrocities committed by Lugard's colleague, Captain Williams, in allowing his Maxim gun to be turned upon Ganda Roman Catholics on Bulingugwe island.[40] Local representatives of the Church Missionary Society, too, were aggrieved at Lugard's political behaviour. 'The policy of the Company had been one which, taking the goodwill of the Protestant party for granted, had always favoured the Papist party', complained George Pilkington shortly after the battle of Mengo; 'most careful had both Captains Lugard and Williams been to let no national or religious prejudices seem in any way to influence them in their administration'.[41] In view of the CMS's very vigorous contribution to the campaign in Britain to arouse public support for the IBEAC administration, such impartiality appeared very ungrateful to Pilkington and other CMS missionaries.[42]

To be sure, Lugard did have one crucially important bargaining counter – precision firearms – and in any final overview of British imperialism's penetration into Africa during the second half of the nineteenth century, these must be accorded due importance, together with those other technological changes which favoured increased European penetration at this time: coal-fired shipping, railways, submarine cables, the telegraph. All these were to link European-dominated empires overseas much more effectively with their metropoles than ever before.[43] Indeed, where the full weight of British imperialism was applied against some still predominantly pre-industrial African polity, technological superiority proved of overwhelming importance.

Such was the case with the Zulu kingdom, where Professor Guy tells us that the British military invasion of 1879 had been intended 'to end the independent existence of the Zulu kingdom with a sudden sharp blow', and was followed by the appointment of 13 chiefs to rule various segments of it, a lengthy and debilitating civil war, and the final incorporation of Zululand into Natal in 1897 and the opening of much of its land to white settlement early in the twentieth century.[44] This did not happen to Buganda. Instead, partly because Buganda was already into its third year of a succession war which might still unseat Mwanga and restore a Muslim king to power in southern Buganda (if Ganda Protestants carried out their threat to abandon Buganda entirely), and partly because the IBEAC itself was so severely undercapitalized, Lugard had insufficient men or *matériel* to manage a proper outright conquest. He only had just about enough rifles with which to defend his own life.

Carl Peters, too, had been concerned about his personal survival in Buganda. Peters was consequently unwilling to hand over to Mwanga any ammunition: that would have been suicidal, in his view.[45] Nor had Peters been willing to 'attack and beat Karema and the Wanjoro in the north': his justification being simply 'I have not enough ammunition'.[46] However, he did have sufficient ammunition to make himself objectionable to Protestant Ganda chiefs generally, and to make friends with Gabrieli Kintu in particular. Kintu, like Kakungulu, had acquired a middle-grade chieftaincy in the immediate aftermath of the storming of Lunguja, as Mwanga's *Mujasi*. Kintu performed various favours for Peters during his brief visit to Buganda, such as checking out rumours of war spread around by Apolo Kagwa. Kintu, wrote Peters subsequently, was 'my particular friend' in Buganda. He was also the person with whom Peters took tea on his last evening there. 'We talked much of Germany and Uganda, and he expressed a wish to visit me one day in Germany. But it would be still better if I should soon return to Uganda, to arrange all matters in friendship between the Germans and the English. I may honestly say, that it was a matter of genuine sorrow for me to part from the distinguished and quiet mannered young Waganda, the only real native gentleman whom I met with in the country'.[47]

Kakungulu subsequently developed a somewhat similar relationship with Lugard.

Lugard's continuing problem in Buganda was his inability to back up his or his subordinate's words with sufficient resources: 'a policy which offers concessions which cannot be carried through because of lack of power', as another CMS missionary typified it during July 1891.[48] Peters's visit to Buganda at the beginning of 1890 had further sharpened party differences between Protestants and Catholics. These were already under considerably more strain than in Nkore, following the equal distribution of chiefships between two politico-religious groupings of unequal size in the immediate aftermath of the storming of Lunguja; for at this time there were far more committed Roman Catholic Ganda converts than CMS-taught ones.[49] Furthermore, Emin Pasha's arrival and activities to the south and west of Lake Victoria at the same time kept the possibility of a German, rather than a British, protectorate over Buganda at some future date alive as a serious possibility in White Fathers' minds right up to the time of Lugard's coming to the kingdom.[50] After Lugard's arrival, the danger that the IBEAC might have to withdraw completely from Buganda, through terminally fatal withering of its metropolitan support, kept alive the feeling amongst at least some White Fathers that Germans might still be their eventual overlords rather than indigent Britishers.

Why White Fathers should also have preferred a German protectorate to a British one, seems clear enough. France was not a serious imperialist partitioner of territory in this part of Africa and, after Bismarck's *Kulturkampf* against Roman Catholicism at home had been replaced by something much less hostile, Germany seemed far less likely than the IBEAC to impose an unfavourable monopoly of religion as well as trade.[51] Admittedly, in late 1889, after the Ganda Muslims' counter-attack had driven Mwanga back to Bulingugwe island in Lake Victoria within weeks of the storming of Lunguja, Father Lourdel and Mwanga wrote beseechingly to Frederick Jackson's first IBEAC caravan for help.[52] But when Jackson declined to supply any immediate help, apart from a somewhat crumpled IBEAC flag, and Mwanga's followers managed to push the Ganda Muslims back into Bunyoro in February 1890, Lourdel and Mwanga started writing very different kinds of letter about a possible future European protectorate over Buganda. This was after assistance had been received, not only from within Buganda but from the ex-CMS missionary Charlie Stokes. Stokes's trading network lay within the more southerly German 'sphere', as too did most other White Fathers' missions which were not situated within King Leopold's Congo State.[53] Then Carl Peters had arrived with his suggestions.

During Peters's visit, CMS missionaries were important in persuading Protestant chiefs to sign his treaty. Christian solidarity against Muslims was their principal argument in favour of this course of action, and probably a more powerful one at the time than posterity has given credit: Kalema's following still posed a very considerable military threat to Mwanga's continuance in power as a Christian king.[54] Furthermore,

Protestant chiefs' signatures to Peters's treaty enhanced their moral authority in signing a subsequent treaty with the IBEAC, when Frederick Jackson arrived a few weeks later. But Jackson appeared to be bewildered by the situation he encountered in Buganda.[55] The best he could do, apart from lending just over a hundred precision rifles to Mwanga, was to take rival Ganda Protestant and Roman Catholic envoys back with him to the East African coast in order to discover within which particular 'sphere' Buganda lay in European governments' eyes. Only when these envoys returned to Buganda did Ganda Catholics realize that, at least for the immediate future, their kingdom would be regarded by Germany as well as Britain as Britain's imperial responsibility.[56]

White Fathers in Buganda could do little about this unless the IBEAC withdrew of its own accord and Britain left nothing behind in its place. Nonetheless, in clause 11 of its charter, the IBEAC was required to adhere to the principle of religious liberty; and in the Final Act of the Brussels Conference of 1889–90 the further duty was imposed on all signatory Powers to protect Christian missionaries 'without distinction of creed'.[57] The Brussels Conference was convened in response to Cardinal Lavigerie's call for 'a great crusade of faith and humanity' against the still-continuing slave trade in Africa and, more particularly as regards East Africa, to provide ideological cover for armed Anglo-German responses to the Abushiri rebellion at the coast. The General Act, to which the delegates at Brussels finally agreed in July 1890, further declared that the slave trade was best countered by 'progressive organization of the administrative, judicial, religious and military services in the African territories placed under the sovereignty or protectorate of civilised nations'. The Brussels General Act has been called by Professor Miers the 'Magna Carta of the colonial powers' rather than of African governments;[58] and its regulation of future importations of precision firearms was, as another historian points out, destined 'to inhibit programmes of military modernization by African rulers, and to ensure the technological superiority of European armies during the decade of conquest' that now commenced.[59] For White Fathers in Buganda, however, the Brussels Act, read in conjunction with the earlier Berlin Africa Conference Act of February 1885, sharpened a more subtly subversive political weapon in their hands: religious liberty.

It was a subversive weapon in Buganda now because in October 1889 chiefly offices had been shared out equally between followers of the Catholic and Protestant politico-religious groupings. Because Mwanga was then considered to be a Roman Catholic supporter, Apolo Kagwa as the Protestant party leader became *Katikiro* and, almost without exception, 'Protestants and Catholics were mingled all over the country in adjoining estates, responsible to different people' of the other denomination.[60] One consequence of this alternation of Catholic and Protestant chieftaincies within a single, highly centralized political system, was greater difficulty in punishing chiefly miscreants. As Captain Macdonald, who was diverted from his exploratory railway survey to enquire into the causes of the battle of Mengo, subsequently reported: 'the detection of offences and offenders was rendered most difficult, and was at once made a party question: and the whole system lent itself to sudden complications between the parties'.[61] Another consequence, White Fathers averred, was suppression of religious liberty.

What was to happen when a Ganda chief switched religious allegiance from Protestant to Catholic? Both Captains Lugard and Williams (who was in charge of Kampala Fort during Lugard's absence for most of 1891) considered that the chief should retain his chiefship, especially when Monsignor Hirth reminded them of the principles of religious liberty enshrined in both the Berlin and Brussels Acts. Ganda Protestants and CMS missionaries thought otherwise. Many more freemen wanted to become 'men of Mwanga' than 'men of the *Katikiro*', and should too many Protestant chiefs become Catholics, Ganda Protestantism would be seriously weakened. In another CMS missionary's words,

> As the king is the head of one party, a good many people want to go over to his party as they get more honour in the country by belonging to the King's party. When men have left the Protestant party to join the King's party & they have refused to turn out of their chieftainships, the Protestants have applied to the I.B.E.A. Co to enforce the law. Now Capt. Williams says he cannot enforce this law, nor can he recognise a man being compelled to leave his chieftainship or possessions on account of a change in his religion ... The Protestants say well, if you will hoist the English flag at Mengo & declare the country to be under English rule we will give up the half of the power of the land for which we fought. The Capt. finds he cannot hoist the English flag. Mwanga and the Catholics won't have it. They don't want the Company in the country at all. Then the Protestants say what guarantee do you give us that the King and Catholics shall not deprive our chiefs of all their power (this has been done in the case of the Gabunga already!) and eventually drive us out of the land? [62]

Such was the slenderness of IBEAC resources, and such the political uncertainty of Roman Catholic support for the IBEAC in Buganda, that Lugard and Williams eventually gave in to the wishes of their most enthusiastic supporters, the Ganda Protestants, over this issue. Macdonald's 'Report' noted that, during Lugard's period as chief IBEAC administrator, 'there was a custom by which anyone changing his religion was evicted from his estate and was provided for by the party he joined, though it is not certain that this custom was universal'. What is certain is that the custom proved deeply unsettling. 'Many of these disputes developed into most serious affairs and nearly led to civil war'.

One such dispute concerned Kakungulu directly. This was in December 1891. As Macdonald's 'Report' summarized it,

> Molondo's case [was] most complicated and nearly resulted in war. It would appear that some shambas [plots of cultivated land] in Molondo's [that is, in Kakungulu's] district belonged to a nominal Protestant who became a Catholic. The Protestants wished to evict him. The Catholics claimed the shamba, hence the usual dispute taken up by both parties.

Molondo was at the capital at the time. News reached Molondo that his village was threatened by the Heathen [party, which Mwanga's forces on Bulingugwe island had befriended earlier but were now hostile to]. He asked the King permission to go to his country seat but was refused. He then went to Capt. Williams who said he might go to defend his village but not to go to the disputed Shamba. Molondo asked no further permission and started off. The Catholics the same night sent a strong party after him to prevent his taking the disputed Shamba. Capt. Williams hearing this went to heads of both parties and got messengers sent off to recall both parties. The Catholics returned and were followed after a few days by Molondo. The Catholics and Protestants had however fought in [the] disputed shamba, the Catholics claim that 13 men were killed [but] the Protestants aver but a few men.

Meanwhile there was very nearly war in [the] capital, the trouble lasted several days, shots were exchanged but fortunately no damage was done ... [63]

On this occasion, as on others during 1891, war was successfully averted. But in January 1892 it was not, when Lugard returned from his march to the west and distributed rifles to the politico-religious grouping in Buganda with the least popular support, but the only one upon which he could unreservedly depend: the Ganda Protestants.

Macdonald's indictment of Lugard was that he had squandered the success of his military expedition against the Ganda Muslims in May 1891, in company with the Ganda Catholics and Protestants, by marching off westwards afterwards. Instead he should have built more constructively upon it by returning immediately to Buganda. Macdonald was not therefore one of Lugard's most fervent supporters. Kakungulu was.

# 3

Lugard has left several tributes on record to Kakungulu. He was one of the 'absolutely loyal men' he had dealings with in Buganda. Indeed, he was one of 'but three men in Uganda whom I thoroughly trusted, but in them I had implicit faith. They were Zachariah (Protestant), Sekibobo (Roman Catholic), and Mlondo (Protestant) – the last was not a Muganda by birth'.[64]

Michael Wright has suggested that the basis of the friendship between Lugard and Kakungulu lay in 'Lugard's impulse towards peace' in the immediate aftermath of the battle of Mengo. 'Semei Kakungulu, Lugard's friend', comments Wright,

> a deeply religious man who had also been heavily involved in the conflict, freely acknowledged this when, thirty years later, he looked back to the great time of troubles. "For when the British Government came to protect our country of Uganda," stated Kakungulu in 1924, "it found that we were killing each other in civil war, Muslims and Christians and also Christians and Christians (Protestants and Catholics), and fighting between ourselves for religion. Then the Government said that it was madness to fight for religion, because religion is God's

affair. Government said that it wished to reconcile us, and it did so, and former enemies became brothers. And because of that peace brought by the Government every man chose the religion which will lead him to God."[65]

But this is a retrospective interpretation. Certainly Lugard was eager to welcome back to Buganda both Catholics and Muslims as soon as practicable after the battle of Mengo, as he realized that failure to do so would make his eventual return to Europe even more uncomfortable. By mid-1892 Lugard thus arranged for the reinstatement of Mwanga II as Ganda king; the regrouping of most returned Roman Catholics within a single substantial area of western Buganda; and the award of three counties to returning Muslims – Busujju, Butambala and Gomba. And Kakungulu was one of the Ganda Protestant chiefs who were of critical importance in holding this mid-1892 settlement together. But what most appealed to Lugard about Kakungulu seems to have been not so much any lack of extremist religious opinion or action on his part – the principal evidence for which comes from the very end of Kakungulu's life, by which time his religious views had altered considerably.[66] Rather, it was Kakungulu's willingness to fight, when most other Baganda Protestant leaders appeared to prefer to stay at home.

Admittedly, one CMS missionary does downplay his role in the military harassment of Ganda Catholics at this time. Travelling back to the capital with Robert Walker immediately after the battle of Mengo, Robert Ashe reported that during the journey 'we heard firing, which turned out to be the end of a desultory attack made by the Protestant Chief Mulondo on the retreating rear-guard of an exodus of Roman Catholics similar to our own, which had taken place from the Roman Catholic province of Kyagwe, under the Sekibobo, a chief of the French faction'.[67] Epic poetry, such as the praise song *Kangabaana, eyawangula abensambya* ('the scatterer of children, the one who conquered those of Nsambya'), which dates from this occasion, might be considered to have exaggerated Kakungulu's bravery – were it not for the comments of Batolomayo Zimbe.

Zimbe, who was present at the time, relates how Kakungulu was commissioned by Lugard to lead an expedition from the capital to evacuate the two CMS missionaries from Masaka. The expedition spent its first night in Butambala county, where it learnt that the Catholic chief, Alexis Sebowa, was also heading for Masaka with followers said to be expressing great hatred for Protestants, 'including little children who were all to be drowned in Katonga'. Katonga was the great river-swamp separating Buddu county from the rest of Buganda. Zimbe says that Kakungulu's men had 650 guns as against Sebowa's 1,300. Kakungulu favoured attacking Sebowa's party before it attacked 'our Europeans'. The first skirmish took place in Busujju county, at a small village called Nsambya. Outnumbered two-to-one in firepower, and by four-to-one in numbers, Kakungulu's followers attacked Sebowa's party first, just after it had struck camp. According to Zimbe, Kakungulu himself was a particular object of

Catholic vilification and counter-attack (presumably in part because the Mulondo case of two months before must still have been fresh in Alexis Sebowa's party's memory). But Zimbe relates that, even when his nearest companions were struck down, Kakungulu was still to be heard firing his distinctive rifle – which fired 12 shots before reloading and was nicknamed *mutesa* – to the very end of the battle:

> God saved Semeyi Lwakirenzi Kakungulu Mulondo because he was our leader. We had fled and all in his lines had been killed but he stayed behind fighting. Sebowa Sekibobo fled to Budu. Next day we met Pokino Sebwato Nikodemu and our teachers the Europeans Rev. R.H. Walker and Rev. Ashe to whose help we had marched, at Kibibi, and Kakungulu our leader offered to take them to Mengo.[68]

So much for a 'desultory attack'!

Lugard was pleased when he heard about it. 'Mulondo seems to have done excellently, also the Pokino [Nikodemo Sebwato, who accompanied Ashe and Walker on the last leg of their journey], but I do not even know whether the rest of the skunks [Lugard's personal synonym for the Protestant party] ever went near the fighting'.[69]

This raises several questions about Kakungulu at this time. Why did he fight so hard when most other members of the Ganda Protestant grouping preferred to lie low in the immediate aftermath of the battle of Mengo? And why should somebody who had fought so bravely as a member of the leading Roman Catholic chief Honorat Nyonyintono's following in late 1889, now be aligned with the Ganda Protestants? As a person clearly close to Mwanga II on Bulingugwe island, and somebody who reportedly refused to accept the second-grade chieftaincy of Mulondo after the storming of Lunguja until it had been personally bestowed upon him by the Ganda king,[70] one might have expected Kakungulu to have converted to Roman Catholicism alongside Mwanga rather than fight fervently on the Protestant side. Furthermore, if the various vernacular chronicles of his life stress any one thing it was his ceaseless quest for honour as currently understood by Buganda's chiefly class. Why therefore did he not also seek, in the CMS missionary's words, to 'get more honour in the country by belonging to the King's party' and converting to Roman Catholicism?

The question is difficult to answer definitively, but interview evidence suggests that personal ties kept Kakungulu within the Ganda Protestant grouping. He had been initiated into Christianity by Alexander Mackay, and Mackay continued to keep in touch with developments in Buganda from the time of his removal to the southern end of Lake Victoria in 1887 until his death there in 1890. Individual Ganda Protestants like Tomasi Semfuma and Tomasi Semukasa also influenced Kakungulu considerably.[71] However, Semukasa was to switch sides between politico-religious groupings in Buganda several times, before ending up as one of the very few Protestant chiefs in the predominantly Roman Catholic county of Buddu during the early twentieth century – Semukasa was 'the Winston

Churchill of Buddu Protestantism', as one of his grandsons engagingly put it[72] – and Kakungulu might so very easily have followed a similar course had his 'crafty man' image, so stressed in oral sources regarding his earlier career as an elephant hunter in Buddu country,[73] applied here too. But it did not. To understand why it did not apply here requires differentiation between the public and private sides of the 'crafty man' image in the traditional politics of honour in Buganda. One must also admit Kakungulu's closer attachment to 'paganism' at this time than his subsequent (and predominantly Christian) chroniclers say.

For Roman Catholicism in Buganda then seems to have been stricter than Protestantism as regards sexual morality – apart from the king, that is, to whom White Fathers granted licence so long as he remained an honorific Roman Catholic. To be sure, Protestant folk wisdom in Uganda nowadays asserts Catholics were more tolerant than Protestants over sexual matters. But the White Fathers' correspondence reveals that this was not so in the early 1890s,[74] while Father Waliggo's detailed reconstruction of Ganda Catholicism in Buddu county during the later 1890s reveals a priest-ridden society in which even minor infringements of sexual morality were severely punished.[75] By comparison, Ganda Protestantism seems to have been initially permissive on polygamy but tougher in preaching against beer parties.[76]

The principal explanation for this situation seems to have been insufficient numbers on the Protestant side. After October 1889 chiefships were distributed, as we have suggested,[77] equally to Catholic and Protestant leaders in Mwanga's following. However, because the Catholic party was so much larger, there tended to be more 'pagan behaviour' in the Protestant party. In the 'Notes on Uganda' which he published in the *Church Missionary Intelligencer* during 1893, Robert Walker wrote that Kakungulu was 'less well taught' than other Protestant chiefs.[78] There is no reason to think that Walker was writing anything other than the literal truth.

Kakungulu was not baptized until after Mwanga's arrival on Bulingugwe island.[79] Admittedly, vernacular chronicles of his life do claim that he had been a Christian from a much earlier date.[80] That is doubtless correct as regards personal interest and commitment. Elephant-hunters are mentioned by the White Fathers as one of the earliest occupational groups to be attracted to Christianity in Buganda.[81] Elephant-hunting was a hazardous occupation even with firearms, yet economically of the greatest importance to the Ganda king. Consequently, those who participated in it entertained fewer fears in the early and middle 1880s of dying at the king's command, but greater ones of dying through doing their job. Several Christian missionaries were also skilled repairers of the very firearms just starting to be used in elephant-hunting, and it would hardly have been sensible for Mwanga II to punish elephant hunters for being friendly with them. We have already noted that one chronicle does state that Kakungulu did worry about being killed during Mwanga's persecution of Christians in the mid-1880s, despite being an elephant hunter.[82] But there was a considerable difference between being a 'secret reader' then, and being still a 'late Christian developer' in the early 1890s. Kakungulu's chroniclers should also be read with particular caution when they refer to his earliest religious opinions. This is for two reasons. One is that they were products of that most powerful transformer of spiritual sensibilities, the literacy introduced by Christian missionaries. The other reason is that the Kakungulu chronicles were not written contemporaneously, but later when his religious views had changed considerably for a variety of other causes.[83]

On one thing, however, Kakungulu's chroniclers seem accurate enough: his increasing personal unpopularity amongst Roman Catholic chiefs as well as with the Protestant party leader, Apolo Kagwa. Throughout the uncertain months preceding Frederick Lugard's arrival as IBEAC administrator, Kakungulu's followers had continued to sing satirical songs about Apolo Kagwa's generalship. That made Kakungulu unpopular with Kagwa. Kakungulu also quarrelled with Catholic chiefs deputed to cooperate with him in fighting Muslims in and near his chiefship in eastern Buganda in 1889–90. Kakungulu accused Ganda Catholics collectively of cowardice. Unfortunately, in Buganda at this time, as in Tudor England, 'men of honour could (and did) lie, cheat, deceive, plot, treason, seduce' and do all kinds of other terrible things without incurring dishonour, but once a public accusation was made implying dishonour there was no easy withdrawal: for too easy withdrawal of the accusation itself implied 'cowardice, the extremity of dishonour'.[84]

Kakungulu's accusation arose in this way. Mulisi Sebwato, another middle-grade chief in Mwanga's following and a Catholic, was appointed by Mwanga to coordinate resistance against the Muslims in eastern Buganda immediately after Mwanga's second flight to Bulingugwe. Mulisi agreed with Alexis Sebowa, Mwanga's county chief in Kyagwe and the overall Catholic party leader by this time, that the Muslims were too strong to be attacked immediately. Mulisi therefore returned with his party to Bulingugwe island. Upon learning of Mwanga's commander's withdrawal, the chief of Bulemezi county, who was also a Catholic Christian, refused to accompany Kakungulu in any attack upon the Muslims. According to his principal chronicler, Kakungulu nonetheless carried on resisting Muslim rule on the Buganda mainland, albeit with heavy losses and an increasingly demoralized personal following.[85] Hearing of his continued resistance, Mwanga appointed Kakungulu his *omugabe* in eastern Buganda. However, Catholic chiefs in Kyagwe county objected strongly to this appointment because Kakungulu had by now accused them publicly of cowardice. They may also have felt that originally Kakungulu had been more concerned to defend his wives and slaves from capture by Kalema's supporters than to cooperate wholeheartedly in fighting against them under Mulisi Sebwato's command. Mwanga accordingly appointed yet another person to overall command of his forces in Kyagwe, and Father Lourdel wrote to Alexis Sebowa and Semei Kakungulu informing them of the king's decision.[86] Around this time, Sebowa was also replaced by Stanislas Mugwanya as overall Roman Catholic party leader.[87]

There the matter appears to have rested. However, when Mwanga's forces felt strong enough to mount a substantial counter-attack against Kalema's followers in February 1890, it was hardly surprising that Semei Kakungulu was not appointed overall commander. Instead Gabrieli Kintu commanded Mwanga's forces at the battle of Bulwanyi, as a result of which the Ganda Muslim army was again pushed back to the borders of Bunyoro.[88]

Later in 1890 Kakungulu was appointed leader of a force sent out against Baganda Muslims after Kalema's death from smallpox. This expedition was much lauded by Kakungulu's followers subsequently for its successful exhumation of Kalema's corpse and its reburial at Mende in Busiro county.[89] But throughout Lugard's period in Buganda Kakungulu occupied a position only on the fringes of the 'king's party' because of his quarrels with middle-grade Catholic chiefs like Mulisi Sebowa and Gabrieli Kintu, who were leading members of it. They were also amongst Kakungulu's fiercest accusers before Mwanga in January 1890 of wrongly condemning Catholic chiefs collectively of cowardice.[90] Subsequent faction fights, such as Macdonald's 'Molondo case' in December 1891, further entrenched Kakungulu's reputation amongst Roman Catholics as an aggressive Protestant party man, regardless of any special personal qualities that might otherwise have moderated his denominational partisanship at this time. Indeed, it was doubtless because of these various 'fights' that Catholics were reported by Zimbe to have shouted so loudly at the battle of Nsambya in 1892: 'Kakungulu – the Catholics will kill you this time!'[91]

Admittedly, during mopping-up operations after this and other engagements, Kakungulu did not pursue Mwanga and Roman Catholic chiefs as vigorously as Captain Williams would have liked, into and through the Sesse islands. Ironically, Kakungulu was still to receive his share of the White Fathers' opprobrium for doing what he and his followers did do in company with Captain Williams's maxim gun.[92] On the other hand, Kakungulu does not appear to have shared the uncertainties of companion middle-grade Protestant chiefs in these operations like Mudiima or Wakibi. They too had been members of the earlier 'king's party' on Bulingugwe island, and their uncertainties nearly led them to move with Mwanga and the Ganda Catholics into German territory.[93] Kakungulu was probably crucial in keeping them and other Protestant party waverers under the IBEAC flag. His principal chronicler asserts that Kakungulu considered that Williams had insufficient supporting forces to pursue Mwanga's forces successfully.[94] This, rather than any inherent moderation in his character, was probably the decisive consideration.

Nonetheless, whatever Kakungulu's personal feelings for Mwanga II may have been, the sharpening of politico-religious rivalries following the post-Lunguja share-out of chiefships, combined with the heightened bitterness between Christian missionaries resulting from the increasing European 'scramble' for colonial territory throughout Africa, meant that the basic political decision now facing Kakungulu was – to which of the three politico-religious parties should he continue to commit himself ? To

Lugard's relief, Kakungulu continued to belong to the Protestant party and, after the battle of Mengo, to act as one of its most warlike leaders.

As a result, he acquired the second highest office in Buganda under the Kabakaship. This happened when the Roman Catholic chiefs together with Mwanga left Buganda after their defeat at the battle of Mengo. Kakungulu was appointed to administer the *Kimbugwe*'s estates during his absence. When the Catholics returned with Mwanga shortly afterwards, Mugwanya no longer wished to be known as Buganda's second minister, but as 'the Catholic Katikiro' equal in status to the Protestant party leader. Apolo Kagwa now became the Protestant *Katikiro*, and Stanislas Mugwanya the Catholic one. Kakungulu was confirmed as *Kimbugwe* or second (or, more accurately, third) minister in the Buganda kingdom. As Lugard's diary jottings indicate, this promoted Kakungulu several notches above senior leaders within the Protestant party.[95]

Needless to say, Kakungulu's chroniclers see this promotion as a sign of his growing honour and worth, as well as evidence of legitimate ambition for something better than yet further middle-grade chiefships, such as Kawuta and Mujasi, which he had also held briefly during the Catholic chiefs' absence in early 1892.[96] Under Lugard's successors, however, even Kakungulu's chroniclers admit that the criteria for promotion to high office became more complicated.

## 4

Some complications arose from the continued uncertainty about Buganda's international status. In August 1892 Lord Salisbury's government in Britain fell, with this issue amongst others still unsettled. Rosebery, the new British foreign secretary, was keen to annexe it and get a railway built to it as quickly as possible. Gladstone, prime minister yet again, opposed embroiling Britain in further African adventures which might provoke 'no end of trouble with the French and Germans',[97] and invoked prime ministerial responsibility as his ultimate argument against annexation. Rosebery threatened to resign. Such was the tenuous electoral basis of Gladstone's new government that a compromise was agreed whereby the British government would provide a further subsidy for the IBEAC until March 1893. By then, European missionaries would have had sufficient time to withdraw completely from this strife-torn part of Africa. But Rosebery fought on, tacitly supporting a wide-ranging CMS-supported campaign for the retention of Uganda as a British imperial responsibility.

This campaign has been written off as a failure by some historians, 'in that it had no perceptible effect upon Liberal opinion and did not compel the cabinet to adopt a clear-cut policy of retention'.[98] But it did make any policy for total abandonment also 'more difficult than ever' and 'demonstrated too the extent to which imperialism had captured the imagination of the upper classes'.[99] Nonetheless, Gladstone and his supporters fought a tough rearguard action in cabinet; and only because Rosebery wrote the instructions for the Commissioner appointed to enquire into the situation on the spot did Sir Gerald Portal haul down the IBEAC flag in Kampala

PUNCH, OR THE LONDON CHARIVARI.—April 21, 1894.

UGANDA

THE BLACK BABY.

Mr. Bull. "WHAT, ANOTHER!!—WELL, I SUPPOSE I MUST TAKE IT IN!!!"

Plate 6. *Cartoon in the British magazine* Punch *on 21 April 1894.*

on 1 April 1893 and replace it with the Union Jack.[100] By the time Portal left again for the East African coast two months later, he had signed another treaty with Mwanga II placing Buganda under British 'protection'. Basically, this treaty confirmed Lugard's final settlement, only amending it with a slightly better deal for Roman Catholic chiefs.[101] Portal appointed the same Captain Macdonald who had just enquired into Lugard's local actions as 'Acting Commissioner in Uganda and its dependencies'. He also left him with a staff of seven Europeans and over a thousand African troops, including those whom Lugard had recruited from among Emin Pasha's former soldiers.[102] But Portal's proposals for annexation were not approved finally by the British cabinet until 22 March 1894, by which time Rosebery had replaced Gladstone as British prime minister.[103]

By comparison with many other British colonial dependencies in Africa at this time the establishment was, as Professor Sanderson remarks, a generous one.[104] But, in Ganda terms, it was not big enough for British officials locally to survive without providing their allies with still greater opportunities for external plunder, supported now with precision weaponry. Thereby further complications quickly arose.

# *Notes*

1. Norman Leys, *A Last Chance in Kenya* (London 1931), p. 115.
2. See P. Lovejoy, *Transformations in Slavery* (Cambridge 1983), pp. 27–8.
3. J.H. Speke, *Journal of the Discovery of the Sources of the Nile* (London 1863); H.M. Stanley, *Through the Dark Continent* (London 1878).
4. M. Twaddle, 'On Ganda historiography', *History in Africa* 1 (1974), pp. 85–100; J.A. Rowe, 'Myth, memoir and moral admonition: Luganda historical writing 1893–1969', *Uganda Journal* 33 (1969), pp. 17–40, 217–19.
5. R. Robinson and J. Gallagher, 'The partition of Africa', *New Cambridge Modern History* Vol. 40 (Cambridge 1962), p. 597.
6. R.Oliver, *The Missionary Factor in East Africa* (London 1952), p. 131, quoting Emin to Mackay, 6 July 1886.
7. G.N. Sanderson, *England, Europe and the Upper Nile, 1882–1899* (Edinburgh 1965), p. 39.
8. I.R. Smith, *The Emin Pasha Relief Expedition 1886–1890* (Oxford 1972), pp. 269–70; J.M. Gray, 'The year of the three kings of Buganda', *Uganda Journal* 14 (1950), pp. 41–2.
9. J.S. Galbraith, *Mackinnon and East Africa* (Cambridge 1972), p. 172, quoting Stanley to Mackinnon, 6 February 1890.
10. Sanderson, *Upper Nile*, p. 44.
11. Margery Perham, *Lugard. The Years of Adventure, 1858–1898* (London 1956), p. 175; Galbraith, *Mackinnon*, pp. 153–5; F. Jackson, *Early Days in East Africa* (London 1930), Chapters 11–18.
12. R. Coupland, *The Exploitation of East Africa* (London 1939) and F.F. Müller, *Deutschland–Zanzibar–Ostafrika* (Berlin 1959) are standard accounts; Carl Peters, *New Light on Dark Africa* (London 1891) is a translation of *Die Deutsche Emin Pasha Expedition* (Munich 1891).
13. Coupland, *Exploitation*, pp. 404–24; Müller, *Deutschland*, Chapters 4–6.
14. J. Iliffe, *A Modern History of Tanganyika* (Cambridge 1979), p. 88.
15. Coupland, *Exploitation*, pp. 424, 472–5; Iliffe, Chapter 4.
16. Coupland, *Exploitation*, pp. 482–3; Smith, *Relief Expedition*, pp. 273–4; Peters, *New Light*, passim.
17. Peters, *New Light*, p. 388.
18. *Ibid.*, p. 452.
19. Müller, *Deutschland*, p. 496: *Wir haben eine Badewanne gegen drei Konigreche eingetauscht.*
20. *Ibid.*, pp. 478–87; Sir John Gray, 'Anglo–German relations in Uganda', *Journal of African History* 1 (1965), pp. 181–297; Wm Roger Louis, *Ruanda–Urundi 1884–1919* (Oxford 1963), p. 15.
21. See J.D. Hargreaves, *West Africa . . . The Elephants and the Grass* (London 1985), Chapter 1; W.J. Mommsen, *Theories of Imperialism* (London 1980), pp. 97–9; R.U. Wehler, 'Industrial growth and early German imperialism' in eds R. Owen and B. Sutcliffe, *Studies in the Theory of Imperialism* (London 1972); and G. Eley, 'Defining social imperialism: use or abuse of an idea', *Social History* 1 (1976), pp. 265–90.
22. Müller, *Deutschland*, pp. 492–6; D.R. Dillard, 'Salisbury's African policy and the Heligoland offer of 1890', *English Historical Review* 75 (1960), pp. 631–53; Sanderson, *Upper Nile*, pp. 53–63; R. Robinson and J. Gallagher, *Africa and the Victorians* (London 1961), pp. 298–300; Louis, *Ruanda–Urundi*, pp. 18–29.
23. Quoted in J. Holland Rose, *The Development of the European Nations 1870–1914* (London 1915), p. 521.
24. Sanderson, *Upper Nile*, p. 64.
25. Robinson and Gallagher, *Africa and the Victorians*, p. 307.
26. Galbraith, *Mackinnon*, pp. 238–9.
27. *Ibid.*, p. 141.
28. Quoting review in *Africa* 44 (1974), p. 109.
29. Coupland, *Exploitation*, p. 483; Muller, *Deutschland*, Chapter 14; Iliffe, *Tanganyika*, Chapter 4.
30 Perham, *Lugard*, p. 223; J.A. Rowe, *Lugard at Kampala* (Kampala 1969).
31. For example, K. Ingham, *The Making of Modern Uganda* (London 1958), pp. 43–52; S.K. Karugire, *A Political History of Uganda* (Nairobi 1980), pp. 75–83; G.N. Uzoigwe, *Uganda* (New York 1982), pp. 57–60, 96–8. The fullest account is Perham, *Lugard*; see Mary

Bull, 'Writing the biography of Lord Lugard', in eds A. Smith and M. Bull, *Margery Perham and British Rule in Africa* (London 1991), pp. 117–36.

32. Perham, *Lugard*, Chapter 4.
33. Quoted by D. Pain in ed. M. Twaddle, *Expulsion of a Minority* (London 1975), p. 229.
34. See below, p. 124.
35. G.K. Baskerville, journal entry for 25 January 1892, Makerere University Library (MUL). Rowe, *Lugard at Kampala*, for the best account.
36. See D.W. Brogan, *The Development of Modern France (1870–1939)* (London 1940), pp. 257–64; F. Renault, *Lavigerie, l'esclavage africain et l'Europe* (Paris 1971), Vol. 2.
37. Published in 1893.
38. Perham, *Lugard*, Chapters 18 and 19.
39. Rowe, *Lugard at Kampala*, p. 1.
40. H. Gründer, *Christliche Mission und deutscher Imperialismus* (Paderborn 1982), pp. 196–200 for a good summary. See also Catholic Union of Great Britain, *Notes on Uganda* (London 1893); [P. Mesnage], *L'Ouganda et les agissements de la compagnie anglaise 'East Africa'* (Paris 1892); and R. Heremans, *L'Education dans les missions des Pères Blancs en Afrique centrale (1879–1914)* (Brussels 1983), pp. 123–4.
41. G. Pilkington, letter of 31 January 1892, quoted in C.F. Harford-Battersby, *Pilkington of Uganda* (London 1898), p. 170.
42. H.Bernt Hansen, *Mission, Church and State in a Colonial Setting: Uganda 1890–1925* (London 1983), Chapter 4, provides essential discussion.
43. See D.R. Hendrick, *The Tools of Empire: Technology and European Imperialism in the Nineteenth Century* (New York 1981).
44. J.J. Guy, *The Destruction of the Zulu Kingdom* (London 1979), pp. 239–47. See also eds A. Duminy and C. Ballard, *The Anglo-Zulu War* (Pietermaritzburg 1981).
45. Peters, *New Light*, p. 284.
46. *Ibid.*, pp. 435–7.
47. *Ibid.*
48. Baskerville, journal, 19 July 1891.
49. Lourdel, letter of April 1890 [no day given] in White Fathers' Archives, Rome (WFA), C14/82.
50. Rubaga Diary (RD): entries for 23 and 30 December 1890.
51. Gründer, *Christliche Mission*, p. 194, quoting a letter of Father Bresson, 14 February 1890.
52. Solomon Wamala, 'Obulamu bwa Semei Kakungulu', unpublished MS in MUL, pp. 72–3; Lourdel, April 1890, C14/82, WFA.
53. *Ibid.* See also A. Luck, *Charles Stokes in Africa* (Nairobi 1972), Chapter 6.
54. Peters, *New Light*, p. 383; Robert Walker, 4 January 1890, WP, noted that 'The Arab party in Buganda seems pretty vigorous & continuously is making attacks on the Xians on the mainland'.
55. Jackson, *Early Days*, Chapter 18; Perham, *Lugard*, pp. 219–27; Rowe, *Lugard at Kampala*.
56. Apolo Kagwa, *Ekitabo kya Basekabaka be Buganda* (Kampala 1952), pp. 155–6.
57. Hansen, *Mission*, pp. 26–7 and Chapter 3 more generally.
58. S. Miers, *Britain and the Ending of the Slave Trade* (London 1975), p. 318, quoted in Hargreaves, *Elephants*, pp. 8–9. See also F. Renault, *Lavigerie, l'esclavage africain et l'Europe* (1971).
59. Hargreaves, *Elephants*, pp. 8–9.
60. 'Capt. Macdonald's Report on Uganda disturbances etc in 1892', 17 April 1893; the copy in A1/1/1891–1892, Entebbe Secretariat Archives (ESA), was used. (Perham, *Lugard*, Chapter 19 on the Macdonald Report, gives little idea of its value as an analysis of Ganda social structure, indeed probably the most perceptive one by a British official throughout the 1890s.)
61. *Ibid.*
62. R. Walker, 5 August 1891, WP.
63. Macdonald, 'Report'. Other accounts of the Mulondo case appear in A. Kagwa, *Basekabaka*, p. 158; *Church Missionary Intelligencer (CMI)*, September 1892, pp. 671–2; Ham Mukasa, *Simuda Nyuma* Vol. 3, pp. 411–12; and Baskerville, journal entries for 4–6 December 1891.
64. British Parliamentary Papers (PP): Africa No. 2 (1893), p. 863; Lugard, *Rise*, Vol. 2, p. 460.
65. M. Wright, *Buganda in the Heroic Age* (Nairobi 1971), pp. 128–9.

66. See below, p. 265.
67. R.P. Ashe, *Chronicles of Uganda* (London 1894), p. 276.
68. Zimbe, *Buganda ne Kabaka*, quoting translation by F. Kamoga in MUL.
69. Lugard, entry for 3 February 1892, eds M. Perham and M. Bull, *Diaries* (London 1959), p. 47.
70. Paulo Kagwa, 'Omukwano gwa Kabaka Mwanga', unpublished MS in MUL, pp. 10–12; E. Kibuga, unpublished MS in the Ndaula papers, Nkoma, Mbale, pp. 3–4; Temuteo Kagwa, 'Kakungulu Omuzira Omuwanguzi', unpublished MS in MUL, p. 5; Wamala, 'Obulamu', pp. 83–4.
71. Oral testimony of Danieri Kato, son of Tomasi Semukasa, Kako, Buganda, 1968. Tomasi Semfuma remained a friend until Kakungulu's last years and was a witness of his will; *Mackay of Uganda*, by his sister (London 1900, 6th edition), p. 287, quotes E.C. Gordon writing to Mackay's father (4 January 1892) that 'Tomasi Semfuma . . . was one of your son's early pupils . . . and he often taught others'.
72. Jasper Bamuta, over lunch one day in 1968 at Kako, Buganda.
73. See above, pp. 20–1.
74. This is a matter of judgment, but greater RC strictness is reflected in correspondence, such as Lourdel of April 1890 [no day given] in WFA, C14/82 ('chez les catholiques on ne peut avoir qu'une femme').
75. J.M. Waliggo, 'The Catholic Church in the Buddu province of Buganda, 1879–1925', Ph. D. dissertation, Cambridge, 1976.
76. WP, 28 November 1891, 18 September 1896. Albert Lugoboli remembered George Pilkington preaching most charismatically against the dangers of drink.
77. See above, p. 74.
78. *CMI*, March 1993.
79. See below, p. 105.
80. See above, p. 23.
81. RD, 10 August 1886, 9 September 1886.
82. See above, p. 27.
83. M. Twaddle, 'The nine lives of Semei Kakungulu', *History in Africa* 12 (1985), pp. 325–33.
84. M. James, 'English politics and the concept of honour 1485–1642', *Past and Present* supplement, 1978, p. 28.
85. Wamala, 'Obulamu', pp. 72–9; A. Kagwa, *Basekabaka*, pp. 154–5.
86. WP, 29 December 1889; RD, 27, 28 December 1889, 10 January 1890; Wamala, 'Obulamu', p. 81; Zimbe, *Buganda ne Kabaka*, p. 225.
87. *Ibid.*
88. A. Kagwa, *Basekabaka*, p. 155.
89. Wamala, 'Obulamu', pp. 84–7. See also Miti (trans. Rock), *History of Buganda*, pp. 636–7.
90. Wamala, 'Obulamu', pp. 78–9; A. Kagwa, *Basekabaka*, p. 159.
91. Zimbe, *Buganda ne Kabaka*, pp. 263–4.
92. See note 40, esp. 'Agissements', pp. 148–9.
93. Wamala, 'Obulamu', pp. 93–7; A. Kagwa, *Basekabaka*, p. 159.
94. *Ibid.* R.P. Ashe, *Chronicles*, p. 306, and Zimbe, *Buganda ne Kabaka*, p. 267, are also relevant; also Miti (trans. Rock), *History of Buganda*, p. 388, where Kakungulu is said to have disapproved of Williams's suggestion on the ground of 'the army not being prepared to make such a long voyage'.
95. Lugard, 6 May 1892 in eds Perham and Bull, *Diaries*, pp. 224–5.
96. Wamala, 'Obulamu', p. 101.
97. Perham, *Lugard*, pp. 405–7.
98. Sanderson, *Upper Nile*, pp. 101–14, upon which this and the next paragraph are based; see also Robinson and Gallagher, *Africa and the Victorians*, Chapter 11; Perham, *Lugard*, Chapters 20 and 21; and the Portal Papers in Rhodes House Library, Oxford.
99. *Ibid.*
100. Sanderson, *Upper Nile*, p. 102.
101. G. Portal, *The Mission to Uganda* (London 1894); H. Bernt Hansen, *Mission, Church, and State in a Colonial Setting* (London 1984), pp. 59–64.
102. Sanderson, *Upper Nile*, p. 103.
103. *Ibid.*, p. 112.
104. *Ibid.*

# Four

# Competing for Honour
# 1893–9

## 1

Kakungulu first heard about his promotion when returning from a joint British–Ganda expedition with three objectives – to replace a Soga chief who had died in a shooting accident, to rescue another CMS missionary in danger, and to keep open IBEAC links with the East African coast. Kakungulu now hastened to Mwanga's court. There he summarized the expedition's achievements and declared to the Ganda king: 'I have defeated the Basoga who rebelled against you'. This declaration, relates his chronicler, pleased the king considerably as 'during the period 1888–92 no Muganda had set foot in their country'. The chronicler also notes that Kakungulu arrived back in Buganda two days after Lugard had left it,[1] evidently on the first leg of his journey back to Britain.

On Kakungulu's way to Mengo, the Bavuma islanders failed to provide sufficient canoes for his warriors to cross into Buganda near the point where the River Nile leaves Lake Victoria. They also attacked Kome island nearby. For all but the reign of Kabaka Suna, the Bavuma islanders had been Buganda's adversaries. It was therefore not surprising that people from Kome island should now appeal to Kakungulu for help. 'In response the Protestant army broke off their voyage [home] and hurried to the rescue of their ally', relate Miti and Rock. 'Lwakirenzi, however, arrived on Kome island somewhat late, and only found that the mischi[e]vous Bavuma had long [since] come, taken up whatever they wanted and gone back to their island home. Lwakirenzi then led his men away from Kome and safely brought them back to Mengo'.[2]

At Mengo plans were laid for a much larger expedition against the Bavuma islanders. Kakungulu was again appointed commander in company with Captain Williams (who stayed on in Buganda as IBEAC leader after Lugard's departure) and Captain Macdonald. But the Buvuma

88

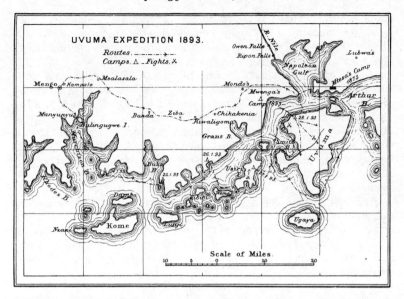

Map 5. *Macdonald's map of the Buvuma campaign of 1893.* (From Macdonald, *Soldiering and Surveying in British East Africa* (1897), p. 146).

campaign of January–February 1893 was not to cause Kabaka Mwanga as much pleasure as the one which had just restored Miro to the chieftaincy of Bukooli. Nor would it prove a crusade about which local CMS missionaries could feel entirely happy.

Mwanga was angry when Williams refused to bring him into the planning of the expedition, let alone take part in the fighting itself. That, comments Kakungulu's principal chronicler, was because Mwanga was 'extremely eager to fight the great country which his own greatgrandfathers and father had failed to conquer'. The chiefs suggested a compromise – that Mwanga should follow this particular plundering expedition by land and at a distance, telling Captain Williams that he 'would he be going on a visit to Kyagwe', the immediately adjacent administrative county on the mainland.[3]

Unfortunately the suggestion backfired. When Kakungulu suggested to Williams that all the captured cattle should be taken to Mwanga's camp in Kyagwe for the customary redistribution of spoils, Williams disagreed. Mwanga had played no part in the fighting. As Ganda commander, it should surely be Kakungulu who divided the spoils. Should Kakungulu himself refuse to divide the spoils, they would have to be returned to their original owners. That was too much for Kakungulu's companions. They now came from all three main politico-religious groups, Catholic and Muslim as well as Protestant, and their representatives complained to Kakungulu that there was no sense in *returning* booty for which they had fought and for which many of their relatives had died. 'Doesn't the Kabaka know that he has no effective authority now and that all powers lie with the European? When the European refused to allow Mwanga to go to war, did he then go to war?' It remained for Kakungulu to attempt to soothe Mwanga's displeasure. This, the chronicler relates, took several days. 'How could you be annoyed with me, your friend? You know that God gave kings cool tempers: they are not as irritable as common people.' With these words, the chronicler relates that Mwanga's displeasure was soothed.[4]

As regards personal relations between Mwanga and Kakungulu, this may have been so. But Mwanga's displeasure with the incoming imperial order would continue because, even more than at Mengo a year before, the Buvuma expedition underlined the extent to which the Ganda king's authority was being eclipsed by the powers of Her Britannic Majesty's representative.

CMS missionaries, too, were unhappy at the manner in which these powers were now deployed. They were especially distressed at the numbers of Bavuma seized as slaves. The Bavuma, reported Robert Ashe in his *Chronicles of Uganda* (1894), published shortly after his final return to Britain, were 'a brave and warlike people' and 'splendid canoe men'. Captain Williams had seemingly decided to attack them in order to secure the IBEAC's communications with the East African coast, but the pretexts for the attack upon the Buvuma islands he considered to be 'more or less frivolous'. He had complained to Captain Macdonald, but been told that Macdonald was only going on the expedition 'to help a brother officer'.

> The attack was made in Stokes' boat and the Company's steel boat and a host of canoes. Two Maxims were employed. The Bavuma, as soon as their enemy appeared, came on splendidly; and had it not been for the frightful effect of the Maxims, which literally mowed them down before they could come within striking distance, it might have gone badly for the Ba-ganda. The islands of this brave people were then occupied and looted. Captain Williams behaved, as was to be expected from an English officer, with humanity and moderation, and was backed up by the Christian chiefs, who returned a vast host of captured women; nevertheless, the Muhammedan Ba-ganda auxiliaries, and no doubt others, carried off numbers of slaves, and openly brought them to the capital.

Soon some of these slaves were marched right past Ashe's house at the capital by Muslim chiefs. Ashe again protested, this time to William Grant, the IBEAC official in charge of Kampala fort. Grant did what he could to stop further slaving, 'but as soon as it became known that the highroads were watched the slaves were conveyed secretly by other means'.[5]

In his own memoir on *Soldiering and Surveying in British East Africa* – more about soldiering than surveying, as a British newspaper remarked upon publication[6] – Macdonald attempted a retrospective rebuttal of criticisms of the expedition, as regards both excessive slave-taking and Ganda territorial aggrandizement more generally.[7] But Macdonald lost the moral argument because the Bavuma expedition had been excessively destructive. Kakungulu's principal chronicler relates that such was the enormity of the slaughter that, not only were certain sections of Lake Victoria 'all blood', there were so many dead bodies bobbing up and down in the water that their heads resembled a multitude of upturned cooking pots.[8] Other vernacular sources, oral as well as written, indicate that many Bavuma were enslaved by Christian Ganda warriors as well as by Muslim ones during this expedition.[9] Kakungulu himself acquired yet another praise name: *Balimwogerako eyawangula Obuvuma* ('They will talk about him as the one who conquered Buvuma'). His followers rewarded themselves by carrying off many more slaves than had been customary during previous plundering expeditions.[10]

Slavery, as we have already noted,[11] was indigenous to Buganda; in Zimbe's words, it was 'our wealth' before the imposition of the British protectorate.[12] Lugard had had quite enough problems to tackle during his period in the East African interior in 1890–2 for him to have added to them by attempting to abolish slavery in Buganda too.[13] When Bishop Tucker told Sir Gerald Portal several months after the Buvuma expedition that Protestant chiefs were willing to abolish slavery within their personal followings, even if Roman Catholic or Muslim chiefs would not, Portal felt uneasy: serious problems might arise thereby immediately as regards labour for roads and other public works.[14] But the Protestant chiefs persisted with their public declaration against slavery; and when Ganda Muslim chiefs rebelled shortly after Portal's departure, Protestant chiefs took full advantage of the customary Ganda rule that slaves running away from masters attached to an opposing side during war could join their followings as free persons.[15]

This rebellion took place in mid-1893, after Portal's departure from Buganda and during the period of Captain Macdonald's acting commissionership. Both CMS missionaries and White Fathers thought that Macdonald did not provoke the rebellion and in fact acted speedily and efficiently in suppressing it. But in London Macdonald did not get much credit. Partly this was because his decision to deport the Sudanese troops' leader, Selim Bey, eastwards along the lengthy caravan road to the East African coast immediately after the rebellion appeared callous. Selim was sick at the time and died before reaching Mombasa. At this very time Selim's friend and recruiter, Lugard, was being lionized in Britain by CMS and non-CMS supporters alike as a leading campaigner for the 'retention' of Uganda as a British imperial responsibility. It was also unfortunate for Macdonald that the British government first learnt the contents of his earlier enquiry into Lugard's conduct in Buganda through a pretty accurate 'leak' of its principal findings in the *Berliner Tageblatt* by a German journalist sympathetic to the Roman Catholic side at the battle of Mengo.

Macdonald had used this journalist's services, injudiciously, during the inquiry itself. That did not endear Macdonald to Gladstone, when the British embassy in Berlin told him about the leak. Gladstone concluded upon receiving the full report that Macdonald was personally prejudiced against Lugard.[16] This was probably untrue – Macdonald is noted in Ganda vernacular sources as being one of the best informed of British proconsuls during the 1890s.[17] Nevertheless, it had been unwise of him to associate Eugene Wolf with his enquiry into Lugard's earlier conduct, and before the end of 1893 Macdonald was recalled to India. In Buganda, his place was taken by Henry Colvile and several other British soldiers who could speak Arabic and thus converse without interpreters with the Sudanese troops earlier recruited by Lugard and compromised by their involvement in the Muslim rebellion of 1893.[18]

The rebellion itself appears to have been the product of political frustration by Ganda Muslims at being restricted to three small administrative counties after negotiating their return to Buganda with Lugard, all the more so after Portal's failure to give them any additional territory such as Roman Catholic chiefs received. The presence of Sudanese troops, both within Buganda and in forts to the west, complicated matters further – particularly when Selim Bey expressed open support for the Ganda Muslims' cause; or rather when Selim seemed to support their cause by stating that he 'would consider hostile action on the part of Mwanga against the Waganda Mohammedans as hostile action against himself'.[19] Macdonald now found himself in a situation similar to Lugard's 18 months before, of being forced to rely upon Ganda Protestants as his most dependable allies.

By this time most Roman Catholic chiefs had fallen back upon Buddu county, *Kabaka* Mwanga having joined the Protestant politico-religious grouping. In Mwanga's presence, Macdonald conferred with Kakungulu and the other Protestant leaders immediately news of likely trouble with the Muslims reached him. Several leading Muslims were then arrested; Sudanese troops at Kampala and Entebbe disarmed; and Selim Bey sent off towards Mombasa. Prince Mbogo was also arrested; he had become Ganda Muslim king upon the death of Kalema in 1890 but renounced his title after negotiation with Lugard. Nikodemo Sebwato was given several hundred musketeers and charged with the security of Mwanga's immediate entourage. He was also told, according to Kakungulu's principal chronicler, 'that when he heard guns firing from the direction of Kampala [Fort] he should take the Kabaka from Munyonyo by lake to Kyagwe. 'However, should you hear that the Europeans have been defeated and we are too, take the Kabaka to Busoga. The Europeans from Mombasa will find him there.'

Meanwhile the main Protestant force was positioned between Rubaga and Namirembe hills – 'in a line about 1500 yards long, but smaller parties were also posted on the north-western prolongation of the ridge', under the immediate command of 'Kakunguru, the brave Protestant leader'. Between Namirembe, Rubaga and Mwanga's palace at Mengo, lay the much smaller outcrop of rock with Kampala Fort upon it. There 'the Maxims were run out to be ready to support the Protestants, should any part of their line be forced'. Macdonald calculated that Muslim Ganda only had 'about 1,300 guns and an equal body of spearmen, while the force at my disposal consisted of about 2,200 guns and perhaps 4,000 spearmen.' However, 'superiority in numbers was partly counterbalanced by the somewhat extended line we had to occupy.'[20]

The battle itself was settled within 30 minutes. However, the first shots were not fired by the Muslims, as Macdonald subsequently reported,[21] but by drunkards amongst Kakungulu's own followers.[22] The battle, once started, too, was extremely fierce; 'terrible', according to Solomon Wamala;[23] 'hot and incessant', in Macdonald's own words.[24] But immediately the Muslim general was slaughtered the mass of Muslims lost heart and fled. Kakungulu pursued them 'unceasingly' as they retreated out of Busiro.[25] Many more Muslims than Protestants died during this pursuit, Solomon Wamala relates. 'Then Kakungulu returned to Mengo and solemnly announced before Kabaka Mwanga, "I have killed the Muslims who previously rebelled against you," and narrated to the king the course of the battle. Then he went to Kampala and told the same story to the Europeans'.[26]

Afterwards Kakungulu was put in charge of operations to prevent Ganda Muslims still at large from linking up with the Sudanese soldiers still stationed in forts to the west, where several British soldiers had been stationed earlier in the year by Sir Gerald Portal. One of them was Roddy Owen, a gentleman jockey who rode the winning horse in the 1892 British Grand National.

Owen was unprepared for the independent manner in which Kakungulu dealt with slaves running away from retreating Muslim chiefs. According to Miti and Rock, Owen was furious that Kakungulu dealt with them without consulting him. For the Protestant Ganda, however, the principal difficulty was that while some Muslim women had been captured by the pursuing Ganda Christians as slaves, others had joined the Christian chiefs' followings of their own accord. As Miti and Rock point out:

> As not all the Mohamedan women in question had been secured as captives, a great many of them having left their Mohamedan master and joined the Christians entirely of their own accord – which class of women was then a free one – it was decided that, as also many of those women had simply been forced to live in conjugal relations with their former Mohamedan husbands as slaves or female prisoners of war they should be given a choice of each lady selecting any one of the three religious parties she preferred and of attaching herself to it without [any] coercion or restriction whatever.

On August 30, 1893, therefore, after each party had presented the number of women that its members had previously held as captives, each of the one thousand such women that there were made her choice and joined either the Protestant or the Catholic or even the Mohamedan group according as each lady chose to do.

93

When Kakungulu reported this, Owen exploded – 'entertaining serious misgivings as to whether after all the Muganda general had not sold the women into slavery among the Banyoro in whose country they were.' This, Kakungulu assured Owen, was not so. According to Miti and Rock, he then 'apologised most sincerely for what he had done' and Owen forgave him, remarking that never again should Kakungulu 'undertake to settle such important matters without first consulting him or even informing him of the position beforehand.'[27]

There is no explicit account of this incident by Owen himself. But Owen's outburst was one which Kakungulu would have accepted without comment: after all, it was the question of *okufugibwa* all over again. However, by the time Owen and Kakungulu got back to the western borders of Buganda, most Ganda warriors under his command had scattered elsewhere – 'in quest of food', as Miti and Rock euphemistically put it.[28] Here Macdonald, in company with Owen, decided upon a final settlement of the Muslim question in Buganda: Prince Mbogo was to be banished to the East African coast, Ganda Muslims would be left in control of only one administrative county, and only those Muslims willing to accept Mwanga's kingship unreservedly under the new British imperial order were to be allowed back into Buganda.[29] Rather than accept these humiliations, many Ganda Muslims left Buganda entirely at this time.[30] Meanwhile Kakungulu, conscious of the greatly reduced number of warriors remaining under his command, appealed to the Ganda king for reinforcements. With these, Kakungulu arrived back at Mengo on 28 September. Then, as Miti and Rock relate, 'Kakungulu, the hero, presented his men to the king in his audience hall in the presence of a large assembly of chiefs, courtiers and other people. He recounted his experience with the enemy in far-off Kizabasenguse and in other places, and in return he received his master's thanks and the praise of all the people who had stayed behind'.[31]

One of the people who had stayed behind was Apolo Kagwa, the Protestant party leader and chief minister. Given the crucial importance now of politico-religious groupings in Buganda, the diminished role within them of Mwanga II since his most recent period of exile, and the continuing dependence of most British officials in the country upon Kagwa's assistance and advice, he was now an extremely important figure. When Macdonald's successor, Henry Colvile, decided upon a war against the neighbouring kingdom of Bunyoro, Mwanga suggested that Colvile himself should be overall commander.[32] When Colvile declined the suggestion and expressed the need for an African co-commander, Mwanga recommended Apolo Kagwa. The Protestant chiefs immediately suspected mischief. With Kagwa absent on a distant battlefield, highly unfavourable things might happen to Protestants in Buganda, especially now that the Ganda king was saying that he might re-join the Roman Catholic politico-religious grouping. Kagwa might die and Ganda Protestants lose their most effective political operator. Protestant chiefs therefore persuaded the CMS missionary John Roscoe to write to Colvile suggesting Semei Kakungulu as field commander yet again. This suggestion Colvile accepted, and so in December 1893 Kakungulu was again commanding a Ganda army on the northern frontier with Bunyoro.[33]

At Kakungulu's investiture as commander, Mwanga is reported by Miti and Rock to have remarked jocularly to his warriors that 'though they had been forbidden to carry off any human beings as part of the booty still he did not think that there was any positive prohibition against their picking up any Banyoro young beauties they might chance to come across during their expedition and keeping them with them in their tents and eventually disposing of them as they pleased.'[34] In fact, this was not to be. Seizing 'Banyoro young beauties' as slaves was to prove a considerable cause of friction between British officials and Baganda warriors during subsequent wars against Bunyoro.

## 2

Like its Ganda counterpart, the Nyoro army consisted principally of a mass levy of the free peasantry mobilized by administrative chiefs. During the last quarter of the nineteenth century, special regiments of musketeers were also raised by the Nyoro king. But because Bunyoro extended over a wide area and was administered in a decentralized manner, these musketeers were stationed throughout the kingdom. They were called *barusura* and, according to Professor Steinhart, their leadership 'was in the royal gift and tended to be distinct from and often in opposition to the regular administrative chieftaincies'. These *barusura* also constituted 'the first experiments with a standing force in this region by an indigenous society' as well as the major instrument whereby the Nyoro king, Kabalega, revived his kingdom's fortunes in the penultimate decades of the nineteenth century.[35] According to an earlier western visitor, they 'were recruited from the deserters of the Egyptian troops, from runaway slaves, and riotous youths from the bordering States … Waganda, Bari, Shooli, Lur, Walegga, Lango, Madi and Bongo men'. They were armed with firearms whose 'incontestable superiority' had been demonstrated by Egyptian troops commanded by Emin's predecessors, Samuel Baker and Charles Gordon. By the time of their victory over Mwanga's invading army under Kibirango in 1886, *barusura* possessed around a thousand guns – 'a large number of Remington rifles, a few Sniders, and a good many percussion muskets, either gathered from the deserters from the Egyptian government or acquired from the Lango, who had several times defeated the soldiers' of the Khedive. To these Kabalega added 'some good breech and muzzle loaders bought from Zanzibari merchants'.[36]

With these arms, the Nyoro army was much better equipped as well as trained than the still temporary levies of most other interlacustrine states including Buganda.[36] Buganda's defeat in 1886 was clear evidence of this. Mwanga responded immediately by building up four special *batongole* chieftaincies, manned principally by unmarried youths whom he stationed close to his royal palace.[37]

Meanwhile, with his *barusura* Kabalega embarked upon the reconquest of breakaway sections of the earlier Bunyoro kingdom. One such was Toro, which had been independent since the early nineteenth century. By 1889 the Katwe salt workings had been recaptured by Kabalega's general, Ireeta.[38] Lugard reestablished Toro as an independent polity during his march to the west in 1891. He put Kasagama on the throne, guarded him with Emin's former troops, and wrote glowingly to London about the Katwe salt workings constituting a veritable IBEAC goldmine.[39] Portal later considered Lugard's reports of Katwe's economic potentialities 'works of fiction'.[40] Portal therefore abandoned Toro and withdrew the Sudanese troops to forts nearer to Buganda – thereby enabling Kabalega to reassert authority over Toro yet again, and helping the Sudanese troops in new forts to attack southern Bunyoro for food and slaves more effectively. In Buganda sufficient Sudanese troops were to be kept at Kampala to hold a balance of power between the principal politico-religious groupings. But no major attempt was made to intervene in Buganda's internal affairs.[41] Upon becoming commissioner in late 1893, Henry Colvile built upon Portal's policies of minimal intervention a major military offensive against Bunyoro.

Colvile's action may have been influenced by Rosebery's secret instructions to extend British influence in the Nile basin and 'to negotiate any treaties that may be necessary for its protection'.[42] But the attack upon Bunyoro was launched at a time when two Nyoro armies were known to be away from Kabalega's capital fighting in Toro and northern Busoga,[43] and Colvile himself felt the need for some dramatic external adventure with which to divert attention in Buganda away from internal tensions. He also wanted to remove at least temporarily from Buganda its most dangerous personalities. For 'the fewer Waganda there were in the country, the fewer throats there would be to cut, and fewer people to cut them.'[44]

Kakungulu was commander of the Ganda levies involved in this offensive. Colvile set out for Bunyoro in December 1893 with 400 Sudanese soldiers; another 300 were left behind to guard the British posts in Kampala and southern Busoga and to secure the grand army's advance base in Singo county. Colvile also took eight Europeans to Bunyoro, amongst them a Major Macdonald again eager to help a fellow British officer and 'Spire my servant'. Frederick Spire was shortly to receive his first post in British protectorate employment as 'Water Transport Officer'. This was when the German official in charge of Bukoba refused to allow more than three canoes with supplies for the Bunyoro expedition to leave without a European in charge.[45] Subsequently Spire would become a senior official in the Uganda Protectorate and a major thorn in Kakungulu's side. But on this occasion he was Colvile's valet and a witness of the way in which, as Colvile himself reported in his book *Land of the Nile Springs*, 'Kakungulu saved me an immensity of trouble by the intelligent arrangements which he made for the concentration of his army on the frontier.'[46]

'This', Colvile continued,[47]

> was no light task. The frontier district, in which I had decided that the concentration of his army should take place, was thinly populated, and

would not support for long the force of 16,000 men that Kakunguru hoped to collect; it was therefore necessary that the concentration should be as nearly as possible simultaneous, so as to allow of the army moving on at once to fresh feeding grounds in Unyoro. As troops were being collected from districts as much as two hundred miles apart, separated by foodless tracts, and connected by only the merest apology for roads, this required a considerable amount of organisation, and I cannot speak too highly of the way in which Kakunguru carried it out.

At the frontier Colvile found a 'sea of huts, which stretched as far as the eye could see'.[48] 'Making our way through the dense crowd of spearmen who thronged the streets of this mushroom town, we came to Kakunguru's headquarters, a large and substantial hut in the middle of a neat enclosure.' There Colvile and the accompanying Europeans were greeted by Kakungulu in the company of George Pilkington, a CMS missionary accompanying Protestant Ganda warriors and behaving much as an earlier medium of a Ganda war god would have done. He had already built a makeshift church.[49] At this meeting Kakungulu was 'dressed in Arab costume', noted Colvile. The following day he 'appeared in European clothes, a check shooting jacket and knickerbockers to match, knitted stockings and shooting boots, the whole surmounted by a turban'. Dressed thus, and mounted on the shoulders of a slave, Kakungulu 'dashed about the camp in all directions, giving orders and trying to get into some sort of form the huge mob under his command'.[50]

In this endeavour, Kakungulu succeeded beyond the commissioner's expectations. The huge Ganda army, with separate Roman Catholic and Protestant contingents,[51] advanced on a broad front with a thousand spearmen preceding it by about a mile. Sudanese troops marched in company with the Europeans and their maxim guns in the centre. Ganda musketeers and other spearmen marched in columns and guarded the flanks. 'Thanks to the distinctive drum beats of the various chiefs', noted Colvile, 'we kept a far better line than I should have expected'.[52]

Professor Steinhart points out that Colvile and Kakungulu expected Kabalega to make a stand at the Kafu river. Instead he fought a series of rearguard actions, ambushing foragers while steadily retreating before the seemingly inexorable advance of the British–Sudanese–Ganda grand army.[53] Kabalega's forces recalled from Toro were anyway in no condition to fight any other kind of campaign, having 'suffered severely from hardships and disease, and returned home in a very dilapidated condition'.[54] Kakungulu told Colvile that he was confident there would be enough food for the whole army in Bunyoro, provided that Kabalega did not lay waste the territory through which he retreated.[55] Kabalega did set the royal capital at Mparo ablaze, but not the 'rich banana groves' behind it. These Colvile found to extend 'as far as the eye can reach'. Bunyoro as a whole he discovered to be 'far more thickly populated and highly cultivated' than Buganda, with 'nice little stores of beans and grain which we found buried in the country' for use during times of famine.[56]

Kabalega then retreated into the Budongo forest and Kakungulu

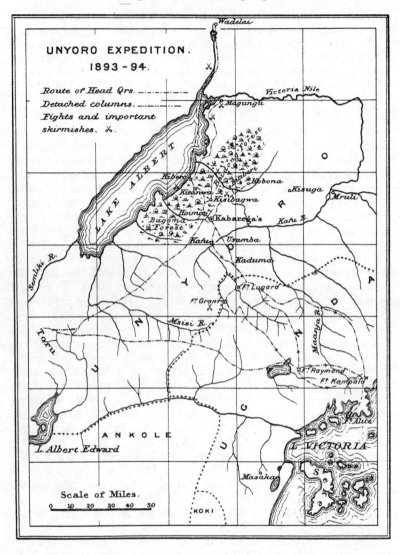

Map 6. *The Bunyoro campaign of 1893–4.* (From Macdonald, *Soldiering and Surveying in British East Africa* (1897), p. 316)

suggested to Colvile that perhaps it was time for the grand army to return to Buganda. 'The country between us and Mruli was said to be very barren, and at the present season badly supplied with water, and even Kakunguru, who had unlimited confidence in the foraging powers of his compatriots, was doubtful whether we could get across'.[57]

Instead Colvile decided to push on. But, as the diary of the medical officer accompanying the expedition makes clear, Colvile had probably already missed the best chance of defeating Kabalega at Mparo. There had been divided counsels in the British high command. Owen advised attack, Macdonald delaying until the following day. By the time Colvile made his decision it was too late. 'There is such a lot of jealousy between these army men … We have lost a good chance, for with the Maxim gun on the hill they could have swept the entire Unyoro camp while they could have sent forces in each side to attack them'.[58] When further skirmishing proved inconclusive and smallpox broke out amongst the Ganda forces, Colvile ordered Kakungulu to stay close to Kabalega in the Budongo forest while he himself set up a further line of forts cutting Bunyoro into two. He then withdrew to Kibiro on Lake Albert in order to get in touch with the rest of Emin Pasha's former troops. Perhaps Colvile hoped to further Rosebery's other ambitions in the Nile valley by moving away from the Budongo forest at this time. If so, it was with little success. A notable at Mahaji who had been disadvantaged earlier by the collapse of the Turko-Egyptian empire, was unwilling to be similarly disadvantaged again – 'how do I know that you will not go away like the other white men, and leave me to be eaten up again by Kabarega. When Kabarega is dead, then I will be your friend, but not before' – very sensible caution, as a year later Mahaji passed under Belgian control.[59]

Colvile was at Kibiro when he received a letter from Kakungulu at the end of January 1894. This reported that Kabalega had left the Budongo forest and was now encamped 10 miles north-east of Colvile himself. Kakungulu suggested an attack. Colvile preferred to finish his forts. He told Kakungulu 'to move out himself with his Waganda and try to surprise the enemy'.[60] By Kakungulu's own account (now only available in Colvile's summary of it), he did precisely that:

> He started next day with about a quarter of his force, bivouacked a few miles to the west of Bitiberi, and next day quite unexpectedly marched into the middle of the Wanyoro. He was in a single file, and it took him a long time to close up his rear; but the enemy was equally unprepared, and a sharp skirmish began between the two advanced parties, gradually developing into a pitched battle, in which the whole of the two forces was engaged. Finally, the Waganda got the best of it and put the Wanyoro to flight, in which Kabarega, running across a bit of open ground from one clump to another, was so hard pressed that he had to drop his favourite rifle.

Colvile remarked that accurate shooting did 'not seem a very common accomplishment in this part of the world, to judge by Kakunguru's statement that the opposing forces were firing at each other for three hours at close quarters, and that, as far as he knew, only three casualties occurred'.[61] Nonetheless, the strategem of encirclement had paid off because, 'deprived of his supplies to the north, [Kabalega had been] forced to make the attempt to break out southwards, which ended in his defeat by the Kakunguru'.[62]

Smallpox was now rife throughout the Ganda army. 'The scene on the road', wrote one of Colvile's companions, 'was both hideous and pitiful, the path being strewn with miserable white objects, masses of corruption, with swarms of flies buzzing round them. These were Waganda sufferers, deserted by their comrades, and hobbling on to a certain and repulsive death'.[63] Nyoro snipers continued to kill stragglers of other kinds who foraged for food or firewood outside the Ganda lines.[64] Ganda in the grand army were therefore delighted to learn that Colvile was now ready for a return to Buganda.[65]

However, the Ganda warriors under Kakungulu's command were less pleased to learn that they would only be allowed to keep about a third of the women they had seized during this campaign as slaves. Macdonald gave 1,174 of their captives back to the Banyoro and only restored 507 supposedly freed Ganda slaves to 'their friends' in the Ganda army.[66] Hardly was this division of captured females complete when news arrived of an impending attack by Kabalega's general, Ireeta. As Colvile later reported,

> Macdonald at once ordered Kakungulu to turn out his men, which he said was done with admirable promptitude, and at four in the afternoon a Waganda force of 2500 guns started to the westward. The manner in which they turned out was the only admirable part of their performance for, on meeting the Wanyoro at eight o'clock the next morning, the force with one accord turned tail and ran away, leaving Kakunguru with only three or four chiefs and a hundred guns.

'Fortunately', added Colvile, 'the Wanyoro were as much impressed by the Waganda as my allies had been by them, and also executed a rapid movement to the rear.' What Colvile did not report, was that this sudden disengagement took place shortly after Ganda warriors had been dispossessed of most of their slaves.[67]

Had the declaration by Protestant Ganda chiefs against slavery in 1892 therefore been basically tactical? In retrospect, this seems likely. The timing of the declaration during Portal's visit had been convenient for the comparatively small grouping of Ganda Protestants closely dependent upon the incoming British protectorate administration for its power. Ganda Muslims had returned to Buganda after negotiations with Lugard, but many Muslim chiefs' free followers were already deserting to other masters and, should the law compelling runaway slaves to be returned forthwith to their owners be repealed, many more runaways from Muslim followings might be attracted into Protestant clientages at a time that *Kabaka* Mwanga was titular head of their politico-religious grouping rather than of the

Catholic one. Catholic chiefs were naturally less keen to abolish the status of slavery, as they had many more slaves than the Protestants, and White Fathers did not share Bishop Tucker's compulsion to end slavery immediately in Buganda.[68]

Protestant chiefs, too, had reservations about abolishing slavery absolutely in their followings. This became evident when Apolo Kagwa returned some runaway slaves from Busoga and the Ganda clergyman in whose enclosure the runaways had sought refuge took the case to Kampala fort. The British official there asked Kagwa if he still had slaves after he and other Protestant chiefs had signed the declaration against slavery several years before. Kagwa replied: 'yes, we still have slaves, lots of them', and the British official was too embarrassed to take the matter further.[69]

British officials, on the other hand, proved increasingly less embarrassed at returning non-Ganda captives discovered on battlefields in Bunyoro as the 1890s progressed.[70] Needless to say, this did little to deepen friendship between British officials and Ganda chiefs.

Lionel Dècle, the representative of the French government who arrived in Buganda at this time after a safari through King Leopold's Congo, considered that slavery would only finally be suppressed by capitalism.

> Bring in railways, and slavery will go out. The policy of the Belgians is exactly the opposite: they drive out legitimate commerce, and inevitably force the Arabs into the slave trade. They have ruined the ivory trade by impossible duties: the Arabs have to pay one tusk out of every five. This is the Congo Free State, whose freedom is all sham and humbug. So far as Africa is concerned, I have no faith left in philanthropists, or missionaries, or foreign governments. I pity the dupes who give their money in Europe to anti-slavery societies and missions. Much better employ the money to find capital for railways and banks.[71]

However, Dècle did not endear himself to White Fathers in Buganda by saying that as a result of his travels in Africa he intended to form an anti-anti-slavery society in Europe. 'The gentleman reminds one somewhat of Parisien farce, without the wit', commented one White Father.[72] Nor did Dècle's sympathy for Lugard's side of the argument about the battle of Mengo find much support in France itself, where the Roman Catholic claim for financial compensation was still being pressed vigorously against Britain. In Britain, however, his views as official French representative paradoxically served further to undermine the credibility of Macdonald's criticisms of Lugard's actions.

Nonetheless, not until Ganda chiefly resentment at British curtailment of slave-taking combined with other grievances to support *Kabaka* Mwanga's armed rebellion against protectorate rule in July 1897, and the Sudanese troops' mutiny of September 1897 further underlined the futility of paying security forces inadequate wages, would the British authorities begin to follow Dècle's advice. Only then would they start seriously to transform Buganda into the region of cash-cropping small farmers, linked by metalled roads and the railway to Mombasa, which it remains today.

For the moment, however, Colvile was content to continue displacing Mwanga II progressively as the principal manager of local gift exchange, excluding only slaves obtained from outside Buganda. From the Bunyoro expedition of 1893–4 Kakungulu and his companions acquired 'three thousand goats, sixty head of cattle, forty guns, ten tusks of ivory, and a great quantity of ammunition, besides recovering five hundred of their countrywomen held as slaves by Kabarega'.[73] Upon the grand army's return to Buganda, much of southern Bunyoro was also added to chiefs belonging to the two Christian political parties.[74] What chiefs in Buganda therefore lost in opportunities for acquiring slaves, they partly made up for with swathes of land from Bunyoro onto which peasant cultivators and herders could be attracted.

Colvile partitioned this territory almost equally between the two politico-religious groupings now dominant in Buganda, Catholics going west into only a slightly smaller area than Protestants acquired to the east.[75] Dècle, who had helped to fire Roddy Owen's maxim gun during a minor expedition against one of Kabalega's allies on the border of Singo county before Colvile and Kakungulu's grand army invaded Bunyoro itself, was most critical to learn that Ganda levies were travelling to join it in separate Protestant and Catholic contingents: 'a very curious result of missionary enterprise which seemed hardly compatible with complete military efficiency'.[76]

However, there was still a marked difference within each politico-religious grouping between leaders and followers. For, as Captain Williams had written earlier, 'nearly all the Chiefs, and certainly anyone of note, [was] outwardly a most enthusiastic professor of the religion to which he belongs', holding evening prayers for all his people about, and does his best to teach his slaves, etc'.[77] But the 'great masses' of their followers were by no means so fervent. As a result, Margery Perham considered that it was 'a misnomer to talk of Christian, Roman Catholic or Protestant armies'. On the other hand, she did consider that national differences between European missionaries in Buganda created 'a cultural and linguistic as well as a confessional division between the two parties. Hence the names of Wa-Ingleza and Wa-Franza came into use . . . [and] seem less inappropriate than the religious ones'.[78] Michael Wright disagrees. He declares that 'the victorious army in Buganda's civil wars deserves to be called Christian', from whatever viewpoint the matter is regarded.[79] Robert Walker, on the other hand, commented at the time:

> in fact I do not think there has ever been much bitterness about religious questions [between the two Christian parties], all the old quarrels were about lands, and public offices. Very, very many people away in their gardens do not know the differences between the two religions [of Protestantism and Catholicism]. They take up whichever happens to be first presented to them. There are very few who are of the one religion or the other from conviction of its superiority.[80]

To be sure, Ganda Christianity in both its Catholic and Protestant forms was already a religion of martyrs, and nothing any subsequent person says can take away from the Christian palace pages of 1886–7, nor from the Christian warriors who fought to restore the repentant Mwanga II to power in 1889–90 (or to plunder Kabalega's kingdom in 1893–4), their deep commitment to their faith. But, with even the most devout Christians amongst them, it was a faith more characteristic of Europe in the ninth than in the nineteenth century; of a time when saints and slaughterers of other human beings were often the very same people, and praised as a result as frequently for their ferocity as for their faith. In Walker's words again, this time from Bulingugwe island in 1890, the Ganda Christian chiefs seemed a curious 'mixture of Christian conscientiousness and heathen cruelty'.

> They believe that God will not give them the victory if they do anything wrong, and therefore they do not like to take any advantage of their enemy. They thought it necessary to write and tell the enemy that they were coming to attack them, lest they should be taken off their guard. Yet when they are victorious they have more than once speared the leader of the opposite side when he was taken prisoner.

'This', Walker remarked, 'is a sort of twilight Christianity'.[81] It does not appear particularly illuminating to argue that 'it was Christianity for all that'.[82]

Two further features of this faith should also be noted. First, Ganda Christianity was still a faith of heroes to whom honour was a major virtue. Secondly, for members of both the Anglican and Roman Catholic denominations, it remained largely an orally transmitted religion, albeit one into which literacy had just started to obtrude at both the functional and popular levels.

In his study of *The World of Odysseus*, M.I. Finley stressed both the competitiveness and the redistributive character of the ancient Greek heroes' behaviour. It was on the field of battle that the highest honours were to be won, through individual combat in which warriors recklessly risked their own lives in order to end the lives of others. Quoting from Veblen's *Theory of the Leisure Class*, Finley pointed out that, under 'this common-sense barbarian appreciation of worth or honour, the taking of life ... is honourable in the highest degree. And this high office of slaughter ... casts a glamour of worth over every act of slaughter and over all the tools and accessories of the act'.[83] Much the same may be said of Buganda immediately before and after the imposition of British colonial rule. The vernacular chronicles of Semei Kakungulu's life, composed for the most part by survivors from the first generation of Ganda Christians, are therefore, along with *The Iliad* of Homer, saturated in blood. Also in late-ninetenth-century Buganda, another 'measure of a man's true worth was how much he could give away in treasure ... The circulation of treasure was as essential a part of the heroic life as its acquisition; and it was this movement, the fact of its existence and the orbit it followed, that set that life apart from any other life of accumulation'.[84] Now Odysseus had his favourite repeating rifle, and sometimes a Victorian shooting jacket too. However, the ending of slavery, the possession of precision firearms, and the acquisition of further swathes of territory and treasures of other kinds made possible by British imperialism and its associated capitalist mode of production, would unhinge this archaic heroic order.

The surviving Kakungulu chronicles indicate accurately enough the main outlines of the ethos of honour of the first Christian generation in Uganda, and their taste for a still predominantly pre-capitalist redistribution of wealth. Where they err is in insufficiently stressing the continuing orality of these first converts' Christianity. Colvile was irritated at the time he was forced to spend during the Bunyoro campaign of 1893–4 in conference with Ganda chiefs still operating in a predominantly oral culture.[85] However, Bible-reading was starting to spread a more popular literacy in Luganda in addition to the limited functional variety already important at military commander level. Walking through the 'masses of Waganda' and their smoke-filled town of grass huts built for the subsequent Bunyoro expedition of April–May 1895, Seymour Vandeleur noticed 'several men studying their Luganda prayer-books' and remarked that 'the missionaries have certainly done wonders in teaching the people to read and write'.[86] George Pilkington accompanied Kakungulu's troops during Colvile's earlier campaign against Kabalega and, whatever reservations one might have about this charismatic preacher stimulating rather than restraining bloodletting by his converts (and acquiring about 250 cows for his own use, according to the White Fathers),[87] his influence in extending popular literacy throughout the Ganda army was considerable.

In time, this literacy would change Kakungulu's own religious opinions profoundly. But for the moment the effect of predominantly oral teaching, combined with an intensive reading of the first fragments of Christian Scripture translated into Swahili or Luganda, was somewhat confusing. As Robert Walker remarked in 1895:

> It is very difficult for these people to understand what the outside world is like: they hear from Europeans privately of the present state of the civilised world & they see the things we bring here – then in our teaching they hear of Abraham, Moses & our Lord & they mix them all up together & not a few think that the New Testament is a history of events in another country not another age & that country & Ulaya (where the white people come from) is all one ... [88]

To be sure, Walker himself was not entirely guiltless here:

> I am afraid I often liken the 'Commissioner' here to Pontius Pilate, Mwanga to Herod, & Queen Victoria to Caesar. I daresay that teachers of the Gospels have seldom had such an opportunity for illustrating the Gospel narratives from the incidents of the daily life of the people. The parties & sects are fairly represented by the Protestants & R.Catholics, & the King's party, the latter being the Herodians.[89]

Kakungulu would later horrify CMS missionaries with his views on misfortune, after reading the Bible in Luganda intensively for 20 years. But in the mid-1890s he was only recently baptized and, at least in Walker's opinion, less well-taught than other Protestant chiefs. In CMS terms, he still had much to learn. He also struck one of Colvile's British military colleagues as 'having embraced Christianity more from his admiration of the social system, education, material comfort and artistic costume, which appear inseparable from it, than from any inward conviction of its Divine truths'.[90]

## 3

Precisely when Kakungulu was baptized and given the Christian name 'Semei' (or 'Simei') is difficult to say. Different sources give different times between 1889 or 1890, when Mwanga II was still living on Bulingugwe island in Lake Victoria,[91] and 1892, by which time Kakungulu had stopped smoking Indian hemp and two of the CMS missionaries at the Ganda capital were Messrs Walker and Millar.[92] Admittedly, Walker was resident on Bulingugwe island as early as September 1889, which makes the matter even more difficult to resolve because the main evidence here is oral, or oral-derived, in character. What is clear, however, is the critical importance for Kakungulu's subsequent career of the territory he acquired as a consequence of the Bunyoro expedition of 1893–4, and why, in contemporaries' eyes, he got it. For, as Ernest Millar explained later to the CMS Committee, 'Kakungulu as he is usually called is a Mukoki by birth & worked his way up by valour in war', becoming successively *Mulondo* and *Kimbugwe*, and then getting 'a piece of Bunyoro called Wunga, which had been given him by the British Govt. for his valour in war'.[93] The British in Uganda were by now far more important patrons than the Ganda king, but Kakungulu's qualification for acquiring new territory remained an ancient one: 'valour in war'.

This new territory, together with the ivory tusks, slaves, guns and cows that he continued to acquire while *Kimbugwe*, by purchase and management as well as through valour and gift, made Kakungulu a man of wealth. In October 1894 some of this wealth was displayed in his second wedding to a Ganda princess, his first royal wife having died by this time of smallpox. As the British official then at Kampala reported:[94]

Kampala
Oct. 15. 1894
Re Kakunguru's wedding

Dear Colonel

Kakunguru this morning sprung the news rather suddenly upon me that he was to be married today. The Archdeacon had told me a long time ago that the Kakunguru intended to marry the former Lubuga Princess Elizabeth Semiramis Nakalema: that he & the C.M.S. men had tried to dissuade the Kakunguru but that the Kakunguru was ambitious to marry a 'princess'. The Archdeacon further explained to me that the reason for dissuading the Kakunguru was that when

Nakalema was the Lubuga [Queen Sister] she had had one of her girl-attendants beaten so unmercifully that the poor wretch died in consequence. Today Mr Millar gave me the further information that she thrashed the girl because she suspected the girl to have had commerce with a man the princess herself happened to be rather in heat of at the time. It appears that in consequence of this ill-advised thrashing & its fatal termination, the Lubuga was formally deposed from the office of Lubuga which has since been vacant. Mr Millar tells me, however, that the reprehensible conduct of the princess occurred when she was a heathen, she has since been converted, is now a Protestant &, Mr Millar adds, sorry for the past.

I had not had time yet to visit the Kakunguru but desired in honour of the occasion (very ill as I was at the time) to pay him today myself a visit.

Not having had time to communicate with you, I hope my presenting to him a silver watch and to his bride a coloured cloth & some silk handkerchiefs as sent by you will meet with your approval. I let the Archdeacon into the secret that I had not had time to get your sanction but asked him to keep it secret. The Archdeacon translated to the bride & bridegroom that the presents were sent by the Colonel and wished them every happiness in their married life.

It is evidently a very grand wedding. I heard the music a long way off (the music reminded one, as the Archdeacon expressed it, of a band tuning up their instruments before beginning to play; unfortunately they never got further). The rows of natives were enormous & the feasting consisted in devouring (I cannot possibly call it eating) huge quantities of boiled & mashed bananas & chunks of meat. In one tent I found a number of big chiefs, Kangawo for one, squatting on the ground so busily digging in that I only gathered when quite near by that they were conveying also the food into their capacious stomachs.

But a most amusing sight was to se the Venerable Archdeacon [Walker], Mr Fletcher & the Rev Mr Millar endeavouring, native fashion, to eat with their fingers from helpings large enough for half a dozen very famished Europeans. The Archdeacon had very cleverly a lad crouching by his side to whom he handed down 3 out of every 4 handfuls, he thus managed to do justice to the occasion; but Mr Fletcher got hopelessly entangled with a lump of mashed bananas as big as his head, & Mr Millar had fairly to give in when a fair-sized joint was expected to be demolished by him.

The Archdeacon kindly translated for me the menu:-

7 bullocks each cut into 17 pieces and under the
distribution of a special chief;
8 goats; (about as many goats as he had to send to the
king for marrying a princess);
80 loads of banana-mash;
30 bowls of milk (curdled & sour);
30 bowls of pombe [local beer].

I felt near fainting (I was really very poorly) several times but could not get at the princess, the bridegroom being too 'shy' to find out whether the ladies had done eating. At last however I got introduced & was presented as your messenger with your gifts. She is rather a stout party & I should say will rule Kakunguru unless I am much mistaken.

One amusing sight was to see 3 boys with a huge bone, all holding it & taking fierce bites at it like ravening wolves.

Another was a big chief loudly complaining that here he was, invited & a guest, but where was the sour milk he was to have. .

The king's soldiers were in 2 rows holding their guns in every conceivable direction when told to present arms.

I forgot to mention '2 kegs of gunpowder' figuring at end of the 'menu'; not to be eaten but to be blazed away in honour of the occasion. Yours sincerely,

W.J. Ansorge

Col. H.E. Colvile, C.B.
H.B.M.'s Commissioner

Ansorge was not the most popular protectorate administrator with Ganda chiefs, as he was prone to punish them with savage sentences, such as throwing them into the chain-gang at Kampala Fort,[95] as well as making racist remarks. He was also, as his report upon Kakungulu's second wedding to a Ganda princess indicates, ignorant of Swahili as well as Luganda. George Wilson, who replaced Ansorge as British official at Kampala at the end of 1894, did have Swahili and two African wives, but as one of them was a Zanzibari and the other a Maasai, and both were kept locked up in Kampala Fort,[96] this hardly improved his Luganda. Wilson was therefore as dependent upon Christian missionaries for translations of conversations with Ganda chiefs in the Luganda language as were other British officials.

CMS missionaries were careful not to exploit this advantage too openly. They also made sure that those of their number (like Robert Ashe) who quarrelled bitterly with British protectorate officials were soon posted elsewhere.[97] White Fathers were less careful. As Frederick Jackson subsequently remarked, the first Roman Catholic missionaries in Buganda were 'semi-political', while early CMS ones only gave political advice when asked for it.[98] As a result, Anglican missionaries were more influential with British officials than their Roman counterparts.[99] As one particularly bitter entry in the Rubaga Diary for the mid-1890s declared:

> It is always the same thing. Whether the representative of the Queen is called Lugard, or Williams, or Macdonald, or Portal, or Gibb, or Ansorge, or Colvile, or Wilson, it is not he who governs Uganda but the Reverends of Namirembe, through the agency of the Protestant Katikiro.[100]

Apolo Kagwa's position in Buganda was certainly now an influential one. Immediately before the British colonial entry, in the hands of a Mukasa, a Nyonyintono, or under Kalema's chief minister, Muguluma, the Katikiroship had been pivotal in the Ganda political system. After

Lugard's arrival the office continued to be influential. But its earlier influence was reduced for a time by the strengthening in corporate identity of the Roman Catholic party opposed to Kagwa, though reinforced to some extent by tightening Protestant discipline supportive of his position. For a time the Katikiroship suffered too from Catholic–Protestant differences aggravated by the interlayered sharing of subordinate chiefships that characterized the earliest part of the Lugardian era in Buganda. Mwanga II sought constantly to strengthen an independent power base. In doing this immediately after Lugard's arrival, Mwanga was aided by Roman Catholic reluctance to fly the IBEAC flag at the very moments that Protestants fell over one another in eagerness to display it. Mwanga was also assisted by the formal necessity for his subjects to approach the IBEAC representative on important questions initially through him. After the battle of Mengo, all this changed. Mwanga fled from the capital with the defeated Roman Catholic chiefs. Though he was restored to his throne within a few months, he never recovered his earlier influence. Kagwa's preeminence within Buganda as Protestant *Katikiro* was now unchallenged – and unchallengeable so long as he retained CMS missionaries' support in dealings with British protectorate officials.

Upon Mwanga's restoration as Ganda king in mid-1892 the Roman Catholic party leader, Mugwanya, was eager to be known as the Catholic *Katikiro* rather than the *Kimbugwe*. After Portal's visit, Mugwanya became the Catholic *Katikiro*, enjoying the estates formerly attached to both Kimbugweship and Katikiroship in Buddu county ('about two-fifths of the province')[101] together with a small estate at the Ganda capital. Nonetheless, in terms of territory within Buganda, Mugwanya now possessed only 'the shadow of the Kimbugweship'; as the CMS missionary George Baskerville put it.[102] Kakungulu, as the new *Kimbugwe*, was to enjoy all the former *Kimbugwe*'s estates *outside* Buddu county, together with all the other earlier powers of this chief, including 'power over the canoes'.[103] That, as we have already noted, made Kakungulu one of the very top chiefs in Buganda. It also sharpened tensions further with Apolo Kagwa, to the extent that Kakungulu acquired a view of the Protestant *Katikiro*'s stranglehold over the Ganda political system essentially similar to that of the White Fathers' diarist.

These tensions are accorded a central place in the numerous surviving vernacular accounts of Kakungulu's career in Buganda, oral as well as written. Kagwa's jealousy of Kakungulu's military success, and the many ways in which Kagwa attempted to make life unpleasant for Kakungulu – the quarrel with Kagwa is one of these sources' continuing themes. One might have expected Kagwa himself to have written about this quarrel elsewhere, for he was a prolific author. But Kagwa's histories are curiously reticent about his dealings with Kakungulu: the references in his published writings are mostly brief and abrupt,[104] while there there is hardly any mention of Kakungulu in his surviving private papers.[105] The evidence for the quarrel between Kakungulu and Kagwa is therefore rather one-sided – respectful of Kakungulu and critical of Kagwa. Yet, when examined

Plate 7. *Apolo Kagwa, chief minister of the Buganda kingdom, photographed in the 1900s.* (From J.B. Purvis, *Through Uganda to Mount Elgon* (1909), p. 158)

within the values of the time and alongside other evidence, the causes of bad blood between the two leaders seem clear.

First, and most important, there was structural opposition within the chiefly hierarchy of the old kingdom. Traditionally, as Roscoe relates, three chiefs 'were admitted into the inner court' of the royal palace 'without first obtaining the King's formal permission': the *Katikiro*, the *Kimbugwe*, and the administrative chief of Kyadondo county in which the palace was situated.[106] Like the *Katikiro*, Queen Mother and Queen Sister, a *Kimbugwe* also had estates scattered in each administrative county of Buganda. 'Both the *Katikiro* and the *Kimbugwe* were called "Kings" by the peasants, because they themselves paid no tribute, but when the tribute was collected, they sent their representatives with the King's messengers, to see that the District-Chiefs returned the correct sums of tribute paid by the people of their district'.[107] The *Kimbugwe* was seen as a check upon the *Katikiro* here as well as on administrative chiefs in general. Ritually, the *Kimbugwe* also had care of Mwanga II's umbilical cord and fetishes as well as responsibility for the royal compound; as Martin Southwold reports, this particular

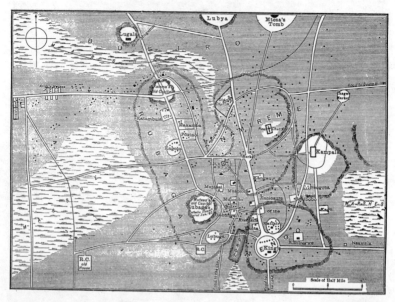

Map 7. *Plan of Mengo and its immediate neighbourhood.* (From Walker, 'Notes', *CMI*, March 1893, p. 197)

Ganda official might be 'aptly described as the *aide-de-camp* of the Kabaka'.[108] As a result of these responsibilties as *Kimbugwe*, Kakungulu inevitably came into conflict with Kagwa as *Katikiro*.

Furthermore, quarrels between leading chiefs were common in Buganda. We saw in Chapter 1 how one such quarrel (between Tebukozoa and Kapalaga) possibly helped Kakungulu to survive danger to his life during Mwanga's anti-Christian persecution of the mid-1880s. Shortly after the battle of Mengo in January 1892, the CMS missionary Robert Ashe also reported that 'no sooner was the English party consolidated [in power] than unmistakable signs of a split began to appear, the two camps ... divided into the Katikiro's and the Sekibobo's, Apolo [Kagwa] and Nikodemo [Sebwato]'. Ashe commented that 'I used sometimes to say to them [the Baganda Protestants] sadly, "I would give you three months of power, after which I should expect to see you split up into two factions so hostile that you would stand face to face with loaded rifles ready for battle."[109] Because the split between the rival factions attached to Sebwato and Kagwa struck him as being so clearly a question of clientage rather than Christianity, Ashe argued that 'the late war [between Catholics and Protestants in Lugard's time] had not been a mere fracas of contending bigots', but a more complicated conflict in which at least CMS missionaries had played a moderating rather than a disruptive role.[110] This was probably true. It was probably also true that Kakungulu rather than Sebwato was appointed *Kimbugwe* because, in the immediate term, Sebwato posed a greater threat to Kagwa's survival as Protestant party leader than a lesser chief like Semei Kakungulu.

To be sure, Kakungulu's followers had extolled his exploits in words distinctly unflattering to Apolo Kagwa in earlier years. Subsequently, they would extol Kakungulu's heroism still further. Oral poetry in Buganda was composed for recitation upon the battlefield and at chiefs' feasts with their followers. After Kakungulu's successful generalship at Kijungute in late 1889, his followers composed a song dedicated anonymously to Apolo Kagwa. Kagwa had been the unsuccessful general in the immediately preceding battle. 'It is fitting', declared this song, 'that you should honour your friend Kakungulu, for he has paid you back the blow you received upon your shoulderblade'.[111] Such poetry probably upset Apolo Kagwa most when, as in this case, it possessed an element of truth. But it would not have upset him as much as a more senior Ganda Protestant like Nikodemo Sebwato being appointed *Kimbugwe* because, once appointed, Sebwato would possess even greater credibility with CMS missionaries – as Kagwa's more likely replacement as *Katikiro*. Kakungulu therefore became *Kimbugwe* in mid-1892, not Sebwato. It was only later, when Kakungulu's conflict with Kagwa intensified still further, that oral poems like '*Nkwakwa*' ('Shoulderblade') struck Kagwa like firewood from an already blazing fire.

Sir John Gray has suggested that Kakungulu might have married a princess in 1894 partly in order to spite Kagwa – 'The fact that Apolo Kagwa had strongly urged the lady's degradation and thereby added to his unpopularity with Mwanga may well have been one of Kakunguru's motives for this matrimonial venture'.[112] There is little evidence to support this suggestion. There is still less for Gray's further view that Kagwa's continuing loyalty to *Kabaka* Mwanga after the battle of Mengo, 'in so far as loyalty was in the very difficult circumstances possible, revealed in him a sense of true statesmanship, which does not ever appear to have entered into Kakunguru's make-up'.[113] In fact, more important sources of friction were probably Kakungulu's very different personality, and his increasing clientage support resulting from increased prominence in plundering expeditions in company with British protectorate officials. For, as Miti and Rock remark, after the Bunyoro campaign of 1893–4,

> Kakungulu was the better loved of the two men and this was particularly noticed when, after Church services, the army leader used to attract a bigger crowd of followers than the King's Prime Minister himself. Kakungulu was liked because he was not only more popular in his dealings with the people but was the more hospitable in his home. Apollo, highest government official that he was, was more feared than loved. He was not easy of access; nor could one feel easy in his presence, especially in his home.[114]

In Buganda interpersonal conflict between chiefs was moderated, as we have already noted, by hierarchical gradings within the various segments of the immediately pre-British political system. Plundering expeditions abroad too, as Colvile correctly perceived,[115] diverted many of the more destructive urges arising amongst Ganda chiefs. Nonetheless, even when there were no wars to fight, it was difficult for a self-respecting Ganda chief not to assert himself in competition for honour with his peers by other means. For in a society of honour public repute is all:

For honour travels in a strait so narrow
Where one but goes abreast.[116]

Sometimes rivalry concerned items of conspicuous consumption. Ansorge records competition between Kagwa and Kakungulu for the purchase of a rickshaw:

There used to be at Kampala a 'jinrikshaw', sent up on spec. by some English firm at the Coast. No one wanted to buy it, so it lay for a long time in the Government store. One day the Kakunguru and the Katikiro came to enquire about it. I happened to be in charge of the Fort and I referred the matter to the Acting Commissioner who sent back word respecting the minimum price that the firm had fixed for the sale of the vehicle. Day after day these two chiefs came and examined the jinrikshaw, pulling it about the courtyard of the Fort. One day the Kakunguru decided finally to buy it and accepted the price mentioned by the Acting Commissioner. He and the Katikiro, both of them heavy men, thereupon got into the jinrikshaw, some scores of men pulled in front and pushed behind, and on throwing the gates of the Fort open for them to pass, they dashed away down Kampala hill full tilt ...

Within half-an-hour one man came to the Fort conveying the shafts of the jinrikshaw, another the wheels, and so on, a mass of splintered wood. Then the Kakunguru arrived and solemnly informed me that he had decided not to buy the jinrikshaw ...

However, eventually Kakungulu did pay for it.[117]

One result of competition for preeminence in nineteenth-century Buganda, as in Shakespeare's England, was to cause men of honour to seek relaxation with their followers rather than with their peers. Peers always posed the possibility of repute being tainted by some trivial indiscretion or minor matter like there not being enough sour milk. Personal followers posed no such problems. So it was in their company that chiefs like Kakungulu spent much of their time relaxing, while they sang their praises, drank their beer and, increasingly, said their prayers.

Sometimes British officials misunderstood what was happening. There were for example a number of quite unnecessary 'alarms' about the stability of the British protectorate during Ansorge's time at Kampala. 'There were at least half a dozen different plots. King Mwanga wanted to get rid of Apollo Katikiro, some of the ambitious chiefs wanted to turn out Mwanga, others longed to oust the British Government', Ansorge wrote afterwards, resulting from what he called a 'turbulent native spirit'.[118] Constant rumours and intrigues, yes, certainly; actual plots, probably not. Abusolomu Mudiima, a Protestant middle-grade chief, for example, was celebrating with followers supplying poles for a new Namirembe Cathedral, evidently with some considerable noise. The noise disturbed Ansorge, who interpreted it as rebellion against the British government. He made arrangements to arrest Mudiima. Apolo Kagwa was irritated by Ansorge's action, but could do little about it apart from defend Mudiima.[119] Needless to say, Ansorge's behaviour was far more destabilizing than Mudiima's carousing.

Personality differences and competition for followers were further causes of friction. The Kimbugweship deepened friction by bringing Kakungulu into almost daily contact with Kagwa. This caused Kakungulu considerable spiritual unease, as Bishop Tucker indicates.[120] It also led to a fear of being poisoned; as when Stanislas Mugwanya woke up the White Fathers at Rubaga in the middle of one night in August 1893 to tell them that Kakungulu had been poisoned, was extremely ill, and the next day they heard that the prime suspect was Apolo Kagwa.[121] In fact, Kakungulu appears to have been very close to death, indeed 'was on the point of being bound up as dead' ready for burial, when Ham Mukasa 'hastily fetched Mr. Roscoe [one of the CMS missionaries] who revived the apparent corpse'.[122]

Two years later, Kakungulu could stand the strain of conflict with Apolo Kagwa no longer. He quarrelled bitterly with Kagwa over some captured cattle and the beating of a servant, resigned his Kimbugweship, and withdrew to recently acquired estates in Bugerere. This was a time of great personal crisis, as his principal chronicler records.[123] It is unlikely, at such a time of crisis, that he was planning a rebellion against the British, as Ansorge's successor at Kampala Fort suspected.[124] For the same reason it is also unlikely that Kakungulu had any very definite plans for the future; still less that he told Kagwa 'You can keep your premiership; let me go and find a kingdom',[125] or words to that effect. In fact, it was the comparatively minor matter of some captured cattle which finally prompted Kakungulu's resignation; though, as the contradiction in Apolo Kagwa's own chronicle-history of Buganda as to its actual date – Kagwa gives both a day in May 1895 and one in the following October – indicates, he only came to a final decision after what Bishop Tucker described as 'almost daily' talks in September.[126]

The cattle in question were captured during further military operations prompted by British protectorate officials against Kabalega during April–May 1895. Cunningham was the British commander, Apolo Kagwa the Ganda one, and Kakungulu the Ganda second-in-command with responsibility to assemble 'all the canoes you can possibly spare'[127] together with William Grant. Grant was now the British official in southern Busoga. Kagwa and Cunningham advanced overland, carrying two maxim guns on litters. Grant and Kakungulu converged by canoe upon Kabalega's new encampment on a promontory above the River Nile overlooking Mruli. In Frederick Jackson's words,

> On the morning of April 22nd, 1894, Grant arrived from Busoga with his 'naval brigade' of 123 canoes, and from the account of eyewitnesses it was a really magnificent spectacle; and one that will certainly never be seen again. It was made up of a company of Sudanese, and a strong

force of Baganda, under the renowned warrior chief Kakungulu; and its formation and the way each canoe kept its position, so impressed Cunningham that he decided to let Grant retain the command, and while the army contented itself with covering the attack with the guns and Maxims, and then supporting it after the landing had been effected.

When that had been effected, with considerable loss to the defenders, the arduous task of following up the enemy in Lango continued for some days, while Ashburnham with a strong patrol followed along the left bank of the river. In the meantime, Grant returned to Luba's ... The main force, though they failed to capture Kabarega, took two thousand head of cattle, and left him a refugee ... [128]

Kakungulu received 'a slight spear wound' during these operations, reported Cunningham.[129] But what is most stressed by vernacular chroniclers and surviving oral testimony is the dispute over cattle with Kagwa. According to Paulo Kibi, Kakungulu's men captured many more cows than Apolo Kagwa's campaigners but Kagwa as commander determined how many of them should be retained by Kakungulu's followers as their share of the spoils. Not enough, inevitably, when Kagwa arranged for the total British share also to be deducted solely from the cows seized by Kakungulu's followers. Kakungulu objected to Kagwa's decision. Cunningham upheld it.[130] Kakungulu was also angered that Kagwa beat Yairo Bina during this campaign upon discovering that Bina was Kakungulu's man.[131] Kakungulu returned to the Ganda capital nearly two weeks ahead of Kagwa's followers,[132] evidently very angry.

According to one of Kakungulu's followers, Mwanga calmed Kakungulu by saying that there would be other campaigns in which he rather than Kagwa would be commander.[133] In fact, another opportunity for plunder soon arose, when the British protectorate authorities mounted a punitive expedition against several groups implicated in the death of a British trader in what is nowadays western Kenya.[134] But it was not to be an expedition upon which Kakungulu would look back subsequently with much satisfaction.

It was commanded by Charles Hobley, the geologist turned official at Mumias, and William Grant from Busoga. Initially, Grant had not wanted Kakungulu to join the expedition ('I think it would be best for himself not to come as he will have so many unnecessary followers') and anyway

The Waganda will not be allowed to proceed as they did in Unyoro. Every man who comes with me will be under my orders and under the same rules and discipline as the Sudanese. I will inform them so before starting from Usoga. It will never do to let them loot from friendly natives. If Kakunguru himself comes it would be well to let him know before starting exactly what he will be expected to do. Also that anything captured by Waganda will first be taken to me. If they agree to all this good and well if not I can get on without them.[135]

At Mumias the expedition was joined by Ansorge and 'about 600 Masai and friendly WaKavirondo',[136] and Kakungulu himself not only came as

Plate 8. *Nubian soldiers with a maxim gun.* (From S. Vandeleur, *Campaigning on the Upper Nile and Niger* (1898), p. 54)

'general of the Waganda army which numbered over 1000' but brought his royal wife too. She 'marched along through fair weather and foul ... accompanied by a large following of female servants.'[137] Kakungulu's warriors fought bravely but suffered many casualties.

Against one village in Kitosh country, Hobley describes how the maxim gun was fired at one entrance:

> This had no great effect on the stout logs which barred it, so we shelled the huts. The Kakunguru then sought permission to storm the gate with his levies, and sanction was accorded. They advanced with great elan and succeeded in forcing an entrance, but the Ketosh spearmen massed inside the village, counter-attacked and drove out the Baganda with considerable loss. Grant then adopted another plan; leaving the large force of Baganda to threaten a second attack on the original gate, he moved the Sudanese Company round to another gate some ninety degrees away in the periphery of the wall. We then cut down a section of the mud wall by Maxim fire and advanced to the attack. The defence then concentrated on this sector; the spears came over like rain and the Sudanese were held up by the ditch. The Baganda were then ordered to renew their attack at the original gate, and eventually the village was taken and burnt, the survivors streaming out by yet another gate.[138]

Captain Sitwell, who also accompanied the expedition, praised the Ganda in his official report: 'The WAGANDA were very useful in capturing cattle & also came into the Boma before the other natives would.'[139] But praise for the Ganda is conspicuously absent from Grant's accompanying report,[140] and his comments upon their activity eastwards in the Kikelelwa forest were distinctly cool.[141] In Hobley's words again,

> The Uganda chief, the Kakunguru, was despatched a day ahead of the Sudanese detachment, which we accompanied, and was ordered to await our force at a certain camp. Upon our arrival at the point of concentration the Kakunguru came and confessed that, under-estimating the opposition to be expected, he had despatched a force to the edge of the forest, which, on its return journey, had been am-buscaded and sixty men and rifles had been lost. This was very annoying, for it was an unwarranted breach of orders and had resulted in a needless loss of life, to say nothing of the bad effect of the loss of the rifles. However the next day we attacked, and, in spite of their recent victory over the Baganda levies, the resistance was nothing like that experienced in Ketosh, and we soon forced our way into the forest.[142]

This was not the stuff of epic poetry, and in fact none survives from this particular expedition. Maxim guns rendered bravery irrelevant.

There was also the food problem. Kakungulu's warriors were now operating outside the banana belt of East Africa. For this reason alone Sitwell decided not to include them in further operations against the Nandi, 'as they do not appear to be very willing to go so far from their own country and ... there might be some difficulty in arranging for the food transport for so large a force.'[143] To make matters worse, upon his force's return to Kampala, Apolo Kagwa accused Kakungulu before Mwanga of negligence regarding the many Ganda who died of sickness as well as wounds. However, relates Paulo Kibi, Mwanga 'did not listen to him'.[144]

Further suppression of slave-taking made 1895 a difficult year for the generality of Ganda chiefs, too. One county chief accompanying another expedition against Kabalega was punished for slaving and thrown into prison well before the expedition returned to Kampala.[145] Another county chief engaged in the campaign was accused of the same offence by CMS missionaries after the expedition's return. But this accusation failed because the British commander was also shown to have been culpable. Ganda Protestant witnesses (and doubtless the British protectorate authorities too) considered it unwise to press charges against a British officer as well as a Ganda chief for forcible slave-taking.[146] Upon his return to Kampala, Kakungulu's relations with Apolo Kagwa were made difficult by Kagwa's continued prosecution of him for losses sustained during the Kitosh expedition. It was therefore not really surprising, after discussions on the way from Mumias with Bishop Tucker and the first CMS lady missionaries to Buganda about 'the prospects of the work in Uganda as well as in the regions beyond',[147] that Kakungulu should have written to Tucker saying that 'as a Christian it was impossible for him to live a life of continual contention with a fellow Christian',[148] and that he therefore resigned his Kimbugweship.[149]

## 4

Kakungulu had already done much to establish a new order in Bugerere. Kabalega's chief there had been removed from power (though later allowed to return as an underling),[150] and a characteristically Ganda structure of under-chiefs and free tenant-farmers installed. In July 1894 George Baskerville heard that the local people were 'keen to be taught & are learning to read' the Protestant Anglican religion. 'They, the Banyoro, were much struck by the fact that the Kakunguru & his people as Christians did not carry off their women.'[151] Kakungulu seems to have kept his existing slaves but not to have forcibly acquired any more following recriminations between British officials and Ganda chiefs in the wake of the Buvuma expedition. Captain Gibb, who commanded military operations against Kabalega's forces in May–June 1894, was struck shortly before Kakungulu's resignation as *Kimbugwe* by the extent of cultivation and order in his new domain and how Kakungulu 'by his wise and considerate conduct [had] induced the Wanyoro to continue in their shambas and work in unity with his people instead of running away to the swamps'.[152]

That was certainly what did happen, however, when Gibb himself installed 20 Sudanese askaris in a small fort in northern Bugerere. Kakungulu quickly complained to Ansorge that these Sudanese 'have been plundering the shambas of the natives, carrying off bananas & sweet potatoes, every food article in fact', and asked for them to be 'recalled'.[153] This, after further correspondence,[154] was done.

After his resignation as *Kimbugwe*, Kakungulu became what one of his chroniclers describes as *Omutaka munsiye*, 'Mutaka in his own country' – a chief who possessed rather more power in Bugerere than an ordinary county chief enjoyed in Buganda proper,[155] and what one of his followers at the time called 'considerable independence of action' (*okutongola ddala*).[156]

Bugerere is bordered on the southern side by the Kyagwe county of Buganda, on the east by Busoga, and in the north by Lake Kyoga. On several islands in Lake Kyoga there were markets where a variety of commodities were traded immediately before Kakungulu's arrival in Bugerere and where, shortly afterwards, several of his chiefs established themselves as market masters. Ivory at the close of the nineteenth century was the most prized commodity in this trade and indeed throughout East Africa. For, as Carl Peters had pointed out,[157]

> The Uganda ivory filters through a thousand channels, apart from the direct exportation of the purchased goods [southwards across Lake Victoria]. It is the great medium of exchange for these regions, and passes through six, seven, or even more hands before it reaches Tabora or Irangi . . . and arriving at the coast, is absorbed into the commerce of the world. This internal trade is engaged in, among others, by the

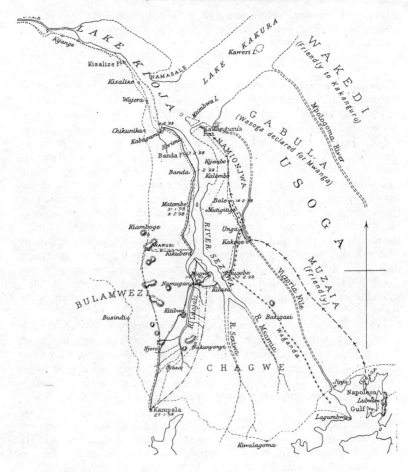

Map 8. *Bugerere and adjacent areas in 1898.* (From map accompanying R.T.
Kirkpatrick, 'Lake Choga and Surrounding Country', *Geographical Journal* 13
(1899))

inhabitants of the island of Bukerebe [in Lake Victoria], whose caravans of traders I have seen myself both in Busiba and also in Usukuma. I think that in estimating the political and commercial affairs of East Africa too little stress is laid on this internal trade among the tribes. In it lies the chief investment of the slave trade.

Alongside these trades lay 'another series of products ... exchanged for centuries between tribe and tribe', such as the hoe and other iron implements supplied by peoples living south of Lake Victoria to those occupying its northern shores.[158] Each of these trades also prospered on Kaweri island in Lake Kyoga, where Kakungulu's veteran follower, Gwantamu, became his representative.

Lake Kyoga also abuts on to several areas of eastern and northern Uganda occupied in the 1890s by a diversity of politically decentralized African peoples. At this time the Kumam seem to have been under intense pressure from the Langi. Earlier, the Langi had allied with Kabalega in support of Kalema against Ganda Christians fighting for Mwanga II in 1890, and it was perhaps not surprising that the Kumam should now have sought support against the Langi from one of Mwanga's most successful generals. It was therefore at one of Kakungulu's forts in Bugerere at the beginning of 1896 that the same Captain Sitwell, who had fought with him against the Kitosh several months before, found 'several Wakeddi chiefs ... [who] all wish for peace. Kwara is the name of the head one', reported Sitwell. 'He wishes a boma [to be] built in his country. He says the Wakeddi further north are always raiding him. I have told him & others with him to try to get in touch with the other Wakeddi & tell them we are quite prepared for peace if they are.'[159]

But who were 'we' ? Clearly not yet the British protectorate authorities, who still felt insecure and undercapitalized for even the modest reform programme which George Wilson was currently reducing to writing in company with Apolo Kagwa and *Kabaka* Mwanga.[160] Besides British officers suffering from what would shortly be termed 'medal fever', and what we have already noted one of them describing as concern 'to help a brother officer',[161] it was upon Kakungulu and his friends that the British protectorate authorities had to depend principally here.

Unfortunately this support sometimes misfired. In May 1896 Kakungulu returned to the Ganda capital to apologize in person for leading an unauthorized plundering expedition into Langi country, as a result of which not only had he himself lost followers, but 30 of Apolo Kagwa's young men and slaves (*baddu*), who had joined in the raid, had also lost their guns as well as their lives.[162] These young men and slaves had been stationed previously in another neighbouring fort in newly conquered Bunyoro territory. It is not clear whether Kagwa's *baddu*, or Kakungulu's, had hoped to become freemen by seizing replacements for themselves straightforwardly as in pre-British days, or whether their ambition had been to acquire other plunder with which to acquire slaves by purchase (*abagule*) now that slaves seized by force (*abanyage*) were prohibited by the British authorities.[163] What is clear, however, is that the whole enterprise was a disaster, firearms notwithstanding. Now Kakungulu had to face yet another case brought before *Kabaka* Mwanga by Apolo Kagwa for needless loss of life and property. It was a case which Kakungulu defended successfully, not least because of his continuing utility to British protectorate officials 'both as being in military command of forts on the Wakeddi frontier and as local Governor' of Bugerere.[164]

In George Wilson's words,[165] Kakungulu reported that

> On hearing of the attack of the Wakedi on Kangao's and the Kisalizi's position, I sent out spies to watch their movements if possible. Meantime I sent special messengers to ask the permission of the King to go out and attack the Wakeddi. The King replied at once, forbidding the attack, and calling me in for consultation. When I received the King's reply the friendly Wakeddi brought reports of the threatening attitude of their hostile countrymen, and begged me to lead them in an attack. Having been called to the capital, and being assured that my absence would expose my district to considerable danger, I decided to accede to the request of the friendly Wakeddi, and to explain my action at the capital on the completion of the operations.
>
> I collected together 200 guns and 300 spears and the friendly Wakeddi brought 3,000 spears. We marched out, the Wakeddi making great demonstrations. On the 3rd day we saw the enemy in villages. On the 4th day we fought from 7 a.m. until sunset; during the day losing 50 men and 27 guns. The friendly Wakeddi having behaved badly, and my own party having expended their ammunition I concluded that we had been beaten and retired during the night and returned to Nyamyonjo [Bugerere]. I have now come in with all speed, and place myself in the hands of the Balozi [British protectorate commissioner] and the King [of Buganda], acknowledging my error, but pleading that the awkwardness of my position may be considered in extenuation.

Wilson told Berkeley that in his opinion Kakungulu

> had in reality made a supreme effort, however misdirected, to recover his status with the [protectorate] government and the country [of Buganda], and I would venture to suggest that the imposition of a fine of a certain number of cattle or the equivalent, to be devoted to the Uganda public fund, would be expedient and beneficial in the present case ... a fine which would be considered deterrent and yet unoppressive, by the Uganda authorities. With my present knowledge of the case, I would submit with some confidence that a fine of *25 cows* would be greeted as a popular verdict.

In fact, the fine was fixed at 40 ivory tusks,[166] and the case became a very bitter one with Mwanga himself now also 'incensed at the disobedience of the Kakunguru'.[167] Mutual vituperation between Kakungulu and Kagwa during the hearing became as intense as it had ever been.[168] However, in the end 'the King, *Katikiro* and chiefs begged that the Kakunguru may be not removed from his post, and that another means of punishment may be awarded; as they submit that the Kakunguru has peculiar qualifications for the control of the Namuyonjo district'.[169] Berkeley was happy to oblige, and Kakungulu retained his position of considerable autonomy of action for another three years.

Afterwards Kakungulu returned to Bugerere. In Buganda, as Walker remarked to his family,[170] Kakungulu was no longer

> the second chief in the land but suddenly he took into his head to give it up & retire into private life. He had, I fancy, acquired a good deal of property & I think must have supposed that though no longer a chief yet everyone wd respect him & honour him. He finds no one thinks of him & he is quite out of it. He comes up to the capital but has no house to live in. Samweli Mukasa has taken pity on him & put him up at his place.

In Bugerere, however, Kakungulu resumed his quasi-autonomous lordship and sent three of his leading followers to establish forts on Namulimuka, Kaweri and Kigi islands in Lake Kyoga. 'From these islands they looked after the whole of Bukedi', boasts one of Kakungulu's chroniclers, doubtless thinking principally of the trade which Kakungulu's men had already started to take over from Kabalega's earlier intermediaries upon these very same islands.[171] From these islands and the immediately surrounding areas, Kakungulu took another 100 or so notables to pay homage to the Ganda king in September 1896. The visit was not a success. As Apolo Kagwa later put it, 'Upon reaching Kabaka Mwanga they said "We wish to come under Baganda rule, and we are asking [you] to give us an army to fight those who are often contemptuously attacking us"'. But the army was not forthcoming. 'We replied, "Well, return home; if we decide to help you, we shall send for you." After this they departed for their home country'.[172] Clearly, while Apolo Kagwa continued as chief minister of the Buganda kingdom, this was likely to be the answer to future requests for military assistance, too.

Back in Bugerere, and on the newly fortified islands in Lake Kyoga, Kakungulu's period of lordship was to be remembered with comparative favour. As Sir John Gray, not notable for unduly favourable comments about him, reported:

> The reputation which Kakunguru left behind him in Bunyala was that, while he was very much of an autocrat, he was in contrast to certain of his immediate successors, just and fair in his dealings with the local inhabitants. Perhaps one of the best tributes to his popularity was that, when he set out to carve for himself a kingdom out of Bukedi, some of his right-hand men were Banyala.[173]

But little is known about the details of Kakungulu's administration in Bugerere.

Here Samwiri Tekiwagala proved the most knowledgeable informant:[174]

How did Kakungulu conquer Namuyonjo?

He conquered him when he was *Kimbugwe*. Namuyonjo was a man of Kabarega, *Kabaka* of Bunyoro. After he defeated him he put his man

Malaki Luganduka in a fort to guard the place at *ekyalo* [village] Kigembo. Then he returned to Buganda. Namuyonjo did not give Kakungulu much resistance.

When Kakungulu went to live in Bugerere, after he had resigned his Kimbugweship, what happened to Namuyonjo?

Kakungulu ruled him.

Who were the chiefs Kakungulu appointed when he lived in Bugerere?

I told you their names the other time. They were all Baganda.

Even the smallest *mutongole* chief?

All the chiefs were Baganda: we had conquered them – the Banyala. All the Baganda chiefs appointed by Kakungulu were given villages (*ebyalo*). Then we called the area we had conquered Wunga.

When Matayo was given Wunga the name was changed to Bugerere by Kagwa; Wunga was the name Kakungulu had given it. The Banyala called it Bunyala.

Was Namuyonjo a *Kabaka*, a small *Kabaka* (*Kabaka omuto*)?

He was just a man of Kabarega (*musajja wa Kabarega*). Not even a prince (*mulangira*). He had a similar relationship to the *Kabaka* of Bunyoro as the *Sekibobo* [county chief of Kyaggwe] had to the *Kabaka* of Buganda – he was his man.

When the Baganda conquered Bugerere and started to rule it under Kakungulu, did they rule it in the same way as Namuyonjo had ruled it, using his chieftainships, or did they use new methods of ruling?

Bugerere was a very small area and there wasn't enough room to invent new ways of ruling! Kakungulu used the same methods he had used in Buganda; the former chiefs of Namuyonjo became our subjects and we ruled them in the Ganda fashion.

Ernest Berkeley, George Wilson, Apolo Kagwa and other leading Christian Ganda chiefs had been in a position of some uncertainty when the question of Kakungulu's disobedience over the abortive raid into Lango had come before Mwanga's court. Wilson was still starting to push through his reform programme which, modest though it was, struck Roman Catholic missionaries as too wide-ranging and before its time.[175] Waswa, the county chief of Singo, was still detained by Ternan's order for allegedly slaving during another recent Bunyoro campaign. Gabrieli Kintu and other middle-grade Ganda Catholic chiefs were free, but were worrying the White Fathers by their backsliding, and would shortly prompt them to write to the British protectorate authorities about their seditiousness. Wilson and Berkeley had sufficient anxieties about seditiousness from other quarters, to prevent them from wanting to turn Semei Kakungulu into another dissident chief. However, when the British protectorate authorities prosecuted the Ganda king himself for ivory smuggling, and were then bounced into reducing radically the size of his palace establishment by Kagwa, Mugwanya, and their respective advisers in the Protestant and Roman Catholic missionary establishments,[176] Mwanga was pushed into open rebellion in July 1897. Then Kakungulu himself very nearly became an open rebel against the British protectorate authorities.

To start with, British officials did not take seriously the White Fathers' warnings about an imminent anti-British rebellion reaching up from middle-ranking Roman Catholic chiefs to Mwanga himself, despite their fears of attack from other quarters throughout the 1890s. Partly it was the legacy of greater CMS success in building up influence with British officials since Lugard's time, partly the British officials' own ignorance of the French language – only after Mwanga's rebellion were the White Fathers visited by several British officers fluent in French.[177] But, partly too, it was unwillingness to accept that *Kabaka* Mwanga really had any alternative to continuing in power as a British client-king, or that the songs sung by his musicians in public about 'Banyoro' were in any way seditious in intent – though in Luganda 'Banyoro' could mean 'the foreigners' in general as well as the inhabitants of the kingdom against which British protectorate officials were still organizing expedition after expedition.[178] Here CMS missionaries, too, were caught unawares by the seeming suddenness of Mwanga's rebellion in July 1897 – their very success in 'managing' their Ganda converts politically by less direct mechanisms than the White Fathers' more confrontational ways with their followers preventing the CMS being as aware of the sheer scale of Ganda chiefly disaffection with the new order.

In retrospect, however, the principal grievances behind Mwanga's rebellion seem clear, as also does the uncertainty of its outcome. 'He and his friends are for a return to heathenism, slavery, polygamy and all the horrors of the past', wrote George Pilkington. 'Ninety per cent of the people are probably with him in their sympathies, but, in the body, they prefer the side which musters most guns and holds the gardens'.[179] As it happened, Apolo Kagwa, Stanislas Mugwanya and their British protectorate allies did manage to muster the greatest number of guns and thus 'hold the gardens' in mid-1897. But it was a close-run thing. Had the second maxim gun jammed, the most crucial battle in Buddu county could easily have gone the other way.[180]

This is reasonably well-established.[181] What is less well-known is that Semei Kakungulu was one of the chiefs who first promised to assist *Kabaka* Mwanga's rebellion against British protectorate rule and then failed to support it.[182] But again, as one of his followers at the time revealed, this too was a close-run thing:

> After Kakungulu went to Bugerere, the quarrel with Kagwa got worse: they quarrelled very bitterly at Bukaleba. Kagwa stood at a distance from Kakungulu, obviously expecting him to go to him and pay his respects in a humble manner. Kakungulu did not go.

> When the two *Kabakas* rebelled [that is, Mwanga II now as well as Kabalega], Kakungulu wanted to join them.

Really?

Yes, Mwanga was Kakungulu's friend when he was *Kimbugwe* – he was very friendly towards him, he even gave his sister Nakalema to be his wife, his legitimate wife.

He wanted to rebel with Mwanga. When they told him to go to Buddu, he refused, saying 'How can I kill my brother-in-law?' So he sent Nziga to go in his place. But then some people persuaded him, saying 'If you rebel, they will kill you also'. So, after a period, Kakungulu helped Kagwa and the Europeans to capture the two *Kabakas* [Mwanga and Kabalega]. What else could he do?

Who were the people who persuaded Kakungulu to cooperate with Kagwa and the Europeans?

Tomasi Semfuma and Tomasi Semukasa, who were both friendly with him. They came from Buganda to Bugerere to persuade him.

How did Samwiri know about these things?

I was his chief! There were two factions (*bitundu ebiri*) among Kakungulu's men, one led by Gwantamu, the other by Nziga. Gwantamu and the drinkers were on Kakungulu's side, favouring rebelling; Nziga and those of us who did not drink were on the side of the *Katikiro*. Then when those who ruled Buganda heard about Kakungulu's desire, they sent Tomasi Semfuma and Tomasi Semukasa to Bugerere to persuade Kakungulu not to rebel.[183]

In October 1895 Kagwa and Mugwanya had been unsuccessful in preventing Kakungulu from resigning his Kimbugweship, but two years later they succeeded in preventing him from joining Mwanga's rebellion. Partly it was a basic question of power – Kakungulu's realization, as an earlier ally of the British protectorate authorities against the Buvuma islanders as well as dissident peoples in western Kenya, that maxim guns and precision rifles gave overwhelming advantages to those firing them. But soon Kakungulu had cause to regret the decision.

For Mwanga's rebellion against the British protectorate authorities in July 1897 was followed by a rising amongst the Sudanese soldiery two months later. By the end of the year, military operations against the Sudanese were concentrated at a siege at Bukaleba in Busoga. Apolo Kagwa was commander of the Ganda troops engaged in the siege. Kagwa's behaviour there irritated Kakungulu considerably. The very frequency with which the phrase '... and I ordered Simei Kakungulu' (*nengaba Simei Kakungulu)* recurs in the account of the siege Kagwa recorded in his book *Basekabaka be Buganda*, indicates one source of irritation.[184] Another is summarized by Miti and Rock. 'Suddenly', they write,

an unpleasant situation had sprung up at Bukaleba between general Apollo and Kakungulu who held the office next in command, arising from the latter's resenting being constantly sent out against the Nubian rebels while the general himself sat in the camp. Kakungulu considered this nothing short of being made use of at the risk of his life while all the praise went to Apollo himself.[185]

In fact, there were several considerations here. First, whatever Apolo Kagwa himself might have thought about the matter, Kakungulu was sent out more frequently to fight at Bukaleba as a result of pressure by other Ganda chiefs. They felt that Kakungulu should do more of the fighting than Kagwa because Kagwa was the more likely of the two to be killed in personal combat, and that would demoralize the Ganda Christian forces fatally.[186] Secondly, Kakungulu was an inspirational military commander who proved himself yet again to be such at Bukaleba. 'He was brave', wrote Ham Mukasa subsequently. Kakungulu 'did not want to hear that so-and-so was afraid. This made them fight hard'.[187] That in turn confirmed Christian Ganda chiefs in their preference for Kakungulu rather than Kagwa to be the more frequent commander in the field. But as far as Kakungulu himself was concerned at Bukaleba, undoubtedly the greatest risk to his life arose from the nature of the fighting itself.

According to Paulo Kibi, it took three months to drive the rebels out of Bukaleba fort, and during this period 'they killed many Baganda'.[188] Basically, this was because for the first time the Ganda friends of the British protectorate administration in East Africa had maxim gunfire directed at themselves. 'The Baganda had not previously witnessed such a fierce battle as this one', related Paulo Kibi. The Sudanese rebels also had better guns and were better shots. Traditional Ganda battle formations anyway were no match for maxim gunfire. 'It was just ridiculous for one to go with 25 rounds of ammunition and return with the same number. People called you a coward. We used to fire anyhow, just to get rid of the ammunition'.[189] Several Europeans were killed at Bukaleba, amongst them the CMS missionary George Pilkington, on one of the days when Kakungulu was field commander of the Ganda there.[190] Clearly, this was fighting in which Kakungulu might well prove inspirational as Ganda field commander, but as a result of which he might also perish in a most unheroic manner.

Ham Mukasa relates that another factor in the quarrel at Bukaleba was talk about the future government of Bugerere:

Kakungulu was heard as saying 'Katikiro, sir, our place Wunga had been given to me by the [British] Government to be my *butaka* [family possession]. I have heard that you are talking about it as though it was *Ntongole* [land only held during chiefly office]. Why?'
Katikiro then said 'No Simeyi Kakungulu. What you are saying is wrong. How can the [British] Government give you a whole country to be your *butaka*? Maybe to stay in while ruling its owners ... OK let us first finish fighting Nubians [and] we shall settle this after we have defeated them.'

However, according to Ham Mukasa, Kakungulu now refused to continue fighting at Bukaleba until the matter had been cleared up by the British protectorate officials present at the siege. This the leading Christian chiefs there considered unwise, because once it became known that they had been quarrelling among themselves their prestige with the British would plummet. Batolomayo Zimbe, who like Semfuma, Semukasa and Kakungulu at this time was a leading member of the Lungfish clan as well as one of the first Ganda Anglican clergymen, was sent to mediate. But his mediation was unsuccessful.[191] 'Still suffering from the old scores of enmity between them', continue Miti and Rock, 'Kakungulu resuscitated old quarrels', refused to play any further major role in the siege, and stated that the only thing he was really interested in fighting for was his land in Bugerere.[192]

But that land was not large enough to satisfy his political ambitions. In 1898 a chance arose of an administrative appointment offering much wider scope elsewhere in the young British protectorate of Uganda, and Kakungulu seized it avidly.

## 5

'Simei Kakungulu has been appointed Katikiro, or chief judge, in Usoga', reported Archdeacon Walker to the CMS Committee in Britain on 1 June 1898. 'He is building a place on a hill near the fort Luba's, and the principal chiefs in Usoga will all have houses near the fort. Some six months of every year these chiefs have to come into residence at Luba's'.[193] According to Samwili Mukasa, the friend with whom Kakungulu had stayed during the case about the unauthorized expeditions into Lango, he too was asked to assist in Busoga. This was because Major Macdonald wanted to divide the area into two or three counties to be administered by Ganda chiefs, 'because Basoga had joined hands with the Sudanese in the rebellion'[194] at Bukaleba. That siege had been broken at the beginning of the year, but Soga Muslims and others who had fought against the British there had to be prevented from doing so again.

Nonetheless, within a month Kakungulu's appointment to Busoga was cut short. There seem to have been three reasons for the ending of his appointment.

One was opposition by William Grant. Grant had built up a personal network of supporters in Busoga before the outbreak of Mwanga's rebellion and the Sudanese mutiny. Basically Grant had done this by excluding as many Ganda as possible from having anything to do with local administration.[195] While happy to have Kakungulu to 'assist me for a month or two', he considered that as a long-term proposition 'no Muganda no matter whom should be placed over the Wasoga'. 'We have got on all right without Uganda [that is, Baganda] interference ... in the past', continued Grant, 'and hope to go on similarly in the future. Uganda for Waganda, and Usoga for the Wasoga. Why a Muganda chief should expect to be made Chief of Usoga I fail to understand.' Grant also argued that it would 'not be wise to have either the Kakunguru or any other Muganda Chief over the Wasoga' because 'once that takes place our power over the Wasoga will not be great'.[196]

Soga notables, too, made clear their opposition to Kakungulu's temporary post being made permanent. If that happened, the Basoga would rebel again 'because they had brought Kakungulu who was not a prince to rule over them'.[197] This news was reported to Apolo Kagwa by one Benyamini Kafumbirwango by letter.[198] According to Miti and Rock, Soga suspected that Kakungulu's coming to Busoga would be the prelude to its annexation to Buganda, on the earlier model of southern Bunyoro. Not only was there therefore open 'hatred of Kakungulu' but a widespread 'spirit of revolt' throughout Busoga. Apolo Kagwa passed this information on quickly to the British authorities. 'The two Governments [Protectorate and Buganda] went into hurried consultation and decided that Kakungulu should be ordered out of Busoga and back to his Wunga territory. This was done and thus another war was avoided.'[199]

Additionally responsible for this sudden backtracking was one of the Ganda chiefs detailed by Macdonald to assist Kakungulu in Busoga – Kakungulu's friend, Samwili Mukasa. Mukasa did not want to work in Busoga. Seizing the opportunity of accompanying Ernest Berkeley, the British protectorate commissioner who was travelling through Busoga towards Kampala during June 1898, Mukasa played the traditional politics of *okufugibwa* with the commissioner during the journey and persuaded him that it would be much better for him to work in Buganda.[200] Mukasa was subsequently appointed to a middle-grade chieftaincy in Bulemezi county, thus further sabotaging Kakungulu's appointment to Busoga as something opposed by his would-be principal Ganda assistant as well as by Soga notables and the local British official.

Back in Bugerere, Kakungulu received a personal letter from the still fugitive Mwanga. Mwanga had worked his way up from Buddu county, through German East Africa, across western Buganda again, then across Bunyoro, and was now with the equally fugitive former king of Bunyoro beyond the River Nile and Busoga. Kakungulu's principal chronicler dates the letter to early 1899, but from other sources it would appear that it arrived in 1898, most probably immediately after Kakungulu's hopes of a major post in the British administration of Busoga had been dashed.[201] Mwanga now told Kakungulu that, though he disliked Europeans, he had nothing against the Christian religion as such; he was doubtless writing to Kakungulu in the hope that he might rebel along with Gabrieli Kintu and other former commanders from Bulingugwe island who were currently engaged in anti-British guerrilla activity on other borders of Buganda.[202] Hence Mwanga's comment to Kakungulu: 'We do not know however whether you like us or not ... an early reply from you will be proof of your love for us'.[203] Nevertheless, remarked Ham Mukasa in words as careful as they were sympathetic to somebody still considered to have been born a fellow Lungfish clansman, 'as Kakungulu was a great chief as well as a very dependable one, he took the letter to Katikiro [Kagwa], whose people passed it on to [the British authorities at] Kampala.'[204] The same chronicler remarks elsewhere, 'it was a difficult time'.[205]

For Kakungulu, the moral difficulties could not have been reduced by the manner in which the Roman Catholic commander whom he had accused of cowardice in 1889–90 now died. Mulisi Sebwato – Morisi Kinyawakyamaggwa *Omusalosalo* as he was currently known – was mortally wounded in both thighs by gunshot from a scouting party on the western fringes of Buganda. Morisi told his fleeing companions to take his gun to Mwanga as it was 'the king's gun', and to leave him to face the enemy alone. When the attackers reached Morisi he was in great pain and, in Father Ddiba word's, 'they just looked at him for though he had joined Kabaka Mwanga they loved him as he was a fellow Christian [*yali musomi munnabwe*]'. While they were still looking at Morisi silently, another fighter joined them. This fighter shouted 'Are you with him just to look at him? Aren't these the people who are causing the trouble?', and shot Morisi in the chest. The remaining members of the attacking party were too shocked to pursue Morisi's companions any further. Instead they spent the rest of the day giving Morisi a decent burial.[206]

In March 1899 the British protectorate authorities organized an expedition to capture the two rebel kings, Kabalega and Mwanga. Kakungulu was one of those asked for help. Kakungulu sent a sub-chief with 100 guns to join the expedition. When this sub-chief reached the Wakeddi Field Force, Kakungulu himself was asked to join it. When he joined it, he became one of its principal commanders.[207] On 9 April 1899 Kabalega and Mwanga were both seized after their whereabouts had been revealed by local Langi concerned to prevent further reprisals by the Wakeddi Field Force.[208] By this 'fine feat of arms' (as the White Fathers, who had become as fervent in their support of the British protectorate administration at the close of the 1890s as they had been critical of it at the start, called the seizure of the two kings),[209] the revolt in Bukedi was brought to an end. Kabalega had part of an arm amputated as a consequence of this clash and was surprised at the care with which Kakungulu treated his wound.[210] Instead of being killed by him, as might have happened in an earlier, more heroic confrontation, Kabalega was carried instead on Kakungulu's orders to Kampala. There George Wilson attempted to photograph him. More hammock than king, remark Miti and Rock, because Kabalega refused to face the camera,[211] though at least one successful photograph was taken of him alongside Kakungulu (see page 129). Meanwhile Mwanga walked, bearded and long-haired, into Kampala, deeply moving the hearts of all Ganda present, Miti and Rock tell us, by the manner in which he was marched into exile with Kabalega in the Seychelles.[212]

On the road to Kampala the captive Kabalega asked Kakungulu to look after his children should he himself be executed by the British protectorate authorities. This Kakungulu agreed to do.[213] Also shortly after the capture of Kabalega and Mwanga, Kakungulu himself asked British officers commanding the Wakeddi Field Force whether he might take over part of the area just traversed. 'I believe he is desirous of adding to his province a portion of the terrain of the recent operations', reported Colonel Evatt to British protectorate headquarters at Entebbe. 'He will doubtless proffer his request himself, and I trust that, if possible, it may be favourably considered.'[214] He did; it was; and thereby arose still further complications.

Plate 9. *Semei Kakungulu guarding the wounded King Kabalega of Bunyoro with one of his wives. Kabalega's arm had been amputated as a result of fighting during his capture in 1899.* (From Sir Harry Johnston, *The Uganda Protectorate* (1902))

# *Notes*

1. Solomon Wamala, 'Obulamu bwa Semei Kakungulu', pp. 113, 102–14.
2. Miti (trans. Rock), *History of Buganda*, p. 389; copies in both SOAS and Makerere libraries.
3. Wamala, 'Obulamu'.
4. *Ibid.*
5. R.P. Ashe, *Chronicles of Uganda* (London 1894).
6. *The Times*, 19 March 1897.
7. J.R.L. Macdonald, *Soldiering and Surveying* (London 1897), pp. 158-9, 167. See also A.T. Matson's Introduction to the Dawson reprint (Folkestone 1973).
8. Wamala, 'Obulamu', pp. 119, 114–26.
9. Rock (trans. Miti), *History of Buganda* pp. 407–9; oral testimony by Paulo Kibi.
10. Wamala, 'Obulamu', p. 130; Paulo Kibi, oral testimony.
11. See above, pp. 9, 12–13.
12. B.M. Zimbe, *Buganda ne Kabaka* (Mengo 1939), p. 310.
13. See Margery Perham, *Lugard. The Years of Adventure, 1858–1898* (London 1956), especially pp. 191–2, for a defence of Lugard on this issue.
14. G. Portal, *The Mission to Uganda* (London 1894), p. 227.
15. *Ibid.*, p. 222; and below, p. 93.
16. Perham, *Lugard*, p. 355.
17. Ham Mukasa, *Simuda Nyuma*, Vol. 3, unpub. ms in Makerere University Library [MUL], pp. 411–12.
18. H. Colvile, *The Land of the Nile Springs* (London 1895), pp. 1–2.
19. Macdonald, *Soldiering*, pp. 238, 171–2. 176–8, 212–71. Other accounts of the Muslim rebellion of 1893 are provided by M. Wright, *Buganda in the Heroic Age* (Nairobi 1971), Chapter 5; Wamala, 'Obulamu', pp. 132–5; Apolo Kagwa, *Ekitabo kya Basekabaka be Buganda* (Kampala 1952), pp. 165–8; and Ashe, *Chronicles*, pp. 394–5.
20. Macdonald, *Soldiering*, pp. 254–5.
21. *Ibid.*, p. 256.
22. Wamala, 'Obulamu', p. 134.
23. *Ibid.*, p. 135.
24. Macdonald, *Soldiering*, p. 256.
25. Wamala, 'Obulamu', pp. 136–40.
26. *Ibid.*
27. Miti (trans. Rock), *History of Buganda*, pp. 432–3; A. Kagwa, *Basekabaka*, pp. 170–2; Wamala, 'Obulamu', p. 143. For Owen winning the Grand National, J.R. Rodd, *Social and Diplomatic Memoirs* (London 1922), p. 276.
28. Miti (trans. Rock), *History of Buganda*, p. 433.
29. M. Bovill and G.R. Askwith, *Roddy Owen* (London 1897), pp. 110–14; Miti (trans. Rock), *History of Buganda*, p. 436; Wright, *Buganda in the Heroic Age*, p. 153.
30. A.B.K. Kasozi, *The Spread of Islam in Uganda* (Nairobi 1986), p. 51; Macdonald to Owen, 23 June 1893, A3/1 & 2, ESA; Ham Mukasa, *Simudu Nyuma*, Vol. 3, p. 422; A. Kagwa, *Basekabaka*, pp. 171–2; Salimini Damulira, interviews.
31. Miti (trans. Rock), *History of Buganda*, p. 439.
32. Roscoe to Colvile, 6 December 1893, A/1/93, ESA.
33. *Ibid.*
34. Miti (trans. Rock), *History of Buganda*, p. 446.
35. E.I. Steinhart, *Conflict and Collaboration: The Kingdoms of Western Uganda 1890–1907* (Princeton 1977), p. 21.
36. G. Casati, *Ten Years in Equatoria*, Vol. 2 (London and New York 1891), pp. 61–2, 80.
37. R.M. Packard, *Chiefship and Cosmology* (Bloomington 1981), p. 135; G.N. Uzoigwe, 'Kabalega and the making of a new Kitara' in ed. O. Ikime, *Leadership in 19th Century Africa* (London 1974), pp. 94–5, and Wright, *Buganda in the Heroic Age*, p. 21.
38. K. Ingham, *The Kingdom of Toro* (London 1975), p. 57.
39. *Ibid.*; Perham, *Lugard*, p. 265.
40. Portal Papers, Ms Afr. s. 109, Rhodes House, Oxford: Portal to Rosebery, 31 March 1893.

41. *Ibid.*
42. 10 August 1893, A 31/1, ESA; quoted by A.D. Roberts, 'The "lost counties" of Bunyoro', *Uganda Journal* 26 (1962), p. 194.
43. Steinhart, *Conflict*, p. 65.
44. Colvile, *Nile Springs*, p. 125.
45. *Ibid.*, pp. 812–9; Gibb to Entebbe 28 December 1893, A3/1 & 2, ESA.
46. Colvile, *Nile Springs*, p.79.
47. *Ibid.*, pp. 79–80. Another tribute to Kakungulu by Colvile is in PP, cd 7708 (1985), p. 68.
48. Colvile, *Nile Springs*, p. 98
49. *Ibid.*, pp. 100–1. Other accounts of this expedition are provided by Wamala, 'Obulamu', pp. 146–51; Macdonald, *Soldiering*, Chapters 19–20; C.F. Harford-Battersby, *Pilkington of Uganda* (London 1898), pp. 229–31; and Colvile, 2 January, and 3 and 8 February 1894, FO2/71, PRO; but Colvile's *Nile Springs* provides the most rounded account.
50. Colvile, *Nile Springs*, pp. 105–6.
51. L. Dècle, *Three Years in Savage Africa* (London 1898), p. 432.
52. Colvile, *Nile Springs*, pp. 127–8.
53. Steinhart, *Conflict*, p. 65.
54. Colvile, *Nile Springs*, p. 110.
55. *Ibid.*, p. 99.
56. *Ibid.*, pp. 115–17.
57. *Ibid.*, p. 119.
58. Moffat, journal, unpublished MS, Makerere University Library (MUL), 6 January 1894.
59. Colvile, *Nile Springs*, pp. 206–7.
60. *Ibid.*, p. 187.
61. *Ibid.*, p. 188.
62 *Ibid.*, p. 199.
63. *Ibid.*, pp. 212–13.
64. Moffat, journal entries for 5 February and 15 March 1894.
65. Colvile, *Nile Springs*, p. 215.
66. *Ibid.*
67. *Ibid.*, pp. 215–16.
67. *Ibid.*
68. RD, 17 February 1894, 23 October 1894.
69. RD, 4 August 1896.
70. See M. Twaddle, 'The ending of slavery in Buganda' in eds S. Miers and R. Roberts, *The End of Slavery in Africa* (Madison 1988), pp. 131–3.
71. Dècle, *Three Years*, pp. 307–8.
72. RD, 17 February 1893.
73. Colvile, *Nile Springs*, p. 188.
74. Steinhart, *Conflict*, p. 70.
75. WP, 13 September 1894; RD, 8 April 1894.
76. Dècle, *Three Years*, p. 432.
77. Perham, *Lugard*, pp. 221–2, quoting PP, cd 6555 (1892), p. 128.
78. *Ibid.*
79. Wright, *Buganda in the Heroic Age*, p. 103
80. Walker to L.B. White, 7 April 1896, CMSA, Acc/F2/3. See further Holger Bernt Hansen, *Mission, Church and State in a Colonial Setting: Uganda 1890–1925* (London 1984), p. 114.
81. Quoted in E. Stock, *History of the Church Missionary Society*, Vol. 3 (London 1899), p. 437.
82. Wright, *Buganda in the Heroic Age*, p. 103.
83. M.I. Finley, *The World of Odysseus* (Harmondsworth 1962), pp. 137–8.
84. *Ibid.*, pp. 140–2.
85. Colvile, *Nile Springs*, p. 125.
86. S. Vandeleur, *Campaigning on the Upper Nile and Niger* (London 1898), p. 78.
87. RD, 12 April 1894.
88. WP, letterbooks, 19 May 1895.
89. *Ibid.*, 28 July 1895,

90. A.B. Thruston, *African Incidents* (London 1900), p. 149.
91. Tefiro Kisosonkole, 'Obulamu bwange', unpublished MS in MUL.
92. P. Kibi, oral testimony; R.H. Walker, 'Notes on Uganda', *CMI*, March 1893, p. 200; Mbale Cathedral baptism register, entry in W. Crabtree's handwriting.
93. Millar to Baylis, 8 May 1901, G3/A7/1901a, CMS archives.
94. ESA A2/3; see also W. Ansorge, *Under the African Sun* (London 1899), p. 103, where he remarks 'The expense must have been enormous'.
95. RD, 2 October 1894, for a Protestant threat to withdraw to Busoga as a result; and Walker to Stockdale 8 August 1897, WP, for subsequent surprise that it did not cause anti-British rebellion.
96. RD, 10 June 1895, for details.
97. See Hansen, *Church, State and Mission, passim.*
98. Frederick Jackson, *Early Days in East Africa* (repr. London 1969), pp 340–1.
99. Hansen, *Church, State and Mission,* is excellent on this.
100. RD, 21 January 1895.
101 Baskerville, journal, 5 April 1892.
102 *Ibid.*, 18 April 1892.
103. *Ibid.*, 15 April 1892.
104. A. Kagwa, *Basekabaka*, pp. 181, 187, 216, 218–19; J.M. Gray. 'Kakunguru in Bukedi', *Uganda Journal* 27 (1963), pp. 33–4.
105. These were scanned in MUL, where they are presently kept, Kagwa Papers: they have been catalogued as far as the 1910s by John Rowe.
106. J. Roscoe, *Twenty-five Years in East Africa* (Cambridge 1921), p. 208.
107. *Ibid.*, p. 236.
108. M. Southwold, 'Succession to the throne in Buganda', in ed. J. Goody, *Succession to High Office* (Cambridge 1966), p. 84.
109. R.P. Ashe, *Chronicles* pp. 347, 368–9.
110. This was Ashe's main theme in *Chronicles*; see John Rowe, pp. xiv–xv in the Cass reprint (1971).
111. Yona Wajja, interview.
112. Gray, 'Kakunguru in Bukedi', p. 32.
113. *Ibid.*
114. Miti (trans. Rock), *History of Buganda*, Vol. 3, p. 454.
115. See above, p. 96.
116. William Shakespeare, *Troilus and Cressida*, Act III, Scene iii, l. 150.
117. Ansorge, *African Sun*, p. 105.
118. *Ibid.*
119. Ansorge to Colvile, 18 December 1894, A2/3, ESA; RD, 16 December 1894; A. Kagwa, *Basekabaka*, pp. 177–8.
120. A.R. Tucker, *18 Years in Uganda and East Africa*, (London 1908) Vol. 2, p. 277.
121. RD, 23–4 August 1893.
122. J.R.P. Postlethwaite to CS, 13 February 1926, SMP 8849, ESA.
123. Wamala, 'Obulamu', pp. 154–8.
124. *Ibid.*
125. *Gwe sigala bwakatikiro; nze ngende nenonyeze obwakabaka*: cited by F.B. Welbourn, *East African Rebels* (London 1961), p. 218. Welbourn gives A.H. Cox as his source, but in a personal communication Cox denied that this was the case. However M.B. Nsimbi, *Waggumbulizi* (Kampala 1952), p. 100, prints the quotation with nearly the same words but without citing any source. In a further communication, Nsimbi told me that he did not acquire the quotation verbatim from any informant, but invented it as 'a literary device to summarize for Ganda readers the conclusions he himself had reached after reading H.B. Thomas, 'Capax imperii – the story of Semei Kakunguru', *Uganda Journal* 6 (1939), pp. 125–36.
126. A. Kagwa, *Basekabaka*, p. 148, says 24 May 1895, p. 190 gives 11 October 1895. Tucker, *18 Years*, p. 277.
127. Grant to Jackson, 26 March 1895, A4/1, ESA.
128. Jackson, *Early Days*, p. 272.
129. Cunningham to Entebbe, 22 April 1895, A4/1. See also PP, *Africa* No. 1 (1896); A.

Kagwa, *Basekabaka*, pp. 180–1; Miti (trans. Rock), *History of Buganda*, Vol. 2, pp. 480–4, for accounts of this campaign.

130. Paulo Kibi, oral testimony; A. Kagwa, *Basekabaka*, p. 181.
131. Paulo Kagwa, 'Omukwano gwa Kabaka Mwanga', unpublished MS in MUL, pp. 21–2, and 'Kakungulu Omuzira wa Uganda', unpublished MS in MUL, pp. 7–10; Y. Wajja reported in *Munno* (1932), pp. 143–4; also Miti (trans. Rock), *History of Buganda*, p. 483, and A. Kagwa, *Basekabaka*, p. 181.
132. RD, 27–28 May 1895, 11 June 1895.
133. Paulo Kibi, oral testimony.
134. A.T. Matson, *Nandi Resistance to British Rule, 1890–1906* (Nairobi 1972), Chapter 4, for a fuller account.
135. Grant to Jackson, 14 July 95, A4/2, ESA.
136. Ansorge, *African Sun*, p. 105.
137. *Ibid.*
138. C.W. Hobley, *Kenya from Chartered Company to Crown Colony* (London 1929), p. 83.
139. Sitwell to Entebbe, 25 August 1895, A4/2, ESA.
140. Grant to Entebbe, 24 August 1895, A4/2, ESA.
141. Grant to Hobley, 14 September 1895, A4/2, ESA.
142. Hobley, *Kenya*, pp. 86–7.
143. Sitwell to Hobley, 14 September 1895, A4/2, ESA.
144. Paulo Kibi, oral testimony; A. Kagwa, *Basekabaka*, p. 187.
145. RD, 22 July 1895; Trevor Ternan, diary, copy in Rhodes House.
146. RD, 23 July 95, for the fullest account of the Protestants' embarrassment.
147. Tucker, *18 Years* (1911 edition), p. 177.
148. Tucker, *18 Years*, (1908 edition), Vol. 2, p. 277.
149. RD, 16 October 1895; A. Kagwa, *Basekabaka*, p. 190.
150. Gray, 'Kakunguru in Bukedi', p. 34.
151. Baskerville, journal, 22 July 1895.
152. Thomas, 'Capax', p. 129.
153. Ansorge to Colvile, 31 August 1894, A2/2/1895, ESA.
154. Ansorge to Colvile, 29 September 1894, A2/3.
155. Paulo Kagwa, 'Omuzira', p. 7.
156. Samwiri Tekiwagala, interview.
157. Carl Peters, *New Light on Dark Africa* (London 1891), p. 391.
158. *Ibid.* I am indebted to Dr John Tosh for advice on Lango.
159. Sitwell to Entebbe, 17 February 1896, A4/4/, ESA.
160. Ham Mukasa, *Simuda Nyuma*, Vol. 3, pp. 426–43; WP, W to R.P. Ashe, 12 May 1895.
161. See above, p. 90.
162. Malumba Zake, interview.
163. See further Twaddle, 'The ending of slavery'.
164. Berkeley to Wilson, 11 May 1896, copy in A11/5/2/96, ESA.
165. G. Wilson, memo, 6 May 1896, A4/5, ESA.
166. *Ibid.*
167. *Ibid.*
168. RD, 13 July 1896.
169. Wilson, 6 May 1896, A4/5, ESA.
170. WP, 3 May 1896.
171. Paulo Kagwa, 'Omuzira'.
172. A. Kagwa, *Basekabaka*, p. 193, quoted in English translation by S.Musoke.
173. Gray, 'Kakunguru in Bukedi', p. 34.
174. Recorded in 1965 at his home at Nakaloke, Bugisu.
175. A. Kagwa, *Basekabaka*, pp. 188; pp. 183–7 prints the 1895 laws signed by F. Jackson; the Lugard Papers in Rhodes House Library contain a commentary on these laws by George Wilson.
176. Miti (trans. Rock), *History of Buganda*, pp. 514–22.
177. For example, Captains Ponsonby and Rumbold; I am indebted to Dr Anne Thurston and Professor Roland Oliver for first drawing my attention to their journals.
178. By extension, the gear-lever in a motor car nowadays is called a *munyolo*.

179. C.F. Harford-Battersby, *Pilkington*, pp. 317–8.
180. Wright, *Buganda in the Heroic Age* (Nairobi 1971), p. 174.
181. Besides Wright, see Viera Pawlikova-Vilhanova, *History of Anti-Colonial Resistance and Protest in the Kingdoms of Buganda and Bunyoro 1862–1899* (Oriental Institute, Czechoslovak Academy of Sciences, Prague 1988), pp. 226–97.
182. A. Lugolobi, *Mbulire* (Lugala 1933), p. 39, lists Kakungulu as one of the conspirators in Mwanga's confidence who failed to fight on Mwanga's side in the eventual armed conflict.
183. S. Tekiwagala, interview, 16 September 1965.
184. A. Kagwa, *Basekabaka*, pp. 216–19.
185. Miti (trans. Rock), *History of Buganda*, p. 579.
186. Ham Mukasa, *Simuda Nyuma*, Vol. 3, p. 477.
187. *Ibid.*, p. 478.
188. P. Kibi, oral testimony.
189. *Ibid.*
190. Ham Mukasa, *Simuda Nyuma*, Vol. 3, pp. 482–6.
191. *Ibid.*
192. Miti (trans. Rock), *History of Buganda*, p. 579.
193. Quoted in *CMI*, October 1898, pp. 755–6.
194. Samwili Mukasa, *Emirimu Gyenakolede*, unpub. ms in MUL, p. 14.
195. Grant to Entebbe, 1 July 1898, A4/11.
196. *Ibid.*
197. Ham Mukasa, *Simuda Nyuma*, Vol. 3, p. 506. See also A. Kagwa, *Basekabaka*, p. 240; Miti (trans. Rock), *History of Buganda*, p. 626.
198. A. Kagwa, *Basekabaka*, p. 240.
199. Miti (trans. Rock), *History of Buganda*, p. 626.
200. S. Mukasa, *Emirimu*, p. 15.
201. Wamala, 'Obulamu', p. 159, says the letter was received on 28 January 1899, but the Rubaga Diary of the White Fathers for 2 August 1898 supports Kakungulu's receipt of it, as too does A. Kagwa, *Basekabaka*, p. 242, for the earlier date.
202. Miti (trans. Rock), *History of Buganda*, pp. 634–5; copies of the Luganda original in A. Kagwa, *Basekabaka*, p. 242 and red folder, Miti Papers, MUL, p. 790.
203. *Ibid.*
204. Ham Mukasa, *Simuda Nyuma*, Vol. 3, p. 510: *Awo Kakungulu olwokubera omwami omukulu era omwesigwa enyo ebaluwa eri Katikiro nibagitwala eKampala.*
205. *Ibid.*, p. 523.
206. J. Ddiba, *Eddini mu Uganda* (Masaka 1967), Vol. 2, pp. 221–2.
207. A. Kagwa, *Basekabaka*, p. 261; Samwiri Tekiwagala, interview.
208. A. Kagwa, *Basekabaka*, pp. 262–3. Lucy Katyanku and Semu Bulera, *Obwomezi bw'Omukama Duhaga II* (Kampala 1950), pp. 26–9, has an eyewitness Nyoro account (see Steinhart, *Conflict*, pp. 93–4). E. Kibuga, unpublished MS in the Ndaula papers, Nkoma, Mbale, pp. 7–10, 13; Wamala, 'Obulamu', pp. 164–7; Ham Mukasa, *Simuda Nyuma*, Vol. 3, pp. 539–45; and Miti (trans. Rock), *History of Buganda*, pp. 674–81, also describe it. The official British accounts are Evatt to Entebbe, 13, 30 May and 3 June 1899, A4/17, ESA.
209. RD, 16 April 1899 ('Le beau fait d'armes ...').
210. Katyanku and Bulera, *Obwomezi*.
211. Miti (trans. Rock), *History of Buganda*, pp. 677–81; Miti, red folder, MUL, p. 839.
212. Miti (trans. Rock), *History of Buganda*, p. 681.
213. S. Kyesirikidde and Y.Wajja, interviews.
214. Evatt to Entebbe, Masindi, 10 May 1899, A4/17/1899, ESA.

# Five

# A Native Collector
# 1899–1901

## 1

Somewhere on the southerly slopes of Mount Elgon early in 1901, Sir Harry Johnston came across an African chief holding 'half a *Nineteenth Century Review*'. 'This the man believed to be a kind of treaty with the white man', commented Johnston during a lecture delivered before a London audience later in the year. But to Johnston the mutilated magazine held another significance. To him it was clearly a relic of Joseph Thomson, the British explorer who had visited Mount Elgon nearly eighteen years before.[1]

That visit had lasted less than a week. Thomson was a sick man at the time, and what energies he did manage to muster during his visit were largely devoted to examining the physical features of Mount Elgon. Its human inhabitants he dismissed with a few disdainful sentences in the record he later published of his trip. 'The only inhabited part of the mighty Elgon is the south side', and even that was only occupied by 'a very small and miserable remnant of a tribe' which was unlikely to survive much longer, wrote Thomson in *Through Masai Land*.[2] It was hardly a very substantial contribution to British knowledge about one of the most densely populated parts of tropical Africa.

Little more was contributed by the first officials of the IBEAC and British protectorate administrations. Frederick Jackson did visit Elgon in 1889 and spent just over a month on the mountain during the following year, but most of his energies were devoted to mountaineering and the collection of zoological specimens.[3] Charles Hobley, the British official at Mumias, devoted nearly a month on Mount Elgon in 1896 and during this period discovered rather more than Jackson about the peoples occupying the westerly slopes of the mountain. He even attempted to open 'preliminary political relations according to their tribal rites' with the members

135

of one Gisu clan and persuade a leader of another to return with him to the recently established protectorate post at Mumias, 'that he might see the station and realise the permanence of our occupation'.[4] But neither expedient came to much. The Sebei and Gisu clans occupying the northerly and westerly slopes of this, the largest single mountain anywhere in the world at base level, remained independent of British colonial control throughout the 1890s, and their perceptions of British intentions appear to have remained most hazy.[5]

Little of this haziness was dispelled by the local behaviour of the Macdonald Expedition, which visited the region around Mount Elgon during 1898.[6] Commissioned to secure the eastern reaches of the Upper Nile for Britain, the leader of the expedition had been instructed 'to establish British influence with the natives as effectually to secure the territories in question against other powers'. This task might entail establishing military posts, but 'the preferable course' was to secure treaties with local chiefs 'by presents and the grant of the British flag'.[7] These instructions were despatched to J.R.L. Macdonald, the leader of the expedition, during June 1897. But, as we saw in the last chapter, there had been Mwanga's rebellion in July 1897 and the Sudanese mutiny in September. It was not therefore until June 1898 that Macdonald, in East Africa again after his interval in India, was able to leave Kampala for the northerly slopes of Mount Elgon, where one of his subordinate officers had been attempting to establish a base camp for the expedition.

On the slopes of Mount Elgon, Macdonald adjusted the aims of his expedition towards more local objectives than the imperial government in London. had originally envisaged. One column was despatched towards Lake Rudolph, while a second proceeded to survey the territory 'west of Turkana' and a third remained in charge of base camp on Mount Elgon. In charge, but not in control: three times in June, September and October, and twice during November 1898, this column was engaged in repelling attacks mounted against it by the Sebei and Gisu clans occupying the northerly slopes of Mount Elgon. 'The theatre of war consisted of broad terraces, in places covered with cultivation and in others covered with dense bush and grass, while the terraces were separated from each other by precipitous cliffs in which were situated numerous caves, used by the predatory natives as places of refuge,' reported Macdonald to London during the following year. 'The agricultural sections were for the most friendly, but there were small robber districts ... which gave a great deal of trouble.'[8] The first and second columns fared little better.[9] In December 1898, shortage of supplies and discontent amongst his porters finally forced Macdonald to abandon the expedition and head instead for Nairobi.[10]

Before reaching Nairobi, Macdonald sent his masters in London a sketch map showing the areas 'secured to us by our treaties' on the Uganda frontier, one of which he claimed to be the 'Region round Mount Elgon'.[11] Around the same time Macdonald also suggested to London the desirability of instituting a regular military patrol to police the areas thus secured.[12]

But it was not an opportune time to make that particular suggestion. 'It will for the present be impossible to undertake any further responsibilities on the Uganda frontier of a costly character,' quickly came back the reply from London by cable and telegraph.[13] Macdonald's treaties might stand, but his proposal for an expensive military patrol was totally unacceptable on financial grounds. Yet, without such a patrol, the treaties concluded by the Macdonald expedition with various representatives of politically decentralized African societies in eastern and northern Uganda were no more meaningful to the persons concerned than mutilated pieces of Victorian magazines left behind by earlier British explorers.

Yet clearly something had to be done about Bukedi. Being the only part of the British sphere of influence in the East African interior not backed by the presence of another European imperial power, it rapidly became a refuge for objectors to British protectorate rule. 'No one knows where Mwanga is', Archdeacon Walker had written to his family during 1898:

> I think if he has not already gone to the Bukeddi country he will go there in the end. Anywhere else he has another European power behind him to prevent him running away. And as long as the Nubians [Sudanese mutineers] are in the Bukeddi country, it will [be] a refuge for all who are disaffected to the European rule. Kabarega retired there & was never caught. The Waganda Mahommedans & others who have a price on their heads will all retire to the Bukeddi country I think. Guns & ammunition will be sold to them stolen here in Uganda.[14]

If British imperial parsimony prevented establishment of a proper protectorate administration in Bukedi, the security of British rule at least demanded that the region be rid of its most dangerous recent immigrants.

That operation, as we have seen, the British authorities at Entebbe had decided to effect in March 1899, and now only the remaining Sudanese mutineers seemed still to be at large. It was therefore not entirely surprising that when Kakungulu told the British officers in charge of the expedition which captured Kabalega and Mwanga, that he would like to extend his activities into Bukedi, rather as he and other Ganda chiefs had been encouraged to expand into southern Bunyoro five years before, these officers were only too pleased to support him in this further adventure. So, after official clearance at Entebbe and the customary ceremonies at the royal capital of Buganda, Kakungulu left for Bukedi with a small force in June 1899. Soon afterwards he received formal instructions from the acting commissioner of the protectorate administration at Entebbe 'to endeavour to induce the mutineers near his district to surrender',[15] and many more Ganda warriors started to join him.

When Sir Harry Johnston came to negotiate the Uganda Agreement of 1900 with the leading chiefs of Buganda, the position of Semei Kakungulu within the overall framework of protectorate administration presented something of a problem. As Johnston explained to the imperial government:

A certain Uganda Chief named Kakunguru first of all assisted Colonel Ternan's force in the capture of Mwanga and Kabarega and the dispersal of the mutineers in the northern part of the Protectorate. This man was then placed in charge of the Bukedi district, north of Lake Kioga and outside Uganda proper, to bring the unruly Kedi or Lango people under control, and further to keep the district clear of mutineers. By right, Kakunguru was chief of Bugerere, one of the counties of the Kingdom of Uganda. His work in Bukedi however has obliged him to give up all control over Bugerere, and we have recently had to allot the control of this county to another Chief. In the ordinary course of events Kakunguru would therefore lose the promised £200 a year salary and receive no remuneration for the excellent work he is doing in Bukedi.

'This work', continued Johnston, was 'so good that it compares favourably with what might be done by a European official'. Unfortunately the protectorate estimates for 'Native Staff' had reached the stage of being no longer susceptible to revision, and so it was impossible to pay Kakungulu any salary under that heading. Johnston therefore suggested, purely as a matter of convenience, that Kakungulu might be remunerated as 'a Third Class Assistant' under the European heading in the protectorate accounts. 'Kakunguru might be regarded as the 13th and receive a salary of £200 a year until such time as I can include him in the schedule for Native Staff. Kakunguru would impose the Hut Tax and Gun Tax on people in his district and I trust will bring in a revenue to the exchequer considerably exceeding the salary of £200 a year.'[16]

About three weeks later, Johnston further rationalized Kakungulu's position in his *Preliminary Report on the Protectorate of Uganda*:

The huge Bukedi peninsula lying to the north of Lake Kioga was formerly a happy hunting ground of these Sudanese mutineers. But an enterprising Muganda Chief who rendered great service during the mutiny was placed in charge of this peninsula about a year ago and supplied with a small number of guns. He – Kakunguru – has succeeded in reducing this peninsula to a perfectly orderly and peaceful condition and has reopened it to trade. I am striving now to encourage this man by getting the Government to permit me to give him from out of our estimates a regular salary as a Native Collector, in return for which he will collect the taxes on his peninsula and transit them to the Administration.[17]

Kakungulu had organized several thrusts into this pensinsula from his small cluster of forts in and around Lake Kyoga before meeting Sir Harry Johnston early in 1900.[18] But, after this meeting, Kakungulu had much stronger British backing for his and his followers' attempts to conquer Bukedi and to incorporate it within the Uganda Protectorate.

## 2

Words with more than one meaning can cause endless opportunities for political debate, especially where the words in question refer to land.

Around 1900 'Bukedi' was one such word. Literally 'the land of the naked people', it was the name applied by both the Baganda and the British to the territory of the Uganda Protectorate lying north and east of the River Nile and Busoga. But the word tended to be used in two rather different ways. Sometimes it was employed for the whole area lying between Lake Kyoga and Mount Elgon occupied by politically decentralized societies,[19] but sometimes it was used only for the most westerly fringes of this region. Sir Harry Johnston evidently understood the word in its restricted sense, as his reference to 'The huge Bukedi peninsula' in his *Preliminary Report* indicates. But Kakungulu chose to interpret 'Bukedi' in the wider way.

'No one knows how far the Bakedi extend', stated a CMS missionary who visited Kakungulu early in 1900.[20] 'They say themselves that Bukedi is ten days long and ten days wide, but that gives only a vague idea of its size.' Nonetheless, declared the missionary, it was 'certainly larger than Uganda [meaning Buganda] and Bunyoro put together'. Kakungulu's reasons for propagating this wider view were mixed, partly the product of unambiguous ambition, partly the result of dietary considerations. 'While Kakungulu was living at Bululu in Kumam', explains one of his chroniclers, 'he heard about the Bamoita of Palisa, about Lyada of Bugwere, and about the peoples living on Mount Masaba [Elgon]. He was informed that these areas produced plenty of banana plantains; he was very happy at hearing that these areas were so attractive, and so he decided to divide them up amongst his chiefs.'[21]

That decision taken, it remained for Kakungulu to take possession of these areas. The method adopted was the traditional Ganda one of the armed expedition. Isaka Nziga, one of Kakungulu's most Protestant and sober followers, was given command of an expedition with 150 guns, a sizeable quantity of powder and shot, and 'a Government flag' (*bendera ya Govumenti*) which Kakungulu had been given by Sir Harry Johnston.[22] Early in 1900 this expedition was despatched eastwards by Kakungulu with orders 'to conquer the territory' (*okuwangula ensi*) of Palisa, Bugwere and Bugisu among other places.[23]

Nowhere in either Palisa or Bugwere did Nziga's men meet much local resistance. In Palisa, it managed to assimilate the only formidable group of dissidents it encountered, a party of Mwanga's followers who had evaded capture when their master had been caught in Lango during 1899.[24] In Bugwere, the expedition even received a nervous sort of welcome. 'At Budaka', comments Paulo Kagwa, 'Lyada welcomed the Baganda very much, gave them many cows and goats, together with plenty of beer', and they enjoyed themselves enormously.[25] But this enjoyment did not last very long. Hardly had it begun when it was abruptly terminated by the arrival in Bugwere of John Gemmill, whom the Ganda quickly nicknamed *Binywera* because of his militant appearance.[26]

Gemmill, a footloose European with a reputation for violence against Africans,[27] found things 'in a very disturbed state' at Budaka. Not only were the Baganda 'robbing' the Bagwere but they were also 'interfering with their women', reported Gemmill to Fowler, the former gold prospector in Canada and naval man who had recently replaced William Grant as protectorate official in Busoga during Grant's absence further east. 'I did my best to settle this shaurie amicable with the Waganda's', continued Gemmill. But those Baganda

> would not listen to rhyme or reason, but turned very cheeky and when I asked them why they were interfering with Liada or his people they informed me that they could muster 130 guns, and also that they had the permission of Bwana Balozie, or otherwise known as Her Majesty's Special Commissioner, and if I did not mind my busines that they would do for me.

Gemmill had managed to disarm the Baganda, in order 'to save bloodshed', and now awaited official instructions as to what he should do with the guns he had confiscated. Some of these bore the Protectorate stamp, noted Gemmill, and some had evidently belonged at one time to the Macdonald Expedition to the Upper Nile.[28]

Fowler was furious when he received Gemmill's letter. 'It is customary', he commented with barely concealed irritation to Sir Harry Johnston,[29]

> for private individuals, previous to leaving a District for the purpose of entering an adjacent country which is known to be in a disturbed state, to ask permission to do so from the Collector of the District. This request Mr Gemmill has neglected to make and in his laudable desire to settle a disturbance in the Wakedi country disarmed a body of Waganda, the MUJASI of which force, ISAKA by name, informs me that he was despatched by the KAKUNGURO with orders to build bomas in LIADA's, NDINWA's, GUERI's and NYOLI's districts and to suppress the internecine feuds which have existed for some years ...
> On inquiry ISAKA informs me that he was directed by the KAKUN-GURO to inform me of his arrival at LIADA's, this order he can give me no definite reason for having neglected.

Isaka Nziga had also admitted that his men had foraged for food throughout the areas traversed by their expedition; 'but this', commented Fowler, 'is I believe the Kaganda custom on such occasions'.[30]

Kakungulu was also highly irritated when he heard about Gemmill's behaviour towards his men. There might have been a massacre had the Bakedi attacked them after Gemmill had removed their guns, he is remembered as having told his followers at the time.[31] 'The Government gave this territory to me' (*Gavumenti yampa ensi eno*), declared Kakungulu. 'How then can a wandering European deprive me of my guns?' (*Omuzungu omutambuye nangaga emundu zange?*).[32] 'I do not know what Kakungulu would have done to this European if he had actually been the one to meet the man in question face-to-face' rather than Isaka Nziga, continues the source from which these quotations are taken. But Kakungulu did not meet Gemmill personally until some time later, so to start with he confined protestations to legal channels.

The British protectorate reply to these protestations appears to have been that since Captain Hornby (*Wombe*, to Kakungulu's chroniclers) and

Fowler (*Fara*) would soon be visiting Bukedi to round up stray Sudanese mutineers still at large, the matter could be settled after their party arrived in the region.[33] Soon Kakungulu received a request from Hornby to meet him at Sambwe and accompany him towards Mount Elgon. This Kakungulu agreed to do, leaving Leubeni Bitege and sixty guns in charge of the fort at Bululu.[34]

Before leaving Bululu, Kakungulu instructed Bitege 'not to allow any European to take his guns away, least of all that terrible European *Binywera*.'[35] Yet within a few days Kakungulu had agreed to lend Hornby – who can hardly be considered to have been one of the pleasantest personalities in view of what one source calls his 'excessive cruelty'[36] – about 150 fighting men to assist in further British military operations against the Nandi people in what is nowadays western Kenya, together with Isaka Nziga as their commander.[37] In retrospect, the second action may appear somewhat inconsistent with the first, even if Kakungulu's statement that he was too sick to accompany this further expedition to western Kenya in person is taken at face value, as the British clearly so took it at the time. Nevertheless, soon afterwards Kakungulu received ample reward for the assistance rendered yet again to the under-capitalized British protectorate administration. First, Gemmill was suitably disciplined by due process of law. As one of Kakungulu's chroniclers puts it, 'The protectorate authorities deported that European from any area controlled by the protectorate authorities in Buganda, and he was warned never to return to this place a second time.'[38] Secondly, Kakungulu was formally requested 'to move, as soon as possible, the women and personnel effects of his men from Kabagambi's [adjoining Lango country] to the settlement in Bukeddi.'[39] In other words, Kakungulu's interpretation of 'Bukedi' was unwittingly gaining recognition from local British protectorate officials at the expense of their Special Commissioner's.

John Gemmill had already blotted his copybook with the British authorities several times because of earlier misdeeds while a caravan leader on the Mombasa road.[40] At his trial at Luba's it also became apparent that Gemmill's associates in Bukedi had forcibly seized at least one woman captive from the Ganda rebels recently surrendered to Kakungulu's advance party – 'she was taken prisoner by Mr J. Gemmill after the slaughter of a number of Bisigoro's (alias Leo) men ... in a night attack'[41] – while when the rifles confiscated by Gemmill were finally given back to Kakungulu's followers by Fowler it was discovered that muzzleloaders had been substituted for breechloaders.[42] Gemmill's business partner, Oscar Smith, was freed in return for turning crown witness – or rather non-witness, as he was ordered to leave immediately by the presiding magistrate, Pordage[43] – and Gemmill himself was sentenced to '1 year's imprisonment with hard labour, and deportation after that time being expired; moreover 300 pounds fine'.[44] 'In considering the sentence', wrote Pordage to Johnston, 'I have taken into consideration that it is necessary to consider other traders who may follow.'[45]

With Gemmill imprisoned, Hornby well on the way to Nandi country, and Fowler back in Busoga, Kakungulu could again settle down seriously to conquering fresh territory. Before the Gemmill case, Kakungulu's followers had clearly experienced great difficulty in subjugating Lango country, and another substantial advance party launched in a more northerly direction than Nziga's expedition also appears to have been aborted, though surviving chronicle evidence suggests that this was as much because of more attractive opportunities for conquest existing in the south and east as because resistance was stronger than expected in the northern areas initially penetrated by this other foray in force.[46] After the Gemmill case, however, Kakungulu constructed a military enclosure at Nabowa in Bugwere, on a site which had been chosen before his departure with Hornby, as being 'quite high and from it you can see Masaba [Mount Elgon]'.[47] This enclosure Kakungulu made his base for a series of co-ordinated raids into Iteso country during the middle months of 1900.

Raiding parties were despatched against the Iteso at Mukongoro, at Ngora, and at Bukedea, mostly under the command of Sedulaka Kyesirikidde, one of Kakungulu's younger brothers.[48] Few serious attempts were made even to find pretexts for these raids. Local notables were simply summoned to appear before Kakungulu 'to make peace' and punished if they did not appear promptly enough.[49] In no case was the punishment dispensed by Kakungulu's warriors during 1900 particularly pleasant. Indeed, at Mukongoro, it seems to have been especially brutal, Iteso captives as well as their cattle being herded into huts which were then fired. 'This was an act of excessive cruelty', admitted one of the Baganda responsible for the atrocity at a later date; 'but it served its purpose in dealing with a primitive community.'[50]

Meanwhile Kakungulu kept in touch with his chiefs in Lango by correspondence. Their forts in Lango country were constantly under attack; hardly had one cluster of dissident Langi been dealt with than another one started fresh difficulties. 'The Bakedi of Lango also had the habit', reports another of Kakungulu's chroniclers, of coming up to the fort at Kikabukabu and reporting to the chief Kago after a skirmish: 'A number of your Baganda soldiers came and attacked us, and had it not been for the Muganda so-and-so who fought bravely, we would have killed them all.' 'But', continues the same chronicler regarding the Langi, 'they were often defeated despite their boasting.'[51] This was because, though the people of Lango were constantly obstreperous, the occupants of neighbouring Kumam country hardly ever gave any trouble and Leubeni Bitege, the commander of Kakungulu's fort there, was able to come frequently to the assistance of Malembwe Bijabiira, his hard-pressed colleague in Lango.[52] Bitege was helped in doing this by the fact that Bululu, the main Ganda fort in Kumam, was constantly being replenished with fresh recruits to Kakungulu's following from Buganda throughout 1900.

By August, Kakungulu was turning his primary military attentions from the Teso plains to the foothills of Mount Elgon. 'All the time Kakungulu spent at Naboa he longed to settle on Masaba', writes Paulo Kagwa; 'and every afternoon he used to sit on a nearby rock and gaze through his binoculars at Masaba'.[53] Then Abudala Makubire, a Muslim in Kakungulu's following, seized several cattle tended by Bagisu in the narrow strip of uncultivated land skirting the foot of Mount Elgon. 'If you want peace, you should come and collect your cattle', was the provocative message Kakungulu ordered to be sent to the Bagisu who had been deprived of these cattle.[54] Soon several Gisu did come to Kakungulu to make peace, mostly members of clans which had migrated into the foothills of Mount Elgon only about a generation before. These locally still somewhat underprivileged groups provided Kakungulu with valuable intelligence about the character of the clans occupying the most westerly slopes of the mountain. In return for this information, Kakungulu advised members of these particular lineages to stay within their huts when the first serious forays by his men into Bugisu began.[55]

These came in October 1900.[56] Yosiya Byatike was despatched with a small force to examine the Nkokonjeru escarpment, which so dramatically overlooks the modern municipality of Mbale, for a suitable site upon which to construct a military stockade, while Kakungulu himself settled temporarily amongst members of the Basoba clan living to the south of this escarpment.[57] But soon Kakungulu was forced to build his principal stockade elsewhere, at a place which he called Mpumudde and is known as Namumali nowadays, because Byatike failed to find any site suitable for a such a stockade on either Nkokonjeru escarpment or Buwalasi hill further to the north; both areas, incidentally, which Kakungulu had been warned would be most resistant to his coming.[58] Besides building his major stockade amongst the Basoba, Kakungulu also had a subsidiary one constructed at Bukonde, close to the modern centre of Mbale municipality.[59]

At first Kakungulu and his followers appear to have been regarded by the Gisu amongst whom they settled 'as visitors',[60] a not unreasonable assumption considering the number of Ganda who had earlier migrated peacefully into the area (amongst them, at an earlier date, most probably some of the 'Bakunta' who had murdered *Kabaka* Junju).[61] But when Kakungulu ordered his follower Esitasio Nkambo to build the fort at Bukonde and other followers foraged through Bugisu for food, the Gisu became 'thoroughly roused', as one European visitor reported subsequently, 'and evidently determined to drive out of their country Kakungulu & his followers whom they no longer regard as visitors seeing they were building stockades ... and looting the shambas partly as a punishment for being arrested by the natives, but chiefly as their principal means of obtaining food.'[62] 'All Bugisu' (*Bugishu yonna*), Eria Kibuga tells us, now turned upon the Baganda.[63] The Bamasikiye, Bakiyende, Basiu and Basukuya clans attacked from the east; the Basano and Baduda from the north, and the Bakonde and Basoba from the west. These attacks were kept up for about a fortnight.[64]

Towards the close of that fortnight, Bishop Hanlon of the Mill Hill Mission arrived at Kakungulu's headquarters in Bugisu 'and begged for a place on which to build'.[65] This request Kakungulu granted, turning it to his advantage by getting the Bishop to mediate on his behalf with local

Bagisu notables to end their attacks upon his fort. 'These chiefs', noted the Bishop six weeks later,[66]

> gave me the idea that they did not understand Kakungulu's position. I asked him to state it to them clearly & fully & to explain the futility of a continued opposition which could only mean more loss of life and property. He explained these things. The chiefs submitted. They made friends with us all & before they left they received some useful presents.

Two days later, the process was repeated with other Gisu notables to similar effect. Bishop Hanlon then departed in a satisfied mood for Buganda. About a fortnight afterwards, he composed the letter from which these extracts have been quoted, declaring that as a result of his visit 'peace was brought about and has remained ever since, as far as we know from Kakungulu who is in charge'.

## 3

Few British officials of the infant protectorate administration in Uganda now believed that Kakungulu's intentions were peaceable, but they were uncertain how to deal with him. Fowler's first reaction to the news about the Baganda advance to Bugwere had been to write: 'The presence of a Government Officer is obviously urgently needed in the Bukeddi country at this moment.' But, six weeks later, he had come to realize that this proposal was financially unrealistic, and was making the more modest suggestion that 'the OCD Busoga should pay a quarterly or half-yearly visit to the Bukeddi country for the purpose of holding a baraza.'[67] Now he was even writing that 'were I asked to name amongst the Waganda chiefs the person most suitable for the the government of Bukedi I should without hesitation select Semei Kakungulu.'[68] Financially, the area of choice was limited.

With Fowler's opinion about Kakungulu being 'most suitable' for Bukedi, Sir Harry Johnston agreed for a time, evidently quite enthusiastically. Kakungulu, wrote Johnston to London during August 1900, was a 'trustworthy Uganda official'.[69] But Frederick Jackson, now Johnston's deputy at Entebbe, was not so sure. As soon as he received information about cattle being confiscated by Kakungulu as punishment for attacks upon his men by Bakedi, Jackson positively suspected the worst. 'I am inclined to disbelieve that Kakunguru was attacked, and I think it far more probable that the attack was by, and not on, the Kakunguru, for the sake of the cattle.'

> I am perfectly sick of hearing of these attacks [continued Jackson] and am beginning to think that Kakunguru and his followers are no better than Masai, or Nandi cattle lifters. When I spoke to H.M. Special Commissioner on Kakunguru's behalf and obtained his sanction to the appointment of the Kakunguru to so important and responsible a post as Assistant Collector of the Bukedi country. It was on the distinct understanding that he would use his utmost endeavours to conciliate the people under him and show himself

worthy of the confidence and high opinion in which he has hitherto been held by the Government, by administering the country in a peaceful and orderly manner. These conditions he has not fulfilled, and his short tenure since his appointment as Assistant Collector has not been conciliatory but a record of fighting and cattle lifting.

Unless Kakungulu behaved himself, concluded Jackson, 'he will receive no further assistance in the shape of ammunition or powder however hard pressed he may be'.[70]

By November 1900, Johnston too was having his doubts. When Kakungulu put in a request 'for large supplies of Martini cartridges' from the British authorities, together with another for permission to purchase other supplies of ammunition himself from the Germans administering other parts of the East African interior at this time,[71] these doubts turned into outright suspicion.

> I should say 'Do nothing for the present; tell Kakunguru to keep quiet pending further instructions'.
> Personally I am not in favour of letting him have more Martini ammunition. He may be storing it up to sell or use in some nefarious project. . .

was Johnston's minute on this matter.[72] For a while Johnston's suspicions appear to have been allayed by a favourable report on Kakungulu sent in during November 1900 by Tarrant, the young protectorate official who had replaced Fowler in Busoga.[73] But by January 1901 Johnston's suspicion had given way to anger. 'J.P. Wilson from Mumia's writes to me complaining bitterly of the Kakunguru's raids in the vicinity of Masawa [Mount Elgon]. I wish you would send to enquire', wrote Johnston to one of his officials during this month.[74] 'In the first place', continued Johnston,

> you might remind the Kakunguru that he never received from me permission to establish himself so far to the East, that I only sanctioned his being employed in the Bukedi country near Lake Kioga. Unless he can give you a very good reason for his behaviour you are to insist on his returning. I am beginning to think that we shall have to withdraw the Kakunguru and leave the Bukedi country to itself, as he is positively worse than having no overseer at all. If you are of the same opinion, then withdraw him without further reference to me . . . the plain result of his work in Bukedi seems to be continual fighting and agitation.

William Grant, who had only recently returned to his earlier position in Busoga, was the official to whom Sir Harry Johnston now wrote. Grant sent off two letters to Kakungulu demanding an explanation of his recent activities, one composed in English, the other in Swahili.[75] Kakungulu quickly showed the English version to W.A. Crabtree, a CMS missionary who had arrived at Kakungulu's headquarters at Mpumudde in Bugisu about a fortnight after the Roman Catholic bishop had departed, and upon whom Kakungulu had already showered 'kindness & goodness'.[76] Crabtree replied to Grant instead of Kakungulu. 'As you have written to Kakunguru in the English language, which language he does not understand, I take the liberty to write to you on his behalf,' wrote Crabtree to Grant.[77] The reports of Kakungulu's raids were merely rumours spread by his enemies. As for the location of Kakungulu's activities, these had been publicly defined by Sir Harry Johnston at a meeting of the Buganda *Lukiko* (or chiefly council, reformed by George Wilson shortly after arriving in the Kingdom and confirmed by the 1900 Agreement). Kakungulu, continued Crabtree,

> was not aware that any further definition of his sphere was made than that it was to be the 'Bukedi' country – understanding by this word a stretch of country up to Ketosh [in what is nowadays western Kenya]. In support of this he would appeal to the leading Baganda present at that Council, such as the Katikiro [Apolo Kagwa] & the Regents Zakariya & Mugwanya.

Furthermore, during that very meeting

> H.M.'s Special Commissioner & Commander in Chief stated that he intended to build two forts at Lake Baringo; to prevent the advance of the Arabs (? Abyssinians; 'Okuziza Abaarabu') – thereby implying that he did not contemplate government officials ('aba Serikali') taking any action on this side of Massawa [Mount Elgon] – Lake Baringo being to the Eastern side of Massawa.

To this neither Grant nor Johnston could make much reply, though Grant did minute ineffectually 'I also wrote him in the Swahili' on Crabtree's letter when forwarding it to Johnston.[78] Black had, on this occasion at least, mated white in very few moves.

It would be wrong to exaggerate the importance of tactical victory at this particular moment between Kakungulu and the British protectorate authorities, as there would be subsequent occasions when white would win much more quickly. Nevertheless, it is instructive to isolate the factors enabling him to confound British officials so effectively during 1900. For an appreciation of these factors deepens understanding of later contests between Kakungulu and Sir Harry Johnston's successors in the same political arena, and also as understanding of how he managed to make a successful movement of men to Mpumudde considering the earlier failures, not only of the Macdonald Expedition in 1898 but of the disastrous plundering expedition despatched into Bukedi at the end of *Kabaka* Mutesa I's reign fifteen years before.

To begin with, there were several factors especially favouring Kakungulu during 1900. There was the presence at Mpumudde of European missionaries whom he found easy to persuade to act on his behalf, simply because they had only recently arrived – the one to soften local resistance to the rigours of his arrival, the other to mollify European objections to the earliest reports about his political behaviour. There was also the straitened financial condition of the British protectorate in 1900, the 'damned economy' which prevented any European official being posted to his headquarters on Mount Elgon and, together with 'crass ignorance', was highly unlikely to lead to any sensible form of British administration in the area, in the opinion of one seconded army captain. 'Apparently the F.O. think that they can develop the country without spending a farthing on it', wrote Captain Rumbold to his brother. 'Johnston's whole energy is at present devoted to the question of endeavouring to cut our salaries and deprive us of any right to leave, and also to make revenue out of officers'.[79] Johnston's commissioning of Kakungulu to conquer an unsubjugated section of Britain's new protectorate in the East African interior was clearly part of this strategy of financial cuts, a strategy designed to reduce regular troops employed in the Uganda Rifles from 1,800 to 1,100 men.[80] Yet, most important of all, in removing possible obstruction of Kakungulu's triumphal progress to Mpumudde in 1900, was the preoccupation of British officials with other matters for most of that year. Had it not been necessary to remove William Grant to assist in punitive operations against the Nandi people for two substantial periods of the year, and replace him in Busoga with officials lacking not only local knowledge but even an elementary knowledge of Luganda, it is inconceivable that Kakungulu would have been as undisturbed as he was by British protectorate officials during his partial conquest of Bukedi.

But Kakungulu had another cluster of advantages on his side during 1900, which resulted from the confusion in British official minds about his official status. What made the confusion more severe was the apparent assumption in protectorate circles that 'any white man of whatever position is more or less treated on terms of equality in this country', as Captain Rumbold also reported somewhat incredulously to his family.[81] Sir Harry Johnston wrote about Kakungulu in letters to London almost as if he was a European official, but clearly Kakungulu was *not* a European and Johnston's treatment of him in person had been quite different. Fowler had called Kakungulu an 'Asst Collector' in administrative correspondence with Jackson,[82] but in personal dealings with Kakungulu had also treated him as an African chief. When he visited Bukedi in June 1900, for example, Fowler took 'the liberty of informing the Bukeddi chiefs', he reported to Entebbe,[83]

> that the Kakungulu is ruling this country under permission from HM Special Commissioner and that the country is *not*, as he (Kakungulu) has apparently informed them, his personal property – further that any important question such as deposition of native chiefs and adjustment of important claims, settlement of feuds, etc, are to brought before me or the Collector succeeding myself at Iganga.

But Tarrant, Fowler's successor at Iganga, had not acted on these lines. Instead, he appears to have tried to treat Kakungulu straightfowardly as a junior protectorate official, making arrangements with him 'for the furnishing of a Report about twice a month so as to keep in touch with events in Bukedi'.[84]

In the mind of Frederick Jackson, Johnston's deputy at Entebbe, ideas about Kakungulu's status were even more confused. 'Kakungulu and his followers are really "settlers" in a country which they have been allowed by the Government to occupy', wrote Jackson to Fowler in August 1900. 'Kakungulu receives a salary as Assistant Collector, but his followers receive nothing.'[85] Given such confusion of roles in British official minds, the extent to which Kakungulu persuaded British officials to advance rather than retard his conquests north and east of the River Nile and Busoga hardly seems surprising.

## 4

Yet, in retrospect, how Kakungulu turned the attitudes and actions of British protectorate officials to his advantage constitutes only one of the questions posed by his triumphal progress to Mpumudde during 1900. Equally deserving attention is how he made any progress at all, considering the spectacular failure of Waliomuzibu's earlier attempt at the close of Mutesa I's reign. Then a major Ganda plundering expedition was defeated ignominiously by the Jopadhola people and Ganda warriors who survived this disaster were considered lucky not to be executed upon their return to Buganda for cowardice or incompetence.[86]

To be sure, to some extent the two questions are linked, an answer to the first contributing to explanation of the second. Successful management – or distraction – of British protectorate officials ensured political tolerance for Kakungulu's activities in Bukedi during 1900. It also provided some firearms for his followers, together with a useful mechanism for ejecting rival European intruders like John Gemmill (for in many ways the ideal allies for British imperialists in Africa, remarks Ronald Robinson, were white settlers).[87] But, by itself, political management of British colonial officials during 1900 provides only a partial explanation of Kakungulu's military successes in this year.

Another part of the explanation lies in the fragmented political condition of eastern Uganda at the start of this century. This contributed massively to the 'continual fighting and agitation' which so worried Sir Harry Johnston by the beginning of 1901 and was to worry his British colleagues still more by the end of that year. Political fragmentation north and east of the River Nile and the Mpologoma swamp also assisted Kakungulu's advance to Mount Elgon in several ways. First, it supplied him with many informers supplying vital information about local conditions, such as the renegade Gisu who assisted the Ganda conquest of lowland Bugisu during December 1900. Secondly, it supplied him with a stream of suppliants urging attacks upon traditional rivals, which Kakungulu was able to exploit when it suited him. When this happened, Kakungulu could also rely upon such suppliants to help in local fighting. Paulo Kagwa relates, for example, how the peoples of Nabowa assisted in the Ganda assault upon Bukedea. There Kakungulu's warriors had to confront one of the most formidable confederacies opposed to them under the warleader Okoce. 'In this battle, there were many Bagwere who took part', relates Paulo Kagwa; 'and this saved them from starvation as they were able to seize millet, groundnuts and dry sweet potatoes which were plentiful there at that time'.[88]

Negatively, political fragmentation helped Kakungulu's advance in other ways. One village in the region might receive the most intense attack from a party of Ganda, but it was unlikely that many (frequently, any) villages would come to its assistance however close geographically those villages might be situated to the victim or victims of attack. Sociologically, this seems to have been because Bukedi formed what Professor Ogot has called an 'ethnic corridor'[89] or shatter-belt between the Bantu-speaking kingdoms of the lakes region of East Africa, south and west of the River Nile and Busoga, and the Paranilotic confederacies of what is nowadays western Kenya and the southern Sudan; contributing to what the commissioners enquiring into the Bukedi riots of 1960 called a 'heterogeneity of . . . tribal groups greater than we have seen in Africa outside what is popularly known as a "detribalised area" '.[90] Or, as one of the more articulate CMS missionaries to travel through Bukedi in the early 1900s, put it: 'Here in Ukedi the chief is almost reduced to position without magnitude, like Euclid's point.'[91] In these conditions it was not surprising to find 'continual fighting and agitation' at local level, but extremely surprising to find fighting and agitation coordinated over anything but very limited areas.

Two areas of eastern Uganda where Kakungulu did encounter exceptional degrees of coordinated resistance in 1900 were at Bukedea, in southern Ateso-speaking country, and amongst the Lumasaba-speaking clans occupying the westerly foothills of Mount Elgon. Around Bukedea, two Iteso scholars see the war leader Okoce managing to coordinate sufficient support amongst the Iteso to resist Kakungulu in an important battle, but not enough to overcome a strategist of genius such as Semei Kakungulu who only confronted Okoce after dealing with lesser opponents in the Serere and Ngora areas, and then approached Bukedea by a surprise route.[92] 'However', remarks one of these scholars, 'Okoce seems to have been so popular with his people that in spite of his resistance, the invaders regarded him as an asset rather than a liability; therefore like Amodan, Oumo and Ijala – the collaborators – Okoce, a resister, was appointed a sub-county chief subsequently at Bukedea.[93] On the westerly slopes of Mount Elgon even more widespread resistance arose to Kakungulu's coming. There the military apparatus for coordinated attack against outsiders existed in the socio-religious shape of circumcision age-sets, which enabled disparate lineage groups to unite for common action as occasion demanded.[94] But Kakungulu was careful to avoid other likely trouble spots until he had broken the backbone of resistance to his arrival in Bukedea and in Bugisu. He was careful to keep his forts in Lango to a merely peripheral presence during 1900, to avoid northern Iteso country entirely (despite at least one approach to him for intervention there at this time),[95] and to avoid for as long as possible Padhola, where the earlier Ganda plundering expedition commanded by Waliomuzibu had come to such grief.

This avoidance of trouble spots was another example of the shrewdness with which Kakungulu directed the Ganda colonial entry into the acephalous societies of eastern Uganda. But Kakungulu's shrewdness was not only the product of his personal qualities, his 'bravery' or heroic achievement (*obuzira*) extolled by his chroniclers and in interviews conducted with surviving followers when this study commenced. It was also assisted by something much rarer in Waliomuzibu's day: the possesion of functional literacy by Kakungulu's leading chiefs. This enabled Kakungulu to plan and direct military operations far more efficiently and intelligently than Waliomuzibu. It also had valuable incidental propaganda effects. 'The Bagisu were very impressed by the way the Baganda used to communicate with one another through letters', commented George Wamimbi. 'They used to say publicly, "Take this paper in this cleft-stick, guard it well because it can speak, and then deliver it to so-and-so". And when the Muganda to whom it was taken read it aloud, it did speak !'[96] In more than one way functional literacy proved a formidable weapon in facilitating the Ganda conquest of previously wholly oral as well as politically decentralized societies at the start of this century.

Then there were guns. These were important, though not as important in one locality as in another. In Lango neither Ganda nor Langi attached too much importance to the possession of firearms in themselves. 'Though the Baganda had guns the Bakedi [of Lango] were not afraid of them', remarked one early European visitor.[97] Yet elsewhere in Bukedi the opposite appears to have been the case. To take the example most empha- sized in interview evidence, the possession of guns by Ganda was clearly of crucial importance in Bugisu. 'The Bagisu surrounded Kakungulu's place and attacked together with spears, arrows and sticks', remembered an elderly Gisu informant who had been an eyewitness of the combined assault upon Mpumudde in December 1900. 'They also had shields. But Kakungulu had guns. Kakungulu killed most of his opponents; the rest ran away'.[98] And what was true of the Gisu was probably no less true of other acephalous societies which Kakungulu confronted militarily during 1900: 'the noise, the mystery and the almost supernatural power of the guns ('the sticks that vomited fire')', remarks one historian of the Iteso, being 'enough to galvanise many resisters into open flight and to turn potential ones into acquiescent collaborators'.[99]

Where did Kakungulu now get most of his guns ? In 1899 the British protectorate authorities in Buganda supplied him with a small quantity of precision firearms, and supplied him intermittently with powder and caps during the following year.[100] But these were by no means the only supplies of guns and ammunition available to him. From the very start of the conquest of Bukedi Kakungulu was able to purchase considerable supplies from local traders. 'Black Swahilis came from Karagwe, from Kitengule across the Kagera river', related Kakungulu's younger brother, Sedulaka Kyesirikidde. 'They sold cloth. Arabs and Somalis also came. They sold cloth, sugar, plates and cups.' These traders also sold guns to Kakungulu and his followers in Bukedi 'privately'.[101] Then even larger supplies of firearms became available to Kakungulu as his following in Bukedi increased in size: by thirty guns when he was joined by a person such as Eria Nsubuga, by another eight when he was joined by somebody like Alexander Njala.[102] In that way, the quantity of guns placed at Kakungulu's disposal by the British protectorate authorities in Buganda was multiplied most probably at least fifty times.[103]

Besides multiplying firearms, clientage was itself the source of an important cluster of factors assisting Kakungulu's military success during 1900. Most obviously, it supplied him with sufficient forces to garrison the increasing number of military forts established straddling the southerly fringes of Bukedi. Less obviously, it provided him with sufficient manpower to allow the despatch of a contingent of 150 or so armed followers to assist British operations against the Nandi without seriously damaging operations in Bukedi. Least obviously of all, it provided him with an important source of intelligence about Bukedi itself. For the force which invaded Bukedi under Kakungulu's command at the start of this century was composed of men who were Ganda by adoption as well as by birth, an important number having actually been born in Bukedi itself. One elderly survivor from that force related, for instance, that its members included several 'Bakedi' who had been seized during an earlier raid into the region, among whom he particularly remembered Masangano, a Munyole, and Mulogobyaire, a Mugwere.[104] In addition many people in Bukedi joined Kakungulu's following in a variety of capacities as the triumphal progress to Mpumudde proceeded. Not only were these various followers as crucially important to Kakungulu's military successes at this time as guns, but they were important to it in a variety of ways.

## 5

Given this importance, one inevitably asked those few survivors from Kakungulu's invading force discovered and interviewed for this study, what attracted followers to Kakungulu during 1900. As far as Masangano and Mulogobyaire were concerned, the answer seems clear. They were his slaves while he was *Kimbugwe* in Buganda during the early 1890s, both of them working in his subordinate chieftaincy of Kitawangula at Buvuma, together with locally born followers like Yairo Bina and Astaliko Kabuzi who also followed him to Bukedi.[105] If not yet manumitted, or 'ransomed' by European missionaries by gift or through the Buganda *Lukiiko* for recognized payments, Kakungulu's slaves would have had little choice in the matter, other than abandoning both Bukedi and Buganda for some other place whenever opportunity arose. A number of persons reduced to slavery through pawnship within Buganda itself also appear to have joined Kakungulu in Bukedi, specifically in order to acquire sufficient resources with which to redeem themselves – as subsequent complaints about excessive numbers of cattle seized for this purpose in government and missionary correspondence at the time make clear.[106] But most of Kakungulu's personal followers who accompanied him to Bukedi in 1899–1900 undoubtedly would have been free persons. While it is true that a number of Kakungulu's free followers did desert him for other patrons when he departed for Bukedi, many of them remained loyal to their old employer and continued to serve him in Bukedi.

Besides personal retainers who remained loyal, and chattel slaves who had little choice in the matter apart from running away (though such slaves could reasonably expect to be able to redeem themselves in due course in the new conditions north or east of the Nile and Busoga), other Ganda abandoned masters in Buganda in their thousands to join Kakungulu in Bukedi. Their motives were varied. First, there were the unpleasantnesses associated with paying the taxes introduced by Sir Harry Johnston in 1900, which protectorate officials later considered the principal reason for the exodus of Ganda from Buganda at this time.[107] These unpleasantnesses seem to have been as persuasive with Banyala in Bugerere as with Ganda further south in Kyagwe county. 'The fear of being taken to the capital to pay their tax has sent thousands across the Kyoga lake to a newly opened up country, Bukeddi, back to their old chief Kakungulu', reported a Mill Hill Father early in the following year.[108]

Other followers were attracted for other reasons. Some came because they anticipated landed wealth, some because they expected administrative office, others simply because they wanted an adventurous life. Typical of the first were the many Ganda who joined Kakungulu 'to get the spoils of lands' and 'to obtain a fortune' during 1900.[109] Representative of the third sort of man was Yoswa Mulinyabigo, a follower who was remembered as 'a very brave man' (*omuzira myo*) and one who enjoyed fighting.[110] In the middle came those Baganda who were attracted by the prospects of political advancement. 'There was the hope of being chiefs', declared one elderly Ganda informant who became a minor chief in Bukedi as a result of Kakungulu's patronage. 'We started from Bululu as mere warriors, but we knew that because Kakungulu had been given this land, we would become chiefs.'[111] Reinforcing each of these desires was a widespread feeling among Kakungulu's followers that life would be much better for them in Bukedi than it had been in Buganda at the end of the nineteenth century. 'When the Baganda heard that Kakungulu had been allowed to go to Bukedi, they rejoiced,' commented Yonna Wajja.[112] In that region, the opportunities for personal advancement appeared to be endless.

Yet some of the men who were attracted to Kakungulu at this time came not so much because prospects for personal advancement were multiplying in Bukedi as because their opportunities in Buganda were contracting. This applied particularly to Muslims. Their prospects for political promotion in Buganda had been reduced to a small fraction of their former extent by the so-called 'Christian revolution' (or rather 'counter-revolution')[113] in their kingdom which finally received British protectorate confirmation in the Uganda Agreement of 1900.[114] This banished to a political wilderness prominent Muslims like Bumbakali Kamya, a man who had held high office under the Muslim king Kalema and his successor Nuhu Mbogo, and who joined Kakungulu's following at this time. But the full brunt of the Christian revolution in Buganda fell upon Baganda who had held less exalted offices on the Muslim side, younger men who had been minor *batongole* chiefs and whose careers still largely lay before them. It was therefore from amongst these younger Muslims that Kakungulu acquired many of his most useful recruits during 1900 – men like Sale Lule, Jafali Mayanja, Abudala Makubire, Sale Kamya and Yosiya Mayanja, whose names recur frequently in the vernacular chronicles recording the Ganda conquest of Bukedi at the start of this century.

Religion was thus a factor stratifying clientage within Kakungulu's following in Bukedi. On the Muslim side, whole segments of the former administration of that group in Buganda appear to have attached themselves to Kakungulu at this time. Salimini Damulira, to take merely one example, remembered the names of at least five sub-chiefs who had worked with him under Musa Lwanga, Mbogo's treasurer, and who joined Kakungulu's following in Bukedi now: Sale Lule and Sale Mulindwa, who had worked with Damulira in the 'big Treasury' (*Eggwanika Ekkulu*), and Jaberi Mayanja, Abudala Makubire and Amiri Mutambala who had worked in the 'small Treasury' (*Eggwanika Etto*).[115] But Protestantism was undoubtedly important too in stratifying Kakungulu's following at this time, as CMS missionaries working in Buganda noted to their disadvantage. Writing regarding Kakungulu in 1901, the Revd G.R. Blackledge commented: 'The departure of this good man has proved a great blow to our work here, for not only have we lost his Christian influence in our midst, and his loyal financial support, but also the very large number of Christian men and women whom he took with him'.[116]

Yet exactly how many of Kakungulu's followers were Protestants at this time, it is impossible to say. All one can hope for are general impressions, since the oral memories from which such impressions must be taken do not allow precise quantification. Nonetheless, several general impressions were forthcoming from the few survivors from Kakungulu's following interviewed for this study. Questioned about the religious composition of Kakungulu's following in Bukedi, several stated that Protestants predominated, followed by Catholics and Muslims sharing second place, and finally by Ganda professing no particular foreign religious allegiance.[117] But one of Kakungulu's former followers questioned was quick to point out the error in the formulation of this question about religious allegiance. 'A Muganda chief does not discriminate for religious reasons', he declared. 'It was simply a matter of personal choice. By the time we left Buganda, it was possible to move about peacefully. Chwa was kabaka.'[118]

Subjected to further questioning, another former follower revealed that religion could operate in a devious way in attracting Ganda followers to Kakungulu. We have already noted that one of the young Muslims who joined Kakungulu at the start of this century was Jafali Mayanja. One might have expected that his arrival would have stimulated other Muslims to join Kakungulu. But that was not the point made by Salimu Mbogo, himself a Ganda Muslim who joined Kakungulu in 1900, when discussing Mayanja's role in attracting other followers. 'Jafali's joining Kakungulu was an important fact', commented this informant; 'it encouraged more of the Mamba clan to come and join Kakungulu.'[119] Much the same point was made by another former follower about Yusufu Byakuno, another prominent Muslim who joined Kakungulu around this time, attracting many of the Lugave clan of Buganda into Kakungulu's clientage.[120] In other words, many prominent individuals in Kakungulu's following in Bukedi appear to have been attracted to him by economic, political and religious considerations which are relatively easy to undertand when the history of the Buganda kingdom during the late nineteenth century is borne in mind; but many of the mass of his Ganda following there seem to have been attracted by a more complex connection of kinship associations.

Nonetheless, whatever these attractions may have been, one thing about Kakungulu's following in Bukedi seems abundantly clear. For the most part it was composed of comparatively young people – which was one reason why it proved possible to interview at least some of them for this study.

## 6

By the close of 1900, Kakungulu's following must have numbered more than a thousand fighting men armed with guns, and nearly as many again equipped with spears. These fighting men were deployed in a line of forts stretching over a hundred miles of swamp, savannah and steppe. At one end of the line lay Bululu, the fort closest to Buganda where most Ganda recruits to Kakungulu's following in Bukedi were collected and equipped. At the other end lay Mpumudde, his military headquarters. Here labourers came in to work from each of the areas controlled from the forts. Here also he began to receive ambassadors from prominent chiefs in what is nowadays western Kenya. 'The importance of this place ... grows on one', wrote the CMS missionary Crabtree in January 1901. 'Mumia recognised Kakungulu as his friend and sent special messengers to him the other day.'[121]

About three months later, Sir Harry Johnston rounded Mount Elgon on his last safari before leaving East Africa at the close of his Special Commission. He met Kakungulu personally at Balimwogerako, the military enclosure Kakungulu was constructing a few miles above Mpumudde. One of Johnston's British companions described this as

a charming situation, a little shut in on the N.E. by the great mass of rock called Busoma ... but embracing on all other sides most magnificent views of the surrounding country, including a very fine one of the main mountain at which you look up a deep long gorge, the bottom of which must be a good 12000 ft below us. To the west, N.W. and SW, we look over the huge plain of Bukeddi which stretches almost unbroken to the Nile, interspersed here and there with large lakes and prodigious swamps, altogether a most undesirable country full of heat and mosquitos, but they tell me full of nice big elephants.

Plate 10. *Semei Kakungulu (centre), photographed at Jinja in the early 1900s. His sister is on the left, his chief minister on the right.* (Crabtree collection)

According to the same source, Kakungulu dined with Sir Harry's party at Balimwogerako, 'behaved like a perfect gentleman, sitting opposite me and using his knife and fork as if to the manner born'. Kakungulu had also 'built quite a nice fort' on the site, 'and has made roads everywhere which is most energetic of him'.[122]

According to the principal Luganda chronicle of Kakungulu's activities at this time, Sir Harry Johnston now told him that the work he was doing in Bukedi was 'a wonder' (*kitalo*).[123] So impressive was this work, declared Sir Harry, that it made Kakungulu 'fit to be called the Kabaka of Bukedi'. He would seek official approval from England for Kakungulu to acquire this new status – on one condition, that Kakungulu abandon the foothills of Mount Elgon for the plains between Mount Elgon and Lake Kyoga.[124] Sir Harry Johnston thus resolved one abrasive ambiguity in British political dealings with Kakungulu, but in so doing he created another one to take its place.

# *Notes*

1. H.H. Johnston, 'The Uganda Protectorate . . .', *Geographical Journal* 19 (1902), p. 15. The lecture was delivered on 11 November 1901.

2. J. Thomson, *Through Masai Land: A Journey of Exploration among the Snowclad Mountains and Strange Tribes of Eastern Equatorial Africa* (London 1885), pp. 507–14 and esp. p. 514.

3. E.G. Ravenstein, 'Messrs Jackson and Gedge's Journey to Uganda via Masai-land', *Proceedings of Royal Geographical Society*, new series, 13 (1891), pp. 193–208; F. Jackson, *Early Days in East Africa* (London 1930), pp. 230–49; H.B. Thomas and R.F.J. Lindsell, 'Early Ascents of Mount Elgon', *Uganda Journal* 20 (1956), pp. 114–21.

4. C.W. Hobley, 'Notes on a Journey round Mount Masawa or Elgon', *Geographical Journal* 9 (1897), pp. 178–85; Hobley to Entebbe, 5 February 1896, encl. Berkeley to London, 21 February 1896, copy in Foreign Office Confidential Prints, Institute of Commonwealth Studies (FOCP), 6849.

5. See further my 'Politics in Bukedi', London University Ph.D. dissertation, 1967, p. 73 and Chapter 3 throughout.

6. This account depends on Robinson and Gallagher, *Africa and the Victorians*, pp. 362–3, and J.P. Barber, 'The Macdonald Expedition to the Nile 1897–1899', *Uganda Journal* 28 (1964), pp. 1–14.

7. Quoted by Barber, 'Macdonald', from Salisbury to Macdonald, 8 June 1897, FO 2/144, PRO.

8. 'Military Report on Operations of the Juba expedition', encl. Macdonald to London, 28 July 1899, FO 2/430, PRO.

9. Barber, 'Macdonald', p. 1.

10. *Ibid.*

11. Macdonald to London, 9 December 1898, encl. memo and map, copies in A6/5, ESA.

12. Barber, 'Macdonald'.

13. Salisbury to Sub-commissioner Craufurd, 19 January 1899; quoted in Barber, op. cit., and FOCP/7400.

14. 15 May 1889, WP.

15. Ternan to Kampala, 23 June 1899, Buganda Residency Archives, unsorted, ESA. Kakungulu was also given a donation of 1,000 rupees, a Martini Henry rifle and 50 rounds of ammunition from protectorate funds: Ternan, 17 May 1899, A5/5/1899, ESA; Wilson to Chief Accountant, 1 June 1899, BRA, unsorted.

16. Johnston to London, 6 April 1900, FO 21/298, PRO.

17. Johnston to London, 27 April 1900, FO 21/298, PRO.

18. Paulo Kagwa, 'Kakungulu Omuzira wa Uganda', unpublished MS in Makerere University Library (MUL), p. 12; Temuteo Kagwa, 'Kakungulu Omuzira Omuwanguzi' unpublished MS in MUL, Vol. 2, pp. 1–3; Simioni Waswa, 'Kakunguru mu Bukedi', unpublished MS, MUL, paras 2–3.

19. H.B. Thomas, 'Tribal nicknames', *Uganda Journal* 12 (1948), pp. 115–16.

20. T.R. Buckley, 'Among the wild Bakedi', *Church Missionary Gleaner*, May 1901, pp. 66–9.

21. Paulo Kagwa, 'Omuzira', p. 28.

22. *Ibid.*

23. Kibuga, *History*, p. 14. This chronicle provides the best account of the conquest of Bukedi during 1900: seen by courtesy of Ibrahim Ndaula of Mbale.

24. P. Kagwa, 'Omuzira', pp. 28–9.

25. *Ibid.*

26. Salimu Mbogo, interview, 14 November 1963.

27. Johnston to London, 27 August 1900, FO 2/299, PRO.

28. Gemmill to Fowler, 17 May 1900, A 21/1, ESA.

29. Fowler to Johnston, 21 May 1900, loc.cit.

30. *Ibid.*

31. Paulo Kagwa, 'Omuzira', p. 31.

32. *Ibid.*

33. Kibuga, *History*, p. 15.

34. *Ibid.*

35. *Ibid.*
36. Paulo Kibi, oral testimony.
37. Numbers vary between 100 and 200 in Ganda accounts.
38. Kibuga, *History*, p. 15.
39. 'Eastern Bukeddi', report encl. Fowler to Entebbe, 1 August 1900, A 10/1, ESA.
40. Jackson, 17 July 1898, A 4/11; Hobley, 11 November 1898, A 4/13, ESA.
41. Fowler to Jackson, 29 June 1900; Tarrant to Fowler, 4 & 5 July 1900: A6/9/Misc., ESA.
42. Fowler to Jackson, 29 June 1900: A6/9/Misc., ESA.
43. Pordage to Johnston, 7 August 1900, with enclosures: A6/9/Misc., ESA.
44. *Ibid.*
45. *Ibid.*
46. J. Tosh, *Clan Leaders and Colonial Chiefs in Lango* (Oxford 1978), pp. 118–19; J. Vincent, *Teso in Transformation* (Berkeley 1982), pp. 96–7.
47. P. Kagwa, 'Omuzira', p. 32.
48. Kibuga, *History*, pp. 15–16.
49. *Ibid.*
50. Daudi Musoke, *Ebyafayo bya Bugisu*, unpub. ms in the care of Kabagozza Musoke of Mbale, p. 9.
51. P. Kagwa, 'Omuzira', pp. 34–5.
52. *Ibid.*
53. Kagwa, 'Omuzira', p. 36.
54. Kibuga, *History*, p. 16.
55. *Ibid.*
56. Hanlon to Entebbe, 4 February 1901, A 25/1, ESA.
57. Kibuga, *History*, p. 16.
58. *Ibid.*, pp. 16–17.
59. *Ibid.*
60. Hanlon to Entebbe, 4 February 1901, A 25/1/, ESA.
61. That, at any rate, was Kakungulu's followers' view at the time. P. Kagwa, 'Omuzira', p. 43.
62. Hanlon, 4 February 1901.
63. Kibuga, *History*, p. 17.
64. Andereya Polo, interview at Busoba, 2 April 1964.
65. Kibuga, *History*, p. 17.
66. Hanlon, 4 February 1901.
67. Fowler to Entebbe, 21 May 1900, A 21/1, and 1 August 1900, A 10/1, ESA.
68. Fowler, 1 August 1900.
69. Johnston to London, 22 August 1900, FO 2/299, PRO.
70. Jackson to Fowler, 30 August 1900, A 11/1, ESA.
71. Johnston to Jackson, September 1900 [no day given], A 10/1, ESA.
72. *Ibid.*
73. Tarrant to Johnston, 13 November 1900, A 10/1, ESA.
74. Johnston to Grant, 14 January 1901, A 11/1, ESA.
75. Minute by Grant, 31 January 1901, on Crabtree to Grant, 27 January 1901, A 10/1/, ESA.
76. Crabtree, Diary, 21 December 1900, Rhodes House, Oxford; W. Crabtree, 'BUKEDI', *Mengo Notes* (May–June 1901).
77. Crabtree to Grant, 27 January 1901.
78. Grant, 31 January 1901, 27 January 1901, A 10/1/, ESA.
79. W. Rumbold, 9 May 1900, East African letters, 1900–2 (copies in SOAS library).
80. R. Oliver, *Sir Harry Johnston and the Scramble for Africa* (London 1959), p. 311.
81. Rumbold, 5 May 1901, East African letters, 1900–2 (copies in SOAS library).
82. Fowler to Entebbe, 1 August 1900, A 10/1, ESA.
83. Fowler, 'Eastern Bukeddi'.
84. Tarrant to Entebbe, 13 November 1900, A 10/1, ESA.
85. Jackson to Fowler, 30 August 1900, A 11/1, ESA.
86. For the abortive plundering expedition of 1884, see R.P. Ashe, *Two Kings of Uganda* (London 1889), pp. 297–8; Apolo Kagwa, *Basekabaka be Buganda* (Kampala 1953), pp.

135–6; and J. Rowe, 'Revolution in Buganda', Ph.D. dissertation, Madison, Wisconsin, 1966, p. 169.

87. R. Robinson, 'Non-European foundations of European imperialism: sketch for a theory of imperialism' in eds R. Owen and B. Sutcliffe, *Studies in the Theory of Imperialism*, (London 1972).

88. P. Kagwa, 'Omuzira', p. 33.

89. B.A. Ogot, *History of the Southern Luo* (Nairobi 1965), p. 96.

90. Uganda Protectorate, *Report of the Commission of Enquiry into Disturbances in the Eastern province, 1960* (Entebbe 1960), p. 2.

91. A.G. Fraser, 'A cycle trip in Usoga and Kavirondo', *Uganda Notes*, November 1902.

92. C.P.P. Emudong, 'The Iteso: a segmentary society under colonial rule 1897–1927', MA dissertation, Makerere University, 1974, p. 72; D.H. Okalany, 'Mukongoro during the Asonya' in *The Iteso during the Asonya* by J.B. Webster and others (Nairobi 1973), pp. 149–56.

93. Emudong, 'Iteso', p. 73.

94. On the Gisu, see J. La Fontaine, 'The Gisu' in ed. A. Richards, *East African Chiefs* (London 1960) and S. Heald, *Controlling Anger: the Sociology of Gisu Violence* (London 1989).

95. Kibuga, *History*.

96. George Wamimbi, interview, 1 December 1965.

97. T.R. Buckley, 'Among the wild Bakedi', p. 67.

98. Andereya Polo, interviews at Busoba, Bugisu, 2 April 1964 and 17 June 1963. Polo was one of the first attenders at the CMS mission in Bugisu.

99. Emudong, 'Iteso', p. 77.

100. Wilson to Entebbe, 27 July 1899, and minute by Ternan, 29 July 1899, BRA, unsorted files.

101. Interview, 27 March 1964.

102. Malumba Zake, interview, 20 June 1964. Zake had been a follower of Zakariya Kisingiri before joining Kakungulu. Njala was previously a follower of Sira Mulondo.

103. This computation is based upon a representative scatter of interview evidence.

104. Yona Wajja, 28 August 1964.

105. *Ibid.*

106. See above, pp. 144–5.

107. Jackson to London, January 1902 (no day given), FO 2/589, PRO.

108. Father L.J. van den Bergh to Mill Hill, 14 February 1901; quoted in *St Joseph's Advocate* (Spring 1901).

109. Malumba Zake, interviews, 12 February 1964, 20 February 1964.

110. Simioni Kalikuzinga, interview at Bulange, 10 December 1965.

111. Sabuli Namwanjam, interview, 7 March 1964.

112. 'Byafayo by'Omugenzi Omwami Simei Lwakirenzi Kakungulu', *Munno* (1933), p. 2.

113. This is the argument of my 'Muslim revolution in Buganda', *African Affairs* 71 (1972), pp. 54–72.

114. See A. Kasozi, *The Spread of Islam in Uganda* (Nairobi 1988), pp. 49–55.

115. Salimini Damulira, interview at Lwakaka, S. Bugisu, 14 August 1965.

116. G.R. Blackledge to London, 30 October 1901, CMS Annual Letters, 1901, p. 225. See also his article on 'Bugerere and the Bukoba mission', *Uganda Notes* (July 1902), noting that Kakungulu's departure for Bukedi was 'simply draining the district of Baganda'.

117. Interviews with Sedulaka Kyesirikidde, 6 December 1963; Enoka Maleza, 7 March 1964; Salimu Mbogo, 18 October 1964; Sabuli Namwanja, 7 March 1964; Malumba Zake, 12 February 1964.

118. Interview with Malumba Zake, 20 June 1964.

119. Interview with Salimu Mbogo, 16 October 1964.

120. Interview with Yona Wajja, 11 August, 1964.

121. Crabtree to Buckley, 25 January 1901, *CMI*, 1901, pp. 369–70.

122. W. Rumbold, 24 April 1901, East African letters, 1900–2 (copies in SOAS library).

123. Kibuga, *History*, p. 17.

124. *Ibid.*

# Six

# Kabaka of Bukedi
# 1901–4

## 1

The first years of this century in Uganda were a time for new kings. Buganda, Bunyoro, Nkore and Toro were all affected; new rulers, mostly juveniles, were installed by British protectorate officials in the hope that they would become adaptable client kings who would cause them less trouble than their predecessors. Daudi Chwa in Buganda in 1897; Yosiya and Andereya Duhaga in Bunyoro in 1899 and 1902 respectively; Kahaya, accepted as ruler of Nkore in 1896, and of an enlarged Ankole kingdom in 1901; Kasagama, placed in charge of Toro by Captain Lugard in 1891 – it was hardly surprising that Ganda in Bukedi should have greeted Sir Harry Johnston's offer of kingship to Kakungulu without excessive surprise. Kakungulu, like the new monarchs of Ankole and Toro, was to be a 'Kabaka-made-by-the-European'.[1] Like those monarchs and the new king of Bunyoro, he was to become 'Kabaka-under-Kabaka'.[2] Besides fitting in with other monarchical movements in Uganda, Kakungulu's elevation to royal office in Bukedi accorded with notions about the primacy of Buganda within the Uganda protectorate which were current in the minds of Kakungulu's most intimate followers at this time.

It also accorded with the political facts of Kakungulu's primacy in Bukedi during the previous eighteen months. While *Kimbugwe* in Buganda during the earlier 1890s, Kakungulu had been accorded respect by his followers as 'a small *kabaka*' (*kabaka omuto*) along with other high ritual functionaries in the same kingdom, and he had employed subordinate officials whose titles paralleled those held by county chiefs owing primary allegiance to *Kabaka* Mwanga himself. When Kakungulu withdrew to Bugerere in 1895, the subordinate officials who stayed with him retained these titles, and still retained them when Kakungulu exchanged Bugerere for Bukedi in 1900. Samwiri Tekiwagala, for example, one of Kakungulu's middle-grade chiefs whose name has already appeared in Chapter 4, successively held the offices of *sekyoyo* to Kakungulu's *kago*, and of *muwemba* to Kakungulu's *mukwenda*, before Sir Harry Johnston made his formal offer of kingship in 1901.[3] Thus, in a sense, that offer adjusted political relations between Kakungulu and the British protectorate authorities more than those between Kakungulu and his Ganda followers.

Coupled with his offer of kingship and the request that Kakungulu confine his activities to 'country without hills' (*ensi etali y'essosi*),[4] Sir Harry Johnston asked Kakungulu to accompany Captain Howard (*Owagi*), one of his special escorts, on a campaign 'to fight the Nubians' further west.[5] This Kakungulu agreed to do, after receiving permission from His Majesty's Special Commissioner to conduct a campaign of his own against the Jopadhola, the people whom in June 1899 at Mengo he had sworn to punish for humiliating Waliomuzibu and the earlier Ganda army. While this campaign against the Jopadhola lasted, they both agreed, Captain Howard would escort the Commissioner and his entourage to Sebei, then return to Budaka in order to link up with Kakungulu before proceeding to Buruli.[6]

Kakungulu spent about a week campaigning against the Jopadhola around the close of April 1901. The first day was occupied 'fighting against the Jopadhola (Badama) from morning till evening', the second constructing a fort at Nagongera.[7] Then Kakungulu departed on a military promenade through Padhola country, leaving Isaka Nziga and a substantial party in control of the fort at Nagongera. This was to protect that fort which, writes Paulo Kagwa, the Jopadhola attacked daily 'because their *lubaale* [deity] called Wakiriga told them that if they really exerted themselves they would be able to defeat Kakungulu'.[8] After completing his promenade, Kakungulu returned to Budaka as planned, again leaving Isaka Nziga in charge at Nagongera, together with Bumbakali Kamya, one of Waliomuzibu's sons as well as one of Kakungulu's most prominent Muslim followers, and about 300 guns.[9]

There Kakungulu found Howard with a hundred soldiers and the information that 'there were 7,000 Nubians at Ganyi who had rebelled'.[10] He also received from Howard a letter which Sir Harry Johnston had evidently written to him on 29 April 1901.[11] 'How are you, my friend ?' begins one translation of this letter.[12]

> I write to give you the following information. [Arise you and your fighting men] and take the best and nearest way to Buruli. There you will receive a letter informing you whether the war is continuing or finished. On receipt you will go to Kiira where you will meet other soldiers. Finish the war completely. Obey all the orders of Bwana Howard until the end of the war. Then return to Bukedi to put Bukedi in order.
>
> I also tell you this. I promised to make you King of Bukedi. Quite so. Do not think I have forgotten this. No. You will receive agreements. First we must ask the King – our Kabaka – and the Government – our Lukiko. I know they will not refuse, but it is well that they should know

first of all. When the Kabaka has assented to your agreements, I will write your name. I will send them to Entebbe to Jackson and will write your name as Kabaka. But first of all help me in this. I will help you by giving you Snider rifles and ammunition to guard your land. When I reach Simoni I will send you a permit to buy your guns because here I have no forms to write this. Of the booty you will receive your share. I have nothing else to tell you. Farewell. God protect you.

I am your friend,
H.H. Johnston.

Kakungulu collected together 200 of his followers armed with guns, then crossed Lake Kyoga with Captain Howard's party in the middle of May 1901.

On 29 May 1901, Howard and Kakungulu managed to meet up with Delme-Radcliffe's forces in northern Uganda.[13] But the following day Kakungulu's services were dispensed with. 'KAKUNGURU despatched to PAOERA with all his mob en route to his own district,' noted the Lango Field Force Diary for 30 May 1901.[14] It has been suggested that Delme-Radcliffe had 'good reasons' for getting rid of Kakungulu at this time. 'Ill-disciplined levies, with strong free-booting propensities,' suggested Sir John Gray, 'were very likely to impede his endeavours and for that reason Kakunguru's contingent, for whom he had never asked and regarding whose despatch he had never been consulted, were not very welcome.'[15] But Kakungulu's chroniclers take a different view of the matter. 'The alleged 7,000 were nowhere to be found,' comments one of them, 'so Kakungulu decided to go back to Budaka, while the European crossed into Bunyoro and returned to Buganda.'[16]

At Budaka, Kakungulu received a tumultuous welcome from his followers, the musicians amongst them composing a special song to commemorate the occasion:

Kakungulu is a man indeed;
No sooner had he conquered Budama
Than he conquered the Seven Thousand,
A man indeed![17]

Then, after catching up with local military matters,[18] Kakungulu set to work to complete the 'enclosure made with mud' which had been started by his *Katikiro* during his absence.

This fort was a large affair. 'The enclosure was very strong', comments one chronicler. 'There were walls six feet high and six feet wide, which stretched a mile round the outside, with windows cut at intervals and places where the earth was piled up for the watchmen to stand on.'[19] This earthwork evidently required a considerable amount of labour to construct. Our chronicler states that labourers came from all over Bukedi to build the enclosure – 'from Lango district, from Teso district, from Bugwere district, and from Budama district.'[20] In another place, he asserts that at any one time these labourers would be collecting water, mixing water with

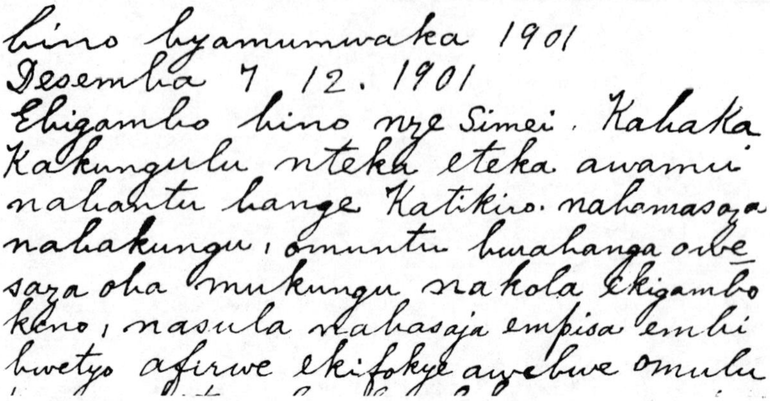
bino byamumwaka 1901
Desemba 7 12. 1901
Ebigambo bino nze Simei. Kabaka
Kakungulu nteka eteka awamu
nabantu bange Katikiro. nabamasaza
nabakungu, omuntu bwabanga owe
saza oba mukungu nakola ekigambo
kino, nasula nabasaja empisa embi
bwetyo afirwe ekifokye ayebwe omulu

Plate 11. *Semei Kakungulu the lawgiver.* (An English translation of these words from his diary is given below)

soil, and building up the walls with the resulting mixture. 'There were so many people engaged on the operation,' he writes, 'that they looked like locusts.'[21] Collecting so many men together had more than one virtue. Besides expediting construction of the enclosure, comments the chronicler, it taught the labourers about 'matters connected with administration' (*ebyobufuzi*).[22] In other words, besides being a massive military operation, it was an exercise in political education.

When it was complete, the enclosure at Budaka became the centre of Kakungulu's administration in Bukedi. Here he received honour from his followers 'by greeting him respectfully, by giving him gifts, and by singing him songs'.[23] Here he held council with his chiefs, in another *lukiiko* which now also kept written records.[24] Here too he dispensed justice to both chiefs and followers as occasion demanded. One of the laws promulgated at Budaka survives in one of his diaries:

> These things I, Semei Kabaka Kakungulu, I make a law together with my people, my Katikiro, Saza chiefs and Bakungu:
>
> Any man who is a saza chief or a Mukungu and commits this offence and does bad customs with his men, he shall lose his position and be given a muluka [parish office] in a kitongole instead.
>
> If he abandons these bad customs and all the people see that his manners show improvement, he will return to chiefly office and be placed in a high position among his men.
>
> If he makes the mistake again, he will be arrested and killed because he must be a very bad man.
>
> If however the position of the offending person is merely a minor one, he will be arrested and sentenced to 2 years' imprisonment. After being released, his conduct would be watched, and if he behaves himself, he will be brought back among the people and returned to his chieftainship. But if he continues in bad ways, he should be arrested and be killed.

What these 'bad customs' actually consisted of was left undefined, perhaps deliberately.[25]

Outside Budaka, Kakungulu's kingdom consisted of a complex of military forts, subdivided into sazas or counties, the centres of which may be seen in Map 9 (below). 'At this time,' remarks one of Kakungulu's chroniclers, 'the counties (*ma-sazas*) had not yet been further sub-divided into sub-counties (*zi-gombolola*). The Baganda used to stay in their forts, from which they would go to their various duties in the villages under their control.'[26] The number of these forts was steadily increasing throughout 1901. In September there were fifteen of them outside Budaka, but by the close of the year they had risen to twenty-five.[27] The number of Baganda stationed within these forts was also increasing. Whereas at the close of 1900 they had numbered one or two thousand, by the beginning of 1902 they had almost certainly reached more than five.[28] This increase Kakungulu naturally welcomed, since the survival of his kingdom in Bukedi as a going concern depended as much on clientship as had its inception. But he was careful to control its expansion in three further related ways.

Map 9. *Seats of Sazas administered from Budaka, December 1901.*

One was through the appointment of county chiefs, which he kept firmly in his own hands. At the close of 1901, Kakungulu had eight of these chiefs administering sazas, the location of which may been seen on Map 9. These eight were Leubeni Bitege, *Mukwenda* of Bwiro in Kumam; Malaki Magongo, *Sekibobo* at Serere; Jafali Mayanja, *Mugema* at Ngora in Teso; Sedulaka Kyesirikidde, *Kimbugwe* at Moita in Pallisa; Isaka Nziga, *Pokino* at Bukedea; Esitasio Nkambo, *Omuwanika* at Bumunza in Bugwere; Yakobo Kieriebuganda, *Kangawo* in Bunyole; and Yosiya Byatike, *Mukungulu* in Budama. Of these eight leading administrative chiefs, three (Bitege, Mayanja and Kyesirikidde) were members of the Mamba clan of Buganda, the same descent group as Kakungulu at this time, while one was also his younger brother (Kyesirikidde). The other five county chiefs were all Protestants like Kakungulu, as also were two among the three of his clansmen who held these offices. Only Jafali Mayanja was a Muslim, and he was remembered by elderly Ganda informants as having been one of Kakungulu's closest friends as well as a prominent member of the Mamba clan.[29] Thus Kakungulu could rely on ties of kinship and religion when dealing with the men who commanded the principal administrative offices in his kingdom, as well as commanding their 'loyalty' (*obwesige*) and 'obedience' (*obuwulize*) in the way any Ganda patron might.[30] But, as a further check upon their loyalty, Kakungulu delayed the investiture ceremony at which these chiefs would formally receive their offices for over a year. 'Kakungulu told us that he was going to hold the ceremony,' testified one elderly informant who had aspired to high administrative office at Budaka; 'but he moved to Mbale before the ceremony could take place.'[31]

Besides careful appointments to county chieftaincies within his kingdom, Kakungulu was careful to control certain appointments within the counties themselves (Figures 1 and 2). Figure 1 lists the officials employed at Ngora in the county of Jafali Mayanja, *Mugema* to Kakungulu during 1901 and 1902.[32] The symbols denote the *batongole* chiefs and personal retainers whose appointments lay directly in the hands of Mayanja (▼) and the middle-grade officials in his county whose positions lay in the direct patronage of Kakungulu (♦). As can be seen, the titles of chiefs in both categories were largely borrowed from Buganda. But it is interesting to note that Leubeni Kagwa, who held the most powerful middle-grade position in Mayanja's county, was a man whose career had been wholly made in Kakungulu's service. A Protestant and a freeman in Buganda, he became one of Kakungulu's clients in Bugerere and achieved military distinction during the Ganda conquest of southern Bukedi. It is also interesting to note that Jafali Mayanja felt it important to control the behaviour of Leubeni Kagwa in turn by placing Assa Mulyanimili, a Muslim and a man who had been one of his personal retainers in Buganda, as a *mutongole* chief under the *mumyuka* of *Mugema*.[33]

This pattern was repeated throughout the lower echelons of Kakungulu's kingdom, as Figure 2 demonstrates. This refers to the officials employed by Samwiri Tekiwagala, an important middle-grade chief who

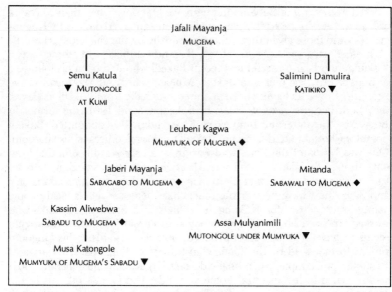

Figure 1. *Sub-chiefs in the Saza of Ngora, December 1901.*

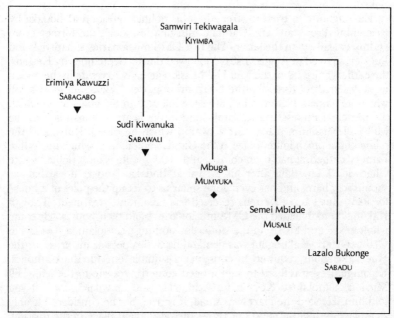

Figure 2. *Sub-chiefs under the Chief Kiyimba in the Saza of Budama, December 1901.*

worked in the *saza* of Budama but employed far fewer men than Mayanja at Ngora.[34] Again the symbols denote the men appointed directly by Kakungulu (▼) and those given their offices personally by the chief concerned (♦).

Besides structuring control of Baganda officials in these ways, Kakungulu was also careful to appoint Bakedi who had been his followers in Buganda to local offices in Bukedi. Mulogobyaire and Masangano have been mentioned as having been acquired originally from Bukedi as slaves: they both became *batongole* chiefs in Bukedi around 1901, the former in Bugwere, the latter in Bunyole.[35] Kakungulu also appointed Bakedi notables who submitted to him in Bukedi to *batongole* offices in his kingdom. One was Lyada of Bugwere, who was given a *mutongole* office in the royal enclosure at Budaka with the title *Muminza*;[36] another was Emokoor, an Etesot appointed to a similar position in Kakungulu's treasury at Budaka;[37] and there must have been many others like them, as well as local people acting as domestics for Kakungulu's chiefs (like Samwiri Kimuda who worked for Yoasi Mivule as a houseboy at this time).[38] Thirdly, Kakungulu seems to have accorded several Bakedi notables a status in his kingdom similar to that held by the *bataka* clan leaders of Buganda.[39] Majanga of Padhola, for example, when finally defeated by Kakungulu's men in 1901, was returned to his ancestral home at Senda, and Ganda officials in the *saza* of Budama were instructed 'to discuss matters with him' and to 'accord him honour because of his age'.[40] In these ways, Kakungulu attempted to make his newly acquired authority acceptable to the local inhabitants of Bukedi.

Kakungulu also tried to strengthen his political position at Budaka by welcoming Protestant and Catholic missionaries, albeit the former more enthusiastically than the latter. The first CMS missionaries, Chadwick and Buckley, arrived in August 1901,[41] followed during September by Kestens, the earliest emissary of the Mill Hill Mission actually to reside in the region for any length of time. To the CMS missionaries Kakungulu gave a hill which he named 'Namirembe', after the hill next to Kampala upon which the principal Protestant cathedral stood in the heart of Buganda;[42] to the Mill Hill Mission a place near a swamp which he called 'Rubaga',[43] the name of the much loftier place at the Ganda capital upon which the White Fathers' cathedral had been constructed. 'Kakungulu is most polite,' wrote Chadwick a few days after his arrival at Budaka, 'and anxious that we should stay here, and has even gone so far as to set up the poles of a house for us.'[44] But Father Kestens received less favourable treatment. Though Kakungulu had helped the CMS missionaries build their houses, 'clear the whole place and broke up the stones for nothing', complained Kestens in October 1901, Kakungulu was demanding 300 rupees as his price for the Hut Tax labour required to construct a suitable one for the Catholics. Kakungulu even refused to sign a deed conferring a site to the Mill Hill Mission, complained Kestens to Grant. 'He said he would sign it if you told him. He said the place was small, it is true, but he considered it only as a place to build on and not yet as the permanent place of the mission. He was not allowed yet to give a proper place.' Kakungulu, complained

Kestens, was 'a CMS man and a rather fervent one'. But as a representative of the Government, he ought not to discriminate so openly against the Catholics. 'He does not like us, as being Catholics', concluded Kestens, '... but as Europeans he might respect us a little and be less offensive.'[45]

Unfortunately, Kestens had behaved highhandedly during earlier service in Busoga. Indeed, Grant complained that he had 'given him a good deal of trouble since he came to the country' by physically assaulting a local chief – 'Luba made the complaint of Kestens having dragged him naked out of a tent and beaten him' – and by burning *lubaale* shrines throughout Busoga.[46] Burning shrines was 'liable to cause general discontent and possibly a rising in the district', admitted one of Kestens's British colleagues in the Mill Hill Mission.[47] Another complained to Nsambya that 'When Kestens came to Luba's Mission on a visit before going to Bukeddi (preceded as usual by his two banners and two drums and crowd of followers – he himself mounted on his mule) he boasted of his having deliberately burnt several balubare huts on the property of some chiefs.' From such behaviour, both Fathers Plunkett and Kirk dissociated themselves.[48] Possibly their protestations were heightened by the British–Dutch differences currently worsening as a result of the Boer War still raging in South Africa. 'For goodness sake, don't send me a Dutchman,' Father Plunkett would write to Nsambya in August 1902.[49] But Kestens was a difficult man for anybody to work with: over six feet tall, he was known as 'Gregory the Great' to his European missionary companions not merely because of his physical size.[50] In Bukedi, Kestens did not appreciate the extent to which Kakungulu was under pressure from British officials to collect tax revenue in rupees rather than cowrie shells ('We do not want shells, we wish to burn them. We are willing to receive sheep and goats but not shells').[51] This made more complicated Kestens's negotiations with Kakungulu for tax labour. This he wanted to construct a larger enclosure for the Roman Catholic community at Budaka than was being planned there for Protestants. But, basically, the problem with Father Kestens was that he did not want to kowtow to any African. 'Niggers put up their houses where and how they like and we Europeans can do nothing and cannot even get a simple hut,' Kestens complained.[52]

Besides exhibiting a markedly Protestant as well as cash ethic in his dealings with Father Kestens, Kakungulu displayed a more diffused kind of Christianity in his operation of royal rituals. He had an ever-burning fire at Budaka, very similar to the one which blazed before the royal enclosure of Buganda,[53] but sometimes it went out. 'Kakungulu was a Christian', explained an elderly Muganda who had been one of Kakungulu's Protestant followers at Budaka:[54]

> If he had had a fire which never went out, he would have been disobeying the Christian customs. The way we did things was therefore a mixture of Christian and old customs, with some European customs as well; Kakungulu arranged things just as he wanted them ... since he was given Bukedi by the Europeans, he had the power as well as the desire to do exactly what he wanted.

But, apart from such innovations, most of the royal rituals observed in Kakungulu's enclosure at Budaka appear to have been very similar to those which had operated at Mengo under Mwanga II. 'When he arrived at court,' commented an elderly Muganda who had worked as 'a page' (*mugalagala*) for Mwanga before joining Kakungulu's following in 1900, 'all present said, "The *Kabaka* has arrived" (*Kabaka azze*). Then they all started bowing and drumming, exactly as they did before Mwanga at Mengo. Then they would address Kakungulu through his chiefs, and afterwards Kakungulu might provide them with food and make laws.'[55] In fact, remarked this informant, 'Kakungulu had nearly everything exactly like the *Kabaka* of Buganda had at Mengo.'[56]

At Mengo itself, the establishment of Kakungulu's kingdom in Bukedi was not greeted exactly with enthusiasm by Apolo Kagwa, Stanislas Mugwanya and Zakariya Kisingiri, the three Regents who ruled Buganda during the minority of King Daudi Chwa. They appear to have been offended, comments one of Kakungulu's chroniclers, when

all the things belonging to Baganda which the Jopadhola had robbed from them many years before, like shields, spears, drums and other things were returned by Semei Kakungulu to Buganda. When the enemies of Semei Kakungulu in Buganda realized what a tremendous feat Semei Kakungulu had accomplished, they became jealous and took words to the Europeans of the Protectorate Government that Kakungulu had robbed many things from the people [of Bukedi], and that he had killed many of them without reason.

'At that time,' continued the chronicler, 'Bwana Jackson was deputizing (*omusigere*) for the Commissioner in Buganda.'[57]

## 2

During the second quarter of 1901, Frederick Jackson at Entebbe corresponded with William Grant in Busoga over the question of Kakungulu's cattle. In April, Grant had telegraphed the information that 'large numbers of cattle are being sold in the Bukedi country' and 'many Baganda proceed to Bukedi for the purpose of bringing cattle.'[58] This movement Grant deprecated, not only because 'they are sold for trade goods, which will be absolutely useless for liquidating Hut and other taxes,' but also because 'if the present drain on cattle is continued in a year or two there will be few cattle in the country.'[59]

In June, Grant was complaining more desperately to Jackson about the cattle he heard Kakungulu had captured during his campaign against the Jopadhola. Remarking 'by whose authority he went I am unable to say', he advised Jackson that the protectorate government quickly take possession of its share of the captured cattle, 'otherwise in a few months the animals will all be reported dead or dying from some unaccountable disease or other.'[60]

In July 1901, Jackson himself was again writing about Kakungulu's cattle in a rather emotive manner. On 13 July he sent Grant 'a list of cattle and goats reported ... to have been purchased from Kakunguru by various Baganda', which had been given him by the Baganda Regents. 'This question having cropped up,' commented Jackson, 'clearly shows what the Kakunguru's methods are of administering the Bukedi country.'[61] He had already in the course of a recent visit to Kampala told the Ganda Regents and *saza* chiefs what he thought about Kakungulu:

> that the Kakunguru and his hordes of ruffians were in my opinion infinitely worse and gave us far more trouble than the Masai, that Sir Harry Johnston has asked the Foreign Office for sanction to instal him as Kabaka of Bukedi, but that I shall oppose the appointment all I can on the grounds that he is a disgrace to the rest of the Baganda Chiefs.

To Kakungulu, Jackson addressed himself by letter.

This letter deserves quoting, because it reveals the flavour of Jackson's political thought at this time. 'I am sorry to have to tell you', wrote Jackson,

> that I have for a long time past heard bad reports about you, and no good ones. You will remember that when you were at Kampala a year ago I had many talks with you and gave you good advice, and that you promised me that you would take my advice. When we parted I thought you were a man of your word. Everyone who knows you told me that you could be relied on. This cannot be so. They were mistaken, and I was mistaken. It may be that you are drifting back to savagedom, now that you are away from Buganda where all the Chiefs and the people are daily becoming more enlightened, and anxious to do what is right. Bukedi is now a harbour for Baganda who don't like doing what is right. They prefer to do what is wrong. You are their chief and therefore responsible for their behaviour. You are an intelligent man and can read and write and you know, in your heart, what is right and what is wrong. There is therefore no excuse for you doing wrong.
>
> I told you that I wanted you to settle down quietly, and govern the Bakedi country properly, and be just and kind to the people, so that they might see for themselves that the British Government is their friend and not their enemy. By your behaviour you are proving to the people that the Govt is their enemy. They know the Govt sent you to Bukedi, & they now say that the Govt is bad; it is our enemy. It is not the Govt that is bad, but you and your people who are bad. I know it and I can prove it by one thing alone out of many others. Four days ago I was at Kampala having a shauri with the Regents & the Abama-saza about the taxes. After the shauri they told me a lot of Baganda had sent you rupees to buy cattle from you, but that Bwana Grant would not let the cattle leave Bukedi. I said, give me a list of people who have sent rupees and how many cattle each man claims from Kakunguru and I will enquire about it.
>
> I have just received this list. There are 75 names, and they claim no less than 420 cattle. Now if you can afford to sell 420 cattle what must the numbers of your cattle amount to? A great many, possibly thousands. Where did you get all these cattle from? Did you buy them? No. Were they given to you becaue the Bakedi liked you & thought you a king and good man? No. You stole them. You sent out some

169

men armed with guns to raid the people. The people had done you no harm. Why then did you raid them? Because some of your followers who are bad, told you some lie about the people having killed one of your people, or something the equal untrue. They wanted an excuse to go on a raid as they knew the people had cattle & they told you a lie. You wanted cattle also and you pretended to believe what you were told. You like cattle. You prefer having a lot of cattle to having a good name.

Let me remind you that you have been placed in an important position by the Government and that you receive pay from the Govt not to raid cattle & kill people, but to maintain peace and order in the country. I say you have thousands of cattle that have been stolen from the Bakedi & other people. You know that half these cattle belong to the Govt. Since you have been in Bukedi how many cattle have you handed over to the Govt and how many have you in Bukedi that belong to the Govt ? How many hut and gun taxes have you collected ? Can you answer these questions ?

Kakunguru I am angry with you & if you go on in your present ways the Govt will no longer be your friend [and] will say Kakunguru is not fit to rule, he & his people are only raiders like the Masai, they live by stealing other people's cattle. When you were at Kampala I gave you powder and I have assisted you in many ways. I will not assist you any more in any way unless you behave yourself properly & keep your Baganda in order. Some day you will get into trouble with the Bakedi & you will ask me for powder. I will not send you any. I will not even send you one cap. Sir Harry Johnston has written to the Govt to ask them to make you Kabaka of Bukedi. If they tell me to make you Kabaka I shall not do so and shall write & tell these very remarks. They will be angry & will say I did quite right

The letter continued in similar vein for several further paragraphs.[62]

Grant forwarded Jackson's letter to Kakungulu, though he himself suspected 'the statements made by the Baganda have been exaggerated to a considerable degree'.[63] But he would pay a visit to Bukedi to resolve the matter 'and find out on the spot whether the country is administered properly by the Kakunguru or not'.[64] Grant left Jinja on 20 August, arriving at Budaka five days later.[65] There he discovered that the statements about cattle had indeed been exaggerated; 'that some of the Kakunguru's men were indebted to people in Uganda previous to their going to the Bukedi country', but that the creditors he interviewed at Budaka 'in most cases ... had no authentic claims for cattle'.[66] Jackson ate his words. 'Please inform Kakunguru,' he replied to Grant, 'that I am quite satisfied with the result of your investigations, and that I am of opinion that many of the stories about, and charges against – such for instance as claims for cattle – are false and trumped up by Baganda who perhaps don't like him.'[67] For the moment at least, the force of rumour had been overruled.

Yet though Grant had cleared up the question of cattle in Bukedi, he could not quite make out what was happening to the human occupants of that region of the Uganda Protectorate. 'So far as the eye can see,' he reported to Jackson, 'everything is conducted beyond suspicion but I regret that I cannot conscientiously think so myself, for the simple reason that without some inducement men who have in the majority of cases land of their own in Buganda would not remain in a foreign country to them without some special reason.' Kakungulu told Grant that that reason was that 'he is loved by his people'. But Grant was sceptical about that, yet could not suggest anything very substantial in its place. The nearest he could get to an explanation was the 'surmise that they have means of paying themselves indirectly from various sources'.[68] What Grant failed to realize was that Kakungulu was indeed 'loved by his people', but in a sociological rather than an emotional way. Grant exaggerated the numbers of Kakungulu's followers qualifying for *mailo* land under the terms of the 1900 Agreement in Buganda, ignored the role of the new Hut tax in prompting young Ganda to join Kakungulu in Bukedi, and also remained ignorant of the complex of other causes attracting men to Kakungulu. He did, however, warn Kakungulu

> that HM's Commissioner would not entertain any laxity on his part so far as the behaviour of his men was concerned, and that in no circumstances was he to organize a punitive expedition without first fully reporting his reasons and obtaining HM Cmmr's sanction. Should this advice be ignored he would be in danger of possibly having his following removed and perhaps himself from the Bukedi country.

This advice, Kakungulu had 'promised faithfully' to observe.[69]

Grant also used his visit to Bukedi to encourage Bakedi to pay the new taxes to the British protectorate administration. 'The Bakedi according to Kakunguru's statements', wrote Grant sarcastically to Jackson five weeks later, 'are averse to paying them', but perhaps 'a European in charge of the Bukedi country would solve and simplify the apparent difficulty experienced by the Kakunguru in collecting taxes.'[70] This suggestion Jackson was forced to refuse. One of his grounds for refusal may well have been the rumour that the Uganda Protectorate's eastern areas were shortly to be transferred to the neighbouring British East Africa Protectorate. 'You may have heard rumours that our Eastern provinces are going to be absorbed by East Africa,' wrote Jackson to Archdeacon Walker on 6 November 1901. 'If this is so, it is possible that we may be deprived of Busoga.'[71] And if Busoga went, Bukedi would certainly have gone with it, plains as well as foothills. But Jackson's stated reason was financial. 'I have to inform you that the Foreign Office are very much averse to any further outposts being established,' he reminded Grant.

> If he [Kakungulu] succeeds in inducing the Bakedi to pay their hut tax and to realise that it will be, if it is not so at present, to their advantage to have a European living in their country, we shall then be in a position to support our desire for this outpost being made permanent by direct evidence of a successful trial. Should the experiment be unsuccessful the people must be left to themselves and Kakunguru can be allowed to do as he likes and if the Bakedi complain to you of ill treatment at

the hands of Baganda or others you must turn a deaf ear to their protests.

Either way, Kakungulu unfortunately had now to be left to his own devices.[72]

About a week after composing that pessimistic reply to Grant, Jackson received a formal request from Kakungulu that the area under his control be enlarged. In August 1901 Grant discovered, apparently for the first time, that Sir Harry Johnston had given Kakungulu 'all termed Bukedi country' as the sphere he was to govern, but had instructed Kakungulu 'not to extend his boundary lines further than they are without the sanction of HM's Special Commissioner and Consul-General' and to avoid the Tororo area completely.[73] Effectively this had meant confining territorial expansion to the areas immediately north of the Ganda forts in Bukedi. This restriction Kakungulu now queried. 'Mr Grant has taken away some of my land without any cause,' he wrote to Jackson.[74]

> Commissioner had given me whole Bukedi country and he stood on a hill and pointed out the boundary of Mr Foaker of Kavirondo, which was plain desert between us ... he said that the Busoga river Mpologoma is boundary of Bukedi and Busoga and Kyoga is the centre between Buganda and Bukedi, which runs as far as Bunyoro ...
>
> He gave all the Wakedi to me (to be under me) up to the second lake Makedonderi. I thanked him in his presence ... he is my witness – he knows everything what he promised me & told me to trust in him ...
>
> I always do the things with the consent of Mr Grant as you have put me under him to work ... I am capable to do my work, I have no command of my own: I am under Government.

Thus, together with the request for a reconsideration of his case, Kakungulu was careful to couple a renewed declaration of loyalty to the British protectorate cause.

Both Kakungulu's letters and the one from Jackson passed through Grant's hands at about the same time as he received Kestens's protests about Kakungulu discriminating against Roman Catholics at Budaka. William Grant was not the kind of man to give in to any of them very easily. On 24 October 1901 he announced to Jackson his decision 'to send Mr Walker to Bukedi to reside at Kakunguru's headquarters for two or three months'.[75] In making this decision, Grant must have calculated that it could hardly make matters worse in that region from a British protectorate point of view. With luck, it might even accomplish the objective which Grant gave to Jackson as the official reason for the trip – 'to get the Bakedi to realise that it is to their advantage to pay the lawful and recognised tax imposed by H.M.'s Government.'

## 3

Had the Ganda Regents' complaints been based principally upon personal animosity, as Kakungulu's chronicler alleged? In retrospect, this would appear to have been only partly the case.

The quarrel between Apolo Kagwa and Semei Kakungulu was 'an old one', as the White Fathers' Rubaga diary had noted during Kakungulu's first abortive raid into Lango country in 1896,[76] and there is no evidence to suggest any lessening of animosity between the two chiefs at this time. However, it was 'Bwana Grant' who had stopped cattle traders buying cheap in Bukedi, shortly after the establishment of Kakungulu's kingdom there, and the Regents had been responding to protests from Baganda traders in raising the matter with Jackson at Kampala in July 1901. Furthermore, Grant's clamp-down on cattle trading had been based upon fear that the British protectorate authorities would not get their now traditional half-share in livestock acquired during protectorate-sponsored plundering expeditions. It was therefore the prospect of having no tax revenue to report back to the British Treasury as a result of Kakungulu's latest adventure which prompted Grant to close the border between Bukedi and Busoga to cattle traders in July 1901. It was largely concern that hut tax revenues were also plummeting in Buganda that led the Regents later in the year to declare that men should be stopped from moving into Bukedi from Buganda.

By 1900 British officials had built a Uganda Protectorate stretching from Lake Albert in the west to Lake Nakuru in the east in alliance with leading Christian chiefs in Buganda. Without this alliance, it is difficult to envisage Buganda surviving as a single entity into the twentieth century. Most probably, it would have torn itself apart as a consequence of the struggle for supremacy between Mwanga's and Kalema's supporters, much as the neighbouring kingdom of Karagwe had broken up shortly beforehand, under stresses associated with the still-growing external trade in ivory and guns as well as internal conflicts.[77] That Buganda survived British imperialist penetration not only intact but territorially much enlarged was, as we have seen, intimately connected with both Frederick Jackson's and Frederick Lugard's earlier policies towards it. That Buganda acquired through the Uganda Agreement negotiated with Sir Harry Johnston in 1900, a treaty permitting a limited degree of internal self-government as well as generous *mailo* land grants to its principal chiefly negotiators and supporters, was of course also partly the consequence of Christian missionary help.[78]

Such help has been seen as a poisoned chalice, initiating the Ganda people into European religious rivalries and wars which otherwise they might have avoided.[79] This, as suggested earlier, seems an over-simplified interpretation, granted the ancient and still lively tradition of interpersonal vituperation and party conflict amongst Ganda chiefs.[80] Christianity, as Kakungulu's own career suggests, initially entered Buganda as an other-worldly cult and, to start with, was a unifying rather than a divisive force. Indeed all 'readers' (*basomi*) of foreign religions in the kingdom initially found themselves under pressure from the adherents of Ganda traditional cults, and it was Islam that made the first close connection between foreign religion and indigenous politics during the turbulent events of 1888–90. European missionaries certainly assisted their converts politically thereafter in a most vigorous manner. In this the CMS only differed from the White Fathers (and, after 1895, the Mill Hill Fathers too) in the degree of formality with which they encouraged party discipline denominationally. In the 1900 Agreement, political competition between Protestants and Catholics in Buganda was basically stabilized.[81] Thereafter Buganda was to be ruled throughout the period of the British protectorate by a Christian oligarchy of chiefs, principally Protestant in character, but with a major Roman Catholic ingredient and a minimalist Muslim one.[82] The major European missionary contribution to the Uganda Agreement of 1900 lay in helping the Christian Ganda chiefs to get a much better deal from Sir Harry Johnston than otherwise might have been the case, despite the massive dependence of British officials upon these very same chiefs for breaking the backs of both Mwanga's rebellion and the Sudanese soldiery's mutiny during 1897–9. 'Considering what power was wielded by the larger land-owners before the Treaty was made and how much we have owed to their influence for the maintenance of the Protectorate during the Mutiny and subsequently for the enforcement of the principle of taxation I think we have come off relatively cheaply in this settlement,' remarked Sir Harry Johnston shortly afterwards.[83]

But therein lay the rub for the Ganda Regents in mid-1901. Support for British protectorate officials during the recent troubles had been a major factor along with European missionary advice in their successful negotiation of the Uganda Agreement. But continuing British regard for it now depended upon effective 'enforcement of the principle of taxation'; and that, personal animosity aside, was principally why Kagwa, Mugwanya and Kisingiri seem to have been so concerned when William Grant stopped the cattle trade with Bukedi and they then discovered that many potential Ganda taxpayers were leaving their kingdom altogether in order to join Kakungulu.

Monetization was another anxiety. British protectorate commissioners initially acquired authority over Buganda as a fully functioning predatory and slave-holding state during the 1890s. While forcible acquisition and purchase of slaves were clearly unacceptable under the terms of the Berlin and Brussels Acts, other forms of plunder were another matter. With the assistance of precision firearms, seizures of cattle abroad were stepped up both in frequency and in extent. Slavery also continued as an important indigenous institution in Buganda for at least a generation. However, slaves now might emancipate themselves by reminding the British protectorate authorities of its technical illegality in British law, or by achieving it through regular payments in cowrie currency through the Buganda *Lukiko*.[84] For the new hut and gun taxes, however, money was demanded in the form of Indian rupees. Initially cowrie shells were accepted by protectorate administrators as sub-divisions of rupees, but by 1901 these had been abandoned by British officials in favour of Indian pice. Unfortunately for some time there were no pice. On 20 July 1901 at the Ganda capital

Pokino wrote a letter to the lukiiko asking how the Bakopi can get rupees to pay the tax. Apollo [Kagwa] says that any one who wants rupees must take his shells to the traders at Kampala and buy them at the rate of 850 or 900 to the rupee.

... Soldiers and scribes of the king [and the Regents, presumably] came to inquire about their pay. It was decided that they should go and decide among themselves what wages they want, and then return and report. The drumbeater of the king was given a jora of cloth.

In September, pice still had not arrived; and Apolo Kagwa told the Mengo Lukiko of his most recent meeting with the British protectorate official at Kampala, who told him 'to instruct the Bamasaza to circulate their rupees and not to keep them in their houses because the people are complaining that they cannot get rupees.'[85] At the beginning of October the Indian pice finally arrived and were circulated in Buganda at the rate of 64 pice to 1 rupee.[86] But there were still problems. A week after the first pice arrived, 'Apollo complained that some crafty individuals had been imposing on the poor peasants by passing off pice as rupees'.[87] It was at this time of monetary transition that Father Gregorius Kestens left Busoga for Bukedi, and started sending back letters to Nsambya extremely critical of Kakungulu's demands for rupees from Roman Catholics.

'Kakungulu is not going to do anything for us,' wrote Kestens on 22 October from Budaka:[88]

The Catholics are going to build a little church. They are about 25 here; the others are spread all over the country. The cleaning of the place I have to do with bapagazi [workmen hired for the purpose]. A budongo house for the priests has also to be buil[t] for money. I asked Kakungulu what he wants for a budongo house and he said 300 rupees. It is rather absurd. He seems to try to get as much money out of us as possible, or rather he is opposing us. I thought 100 rupees a fair price ... I asked Kakungulu to clean our place from high grass. He wanted payment. I offered to pay the Bakedi in beads, shells or cloth. For that he also wanted rupees. I explained him that I had not got sufficient rupees and would not get many, to pay for everything in rupees. Besides if I have to pay, it is better that the Bakedi who do the work, get daily wages. If some Muganda chief gets the rupees he'll work with Bakeddi; they'll get nothing and he'll spend the rupees to pay his taxes. The Bakeddi get displeased with us and think that we force them to work for nothing.

When Kestens had arrived at Budaka during September, he evidently got on well with Kakungulu. Kakungulu allowed him to chose a second site for the Roman Catholic mission at Budaka ('a nice place just opposite Kakungulu's mbuga [main enclosure], near good water and with a nice view'),[89] while at Mpumudde Kestens considered Kakungulu's withdrawal to have had a most unfortunate effect on Catholic missionary work there. 'If only Kakungulu here was in power, the work would be all right and we could take possession of our place'.[90] But, in October, the question of payment in rupees preyed on Kestens's mind. Kakungulu told Kestens he could not accept the suggestion to pay Bakedi day-labourers directly. 'He pretended to be offended by that and sent me a messenger to tell me that he was going to do nothing for us. He would not tell the Bakeddi to come here to kupagaza. He was man of the government and had nothing to do with the work of Basomesa [church teachers].' In fact, complained Kestens, Kakungulu was 'working for the CMS', had 'worked some months to break the stones on their hill and cultivate it without payment' and he was 'also building their kanissa [church].' Kakungulu's Bakedi worked on the Protestant compound without charge; Kestens's Bakedi had to be paid for. 'I get rather disgusted with the work here' at Budaka, complained Kestens 'amongst those bigitive Protestants.'[91]

Kakungulu and Kestens approached the question of church labour from opposing principles. Personality differences aside, Kakungulu considered it legitimate, as a CMS supporter himself, to provide free assistance from his following to Messrs Buckley and Chadwick for both constructional and agricultural work;[92] but wrong for him, as the impartial and efficient protectorate official which William Grant had stressed so recently that it was imperative for him to become, to provide similar assistance for somebody to whom he had no confessional connection. Kestens, on the other hand, tried to extract as much official assistance as possible from Kakungulu on the 'religious equality' argument, as there were not enough Roman Catholic chiefs within Kakungulu's following as a whole to arrange for work upon Kestens's compound to be done free of charge. Protectorate pressure upon Kakungulu to collect taxes in rupees undoubtedly made life still tougher for Father Kestens, though it must be admitted that Kestens himself was the author of many of his frustrations at Budaka.

In Buganda, too, there was confusion between public duties performed, and private benefits enjoyed, by administrative chiefs and their followers. In November 1901 Tompkins, the British official at Kampala, told the Baganda Regents and county chiefs not to levy 'more than one' month's work from their men; but the chiefs were not pleased with this and wanted to levy their own addditional 'tax of Rs 2 from their men in lieu of work'.[93] Tompkins also told Kagwa not to force Catholic converts to work on the rebuilding of Namirembe Cathedral in the same month, much to Kagwa's disgust.[94] But the major problem facing both British officials and Baganda Regents at Kampala in 1901 was to remain 'enforcement of the principle of taxation'.

In retrospect, this problem would seem to have been only partly monetary in character. To be sure, when Stanley Tompkins asked Apolo Kagwa in September 1901 'how things were going in Buganda' and Kagwa replied that 'the only thing that disturbed the Baganda at present was the getting of rupees to pay the hut tax', Tompkins replied that pice would soon solve that problem.[95] It did not. In December 1901, when it became clear 'that the hut tax was not coming in as well as he had expected', Tompkins repeated the same advice. Chiefs were ordered to 'advance money to their people', as 'Government work in lieu of the money tax is finished at Xmas, consequently all not already paid in work on the roads, or at Ntebe or Kampala will now have to pay in rupees.'[96] But in September and October 1901, Apolo Kagwa went on safari in eastern Buganda and discovered that many of the previous year's taxpayers had simply disappeared: '80 men had left Kauta, 40 his (Apollo's) places, 160 Mutyuwa ... It is a common practice for a man to take his wife and leave her at her father's, and then to disappear.' 'This,' Kagwa declared upon his return from safari, 'must be stopped.'[97]

But how was it to be stopped? In retrospect it also seems clear that a major problem for Ganda chiefs in 1901 was that the new hut tax was an annual tax. Ganda cultivators were accustomed to earlier rulers seizing goods in lieu of tax; indeed one of the customary tasks of a Ganda chief had been levying tax for the Ganda king as well as 'cutting cases' and waging war on his behalf. Tax labour was a possibility for a time, but produced no immediate cash. Livestock could hardly be seized on an annual basis, however, if only because peasants were now pre-empting this possibility by eating their goats and sheep themselves before tax-collectors could arrive for a second-year cull.[98] Migrant labour to South Africa was a possible additional revenue-earner for the Uganda Protectorate, and was in fact actively discussed in 1902 as a source of long-term tax revenue but rejected because, as Apolo Kagwa said, 'the Baganda will not consent to go there.'[99] Cash-cropping was yet another money-raising device suggested by George Wilson in 1902[100] and subsequently was to become (first seriously with cotton, later with coffee) Uganda's principal source of tax revenue throughout the twentieth century. But in 1901 this still lay ahead. For the moment, stemming the haemorrhage of tax-payers migrating out of Buganda seemed the most necessary action to Apolo Kagwa.[101] To Stanislas Mugwanya, too, it seemed pointless to worry excessively about gun tax when so many guns had either worn out or 'gone to Kakungulu, the Germans and elsewhere'.[102] Little could be done about 'the Germans and elsewhere'. But something might be done about Kakungulu; or so William Grant now thought. It was therefore to the new mud palace at Budaka that W.R. Walker made his way during November 1901, a time to be remembered locally as one of most grievous famine.

## 4

W.R. Walker had been employed on clerical duties in the Uganda protectorate administration since 1899. Two years later he was transferred to Jinja after 'maltreatment of Chiefs and several other mistakes' at another protectorate station.[103] Little is known of his earlier life, but the little that is suggests a background very similar to John Gemmill's.[104] Despite this background he was, however, as Jackson later reported to the Foreign Office, 'an Englishman',[105] and as such presumed suitable for dealing with 'the Kakunguru the native collector and his horde of undisciplined followers'.[106] After collecting several loads of beads and americani cloth 'to distribute as presents to deserving chiefs',[107] Walker therefore left for Budaka early in November 1901.[108]

On 13 November 1901 Walker arrived at Budaka and for a few days, states one of Kakungulu's chroniclers, a friendly atmosphere prevailed. 'Each afternoon Kakungulu used to go for a talk with Bwana Walker, and sometimes the European called Kakungulu for a conversation at other times when the need arose.'[109] But then they began to quarrel. Four days after his arrival at Budaka, Walker dined with Fathers Kestens and Kallen at the Catholic Mission, and the following day the two missionaries visited Walker 'to settle scores'. 'Two men as slave[s] of the Kakunguru are left free. Kakungulu promises to treat us with more respect.'[110] The next day Father Kestens left Budaka for Iganga, to be replaced by Father Drontman from Iganga three weeks later 'in good health and spirits'.[111] Two days after Father Kestens's departure, Walker held a 'meeting of the Bakedi chieves' at Budaka. Buckley of the CMS and Father Kallen were also present. In Father Kallen's words,[112]

> The chieves all get a present from Mr Walker, but were told to bring no tax. Mr Walker told them he came in name of the English government to make friends with them. Father v.d. Kallen asked Mr Walker that tell them that being a Catholic does not interfere with their being chieves. Mr Walker kindly told them.

In a letter to Nsambya next day, Kallen reported that Walker had told the Bakedi notables present to 'pay a tax of 3 Rps if they could', and told Buckley and Kallen publicly 'to keep down the Islam'. He also reported that as a result of the meeting one of Kakungulu's chiefs had converted from Protestantism to Catholicism: 'his name is Singoba and he has a fort in Kakabukabu'. 'Three Bakeddi chieves have declared themselves Catholic [also] and appeared this morning at the Barassa with their medals.'[113]

Kakungulu's response to Walker's *baraza* was to order all Protestant Baganda to work next day on the Protestant church at Budaka ('if they refuse they will be ordered to make bridges over the swamp'),[114] and even some Catholics as well. When asked by Father Kallen for 'the map of our place at Masaba', Kakungulu declared that he could not find it, a difficulty he was still experiencing several days later when told by Walker to give it to Kallen.[115] Then Kakungulu moved to the offensive. Father Drontman he received in a 'very kind'[116] manner, but a few days later Father Kallen heard from Walker that Kakungulu had accused Kallen of stealing land from a Mugwere chief. Kallen denied the charge, and as Kallen appears to have acted as Walker's interpreter while the case was heard ('the poor man cannot even understand his interpreter', reported Kallen to Nsambya),[117] it was perhaps not surprising that in the end Walker 'wrote a letter to the Kakungulu not to give any more incorrect information'.[118]

Another dispute concerned a Catholic convert at Budaka accused of committing an offence by a Nyole chief. Walker considered the Nyole chief's case 'not entirely proved', and only gave Kidza 'a small punishment'. However, as Kallen soon learned, 'Kakungulu however did not obey Mr Walker and gave Kidza the full punishment of 10 cows 10 sheep 10 nkumbis [hoes]'.[119] Later Kidza was also taken prisoner by Kakungulu, presumably for non-payment of the fine, and Kallen wrote Kakungulu a letter of complaint. Kakungulu responded with what Kallen called 'a very strong measley [letter] telling me to mind my own business'.[120] Kallen contacted Walker, who sent askaris to free Kidza. Kakungulu said Kidza was not in his custody, but Kallen dscovered that this was untrue and told one of Kidza's household 'to go to Mr Walker and bring the soldiers to the house where he was imprisoned'. This the lady quickly did and Kidza was duly delivered. According to Kallen's account,[121]

> Kakungulu was not at home at that time, and had gone out to hunt a leopard [and] when coming home and hearing the news he said the Bafranza have done me wrong. But he had forgotten the insulting letter he wrote, and the lie he told before Mr Walker. Kidza having no home comes on our hill [now] to live.

Dr Gale treats Kakungulu's comment 'The Bafranza have done me wrong' as evidence of denominational bias,[122] but it was also the remark of a Ganda chief who had now suffered three times from Roman Catholic missionaries interfering with his following at Budaka: Father Kestens, who had given sanctuary to a runaway slave from Kakungulu's household before Walker's arrival and aided at least another slave to be set free before himself leaving for Iganga,[123] and Father Kallen, who had now interfered in disciplinary action between Kakungulu and another follower who was possibly also a slave as well as a Roman Catholic.

Besides coming into conflict with W.R. Walker over the treatment of Catholics in this way, Kakungulu also clashed with Walker over a variety of other matters. The most bitter dispute concerned the flagstaff. Who had the right to fly the Union Jack at Budaka – Walker the 'unestablished' British protectorate official, or Kakungulu the accredited 'native collector' who now considered himself to be *Kabaka* of Bukedi too?[124] Walker evidently came to feel quite strongly that the right was his alone after an acrimonious quarrel took place between a Mugwere and a Muganda over a goat. The Mugwere complained to Walker, who promptly attempted to have the Muganda arrested. But the Muganda evaded capture by telling one of Kakungulu's bodyguard that he was not going to get a proper trial. 'The European was most annoyed over this,' reports one of Kakungulu's chroniclers.[125]

> He rode his horse to Kakungulu's place. But Kakungulu was having a rest so Walker moved about the courtyard in a quarrelsome sort of way. Eventually Kakungulu came out to meet him, and Walker told him about Wairagala accusing Amuli Kiso for eating the goat and then having been released by Kakungulu's men.
> 'I suspect they did this on your order,' said Walker.
> 'This is the first I have heard about this matter,' replied Kakungulu. On hearing this Walker became even angrier and more quarrelsome.
> Kakungulu asked Walker, 'Why didn't you send them both to me so that I might hear the accuser ?'
> The European then asked, 'Which of us is superior?'
> 'The same government that gave you power, gave it to me too. You have a flag, so have I. First cases should pass here, then move on to you,' was Kakungulu's reply.

On 2 January 1902, Walker asked one of the CMS missionaries to tell Kakungulu to lower the flag in his fort.[126] 'Then I was present there,' recorded Kakungulu in his diary entry for that day,[127]

> he Walker came himself to cut down the flagstaff. When I saw him coming, I ordered my people to remove the flag. Then I wrote to Bwana Grant a letter to explain that thing.

'Has Kakungulu permission to fly Union Jack at Budaka where Walker is now stationed and flying the Jack?', telegraphed Grant to Entebbe on January 5.[128]

> There is at present a misunderstanding on the subject as to whether the Kakunguru who erected a flag pole on the 1st inst. and flew the Jack while Walker flew a short distance from it. Is he at liberty to fly it or not, the question has been referred to me for decision. The Kakunguru's flag meantime is down, is apparently much offended. Please instruct me what your orders on the subject are ...

'While Walker is at Budaka,' came back Jackson's uneasy reply, also by telegraph, 'he is in charge and therefore flies the flag. When he leaves Kakunguru as Collector flies Union Jack.'[129]

That Kakungulu accepted this verdict without resistance of any sort was partly due to diplomacy by European missionaries at Budaka, of both Catholic and Protestant persuasions. 'After a heated wrangle over the matter,' writes Solomon Wamala, 'Buckley, the missionary who had given himself the name Ssebowa when preaching at Bulemezi, Chadwick (Kyadoki), a Catholic missionary and Father Kirk (Perekeki) requested and eventually persuaded Kakungulu to pull down the flag.'[130] However, as Father Kirk was not yet stationed at Budaka, it is highly likely that Perekeki in this account is confused with either Father Drontman or Father Kallen, who were still there.[131]

There was an almost equally bitter dispute between Walker and Kakungulu over the collection of hut tax, the question which Walker had specifically been sent to Budaka to settle. On the same day that Kakungulu lowered his flag, he summoned a special *baraza* at which about twenty Bakedi notables were questioned by Walker, through his interpreter, on their attitudes towards hut tax. In all cases these proved negative, the notables pleading poverty, ignorance, or inability to enforce political decisions as their reasons.[132] Walker complained to Grant. 'Considering that my influence with the Bakedi with regard to paying the Hut tax must filter through the Kakunguru first,' he wrote,[133]

> I am not surprised at the result of this baraza. I have heard stories from more than one source that the Baganda advise the Bakedi not to pay to me the Hut tax (that is to a European) – then the Mzungu will leave the country and the Kakunguru will have peace, that our Kabaka is your master or chief. These words I have no doubt are inspired by a Likiko (the inner council at which no outsiders are admitted).

About the famine still raging around Budaka at this time, Walker wrote nothing.

Grant, too, was annoyed with Kakungulu at precisely the same time that he received Walker's complaints. He had just got hold of information about what he considered an unduly extravagant shopping list for a throne (*entebe enungi eyekitibwa*), a bicycle (*akagali*), a typewriter (*tepulaiti*), and an instrument which he assumed to be the latest musico-mechanical gadget, a phonograph (*ekyuma ekikwata edobozi*), all of which had been ordered recently by Kakungulu. Other orders on this list were for a bicycle-pump (*bomba eyompa*), a high quality razor (*ewembe enungi enyo*), a sewing-machine (*ekyuma ekitungu engoye*), and an iron bed (*ekitandakye kyuma*).[134] How could Kakungulu afford to purchase such luxuries if there was – as Kakungulu had evidently claimed to Walker – insufficient money in Bukedi to provide revenue for Hut Tax? Like Walker, Grant resorted to a conspiratorial explanation of his suspicions: Kakungulu had 'some private source of revenue'.[135] Furthermore, Grant had been reconsidering the whole question of Bukedi. 'I would venture to suggest', declared Grant as a result of further enquiries in Busoga,

> that districts belonging to undernoted chiefs viz Riada, Mangoli, Dube, Ingoghe, Dugu, Ndingwa, Funyeko, Vinule, Namansa, Kirunda, Wai-gondo, Kainga, Badama were quiet and the inhabitants had friendly transactions with Busoga before ever the Kakunguru or his people set foot in the country. The country was open to traders since 97, all sorts and conditions of men used to go there, to purchase ivory, sheep and goats. Some of the chiefs used to come to Luba's and others paid tribute to Basoga chiefs. They are besides almost identical with Basoga in their habits and customs, with exception of the Badama [Jopadhola] who are more akin to the Lango tribe.

But 'while the Baganda are in the districts of those chiefs I enumerated,' concluded Grant, 'the tax collected by them on account of the Uganda administration will be nil.'[136]

Grant complained to Jackson. It so happened that Jackson was also again irritated with Kakungulu because, in addition to the complaints he had been hearing throughout the year about Kakungulu from the Ganda Regents, he had just received information that Kakungulu had recently written these Regents a very rude letter, in which he stated that as he was now king of Bukedi he could invite to Bukedi anybody he pleased.[137] The Regents had presumably written earlier reporting Stanley Tompkins's request to them in November 1901 that no more Ganda should go to join Kakungulu in Bukedi as 'a lot have been going lately';[138] an order repeated in January 1902, when Andereya Luwandaga was also ordered 'to prevent all unauthorized persons entering Bukeddi' from the west.[139] 'The Kakunguru,' Jackson now complained to London, 'has been a veritable thorn in the side of Mr Grant and the Regents.'[140]

Grant and Jackson now met again in order to decide what further to do, and agreed upon an elaborate stratagem to bring Kakungulu to his senses and restore the delicate balance of British protectorate power in eastern Uganda. Immediately on his return to Jinja, Jackson reported to the Foreign Office in London,[141] Grant was to write a letter to Kakungulu

> and inform the Kakanguru that he had just paid me a visit, that I knew nothing of his appointment as King, that he had no right to give land to his people that belonged to the natives of the country; that such land would not be acknowledged by the Government as belonging to any of his followers; and that he must withdraw all his people from the eastward of a place called Budaka and return with them to the vicinity of Lake Kioga.

'Mr Grant is of opinion,' continued Jackson,

> that when it is known amongst the Kakanguru's followers that he is not their King, but only holds the same rank as a County Chief in Uganda, and that he has not authority to give them land, large numbers of them will return to Uganda, through fear of losing the estates which have already been allotted to them [under the *mailo* regulations following the 1900 Agreement].

By these means, Kakungulu would be dethroned, in effect, as *Kabaka* of Bukedi and brought to a more sober knowledge of his official limitations.

But Kakungulu did not react according to plan. After receiving a letter from the British protectorate authorities and conferring with his principal chiefs, Kakungulu left for Jinja to discuss the matter personally with Grant.[142] There he was told again 'that officials had to go where they were ordered', but replied that he did not wish to leave Budaka.[143] He was prepared to accept his removal from British protectorate office at that place, but resolutely refused to move to Lango. Instead he asked for a grant of land in Bukedi upon which to settle with his followers.[144] 'I am tired, I no longer want to wage wars,' he told Grant;[145] rather than move westwards as requested, he preferred 'to retire'. First he asked for a place around Budaka, then compromised by requesting an area between Budaka and Mount Elgon.[146]

This was certainly not the decision expected by William Grant, nor by Frederick Jackson. But once it had been made, both accepted it, because there was little else they could do. For to refuse Kakungulu's request would have been to provoke possibly yet another rebellion in the Uganda Protectorate, and another rebellion would have made them both unpopular with the Foreign Office in London, as well as being extremely difficult for the British protectorate administration to suppress.

Nor should one underestimate the danger of rebellion at this time. Rebellion was something British protectorate officials had to live with in the early 1900s and the thought of it was constantly in their minds. Rebellion was also publicly discussed by Kakungulu's followers on this and several other occasions.[147] On this occasion, according to Samwiri Kimuda who was present at the time, Kakungulu responded to Grant's arrival with a Sikh military escort and the request for him to leave Budaka, by calling two meetings with his chiefs. At the first one 'Magongo was the first to speak, advising not to fight the white man. Kitunzi supported this view, as also did the county chief Isaka Nzi[g]a and Lazalo, Kakungulu's Katikiro.'[148] The arguments were much as they had been in Bugerere at the outbreak of Mwanga's rebellion five years before, or during the flagstaff dispute five weeks before. However, regarding the flagstaff dispute, another survivor from Kakungulu's following remembered Nziga's memorable categorization of W.R. Walker as 'a small vulture' (*nsega nto*) – the point about vultures being that they all looked prematurely aged and bald like Walker, but one could never tell a young, incompetent one from an older, powerful one in predicting the trouble they might cause.[149] Nziga again argued in favour of continued cooperation with the British protectorate authorities, and against armed resistance; and this view again prevailed. Then Kimuda remembered Kakungulu calling a second meeting to decide where he should move to. 'Kakungulu asked whether they should return to Buganda. The meeting decided that they should be allowed to settle in *kalungu* [an area of deserted land] now known as Mbale.'[150] And for an administration as impoverished as the Uganda Protectorate at that time, a land grant there must have appeared an astonishingly cheap form of compensation for Kakungulu's loss of office at Budaka.

As a first offer, Jackson suggested a grant of eight square miles,[151] assuming that Kakungulu would still want to act as the equivalent of a Ganda county chief in Bukedi on his retirement as its king. But when Kakungulu asked 'to retire', Jackson appears to have decided to cut his losses by offering him twenty square miles and discontinuing his official salary.[152] This Kakungulu accepted, after checking that all the allotted land would be his personal private property[153] and making sure that he received full payment for all the previous service he had rendered to the British protectorate administration.

By this settlement, Kakungulu certainly lost the allegiance of a substantial number of his followers, as William Grant had predicted and we shall shortly see, as well as relinquishing his official salary; though, ironically enough, Kakungulu does not appear to have actually received his salary as 'native collector' until now officially relinquishing the post.[154] Yet Kakungulu himself remained a *kabaka*, and his political power in Bukedi was still considerable.

5

Exactly where the land grant was to be taken up was left to Kakungulu's discretion. The only condition made by the British protectorate officials concerned appears to have been that, if possible, the choice should be restricted to 'small deserted areas of land' (*obulungu*).[155] Kakungulu sent out several parties to inspect various sites around Kumi and on the Teso plains before finally selecting Mbale as the site for his settlement.[156] The reason he chose Mbale in preference to these other sites seems clear. It was a joint decision taken by him in company with his chiefs. 'Kakungulu asked the chiefs, "On which of these small deserted areas of land shall we build?" … All the chiefs agreed to build on this place because it was near the plantain trees. "Where shall we buy plantains if we go to the other places?", they said.'[157] The decisive factor was diet. Mbale had the clear advantage over the more northerly sites considered of being close to *amatooke*, the staple diet of the Baganda; it was within the banana-growing belt of East Africa.

Nor is it really surprising that Kakungulu and his followers should have attached so much importance to that particular factor when selecting their site. They were a warrior community, and it was a well-known fact that the efficiency of Ganda as warriors deteriorated rapidly outside the plantain zone of East Africa, because bananas formed part of their basic diet.[158] Kakungulu's followers also had the more private knowledge of their relative ineffectiveness in Lango country during 1899–1900 to remind them of the importance of the diet factor in the most emphatic manner.

In the same month as the Ganda chose Mbale as their site, they began to construct their settlement.[159] First they erected 'big European tents' (*ewema enene ezekizungu*) for Kakungulu and his principal chiefs, as well as others made with barkcloth from Busoga and machine-spun cotton from abroad for themselves.[160] Then they set about building a more permanent settlement, and gradually a pattern began to emerge.

Naturally the largest house was the one built for Kakungulu. Though it was difficult to get any exact idea of its architectural proportions from interviews with some of the last survivors from Kakungulu's following at Mbale, and though no photographs of it seem to have survived, it was by all accounts an extremely large building. One former follower remembered it as having been 'big, longish, but not roundish. It had reeds round it like the palace [at Mengo]. Inside there were seven huts as well as a very large house.'[161] This house provided the focal point of the settlement: the houses of Kakungulu's chiefs were built round it in a regular series of concentric circles, and the roads inside the settlement radiated from it. As another survivor remembered it, 'There were roads converging on Kakungulu's place like the spokes of a bicycle wheel. The chiefs lived around Kakungulu, and their shambas extended outwards.'[162]

The oral sources recorded stress that this pattern of settlement was largely determined by strategic considerations. Defence, rather than any conscious imitation of the royal capital of Buganda, was said to have been the most immediate consideration in the minds of its builders.[163] Even so, Kakungulu's settlement at Mbale seems to have been remarkably like Mengo in physical appearance.

There were also political resemblances.[164] 'After we had finished constructing Kakungulu's house,' writes one of his vernacular chroniclers, 'we set about building a reed enclosure which we called "lubiri". All Kakungulu's chiefs retained their titles, such as Sekibobo, Kago and so on, which they had possessed when they had actually ruled sazas.'[165] But the areas now under their control were of course much smaller: simply sections of Kakungulu's estate around Mbale. Kakungulu was still a *kabaka*, but now only a small one again.[166]

Inevitably the number of Kakungulu's followers at Mbale shrank together with the size of his kingdom. No exact figures exist, but oral testimonies suggest that Kakungulu's following of 5,000 fighting men had roughly halved by the time it reached Mbale.[167] Among the followers who

left Kakungulu for more attractive patrons in Buganda at this time were
Enoka Kamya and one Saulo, who had held the middle-grade offices of
*sabawali* and *namutwe* to Malaki Magongo, formerly *sekibobo* to Kakungulu
in Serere.[168] 'There were also many others,' remembered one Muganda
who decided to stay, 'both chiefs and peasants who left for Buganda at
that time saying "We shall all starve in such a small deserted area"; but
they were so many that I cannot possibly remember all their names.'[169]

The Ganda who continued to acknowledge Kakungulu as their patron
were quite clear about the causes of their master's predicament. Asked if
Kakungulu was still respected as *kabaka* by his followers, a man who had
remained in his following at Mbale as a *mutongole* chief retorted: 'What else
could they do? They knew that the whole thing which had happened to
Kakungulu was largely due to Gulemye [Apolo Kagwa] who had poisoned
the Europeans' minds.'[170] What was evidently required was an antidote to
that poison. This Kakungulu attempted to provide by paying a personal
visit to Entebbe during May 1902, in order to petition James Hayes Sadler,
the incoming Commissioner of the Uganda Protectorate by promotion
from British Somaliland, about his case.

'I went and saw Commissioner Sadler when I reached the place where
he stayed,' noted Kakungulu in his diary after the visit.[171] The Commissioner was pleased to see him, and asked why he had resigned from
protectorate office. Kakungulu replied that he had not resigned, he had
been dismissed, and he would very much like to know why the Europeans
had decided to dismiss him. The Commissioner replied that he would look
up the relevant papers on the question. Kakungulu gave him eight days
to do this before reminding him about the matter by letter. When Hayes
Sadler saw Kakungulu again, he told him that he had committed no
particular crime, but that the Europeans simply wanted to rule the area
concerned themselves. He refused to reconsider the question, but suggested
that Kakungulu return to Mbale and live quietly on his personal estate.
Kakungulu then left Entebbe, staying a few days around Kampala before
reaching Mbale in the middle of June.

Back at Mbale, Kakungulu decided to make one more appeal to the
Protectorate Commissioner at Entebbe. 'I wish you my master to lift me
up and not throw me aside altogether,' he wrote on 3 August.

> I am entirely your child. I have done the Government work better than
> the rest of the Waganda. I do not wish to boast but every European in
> Uganda knows the work I have done for the Government and the
> Company ... My being made Sultan is not my doing but that of Sir
> Harry Johnston Commissioner when he saw the good work I had done
> for the Government he made me King of the Wakedi but he said I
> must first go and ask King Edward and his parliament and Ministers
> that they may agree to what I have given you, they will not refuse and
> I accepted his words in good faith as the words of truthful people are
> always to be believed.

'My master,' concluded Kakungulu, 'do not throw me away altogether and remember I am your slave and I have done nothing bad.'[172] But it was to no avail. The protectorate administration of Uganda clearly did want to throw Kakungulu aside in 1902.

While Kakungulu had been composing his last appeal to Hayes Sadler, he had brooded over his political eclipse. 'I was sent away from my country Bukedi by my masters the Europeans, who ordered me out: they accused me for nothing,' he confided to his diary, most probably during July 1902.[173] To compensate for his political misfortune, Kakungulu increasingly took refuge in his religion. 'Though the Europeans and my other friends wrongly accused me,' he confided in his diary, 'God [*Katonda*] has pitied me and supplied my every need.' On 20 July 1902 he gathered many of his followers at Mbale together in order 'to thank God, because he has delivered us from the fear of famine, and supplied us with the first fruits of our labours in this small deserted place.' But, besides seeking spiritual solace for his misfortune in this way, Kakungulu was soon turning his religion again to his political advantage.

'The Muganda chief Semei Kakungulu, one of our converts, who had charge over a large country East of the Nile and North of Usoga,' wrote Archdeacon Walker of the CMS to London in February 1902,[174]

has been removed from his position. We do not know what changes will now be made or how the government of the province (called by most people Bukedi) will be carried on. Semei Kakungulu himself has been given 20 square miles in another country & has retired into private life. The Baganda will mostly follow Semei & their influence over the Bukedi country will cease. We were free to go wherever Semei ruled, now all will be changed.

Clearly the CMS had cause to regret the situation. But Crabtree, their local representative, did not agree; possibly because of the way Kakungulu had treated him upon his first arrival in Bugisu, possibly because Kakungulu's followers did not quite live up to the ideals of this pioneer missionary linguist. 'Kakunguru's occupation – of which we had better say little,' commented Crabtree in January 1903. 'The desire to get goods far exceeded the desire to learn who & what various peoples were.'[175] Yet in October 1903 Crabtree was replaced by J.B. Purvis,[176] who quickly became an ardent admirer of Kakungulu and all his ways. So too did A.G. Fraser, who visited Kakungulu before Crabtree's departure and a few months later published an account of his visit which must have been read by British protectorate officials at Entebbe, considering that it was printed in the only locally produced news sheet circulating in Uganda at that time, *Uganda Notes*.[177]

'KAKUNGULU,' wrote Fraser in that journal, 'is the most able and polished of the Baganda.' But now he was

confined to a tiny estate with no jurisdiction whatsoever without it. With him dwell his chiefs with the titles of their departed glory, and he himself, the greatest and most ambitious of the Baganda, has not a vestige of power. Personally he is a most attractive man, quiet, dignified, handsome, courteous, a most kingly figure, and however just his fall may have been necessary one can only be sorry for him. Now too that he has no power the natives are turning on him. Recently he has lost over 50 head of cattle, 2 women on his estate have been killed when going to draw water, the chief of his cattle men was speared through the body, and 4 others of his followers badly wounded with stones. At any rate such is the tale his chiefs told me.

Kakungulu himself told a similar tale to William Grant, the protectorate official at Jinja, on several occasions during 1902.[178] But Grant appears to have been as much impressed by the increasing evidence of Kakungulu's power in eastern Uganda as influenced in his favour by considerations of pity.

To begin with, there was the evidence of numbers. The Collector at Budaka had less than a hundred askaris under his command,[179] and consequently, as Grant's successor reported in 1904, 'the influence of the Government... was only felt within a few miles of the station at Budaka.'[180] But Kakungulu's armed following at Mbale still ran into thousands, as we have already noted. Inevitably this had an adverse effect upon the balance of British protectorate power in eastern Uganda. An elderly Mugisu who had been a youth when Kakungulu moved to Mbale was asked why he thought Kakungulu had moved to that place. 'Because it seemed the best place to him,' was this elderly Mugisu's reply. 'His rule was so widespread that he could choose where to go.'[181]

Kakungulu's influence around Mbale was also strengthened by the arrival of Asian traders. In 1901 the Uganda railway had finally reached Lake Victoria, and during the following year Gujerati-speaking traders moved towards Mbale in ever-increasing numbers. In 1902, William Grant was writing: 'practically no trade at Budaka now. The traders have moved up in direction of Mubale, where the Kakunguru is settled and are establishing themselves by degrees there.'[182] By 1904, Mbale had become an important route centre. 'Several important routes converge on Mbale,' commented a visiting missionary during that year:[183]

an excellent road connects Mbale with Jinja to the south-west. A caravan route, very far from excellent, connects it to Mumia's to the south. Caravans to and from Mbale to the north-east pass through Mbale, laden for the most part with ivory. And to the north-west a caravan route passes through Serere and Bululu to the Nile provinces: so that for trade purposes Mbale is a natural centre.

Inevitably this too had an adverse effect on British protectorate influence in eastern Uganda. In disputes between the Collector at Budaka and Kakungulu at Mbale, 'the strangers' (*abalungana*) and 'the Indians' (*abayindi*) at the latter place naturally supported their patron Kakungulu in preference to his less powerful European rival as did the Baganda surrounding them.[184]

William Grant, the British official in Busoga, also increasingly appreciated the political importance of Mbale. Almost unconsciously, he himself increasingly came to depend upon Kakungulu rather than Walker to achieve his more ambitious objectives in the region. When he felt punitive measures were necessary on Mount Elgon in November 1902, Walker supplied him with 25 askaris as well as himself, while Kakungulu came with more than two hundred of his warriors armed with guns.[185] When Grant campaigned around Tororo in May 1903 against the southern Iteso, Kakungulu supplied him with a similar number of men under the command of Bumbakali Kamya, one of the most important Muslims among the Baganda at Mbale.[186] Most significant of all, when Grant travelled to Karamoja later in 1903, not only did Kakungulu again supply him with a substantial number of fighters but Kakungulu also acted as Grant's forwarding agent for important correspondence.[187] Not only was Kakungulu therefore more powerful than the offical local representative of the protectorate administration in eastern Uganda, he was also fulfilling several of his most important administrative functions.

However strange this may have appeared at the time, it seems still stranger in retrospect. Granted his power was greater than that possessed by the official British agents of the protectorate administration, and granted that he laboured under an intense sense of grievance against the political treatment he had received from those very same agents, one inevitably wonders why Kakungulu still wanted to cooperate with them rather than to rebel against them, since he would certainly have been able to give the protectorate authorities in Uganda a considerable run for their money.

Probably much of the answer to that question lies in what Kakungulu discovered during the ten days which Ham Mukasa spent with him at Mbale in June 1903.[188] Mukasa had visited Europe in 1902–3 in company with Apolo Kagwa, principally in order to attend the coronation of the new British king, Edward VII. Kakungulu was evidently sufficiently impressed by Mukasa's report of this journey, to copy the names of a number of foreign countries into his diary: England, France, Italy, Russia, Belgium, Holland, Denmark, Norway, Sweden, Austria, Switzerland, Spain, Portugal, Turkey, Greece, and 'America' (*Emerica*).[189] What exactly Mukasa told Kakungulu about these places we do not know. But we do know what Mukasa wrote about the immense might of the Europeans in the book he compiled about his European tour,[190] and it is unlikely that the information he gave Kakungulu in private would have differed substantially from the impressions he recorded in that book. Certainly, this information did not diminish Kakungulu's desire to collaborate now with the British in Uganda as best he could.

The British, for their part, were now anxious to oblige. By November 1903, William Grant was writing to Entebbe about the desirability of reincorporating Kakungulu within the British protectorate administration of Uganda. 'What was once a dreary waste' at Mbale, he wrote to Hayes Sadler,

> is now flourishing with gardens, teeming with life. Good wide roads have been cut, rivers have been bridged and embankments made through marshy ground, all at his own expense and for the public use. His past services cannot be over-estimated. Since my coming into the

country in 1890 I can testify to the good work he has done. He has done more, I should say, in assisting the Government in troublesome times than any other Chief in the country. He was misplaced when he considered himself Kabaka of Bukedi, but all that was due to some misunderstanding on his part.

But apart from that, there were the brutal facts of the contemporary political situation. 'The private estate given him is apparently not large enough to enable him to give ample scope to his energies,' wrote Grant in a masterly understatement. 'His influence is great, [but] he *could* be of immense assistance ... if judiciously employed.'[191] The reverse, by implication, would also be the case.

In December 1903, Hayes Sadler paid a personal visit to eastern Uganda. Directly rumours of his impending arrival reached Mbale, Kakungulu set about preparing for the Commissioner's visit. Special structures were erected at Mbale to cover the Commissioner's tents, and special bridges built for his convenience between Mbale and the Namatala swamp.[192] As soon as the Commissioner's party approached Bukedi, Kakungulu departed from Mbale to greet him personally at the Mpologoma crossing.[193] Hayes Sadler was impressed by the treatment he received around Mbale. 'Here,' he wrote to London, 'one seemed to be back again in the civilization of Mengo or Toro. Neatly dressed Baganda wel-

Plate 12. *Semei Kakungulu photographed at Mbale in the 1900s.* (From J.B. Purvis, *Through Uganda to Mount Elgon* (1909), p. 238)

comed us along the road, and on all sides were flourishing plantations and substantially-built grass-roofed houses.'[194] Sadler particularly noted that wherever he went around Mbale with Kakungulu, the local people paid their respects to him before saluting His Majesty's Commissioner.[195] Clearly something had to be done to bring the official situation into line with local realities, some political adjustment had to be arranged.

In the official letter he sent to London describing his journey through eastern Uganda, Hayes Sadler mentioned his solution to this problem without elaborating in any great detail its principal cause:[196]

> I reinstated the Kakunguru in his position as Saza, under the Assistant Collector, making him responsible for the collection of hut tax over his own people, but giving strict injunctions that he was not to have anything to do with hut tax collections outside his settlement unless desired to do so by the Assistant Collector, under whose orders he was to be. As an intermediary with the Bakedi and the tribes of the outer slopes of Mount Elgon who trade with Mbale he can be of great assistance to the Administration, and during the three weeks he was in my camp I had plenty of opportunity of seeing the tact with which he dealt with the natives, who all referred to him and looked upon him as their Chief.

Hayes Sadler was also careful to appoint a new Assistant Collector to work with Kakungulu: A.H. Watson, a young official with experience of Canada and service with Canadian troops in the South African war.[197] W.R. Walker was quietly and conveniently sent on overseas leave.[198]

# Notes

1. Sabuli Namwanja's words. Interview, 7 March 1964.
2. Interview with Sedulaka Kyesirikidde, 27 March 1964. 'The Europeans made him a *kabaka*, and he became the fourth one', the others being Ankole, Bunyoro and Toro.
3. S. Tekiwagala, interview, 17 August 1965.
4. S. Tekiwagala, interview of 16 September 1965, though confusing Johnston with his successor, Sadler.
5. Kibuga, *History*, p. 17.
6. *Ibid.*; Paulo Kagwa, 'Kakungulu Omukwano gwa Kabaka Mwanga', unpublished MS in Makerere University Library (MUL), pp. 49–51.
7. Kibuga, *History*, see pp. 18 and 156; P. Kagwa, 'Kakungulu Omuzira wa Uganda', unpublished MS in MUL, p. 47, though mistakenly giving the date as December 1900.
8. P. Kagwa, 'Omuzira', p. 47.
9. P. Kagwa, 'Omuzira', p. 48; Kibuga, *History*, p. 18.
10. P. Kagwa. 'Omuzira', p. 48, though this time confusing Hornby (Wombe) with Howard (Owagi); Kibuga, *History*, p. 18.
11. T.N. Howard to Delme-Radcliffe, 30 June 1901, encl. Johnston to London, 23/12/01, FO 2/464, PRO.
12. By the Revd J.B. Purvis, a later missionary of the CMS in Bugisu, and printed by Sir John Gray as Appendix I to his 'Kakunguru in Bukedi', *Uganda Journal* 27 (1963), pp. 55–6, with comments on its veracity at pp. 45–6. In both places Gray reproduces material previously presented in the report he compiled on Kakungulu's grievances in 1924 while acting as district magistrate at Mbale: see below, p. 294. Most acutely, Gray suggested that 'Arise' is a better translation of *Situka* in this context than 'Now I am not coming to you' which Purvis provided ('Kakunguru in Bukedi', p. 56).

13. Diary of Lango Field Force, encl. Jackson to London, 23 December 1901, FO 2/464, PRO.
14. *Ibid.*
15. Gray, 'Kakunguru in Bukedi', p. 44.
16. P. Kagwa, 'Omuzira', p. 48.
17. P. Kagwa, 'Omuzira', p. 40, provides this version of the song and it was the one remembered by most survivors from Kakungulu's following interviewed for this study.
18. Kibuga, *History*, p. 18.
19. P. Kagwa, 'Omuzira', p. 49.
20. *Ibid.*
21. P. Kagwa, 'Omukwano', p. 62.
22. *Ibid.*, p. 63.
23. Malumba Zake, interview, 5 August 1965.
24. These records were kept by Eria Nsubuga at Budaka: Salimu Mbogo, 17 August 1964.
25. Kakungulu, *Diary*, [microfilm, MUL] Vol. 1, p. 6, dating it during December 1901.
26. P. Kagwa, 'Omukwano', p. 63.
27. Grant to Entebbe, 7 September 1901; Walker, 'List of Bamasaza of the Kakunguru within his limits in Bukedi District, December 1901', encl. Grant to Entebbe, 21 March 1902; both in A 10/2, ESA. In September Grant had counted 16, but this would have included Budaka.
28. The executive committee of the CMS in Uganda put Kakungulu's following at Budaka at 5,000 in 1902: Minutes, 30 June 1902, G3A7/1902b, CMS archives.
29. This is based upon Walker's 'List of Bamasaza', but analysis of it depends on information collected from elderly Ganda informants interviewed for this study in general and from Salimi Mbogo, Salimini Damulira and Samwiri Tekiwagala in particular.
30. See further L.A. Fallers, F.K. Kamoga and S.B.K. Musoke, 'Social stratification in traditional Buganda' and A.I. Richards, 'Authority patterns in traditional Buganda' in ed. L.A. Fallers, *The King's Men: Leadership and Status in Buganda on the Eve of Independence* (London 1964), pp. 67-85, 270-4.
31. Samwiri Tekiwagala, 16 September 1965.
32. Interview with Salimi Damulira, 21 August 1965.
33. *Ibid.*
34. S. Tekiwagala, 16 September 1965.
35. Interview with Malumba Zake, 20 February 1964, and Asumani Mwanga, 28 November 1965.
36. Kibuga, *History*, p. 18, for the title: Walker, 'What happened in baraza in connection with Hut Tax Bukedi', 3 January 1902, encl. Grant to Entebbe, 21 March 1902, A 11/2, ESA, for the information.
37. Interview with Eria Emokoor, 28 April 1964.
38. Taped testimony from Samwiri Kimuda, 1970; I am indebted to Ron Atkinson, then a US Peace Corps volunteer, for introducing me to this informant.
39. On these leaders, see Fallers, Kamoga and Musoke, 'Social stratification'.
40. Kibuga, *History*, p. 19.
41. A.B. Fisher to London, 18 August 1901, G3A7/1901b, CMS archives.
42. P. Kagwa, 'Omuzira', p. 49.
43. P. Kagwa, 'Omukwano', p. 64.
44. *Mengo Notes*, October 1901.
45. Kestens to Grant, 27 October 1901, A 10/3, ESA.
46. Plunkett to Nsambya, 7 November 1901; copy in Nsambya Diary [ND], UNL, Box 18, Mill Hill Mission archives, London.
47. Kirk to Nsambya, 2 October 1901, ND.
48. Plunkett to Nsambya, 3 November 1901, ND.
49. *Ibid.*, 26 August 1902.
50. Fr. Prendergast, 13 June 1898; *St Joseph's Advocate*, Autumn 1898, and obituary, *ibid.*, Autumn 1905.
51. ND, 2 July 1901.
52. Kestens, 4 November 1901, ND.
53. Interview with Malumba Zake, 20 June 1964.
54. Enoka Maleza, 22 August 1965.

55. Salimu Mbogo, 7 August 1965. Mbogo had served Mwanga as a page immediately before his flight from Mengo in July 1897; he became a member of a roving band of marauders after Mwanga's capture in 1899, joining Kakungulu's following in 1900.
56. *Ibid.*
57. Kibuga, *History*, p. 20.
58. Grant to Entebbe, 29 April 1901, telegram, A 10/1, ESA.
59. *Ibid.*
60. Grant to Entebbe, 1 June 1901, A 10/1, ESA.
61. Jackson to Grant, 13 July 1901, A 11/1, ESA.
62. Jackson to Kakungulu, July 1901. This quotation comes from a copy of the English version preserved in Jackson's handwriting in A 11/1.
63. Grant to Entebbe, 5 August 1901, A 10/1, ESA.
64. Grant to Entebbe, 7 September 1901, A 10/2, ESA.
65. *Ibid.*
66. *Ibid.*
67. Jackson to Grant, 26 September 1901, A 11/2, ESA.
68. Grant to Entebbe, 7 September 1901, A 10/2, ESA.
69. *Ibid.*
70. Grant to Entebbe, 14 October 1901, A 10/2, ESA.
71. Jackson to Walker, 6 November 1901; copy in G3A7/1901b, CMS archives.
72. Jackson to Grant, 17 October 1901, A 11/2, ESA.
73. Grant to Entebbe, 7 September 1901, A 10/2.
74. Kakungulu to Jackson, 22 October 1901, A 10/2.
75. Grant to Entebbe, 24 October 1901, A 10/2.
76. RD, 13 July 1896.
77. On Karagwe's fate, see J. Ford and R. de Z. Hall, 'The history of Karagwe', *Tanganyika Notes and Records* 24 (December 1947), pp. 15–26.
78. See D.A. Low in Low and R.C. Pratt, *Buganda and British Overrule* (London 1960), *passim*.
79. R. Oliver, *The Missionary Factor in East Africa* (London 1952) is one of the best accounts.
80. See further my comments in *Journal of African History* 29 (1988), pp. 81–92.
81. D.A. Low in Low and Pratt, *Buganda and British Overrule*.
82. My account of 'The Bakungu chiefs of Buganda under British colonial rule, 1900–1930', *Journal of African History* 10 (1969), pp. 309–22, develops this further.
83. 'Memo. by H.H. Johnston on the land settlement in Uganda', 2 March 1903, FO 2/741, PRO.
84. My discussion of 'The ending of slavery in Buganda', pp. 119–49 in eds S. Miers and R. Roberts, *The End of Slavery in Africa* (Madison 1988), develops these points.
85. ND, 27 September 1901.
86. ND, 1 October 1901.
87. ND, 8 October 1901.
88 Kestens, 29 October 1901; copy in ND.
89. Kestens, 26 September 1901, ND.
90. *Ibid.*
91. Kestens, 22 October 1901, ND.
92. *Ibid.*
93. ND, 12 November 1901.
94. ND, 17 November 1901.
95. ND, 19 September 1901.
96. ND, 19 December 1901.
97. ND, 25 October 1901.
98. *Ibid.*
99. Twaddle, 'The ending of slavery', p. 142.
100. ND, 27 October 1902.
101. ND, 8 October 1901, 25 October 1901.
102. ND, 1 October 1901.
103. Johnston to Tarrant, 5 January 1901, A 11/1, ESA.
104. Interview 3 March 1965 with E.B. Haddon, who worked with Walker at Kampala in 1905.
105. Jackson to London, 4 January 1902, FO 2/589, PRO.

106. *Ibid.*
107. Grant to Entebbe, 25 October 1901, A 10/2, ESA.
108. Grant to Entebbe, 9 November 1901, A 10/2, ESA.
109. P. Kagwa, 'Omuzira', p. 50.
110. Budaka Diary (BD), UNL, Box 21, Mill Hill Mission archives, London. An earlier account is in H.P. Gale, *Uganda and the Mill Hill Fathers* (London 1959), pp. 227–9.
111. BD, 19 November 1901, 9 December 1901.
112. BD, 21 November 1901.
113. BD, 20 November 1901.
114. BD, 22 November 1901.
115. BD, 30 November 1901, 4 December 1901.
116. BD, 12 December 1901.
117. Kallen to Nsambya, 9 December 1901, ND.
118. BD, 15 December 1901.
119. BD, 23 December 1901.
120. BD, 30 December 1901.
121. BD, 31 December 1901.
122. Gale, *Mill Hill Fathers*, p. 228.
123. BD, 8 November 1901, 18 November 1901.
124. Walker did not become an established protectorate official until 1 April 1902 (FO to Walker, draft, FO 2/597, PRO), but Kakungulu had been treated by now in protectorate correspondence as an Assistant Collector for two years.
125. P. Kagwa, 'Omuzira'.
126. Kakungulu, *Diary*, Vol. 1, entry for 2 January 1902.
127. *Ibid.*
128. Grant to Entebbe, 5 January 1902, telegram, A 11/2, ESA.
129. Jackson to Grant, 7 January 1902, telegram, A 11/2, ESA.
130. Wamala, 'Obulamu', p. 208.
131. This is based on a perusal of the Budaka Mission Diary in the Mill Hill Mission archives in north London (UCL, Box 21).
132. 'What occurred in baraza in connection with Hut Tax Bukedi', memo by Walker, 3 January 1902, encl. Grant to Entebbe, 21 January 1902, A 10/2, ESA. A parallel account is contained in the first volume of Kakungulu's diaries.
133. Walker, *ibid.*
134. Grant to Entebbe, 6 January 1902, A 10/2, ESA.
135. *Ibid.*
136. *Ibid.*
137. Jackson to London [25] January 1902, FO 2/589, PRO.
138. ND, 22 November 1901.
139. ND, 17 November 1902.
140. Jackson to London [25] January 1902, FO 2/589, PRO.
141. *Ibid.*
142. Kakungulu, *Diary*, Vol. 1, p. 7. This was on 28 January 1902.
143. 'Memo re Kakunguru', no date, A 11/2, ESA.
144. Grant to Entebbe, 3 February 1902, telegram, A 10/2, ESA.
145. Kakungulu, *Diary*, Vol. 1, p. 7.
146. Grant, 3 February 1902; Kibuga, *History*, pp. 21–3; Kakungulu, *Diary*, Vol. 1, p. 7; P. Kagwa, 'Omuzira', pp. 54–5.
147. E.g., Johnson to London, 17 March 1900, quoted by D.A. Low in Low and Pratt, *Buganda and British Overrule*, p. 94; Jackson to London, 7 February 1902, FO 2/297, PRO; 'Memo by H.H. Johnson on the Land Settlement in Uganda', 7 March 1903, FO 2/741, PRO. The danger of rebellion when Kakungulu was ordered to move from Budaka has been mythologized by European tradition into a story about Walker being instructed to remove Kakungulu when he was appointed at Budaka. The story seems to have been started by P.W. Perryman, 'History of Kakunguru' (1920), para. 7, and is purveyed by most European writers on Uganda, including Sir John Gray, 'Kakunguru in Bukedi', p. 47. It is of course wrong: it inverts cause and effect.
148. S. Kimuda, 1970. Kimuda had been a servant of Semei Serwanga, a follower of Yowasi Mivule.

149. *Ibid.*
150. *Ibid.*
151. Jackson to Grant, 3 February 1902, telegram, A 11/2, ESA.
152. Jackson to Grant, 5 February 1902, telegram, A 11/2, ESA.
153. Grant to Entebbe, 6 February 1902, telegram, A 10/2, ESA. Kakungulu received the formal deed of ownership from Grant on 16 March 1902.
154. 'Memo re Kakunguru', n.d., in A 11/2, and H.B. Thomas, '*Capax imperii* – the story of Semei Kakunguru', *Uganda Journal* 6 (1939), p. 132.
155. Interview with S. Mbogo, 17 August 1965.
156. *Ibid.*, 4 August 1965.
157. *Ibid.*, 3 August 1965.
158. See P.B. Haig, 'Medical report on the Nandi expedition', FO 2/461, PRO; and R.W. Beachey in *Uganda Journal* 28 (1964), p. 112.
159. Kakungulu, *Diary*, Vol. 1, p. 9; Crabtree, Diary, entry for 26 February 1902; Grant to Entebbe, 21 March 1902, A 10/2, ESA.
160. P. Kagwa, 'Omuzira', p. 57.
161. Interview with Sedulaka Kyesirikidde, 27 March 1964.
162. S. Mbogo, 18 October 1963.
163. *Ibid.*
164. It was also similar to Mengo economically. See my account of 'The founding of Mbale', *Uganda Journal* 30 (1966), where this aspect and others are developed further.
165. P. Kagwa, 'Omuzira', p. 59.
166. S. Mbogo, 17 August 1965.
167. E. Maleza, 22 August 1965.
168. Interview with S. Tekiwagala, 17 August 1965.
169. *Ibid.*
170. Interview with S. Mbogo, 17 August 1965.
171. Kakungulu, *Diary*, Vol. 1, pp. 11–13, from which these remarks are taken.
172. Kakungulu to Sadler, 3 August 1902, A 10/2, ESA.
173. Kakungulu, *Diary*, Vol. 1, pp. 13–15, upon which the following sentences also depend.
174. Walker to London, 27 February 1902, G3A7/1902a, CMS archives.
175. Crabtree to London, 29 January 1903, G3A7/1903a, CMS archives.
176. Purvis arrived in September 1903, Crabtree left during October: *Uganda Notes*, October 1903, July 1904.
177. A.G. Fraser, 'Cycle trip in Usoga and Kavirondo'.
178. Grant to Entebbe, 27 October 1902, A 10/2, ESA.
179. Walker's askaris were reported by Wilson to London as numbering 49 in 1903 ('Uganda Constabulary return for half-year ending 31 December 1903', FO 2/856, PRO).
180. A point repeated in Boyle to Entebbe, 27 May 1904, A 6/17, ESA.
181. Interview with Andereya Polo, 17 June 1963.
182. Quoted in Twaddle, 'The Founding of Mbale'.
183. *Ibid.*
184. Kakungulu, *Diary*, Vol. 1, pp. 18–22.
185. Grant to Entebbe, 18 November 1902, telegram, A 11/2; same to same, 8/1/03, A 27/6, ESA.
186. Kakungulu, *Diary*, Vol. 1, p. 24.
187. *Ibid.*
188. *Ibid*, p. 7.
189. *Ibid.*, pp. 24–5.
190. H. Mukasa, *Uganda's Katikiro in England* (London 1904).
191. Grant to Entebbe, 13 November 1903, copy in SMP 1760/08, ESA.
192. P. Kagwa, 'Omuzira', p. 62.
193. *Ibid.*
194. Hayes Sadler to London, 27 February 1904, FO 2/856, PRO.
195. *Ibid.*
196. *Ibid.*
197. Obituary, *East Africa and Rhodesia* (3 July 1958); FO to Watson, 23 April 1902, FO 2/597, PRO.
198. Hayes Sadler to London, 3 June 1904, FO 2/857, PRO.

# Seven

# Expansion & Resistance
## 1904–6

1

Before leaving for Buganda, Hayes Sadler composed a memorandum. In it he noted that he had made Kakungulu 'omusaza [county chief] of the country of which ... the boundary is a line from Mbai to Lake Norman thence to Lake Mpologoma down that lake and following the Nambale river until it issues from the Elgon range'. Within this area, Kakungulu would 'be personally responsible for the payment of Hut Tax for all huts on his private estate' and also of 'any Waganda who might choose to settle down not far from but outside his private property and who would still be liable to his jurisdiction'. As for the remainder of Mbale county, Kakungulu was 'not to interfere with hut tax collections unless and only so far as the Collector of the district might wish'. Kakungulu 'would in fact act as an intermediary and Assistant to the Collector'. In return, he 'would receive back his pay as a saza from April 1st 1903 at the rate of £200 per annum', which would also be his future rate of pay. The rest of the memorandum was concerned with protectorate rights with regard to land around Mbale.[1]

The memorandum was not without ambiguities, but its general meaning was clear: Kakungulu's future position was to be like that of a county chief in the post-1900 kingdom of Buganda.

Sadler's speech conveyed a different message. It was translated from Swahili by Salim Bwagu, who had accompanied the protectorate commissioner from Busoga.[2] In Luganda, it was to the effect that the British colonial authorities 'had returned Kakungulu to his administrative duties in Bukedi as they had been before' (*Gavumenti ekuwadde ensi ye Bukedi okufuga nga bwe wagifunanga edda*), but that Kakungulu would have to keep away from Lango and Kumam districts. These areas were to be administered directly from the protectorate office at Jinja. Instead Kakungulu would be

Map 10 *Seats of Sazas administered from Mbale, January 1904.*

| | | |
|---|---|---|
| *Omuwanika* | Esitasio Nkambo | Bunkoko |
| *Omujasi* | Yosiya Mayanja | Bubulo |
| *Omukungulu* | Malaki Magongo | Buyobo |
| *Kitunzi* | Malembwe Bijabira | Mbai |
| *Kago* | Eria Nsubuga | Kadama |
| *Kangawo* | Yakobo Gafabuganda | Bunyole |
| *Kimbugwe* | Sedulaka Kyesirikidde | Palisa |
| *Sekibobo* | Yosiya Byatike | Serere |
| *Kyambalango* | Bumbakali Kamya | Bukedea |
| *Mugema* | Jafali Mayanja | Ngora |
| *Mukwenda* | Leubeni Bitege | Soroti |
| *Kiyimba* | Yairo Bina | Mani Mani |

Figure 3 *List of Kakungulu's saza chiefs, January 1904.*

196

allowed to expand again into the western foothills of Mount Elgon.[3] In general, Sadler's speech suggested that Kakungulu's kingdom would be restored to something like its earlier extent.

Temuteo Kagwa relates that, as soon as he returned to his enclosure after hearing Hayes Sadler's speech, Kakungulu ordered his drum *kungula to* be sounded as a sign of rejoicing. The next day he called a special meeting with his followers to reallocate chiefships.[4]

The principal offices which emerged from this meeting are set out in Figure 3. Of the twelve county chiefs appointed, seven had held similar offices under Kakungulu at Budaka; the office of the eighth (the *Pokino*) was kept vacant during Isaka Nziga's absence on an ivory-collecting expedition in Karamoja. Regarding Kakungulu's five other appointments to *saza* offices within his kingdom in January 1904, two (Yosiya Mayanja and Yairo Bina) were Protestants like Kakungulu, while another two (Malembwe Bijabiira and Eria Nsubuga) were his clansmen as well as his co-religionists. Only Bumbakali Kamya among these appointments was tied to Kakungulu by neither clanship nor by religion. But he was one of the two most prominent Muslims in Kakungulu's following and had assisted William Grant in a punitive expedition around Tororo in 1903.

The areas to which these chiefs were sent by Kakungulu during January 1904 are shown in Map 10 on page 196. *Kangawo, Kimbugwe, Sekibobo* and *Mugema* were returned to their old counties of Bunyole, Palisa, Serere and Ngora. The new *Sekibobo* was Yosiya Byatike; the previous one, Malaki Magongo, now became *Omukungulu*. *Mukwenda* now had headquarters at Soroti rather than in Kumam, *Omuwanika* in Bugisu rather than Bugwere, his place near Budaka being taken over by *Kago*. *Kitunzi, Omujasi* and *Omukungulu* were also now despatched into the western foothills of Mount Elgon. Two new *sazas* were created for Kyambalango and Kiyimba at Bukedea and Mani Mani respectively. However, whether Kiyimba actually took possession of his area in January 1904 is highly unlikely, since Yairo Bina was still absent collecting ivory in the direction of Ethiopia with Isaka Nziga at that time. Nonetheless, the other county chiefs certainly took possession of their offices. Together with deputies and other subordinates, they were formally presented by Kakungulu to the new Collector at Mbale and then despatched to their respective areas. Meanwhile, other functionaries were deputed to keep their plots at Mbale clean and tidy during their absences from Kakungulu's headquarters.[5]

## 2

In February 1904 Hayes Sadler was told of 'an affray' involving 'Mujasi, a Uganda sub-chief [who] had been placed by Kakungulu over some Wagesho tribes who dwell about twelve miles beyond the CMS station on the side farthest from here, and within an hour's march from the boundary line of the two Protectorates [of Uganda and what is nowadays Kenya].'[6] Hayes Sadler was astonished, and blamed Watson. 'Warn him distinctly,' he telegraphed to Alexander Boyle, who had recently replaced William Grant as sub-commissioner at Jinja, 'not to send police to the Elgon tribes, to be very careful as to calling in any of the Elgon chiefs and to use the Kakunguru in his communications with them. I cannot have him involving me with the hill tribes, and incidents of this kind frustrate all the good done by my tour.'[7]

Boyle agreed that Watson was to blame, but put a rather different interpretation upon the affray. 'The point in the report which I consider requires explanation,' wrote Boyle after re-reading Hayes Sadler's memorandum,

> is the fact that the Kakunguru had placed an agent of his own over a section of the Bagesho tribe apparently for the purpose of collecting taxes from the natives of that part. The Kakunguru was himself given clearly to understand by you when you were at Mubale that he was not to have or to exercise any direct control over the natives, but was merely to act as intermediary to the Officer in charge of the Bukedi district and it is therefore inexplicable to me how such an appointment had been allowed and [I] can only presume that Mr Watson had not realised the actual condition of affairs nor the conditions of the appointment of Kakunguru.

Boyle had therefore ordered Watson to withdraw 'any agents that the Kakunguru may have sent into the district ... if they have received instructions to collect taxes'. He had hedged the order in that way, he told Sadler, 'as you will doubtless remember the Kakunguru was told that he should help the natives by instructing them what they should plant and how they should plant it.'[8]

But Boyle's instruction was not obeyed. Instead Watson suggested 'frequently changing the Waganda chiefs from place to place' to prevent them acquiring excessive local influence.[9] Boyle would have nothing of it.[10] Sadler agreed. Watson was again ordered to withdraw Kakungulu's chiefs to Mbale.[11] This time Watson complied, and Kakungulu withdrew temporarily to Mbale the county chiefs ruling the most distant parts of his kingdom.[12] But soon Watson was again writing in defence of 'the system in force', this time requesting that his proposals should be forwarded for the protectorate commissioner's personal perusal. His arguments were as before, but put more strongly. There were no real chiefs at Mbale.

> When HM Commissioner was here several persons were presented to him and described as chiefs; yet these men are coming in daily to complain of the people who are nominally their followers. One may talk for hours with such men and try to make them familiar with our aims and objects, but after doing so we have not advanced one iota with the people whom they are supposed to represent, for, when they return home, no one dreams of listening to what they say.

If the Commissioner insisted that all the Baganda be withdrawn to Mbale, 'the more outlying districts,' concluded Watson, 'in which already some signs of progress are discernible, would at once lapse into their former condition of savagery pure and simple.'[13]

Such language, Sadler admitted, 'puts the matter in a different light ...

it now appears that he was utilising the Baganda chiefs in the interests of the country, which is a different thing from their perambulating on their own account. How far it will be desirable to use the Baganda chiefs for this purpose I must leave entirely to your discretion.'[14] Boyle took the hint. 'In order to get any systematic government among these people we shall have to have recourse to Baganda capable of advising them,' he was soon writing. These men would be unpaid. However,

> understanding as they do the ways of the Administration, [they] will by their advice gradually introduce method into the government of the local chiefs; they will see that the roads are kept clean and repaired, that information of all events is sent in to Mubale; that traders and others do not impose upon the natives and they will also act as a check upon the local chiefs both in their dealings with their own people and with the Administration.[15]

Soon rationalization of reality went further. 'The month of January of this year marks, I consider, the real commencement of effective administration in Bukedi,' wrote Alexander Boyle in his annual report for 1903–4,

> namely when the Kakunguru was appointed Assistant to the Collector of the District, and when it thus became possible to extend the influence of the Government, which previously was only felt within a few miles of the station at Budaka, throughout nearly the whole district by making use of Baganda from the Kakunguru's following as agents and advisers to the local chiefs of the outlying districts.[16]

Effect was now being turned into cause, and the reconstitution of Kakungulu's kingdom in eastern Uganda passed off as a conscious product of British protectorate policy. Yet, in so doing, Boyle missed an opportunity to transform Kakungulu's kingdom into an actual bureaucracy.

Towards the end of April 1904, Boyle had been making his way to Mbale to find out what was really happening there when he was informed of serious dissension within Kakungulu's following:

> that six of Kakungulu's men had come to [Watson] privately to say that they did not wish to work under him any longer but to work directly for the Government, and afterwards I learnt from Mr Purvis that some of them had been to him to try to intercede for their employment by the Administration, putting forward their wish to assist in religious work as an inducement to urge him to intercede for them.
>
> Under these circumstances, I informed Kakunguru in full baraza of the disloyalty of his chiefs to him and told him that I did not consider such men to be suitable persons either to represent him or the Government in outlying districts.[17]

Yet, as Boyle himself admitted, the men concerned were the 'largest chiefs' in Kakungulu's following. From other sources[18] we know there were actually seven of them: Sedulaka Kyesirikidde, *Kimbugwe*; Leubeni Bitege, *Mukwenda*; Yosiya Mayanja, *Omujasi*; Bumbakalai Kamya, *Kyambalango*; Jafali Mayanja, *Mugema*; Yosiya Byatike, *Sekibobo*; and Eria Nsubuga, *Kago*, as well as several lesser dignitaries. Two questions inevitably arise. First, what prompted these chiefs to make their advances to the protectorate administration? Second, whatever made the leading British official spurn the advances?

In retrospect, the answers to both questions seem clear. Regarding the first, the chiefs concerned calculated that it would be better for them 'to leave friend Kakungulu and become officials for the Europeans ... like those at Mengo [who] receive pounds'[19] as a result of what happened during the previous month.

One incident was Watson's temporary withdrawal of Ganda chiefs to Mbale in response to repeated demands to do so from his protectorate superiors. Another was the speech Kakungulu himself delivered to his followers after an embarrassing difference with Watson over petty taxes: in future they should pay respect to the Collector rather than to himself, because that was the only way they could ensure their continuance in power in Bukedi.[20]. The third factor was that Abudala Makubire, the Collector's interpreter,[21] and Bumbakali Kamya, the only county chief in Kakungulu's following unattached to him by either religion or clanship, were Muslims and remembered by Kakungulu's surviving followers as intriguers. Intrigue apart, as Ganda Muslims both Makubire and Kamya had lived through the earlier collapse of Kalema's kingdom in Buganda ten years before: kingdom collapse was no novel experience for them. It would appear to have been the conjuncture of this third factor with the first and second that caused the chiefs, who were Kakungulu's brothers by religion and clanship, to consider their options. In the light of their near-annihilation politically at Budaka just over two years before, these chiefs considered approaching the British authorities. Nonetheless, according to Solomon Wamala, it was Abudala Makubire who persuaded them finally to make their advances, saying he was sure they would please their British superiors thereby.[22]

That these superiors were not pleased, seems to have been as much due to the linguistic ignorance of Watson and Boyle as to tactless diplomacy by some of the chiefs themselves with the CMS missionary at Nabumali (as Mpumudde was now called). Conversation with Boyle took place in Swahili, with Bumbakali Kamya acting as spokesman for the chiefs because of his knowledge of it.[23] But, despite fluency in Swahili, Kamya failed to persuade Boyle of the reasonableness of turning Kakungulu's county chiefs into salaried officials directly responsible to the Protectorate authorities and enjoying conditions of service comparable with their counterparts in Buganda. Had the sub-commissioner concerned been an old IBEAC hand, with a more intimate knowledge of local life and language rather than a more polished but ignorant official, the result might have been different. But the official now was Alexander Boyle, not William Grant. Where Grant might have seen the chance for a deal, Boyle saw evidence of evil. 'There is something bad in you,' he is remembered as telling the dissident chiefs. 'I cannot understand why you are abandoning the friend who has looked after you from childhood, and with whom the Europeans first found you.'[24] Boyle therefore ordered Kakungulu to provide him with the names of six new chiefs within two days.[25]

## 3

Pressure of work and illness kept Watson at Mbale for most of the middle months of 1904.[26] Though he did manage to spend a fortnight travelling to Ngora and Mbai in June, he was unable to get to Serere or Soroti.[27] When fighting broke out between 'unfriendly' groups there in August, he was at a loss regarding what to do. If he had a clerk, he said he might be able to visit the area.[28] Boyle thought of a more economical remedy:

> to send the Kakunguru to investigate the matter and I have informed him that in my opinion it would be well for the Kakunguru to make periodic tours of inspection of his outlying agents in the Bukedi District. He has a great deal of influence with these people and is generally liked by them and it will also tend to show the natives that they are still being looked after by the man who originally conquered them and the force of whose hand they have felt more than once.[29]

Kakungulu accordingly left Mbale for a safari to Serere and Soroti on 18 August.[30]

At each of the places visited during this safari, Kakungulu delivered a speech. Some time later, one of his clerks copied a summary of it into one of his diaries.[31] This deserves quoting here in translation, since it is as revealing about Kakungulu's attitudes towards Europeans as the letter by Frederick Jackson, quoted earlier, was about the latter's attitudes towards Africans:

> First of all, I am delighted to see you Bakedi, both chiefs and peasants, who are all my friends. I am delighted really because of the reason which has brought me to see you, my friends. For I have been sent by the Government Europeans (*Abazungu abagavumenti*) to see how you are getting on and to explain the many things that need to be done by you. I have been sent to you, not to stir up trouble or to fight, but to visit all of you my friends who live in the places I have already visited and those to which I am going.
>
> You know how that when I first came here, I came as easily as a child. All the Bakedi, every one who was a fighting man from Bululu to Masaba, came and fought against me. Where now are the people who defeated me? Nevertheless, you must understand that both I and the European want peace, not warfare (*Nze nabazungu tetwagala kulwano, wabula emirembe*). Wars are not good things: they devastate the countryside. There are many among you who feel like killing people when you drink too much beer. But what is the value of fighting in this way?
>
> You must understand that the Europeans will rule many countries (*Abazungu baja bafuga ensi nyingi*). They already rule many tribes. You know how the Europeans captured the two kings who did not want to acknowledge their authority. When they rebelled, the European fought them until he conquered them. Those kings were Mwanga, the king of the Ganda people, and Kabalega, the king of the Nyoro people.

Yet you should also realize that the Europeans have learnt how to be merciful. Therefore if you have any matter you want to raise, or if some Muganda has harmed one of you, do not say 'As they are all Baganda, how can they judge the Mukedi's case fairly?' Rather bring your case before the chief appointed for your area. Should that chief fail to deal with the case to your satisfaction, he will bring it to me – I, Kakungulu. If I fail to solve it, I will take it to the European who rules this area. If the European fails to resolve the matter, he will take it to the one at Jinja, the one at Jinja to the Commissioner, and so on until the case is decided, and we know who is actually in the wrong.

The Government wants people to work ... That is what we Baganda do at home ... Remember how in the past I told you to cultivate chillies, groundnuts, sim sim and to prepare sisal fibre. When these come to maturity, that will help your payment of taxes considerably. For how long can you pay your taxes by cows?

So we should all be friends. We are all of the same flesh, though we ourselves usually tend to think otherwise. There is no distinction between Muganda and Mukedi (*Tewali Muganda namukedi*). The European has suggested that if a chief gives a cow for tax, he should take goats from his men, since tax is for huts in general, not only those of certain individuals. If there is anyone present who has been wronged by a Muganda or a Mukedi, let him stand up and say so. Indeed, anyone who has anything to say, let him speak.

That is all I have to say now.

The clerk who copied this summary into Kakungulu's diary comments that as a result of that speech Kakungulu acquired an enhanced reputation as a lawgiver in the areas visited by his safari. He also records that Kakungulu received more than twenty cattle in the same areas from satisfied litigants.[32]

Besides enhancing his legal reputation, the safari enabled Kakungulu to increase the number of forts under his command. In August and September 1904, new stockades were constructed under his direction at Tira for the *sabagabo* of his *sekibobo* administering Serere; at Gweri for the *mumyuka* of the *mukwenda* now ruling Soroti; at Kachede for Isaka Nziga, the *pokino* who had recently returned to Mbale from Ethiopia; at Kapiri for the *sabagabo* of Kakungulu's *mugema*, this functionary acquiring new headquarters at Kumi (his previous ones at Ngora coming under the control of his sub-chief *senkezi*).[33] When Kakungulu returned to Mbale from the safari in September 1904, his political power in eastern Uganda was substantially greater than it had been two months before.

This power was not, however, universally effective. The Bukedi plains were more effectively policed from Kakungulu's forts than the foothills of Mount Elgon. One CMS missionary who visited the mountain during 1904 comments how ineffective Ganda influence appeared on its south-westerly spurs. 'Beyond Nabumali,' wrote this missionary,[34]

Kakungulu felt it necessary to supply us with an escort of twelve native police, armed to ensure a safe passage through the then independent tribes known as the Ketosh. Camped for one night in the country of these as yet untamed people, I went round to see that the porters (natives of Buganda) were safely housed. I found them occupying the huts of the villagers, and to my question, Where are the people of the village? the Baganda proudly replied, They have fled from the glory of the Baganda. But the next night, when the escort had left us, and we were considered to be beyond the danger limit, I found the same Baganda porters taking shelter as best they could, not in the huts of the people, but under the granaries in the open. I asked them why they had not gone into the huts for the night? to which they replied, They will not let us in! I could not help retorting ... Whence is the glory of the Baganda?

Yet, weak as it was, Kakungulu's influence on Mount Elgon over-shadowed British authority in the area. When the protectorate authorities instigated punitive measures against the Baligenyi clan of Bugisu during September 1904, Boyle was careful to include Watson in them despite his sickness. 'Owing to the influence of the Kakunguru it is difficult to impress on the natives that he is only second to the Collector ... had Mr Watson been left behind, while the Kakunguru accompanied the expedition, it would have been thought by the natives that Mr Watson was of secondary importance only.'[35]

Nearly a month later, Watson was complaining about the same thing. 'Kakunguru, I have reason to believe,' he reported,[36]

secretly encourages throughout Bukedi the idea of his Kingship. Openly he accepts without demur the title of 'Omusaza' but as you know it is quite a common thing for the Baganda to call him 'Kabakka' and it would be absurd to suppose that this custom would exist if he enjoyed among his familiars the title 'Omusaza'.

Absurd indeed; especially since the manner in which Boyle responded to Watson's complaints revealed that Kakungulu's continuance in power depended as much upon his deference towards the sub-commissioner at Jinja as upon his personal authority in the field.

'Only three days ago,' wrote Watson in the same letter,

Kakungulu again gave trouble. A report had reached me that the house of the police near the CMS station had been burnt by the Ba-Gesho. Having some reason to suppose that the Muganda agent in that part was not getting on satisfactorily with the natives, and believing that he was in part at least to blame, I sent at 10 am to Kakunguru desiring him to go at once and make enquiries. He replied that it was unnecessary that he should go in person, but that he would send his men. Three times during that day did he refuse to attend to my message, and only at 5 pm when I finally told him that, failing his immediate compliance, I would report him to you as guilty of gross insubordination, did he give way and go off.

Six days later, Kakungulu sent his own version of events. 'My dear friend Mr Boyle (*Munange Bwana Boyle*),' began the English translation which Kakungulu enclosed together with the Luganda original for the sub-commissioner's convenience:

Once on Monday 31st day of Oct news was brought in to us that the Police camp which was at Mpumude had been burnt by native (Bageshu) of state. Without delay Mr Watson sent me to find out the matter. When I got there I caught two men who actually destroyed the huts. After two days I returned home with these prisoners whom I handed to the Collector.

Ending the letter 'Yours very affectionately' (*Nze mukwano gwo*), Kakungulu mentioned incidentally that he was enclosing one or two gifts. 'Herewith I am sending you caps one of them covered with strings of shells and the other with Leopard piece skin, one bow, one (wooden) quiver containing arrows and one shield.'[37] On November 16th, Boyle forwarded Watson's letter complaining about Kakungulu to Entebbe with the comment 'I have received a report that K's visit was quite satisfactory, the chiefs & people assisting him to arrest the culprits.' He wrote at the same time to George Wilson, now Acting Commissioner during Hayes Sadler's absence, suggesting 'a letter from yourself, addressed to the Kakunguru, congratulating him on the progress he has made in the district'.[38] The politics of *okufugibwa* were still proving highly adaptable to colonial conditions.

But Boyle was not hoodwinked completely. 'This district undoubtedly wants careful handling,' he had commented to George Wilson more than a month before when suggesting that the British official sent to relieve Watson should be 'a fairly experienced man'.[39]

With care it will pay well, with carelessness it might be a thorn in the flesh. I needn't say for you know him better than I do, that Kakunguru is a man who may be invaluable if well handled but if the Collector saws too much at the bit he might be vicious in a quiet way, namely by hampering everything while apparently helping. I like the man in a way but I know he wants a lot of watching.

What Boyle failed to appreciate fully was that Kakungulu could be as 'crafty' (*mukujjukujju*) with the sub-commissioner at Jinja as with the Collector at Mbale.

Besides playing traditional Ganda politics with British officials, Kakungulu improved his informal alliance with the CMS too. This he did when Bishop Tucker again visited eastern Uganda in the middle of 1904. Kakungulu accompanied 'the Bishop and his friends' from Mbale to Nabumali;[40] contributed with his followers £20 'for religious purposes' around Mbale;[41] and helped to arrange a special communion service for Ganda at Mbale itself.[42] 'During the whole of Mr Crabtree's residence at Masaba (some 2½ years)', reported Bishop Tucker to the CMS Committee in London, 'he only once I think arranged a Communion service for them.' Yet, in the bishop's opinion, 'Christian Baganda must be evangelists for the regions beyond' Mbale. 'Mr Crabtree however will have none of them. The fact is he dislikes the Baganda and I am bound to say the Baganda cordially reciprocate the feeling.'[43] The CMS commitment to Kakungulu was now greater because of its relative neglect of him during the previous two years.

Strengthened by this commitment, Kakungulu set about fulfilling more material ambitions. On 6 November 1904 he wrote to his friend Ham Mukasa in Buganda, 'explaining that the residence he was going to build for himself at Mbale would have 44 doors and 34 windows on the ground floor, 22 doors and 17 windows on the top floor, and many other features.'[44] Evidently he had learned more than one lesson from Ham's visit in the previous year.

## 4

One Sunday in 1905, Alikizanda Njubirese and Zakayo Katono, two evangelists of the CMS connection, were trying to hold services in one part of Padhola, while Merekizadeki Tebadagamu, an unofficial government agent, was attempting to collect taxes in another. Before the day was out, all three had been killed by Jopadhola, together with most of the occupants of the government fort at Mulanda. Had reinforcements not been rushed from Mbale the next day, their companions at Peta, the principal government fort in Padhola, would most probably have suffered a similar fate.[45] 'Believe me,' declared the Reverend J.B. Purvis to Bishop Tucker during the following month, 'every Muganda and the whole of Mbale has for some time been living on the edge of a volcano. The lack of combination on the part of the natives has alone saved you from receiving a much more severe shock than the massacre of 80 or 100 men, women and children at Budama has given you.'[46]

Only three days before the killings in Padhola, Purvis had warned the Collector at Mbale about the danger of a social disturbance in Bugisu, should the custom of raiding cattle for hut tax continue. 'The industrious man', Purvis had written,[47]

who has gathered together a few cows, and trusting in the protection of the European Government, has moved down from the hills, given up warfare, is willing to pay a reasonable tax, has helped to make roads, is raided by Baganda in the name of H.M. Government for hut tax, and loses a number of cows. The result is retaliation; and stray Baganda are murdered when they go to demand labour from the very people who have had cows taken as hut tax.

When the killings of Baganda took place in Padhola, Purvis naturally assumed that they had a similar cause: 'the present system of collecting what is called Hut Tax', he wrote to Bishop Tucker on 17 July, 'is responsible for the massacre and also for the marked spirit of unrest and discontent among the natives in this district.'[48]

There was much truth in what Purvis wrote. Distaste for taxes paid in confiscated cattle appears to have been as widespread in Padhola during 1905 as it was in Bugisu. 'They say they have now paid cattle as Hut Tax for three years,' reported the Mbale Collector to Jinja on 10 July, 'and as the cows they paid would by now have borne calves and increased, they are unable to see why they should continue paying every year.'[49] About three weeks later, the sub-commissioner from Jinja discovered for himself how many Jopadhola were incensed about this practice. Interviewing a group of Padhola notables intimidated by the instigators of the massacre, he discovered that they had been told, in effect, 'we will kill you if you refuse to rebel with us ... since you are the ones who took our cows to the Europeans.'[50] But in addition to uncovering this grievance about hut tax, the sub-commissioner unsurprisingly unearthed a distaste for its collectors – and it was that distaste which impressed him as being the most likely cause of the massacre at Mulanda.[51]

Distaste for Baganda was certainly as widespread amongst Jopadhola during the 1900s as distaste for paying poll tax in cattle. Of this there can be no doubt: it is even admitted by Ganda sources hostile to the Jopadhola. One such source remembers 'Winokiko', one of the instigators of the 1905 disturbances, having declared at the time: 'The Baganda are killing us: do they want to rule us for ever?'.[52] At least some Jopadhola of his generation were determined that they should not.

Another inflammatory factor concerned contradictory attitudes exhibited by local Ganda towards consumption of beer. The day the massacre at Mulanda took place, Alikizanda Njubirese and Zakayo Katono broke up a beer party in one part of Padhola, ordering the participants to leave and 'telling them they were not allowed to drink', while in another part Merekizadeki Tebadagamu seized supplies of beer for his own enjoyment.[53] This incensed local people. 'Who are these Waganda that they rob our goods, take our women and now stop our drink?', the rebels are reported to have declared.[54] The massacre at Mulanda and the raid on the fort at Peta followed almost immediately.

That these disturbances did not spread further in Padhola was in part a consequence of the politic stance adopted towards them by the young Majanga, son of the Majanga who had formed the Jopadhola into such fighting trim immediately before Kakungulu's arrival in eastern Uganda in 1899–1900.[55] Had the young Majanga joined the rebels in 1905, British officials might have had a large-scale rebellion on their hands, because his influence with the Nyapolo clan of Padhola and his ritual access to the cult of Bura could have provided it with an indigenous organization and dynamic extremely difficult to destroy.[56] But in fact the young Majanga cooperated with the Collector at Mbale, the sub-commmissioner from Jinja and the troops under their command – 87 rank and file Kings African Rifles (KAR), 71 rank and file Uganda Constabulary, 49 'Wasoga Friendlies', 3 sepoys with a maxim gun, besides commissioned and non-commissioned officers – in putting down what remained of the rebellion in Padhola three months later.[57] Not that there was by then very much to put down. 'Before entering the Budama country', reported the military commander of the Budama punitive column, 'I was given to understand that they would probably resist strongly and the experience of the cattle collecting parties confirmed this. They were however, owing to their total lack of organization and primitive weapons quite unable to cope with our forces.'[58]

The young Majanga's collaboration with the British forces was clearly one factor in their defeat. 'The old Majanga, father of the present Chief,' reported the sub-commissioner from Jinja subsequently, 'was evidently a far-seeing man, as I was told that he told his son and the chief men that whatever happened they must keep in with the Europeans.' This advice the young Majanga had followed 'most excellently'.[59] Towards the end of September 1905, he received his reward: he was appointed protectorate agent for Padhola in place of Misa Kisaka, the Muganda who had ruled the area previously.[60] Within a week of this appointment, the sub-commissioner from Jinja passed through Padhola and was pleasantly surprised 'to see all the people in their houses and working in their shambas'.[61] The rebellion, such as it was, was over.

Yet, though putting down the rebellion in Padhola caused British protectorate officials in Uganda few practical problems, getting over the shock it induced in their minds was quite another matter. Of course there had been punitive expeditions around Mbale and Tororo before, but none for reasons like this. The earlier expeditions had been directed against politically decentralized societies not then administered by British protectorate officials in eastern Uganda. This one was directed against one such society subjected to protectorate taxation for several years. To be sure, before 1901 Padhola had been in several regards a centralized society but, after Kakungulu's conquest, it had reverted to a much more decentralized condition.[62]

To begin with, the protectorate commissioner at Entebbe had reacted by suspending collections of hut tax in all areas of Bukedi lying south of Mbale. He had also ordered all Baganda operating in these areas to be withdrawn to Kakungulu's private estate.[63] Cubitt, the acting sub-commissioner at Jinja, was ordered to discover whether Kakungulu's followers had been exceeding the instructions he had given them at the start of the previous year. 'It was particularly impressed on the Kakunguru when I visited Mbale,' wrote Hayes Sadler to Cubitt, 'that he was on no account to collect Hut Tax outside his allotment without the direct orders of the Collector, and you should report on whether it was with the Collector's orders that Kisaka had been levying cattle.'[64] But before waiting to learn Cubitt's conclusions, Hayes Sadler selected his scapegoat. 'I think it will be found,' he wrote to London on 27 July, only two days after composing his instructions to Cubitt, 'that the attack was due to the Chief Kis[a]ka, who was not at his station when the attack took place, exceeding his instructions and collecting cattle from the Budama [Jopadhola] in the name of the Government Hut Tax.'[65]

Three weeks later, Cubitt reported that there was local resentment in Padhola about paying protectorate taxes in cattle. But to view such resentment as the principal cause of the killings was 'absurd' because 'only one hundred cattle have been received as Tax during the past two years' and the country was 'the richest that I have ever seen'.[66] In Cubitt's opinion, the principal cause of the trouble was Ganda misbehaviour, with possibly sexual associations: 'this revolt by some of the Badama,' he wrote to Hayes Sadler on 16 August, 'was caused by their long standing hatred of the

Baganda brought to a sudden head by the beating of a Chief's wife.'[67]

Cubitt recommended that several changes should be made in local administration. 'The time ... has now come,' he commented in another letter,[68]

> that we should make it clear to the natives that we are at the head of affairs and not the Kakunguru, and in order to make this evident I would recommend that we should appoint our own Agents and no longer give them the titles which they bear, such as Mukwenda, Mugema and other Uganda Saza names, given them by the Kakunguru only to keep up the impression that he is Kabaka. In the past he has been allowed to appoint his own men and I think that this should now be stopped ... the men we now appoint as our Agents might receive a refund of 5% on the tax collection.

Kakungulu's patronage should give way to a percentage rebate system.

Hayes Sadler approved of Cubitt's proposals, in much the same way as this 'charming old gentleman'[69] had approved of successive proposals put forward by Cubitt's predecessors on the same subject. 'When I reinstated the Kakunguru as Saza he was distinctly made to understand that he was in no way to interfere with Hut tax collections outside his allotment of 20 square miles unless especially desired to do so by the Collector.'[70] In October 1905, Cubitt announced his proposals to a large meeting of Kakungulu's followers at Mbale. 'On Tuesday the 17th, at 10 o'clock in the morning,' dictated Kakungulu to his diarist,

> there was a meeting attended by many Baganda and Bakedi. Mr Cubitt and Mr Ormsby announced that the campaign of Budama was caused by the Baganda, because they stole things from the Jopadhola [Badama] daily. But from now on, the names of *Sekibobo* and *Mugema* are no longer to be used. Whoever is appointed to offices will receive Rs 5 out of every Rs 100 of tax collected if he is a Muganda, Rs 10 if he is that Muganda's Mukedi assistant; he will also have three or four other men to help him in his work, and he will just be known by his own name.[71]

In other words, what seven of Kakungulu's chiefs had failed to achieve 18 months before, a rebellion among a section of their Jopadhola subjects had almost achieved on their behalf. Almost, but not quite: Ganda henceforward employed as government agents among the acephalous societies of eastern Uganda were to receive percentages, but not yet 'pounds'.

Yet it would be wrong to suggest that this partial bureaucratization was simply a response to the Padhola rebellion earlier in the year. It was also influenced by two other considerations: Kakungulu's failure to participate himself in the punitive operations against the Jopadhola – basically because of conflicting ceremonial demands associated with his wedding to yet another Ganda princess[72] – and because of 'certain implicit assumptions' held by the man whom Cubitt installed as British protectorate administrator at Mbale roughly halfway through the troubles in Padhola.[73] For, immediately before patrolling Padhola with Cubitt and the KAR during September 1905, this official had written to his family: 'We have to inflict a fine on a tribe of natives who murdered a lot of Baganda lately. The latter brought it on themselves thro' their looting so I have little sympathy for them.'[74]

## 5

Sydney Ormsby was a footloose Irishman. Before the railway reached Lake Victoria, he had been a trader and transporter for the infant administrations of both the Uganda and East African protectorates.[75] When the railway was complete he abandoned trade for administration, becoming an official in Toro and a tax-collector in Buganda.[76] By the time he became a full member of the British administration in Uganda, he could claim 'a working knowledge of five native languages spoken in the Protectorate' and 'many years experience of the country'.[77]

This experience left Ormsby with decidedly negative views of young Africans assisting European colonial administrators. 'In picking a Chief among savages,' he wrote for Coote, the British official sent to work under him in 1906,[78] 'choose an oldish man who has been looked up to for some quality & back him up for all you are worth. He will be less likely to deal unjustly than a young tho' more intelligent native. Never place implicit confidence in an interpreter & endeavour to understand sufficient of the language to chuck him off as soon as possible.'[79] Regarding missionaries, unfortunately they saw things from their point of view. 'They can only ask. We have to command obedience.'[80] Clearly such a man was likely to be hostile to Kakungulu and his followers as well as towards any Christian missionaries with whom he came into contact.

J.B. Purvis, the CMS missionary at Nabumali, sympathized more with Kakungulu than with Ormsby. Several years later, he reported that

> One of the greatest difficulties that we have had to contend with in the work at Masaba was the unsettling of the native mind and mode of life by the incoming of Government administration.
> In 1903 the actual work of dealing with the natives was done by the Muganda chief, Semei Kakungulu ... He had placed his agents in various parts of the country to rule it on lines similar to the feudal system of Uganda [meaning Buganda], and he was answerable for the general condition of the district to the British official at Budaka, situated some twenty miles from Masaba.
> It was the express wish of the then Commissioner of Uganda that the raw natives in this eastern portion of the district should be 'brought into line', as the expression goes, very gradually; and probably to make sure that the Muganda chief and his men played square with the native and the Government the official post was moved from Budaka to Mbale, a Uganda colony brought into existence by the dogged perseverance of the chief Kakungulu and his people.
> New assistant collectors were appointed from time to time, and gradually a new order of things was evolved which brought the Baganda in outlying places directly under the control of the Government officer.
> I am convinced that this step was taken for the good of the Bagishu;

but after some four years' residence in the district I am bound to say, having earnestly and carefully weighed the seriousness of the statement, that during the years of my residence which mark the introduction of law into Masaba there seems to me to have been less peace, less security of property, and more, very much more, bloodshed than during the period I lived there without direct British administration.

The principal reasons for this appalling situation were the 'method of collecting hut-tax' introduced by British protectorate administrators, and 'punitive expeditions as a means of meting out punishment'.[81]

Many of the worst atrocities occurred after Kakungulu had left Mbale in 1906.[82] But who was to be condemned for this greater bloodshed – British officials, who encouraged increased livestock seizures as temporary expedients before cash-cropping, plantation or migratory labour could be introduced as longer-term sources of tax revenue, or Kakungulu's followers acting as protectorate middlemen? Some modern commentators blame Kakungulu's followers as 'imperialists' or 'mercenaries'.[83] But that was not Purvis's view. Nor, of course, was it Kakungulu's.

In fact, Kakungulu was angry when Dashwood, an assistant collector at Mbale, described local Ganda chiefs at the time of the Padhola disturbances as 'bad people' and said that the reason they dressed so smartly was because they robbed people. 'Replace us by other chiefs, if you regard us as thieves,' was Kakungulu's reply. In Padhola his followers had been obeying Dashwood's instructions on collecting hut-taxes – that was why there were now disturbances. Dashwood ignored Kakungulu's challenge to replace all chiefs. Instead he ordered Kakungulu to write to the various forts instructing their occupants not to collect any further taxes for the time being but to remain in position until told what to do.[84] As noted already, fresh instructions were not issued until October, when Ormsby and Cubitt introduced the system of paying hut-tax collectors by percentages.

At this time Ormsby and Cubitt also visited Kakungulu privately to tell him that in future nobody in the various forts in eastern Uganda should act as his chiefs. 'And this,' continues Kakungulu's diary for 18 October 1905, 'was what Kakungulu now most wanted. He was already in the process of writing a letter explaining that they should no longer keep these people [in the forts] in his name, and they came before it was completed.' Conquering new lands and peoples with British protectorate support was clearly one thing. Acting as an intermediary implementing unpopular policies which sparked off rebellions – for which he rather than British officials would be blamed, without having any effective say in the formation of policy – was quite another. It was no wonder that, quite independently, Kakungulu was already considering the desirability of dismantling his kingdom in Bukedi.

Outwardly, however, the kingdom still appeared to be prospering. Certainly it so appeared in the eyes of Ganda chiefs elsewhere in the Uganda Protectorate. In February 1905, indeed, James Miti had told the protectorate administration of Uganda that he no longer wished to keep his advisory position in the kingdom of Bunyoro; instead he wanted to obtain a portion of territory to the west of Kakungulu's domain, which he might rule 'like Kakungulu'.[85] The saga of Kakungulu's secular divorce from the Princess Nakalema and his subsequent remarriage to the Princess Dimbwe on Ganda customary terms, must also have suggested to many that Kakungulu was getting the best of all possible worlds, CMS missionaries notwithstanding.

It so happened that Bishop Tucker and the Reverend J.B. Purvis both left Bukedi for Busoga on the very day that Dimbwe arrived from Busoga to marry her new husband.[86] What Bishop Tucker thought of this marriage is not known, but that it was taking place after divorce meant it was hardly a wedding of which he could approve. Dimbwe had been brought up as a Muslim. She was a daughter of Kalema, the former Ganda Muslim king. She was escorted to Mbale in September 1905 by Nuhu Mbogo's *Katikiro*, who was also a Muslim. Remarriage to a Muslim was a matter of controversy in Ganda Christian circles at this time.[87] Henry Wright Duta, the veteran Ganda pastor, wrote to Kakungulu warning him specifically against the wedding and suggesting future dietary problems.[88] The wedding was also unusual in that it was taking place after Kakungulu had become the first African in the Uganda Protectorate to get divorced under British law – and that had required several visits to Entebbe after Nakalema had been caught copulating with a youth from Kakungulu's following at Mbale, before the necessary authorization for remarriage under protectorate regulations was obtained.[89] The marriage itself, however, was customary. It was also expensive; so expensive, noted Kakungulu's private secretary, and involving so many different dancers, drummers, and musicians from Buganda, that even he had no idea of its total cost.[90]

According to Solomon Wamala, 90 cattle were slaughtered during the wedding celebrations.[91] Dimbwe, according to Kakungulu's diary, was 18 years old at the time; Kakungulu 37 years 'since he was born by his father Semuwemba of the Mamba clan'.[92] Dimbwe also arrived in Bukedi on the same day that Esitasio Nkambo, Kakungulu's *Katikiro*, took a number of Kakungulu's warriors off with the Budama punitive column. When Cubitt and Ormsby returned to Mbale a month later, the wedding celebrations were still in full swing.[93] What precisely Ormsby or Cubitt thought of this most public display of Kakungulu's wealth and affection is not known. However, several days before the wedding celebrations finally ended, the two protectorate administrators made their statements about payments to collectors of hut taxes being in future by percentage rebates, and collectors no longer being known as Kakungulu's chiefs.

From Ormsby's private papers, it is clear that a crucial word in his political vocabulary was 'obedience'. However, Ormsby possessed sufficient shrewdness to ensure that he exacted obedience from Kakungulu's followers before attempting to tackle Kakungulu himself.

On 21 October, he set off on a lengthy safari in company with the sub-commissioner from Jinja and many of the soldiers who had recently patrolled Padhola.[94] Malembwe Bijabiira, who had earlier been county chief *kitunzi* under Kakungulu, was reappointed *Muganda* Agent for Mbai, but severely pruned of his following and told not to press the Sebei people too severely for hut tax.[95] But not all Bijabiira's companions got off so lightly. Misa Kisaka, as we have seen, was replaced as ruler of Padhola by the young Majanga, son of the earlier paramount chief. Most of the men Kakungulu had appointed as county chiefs on Boyle's instruction in May 1904 were also replaced. 'Eriya' of Soroti was dismissed on the (surely self-contradictory) grounds of having 'no control whatsoever over the natives' and having 'used his power for his own benefit'; 'Luminze' in Serere was replaced for being 'much too young' and having 'no idea how to deal with the people by whom he is surrounded'; Luka Lukanda at Bukedea was dismissed for dacoity, and 'Yowasi' in Palisa was warned that unless his work showed distinct improvement 'his place will be given to a better man'.[96] Only Isaka Nziga at Ngora earned Ormsby's unqualified praise. 'Of all our agents in this District "Isaka" of Ngola is the most capable man appointed,' reported Ormsby. 'The roads through his district are excellent, the natives appear contented and are certainly well under control.'[97] Tax collecting apart, he came out on top in the three tests of early British rule in Uganda.

Around the same time that Ormsby replaced the county chiefs Kakungulu had appointed in May 1904, he gave back important jobs to the very chiefs those men had replaced. Sedulaka Kyesirikidde was given charge of Bugwere as regent to Wakida, his father being considered 'besotted with drink'.[98] Eriya Nsubuga was given a similar position in Padhola, when the previous adviser was dismissed early in 1907 for being 'sulky and ill-conditioned'.[99] Yosiya Mayanja was appointed *Muganda* Agent at Soroti around the same time.[100] Jafali Mayanja was appointed *Muganda* Agent in South Bugishu soon afterwards, and Bumbakali Kamya was given the task of guarding the most westerly approaches to Lake Kyoga.[101]

Having dealt with Kakungulu's chiefs, Ormsby turned upon Kakungulu. First, he requested that a protectorate surveyor mark the boundaries of Kakungulu's private estate around Mbale once and for all, a request his superiors at Jinja and Entebbe quickly approved.[102] Then he asked Kakungulu himself to hand in his guns 'for checking'.[103] But over the question of Kakungulu's guns, Ormsby complained, 'great difficulty has been experienced in getting the guns in'.[104] Moreover, while Kakungulu stalled over registering his guns, George Wilson intervened on his behalf. Now deputy commissioner at Entebbe, Wilson reminded Boyle, sub-comissioner at Jinja again, of Kakungulu's importance in the wider politics of the Uganda Protectorate. 'I am greatly desirous of your personally directing the negotiations dealing with Kakunguru's property or rather his sphere of influence,' wrote Wilson to Boyle.

> You are so thoroughly conversant with the somewhat extraordinary character of his affairs in relation to the Government and have been so obviously sympathetic with Colonel Sadler's desire to gently soften the influence of actions which from time to time emanate from the uncertainties of preliminary administrative measures, that I am diffident

in impressing upon you the need of continuing Colonel Sadler's policy. But the matter is very serious and after our experiences with Kakunguru, it is so obvious that there will be no excuse for any further unconsidered measures that we must not risk indiscretions.

There was another point. 'You well know that I hold Kakunguru's presence in the Protectorate as a welcome restriction on undue pretentions by Apolo Katikiro, who though loyal and most admirable in his conduct, has on one occasion at least exhibited aspirations suspiciously regal in tone.'[105] In other words, Kakungulu's continuance in power outside the kingdom of Buganda was a useful counter-weight to the political power of Kakungulu's old rival, Apolo Kagwa, within that kingdom. Ormsby had therefore to wait until a new commissioner arrived in Uganda before again complaining about Semei Kakungulu.

## 6

In April 1906, a new British commissioner arrived at Entebbe. Apart from four sickly years on the West Coast, Hesketh Bell had no previous experience of Africa. He was 41 and a bachelor.[106] Browsing through the library at Government House, Antigua, he thought he would have fewer frustrations politically. 'I see that there are no Councils or anything of that sort to hamper action, and that I shall have full responsibility. It will be "Empire building" on a fine scale.'[107] This illusion survived London unscathed. King Edward VII was friendly but ignorant. The Colonial Office was scarcely more helpful. 'I gathered that the people at the C.O. do not know very much about Uganda', wrote Bell. 'Up to quite recently the country was under the Foreign Office [the transfer of metropolitan responsibility to the Colonial Office took place in 1905] and was administered on rather rudimentary lines. I conclude that the Commissioner is given very wide discretionary powers and that, provided I run things smoothly, I shall be given a fairly free hand'.[108]

At Entebbe, Bell encountered reality. Within days of arriving there, secretariat officials told him that the policy in Uganda was 'to run the territory, so far as possible, as a purely native state and to see whether the people are really able to govern their country with honesty and justice.' So much for empire-building on a fine scale. However, climatically and culturally there were compensations. 'Having imagined that I should find in Uganda nothing but primitive conditions, I was greatly surprised to see, all round me, evidence of comfort and refinement.' In May 1906 he attended a garden party with 25 Englishwomen present, 'dressed very smartly and with complexions not often seen in the tropics'. Also in May at Entebbe, he welcomed Baganda chiefs who came from Kampala on bicycles and in rickshaws as well as by foot. In the same month, Semei Kakungulu came to see him by lake steamer.[109]

Kakungulu was still working as county chief at Mbale at this time. The protectorate administration had reduced his power considerably by separating much of his following in Bukedi from protectorate service. But despite these political defections (for that is how Kakungulu personally regarded them), he still commanded a sufficiently large clientage to cause British officials concern. In April 1906, when news of the new commissioner's arrival reached Mbale, Kakungulu said he would pay his respects in person. On 27 April, Alexander Boyle telegraphed this information to Entebbe, and ten days later Kakungulu left Mbale on the first leg of his journey.[110] On the same day, Sydney Ormsby posted off another letter of complaint.

Officially writing about the delimitation of Kakungulu's estate at Mbale, he took the opportunity to comment upon the 'false position' Kakungulu occupied in the district of which he was Collector. 'It seems a great pity that a man of Kakungulu's ability should be wasted in his present position,' wrote Ormsby. 'As a Saza [county chief] among the Baganda, I have no doubt he would prove invaluable, but here he is quite useless proving a hindrance rather than a help to the Collector owing to his inability to accept his altered position.' To strengthen his case, Ormsby argued that Kakungulu's personal following was now quite small: 'not more than 500 Baganda'. 'The Baganda are gradually leaving Bukedi as they can no longer exist by raiding and only return on a legitimate trading trip.'[111] If Kakungulu's following was now so small, one inevitably asks, how could he prove a great hindrance?

Nevertheless, Ormsby had played a strong hand on paper and Alexander Boyle, sub-commissioner still at Jinja, supported him. A few weeks before, Boyle and Ormsby had been on safari together. 'I fully concur with Mr Ormsby's remarks on the subject of the false position occupied by Kakunguru,' Boyle now wrote to Bell. 'At present he is paid £200 to do little or nothing and owing to the people surrounding him it is impossible to make use of him.' Boyle suggested, doubtless with Wilson's instructions in mind, that Kakungulu 'be given a position more suitable to his ability which is undoubtedly of a high order, and which would give him an enlarged sphere of influence.'[112]

Bell was aghast. Overawed as he was by his new post, and inclined as he was to trust secretariat officials and to leave the *status quo* undisturbed, he queried this suggestion. 'What sort of post could such a man fill? Has he a sound claim against the Government? I doubt the advisability of putting a man who appears to be so turbulent and to have rather a "swelled head" in the neighbourhood of Mbale !' He ordered a special report on the subject.[113]

Stanley Tompkins reported to Bell about a fortnight later. Kakungulu, commented Tompkins, 'did a lot of fighting for the British Government under General (then Captain) Lugard' and 'rendered the greatest assistance to the Government' during the troubles of 1897. 'He was not appointed a Regent, and Uganda [meaning Buganda] was not large enough to hold both Sir Apolo Kagwa and himself.' Since receiving the commissioner's instruction to report upon the matter, he had consulted Alexander Boyle. Boyle suggested 'that the Kakunguru could be usefully employed as President of the Usoga Lukiko, and I submit this as an excellent suggestion.'[114]

The suggestion was considered excellent for several reasons. These were not recorded officially at the time, but are clear from what the British protectorate officials concerned wrote later and in private. First, Kakungulu could not be dismissed outright because of the continuing danger of rebellion. He had an unknown number of guns under his command and was thought to possess 'great stores' of buried ivory with which he could purchase many more.[115] In Bell's own words, 'In spite of his earlier loss of dignity the Kakunguuru was still one of the most powerful natives in the Protectorate and it was believed that he could, at any time, raise a large following and create a serious situation.'[116] Kakungulu was also believed to be touchy as well as powerful. 'When I arrived here in 1906, I was informed that he was nourishing a feeling of deep grievance against the Government on account of his unmerited degradation' from his earlier position of paramount power in Bukedi.[117] If Kakungulu was not handled delicately, there really did seem every possibility of yet another anti-colonial rebellion in Uganda.

Ormsby had suggested transferring Kakungulu back to Buganda, but that was impracticable. Several years before, Kakungulu had refused to accept a similar transfer and caused great trouble by 'retiring' from protectorate employment altogether. As Wilson had recently hinted to Boyle, that mistake should not be repeated. There was also Wilson's other point about Kakungulu acting as a counterweight to Kagwa, chief minister of the Buganda kingdom. So Kakungulu could not be dismissed from protectorate office for fear of provoking rebellion; he could not be allowed to retire lest other complications ensue – he would have to be promoted. But where in the protectorate could he be promoted? Not in Bukedi. Not in any similarly decentralized area where he might yet again grow into an overmighty subject. Not in Buganda, where Sir Apolo Kagwa was unlikely to prove cooperative in providing him with a suitable position. Not in the other kingdoms of Ankole, Bunyoro or Toro, where by this time other Ganda chiefs were advisers and difficult to dislodge. No wonder Stanley Tompkins considered the presidency of the Busoga district council 'an excellent suggestion' in June 1906.

Now the problem arose of persuading Kakungulu to accept this position. In March 1906 Kakungulu had been told of the new commissioner's impending arrival. In May he met him twice. By Kakungulu's account, at the first meeting Bell said, 'I have heard a lot about your name and what you have done for the government. In fact, this is the reason I sent for you. Now you can go back to where you are staying for the night and tomorrow morning we shall meet again and I shall say goodbye to you formally.' The next day, very little happened. 'After words, the commissioner presented me with a big mirror, a good watch, and a lantern. Then he told me to go back to my country and said that he would be happy to visit me there when God allowed.' The next day, Kakungulu set off for Bukedi.

At Jinja, Boyle told Kakungulu about his promotion. 'We would like you to come and help us at Jinja because the European protectorate officials are tired of the Basoga, who will not do what they are told.' To that, Kakungulu answered: 'It is not possible for me to leave my people

Plate 13. *Ganda canoe and British steamer on Lake Victoria in the 1900s.* (From C.W. Hattersley *The Baganda at Home* (1909) p. 148)

in Bukedi and come to Jinja.' Boyle replied that the promotion had been approved by the new commissioner shortly after Kakungulu's departure from Entebbe and Kakungulu's following at Mbale would not necessarily disperse upon his acceptance of it. 'All that we are suggesting is that you should appoint a deputy to rule your followers in Bukedi when you come to Jinja.' It was shrewdly put, but still Kakungulu demurred. Only after another visit to Entebbe, and a hint that if he refused the promotion another chief would be placed over him, did Kakungulu agree. Even then, the deal nearly fell through when Kakungulu discovered that protectorate surveyors had reduced the size of his Mbale estate.

To this, Kakungulu objected.

> Then the commissioner and sub-commissioner talked together in their own language. Eventually the commissioner said that the sub-commissioner had thought that since there were so many people in the area, your deputy would not be able to administer them all properly; that is why the area of your responsibility has been reduced.
>
> I replied, 'Sir, it has not been my own desire to leave Bukedi; this suggestion has come from you. I do not see any reason why I should lose my area of influence at Mbale. Perhaps there is some reason on the protectorate side?'
>
> 'There is no reason to worry you. We can negotiate over these things between ourselves; you can get some *mailo* in Busoga to compensate for your loss of land in Bukedi.'
>
> I then said, 'If that is the case, I shall accept what the protectorate administration proposes.'[118]

The British had got their way.

Kakungulu returned to Mbale to pack up. In July 1906 he took up residence at Jinja. On 28 July, he again greeted the commissioner's lake steamer. 'As soon as we landed,' wrote Bell subsequently,

> Kakunguru advanced to meet me, and I was at once impressed by the personality of this man. His great height, dignified demeanour and pleasant countenance marked him out at once as being of greatly superior breed to the ordinary folk. Although he saluted me in the usual Uganda fashion, by kneeling before me and taking my hand between his, there was not the slightest sign of servility in his salutation ... a person of much natural courtesy and ready wit.[119]

# *Notes*

1. 'Memorandum by HMC', 16 January 1904, A/10/3, ESA.
2. Y. Wajja, *Munno* (1933), p. 222.
3. *Ibid.*
4. T. Kagwa, 'Kakungulu Omuzira Omuwanguzi', unpublished MS in Makerere University Library (MUL), Vol. 2, p. 30.
5. Paulo Kagwa, 'Kakungulu Omuzira wa Uganda', unpublished MS in Makerere University Library (MUC), p. 64.
6. Watson to Boyle, 10 February 1904, A/10/2, ESA.
7. Sadler to Boyle, 15 February 1904, A/11/2, ESA.
8. Boyle, 15 February 1904, A/10/3, ESA.
9. Watson to Boyle, 9 March 1904, A/10/3, ESA.
10. Boyle to Sadler, 14 March 1904, A/10/3, ESA.
11. Sadler to Boyle, , 23 March 1904, A 11/2, ESA.
12. Watson to Boyle, 5 April 1904, A/10/3, ESA.
13. *Ibid.*
14. Sadler to Boyle, 17 April 1904, A//11/2, ESA.
15. Boyle to Sadler, 7 May 1904, A/10/3, ESA.
16. Boyle, 27 May 1904, A/6/17, ESA
17. Boyle to Sadler, 7 May 1904, A/10/3, ESA.
18. Kakungulu, *Diary*, Vol. 1, pp. 75–7, KP, provides the fullest account; P. Kagwa, 'Omuzira', pp. 65–6, describes it in a more confused manner.
19. Kakungulu, *Diary*, Vol. 1, p. 75, translated.
20. Watson to Boyle, 14 March 1904, A/10/3, ESA.
21. P. Kagwa, 'Omuzira', p. 60.
22. Solomon Wamala, 'Obulamu bwa Semei Kakungulu', unpublished MS in MUL, p. 213.
23. Kakungulu, *Diary*, Vol. 1, pp. 75–7.
24. *Ibid.*
25. Boyle to Sadler, 7 May 1904, A/10/3, ESA.
26. Boyle to Wilson, 8 October 1904, A/10/3, ESA.
27. Watson to Boyle, 16 July 1904, A/27/6, ESA.
28. Watson to Boyle, 7 August 1904. A/27/6, ESA.
29. Boyle to Sadler, 15 August 1904, A/27/6, ESA..
30. Kakungulu, *Diary*, Vol. 2, p.1.
31. *Ibid.*, pp. 5–7.
32. *Ibid.*
33. Besides Kakungulu's diary, Paulo Kagwa, 'Omuzira', p. 65, provides a list. Nziga returned from Ethiopia in August.
34. J.J. Willis, 'Recollections', unpublished MS in Royal Commonwealth Society Library, p. 33; for 'Ketosh' here, read 'southern Bugisu' nowadays.
35. Boyle to Entebbe, 8 October 1904, A/27/6, ESA. This file contains correspondence on these punitive expeditions, summaries of which were forwarded to London on 17 November 1904 (PRO: Fo 2/860).
36. Watson, 8 October 1904, encl. Boyle to Entebbe, 16 November 1904, A/10/4, ESA.
37. Kakungulu to Boyle, 9 November 1904; copy in Kakungulu, *Diary*, Vol. 2, pp. 11, 38–9.
38. Boyle to Entebbe, 16 November 1904, A/10/4, ESA.
39. Boyle to Wilson, 8 October 1904, A/27/04, ESA.
40. Kakungulu, *Diary*, Vol. 2, p. 1. The other missionaries were J.J. Willis and J.B. Purvis.
41. *CMS Report 1904–1905*, p. 127; J.B. Purvis, 'Masaba and its people', *Uganda Notes* September 1904.
42. Tucker to London, 28 July 1904, CMS Archives G3A7/1904b.
43. *Ibid.*
44. Kakungulu, *Diary*, Vol. 2, p. 37.
45. The day was 25 June 1905. The principal sources from which this account is drawn are: (i)'Correspondence relating to the Budama raid', A/27/6, ESA; Kakungulu, *Diary*,

Vol. 2, pp. 81–3, 98–112; P. Kagwa, 'Omukwano gwa Kabaka Mwanga', unpublished MS in MUL, pp. 76–8, and 'Omuzira', pp. 71–2, 88–9; and interviews with A. Oboth-Aripa and P.C. Ofono. I am indebted to Professor B.A. Ogot for early advice: his own forthcoming book will be a major contribution to this subject.

46. Purvis to Tucker, 17 July 1905; copy in ESA, A/27/6.

47. Purvis to Dashwood, 22 June 1905, ESA, A/27/6.

48. Purvis to Tucker, 17 July 1905, ESA, A/27/6.

49. Dashwood, 10 July 1905, ESA, A/27/6.

50. Kakungulu, *Diary*, Vol. 2, p. 106, reporting Cubitt's enquiries in Padhola on 27 July 1905.

51. *Ibid.*

52. P. Kagwa, 'Omukwano', p. 78.

53. Cubitt to Entebbe, 16 August 1905, A/27/6, reporting testimony of Jopadhola prisoners he had interrogated.

54. *Ibid.*

55. See above p. 160.

56. See the seminal studies of T.O. Ranger, 'The role of Ndebele and Shona religious authorities in the Rebellions of 1896 and 1897' in eds E. Stokes and R. Brown, *The Zambezian Past* (Manchester 1966); J. Iliffe, 'The organization of the Maji Maji rebellion', *Journal of African History* 8 (1967), pp. 495–512; and Ranger, 'The death of Chaminuka: spirit mediums, nationalism and guerilla war in Zimbabwe', *African Affairs* 81 (1982), pp. 349–69.

57. 'Report on Punitive operations in Budama', encl. Ward to Entebbe, 16 October 1905, A/27/6.

58. *Ibid.*

59. Cubitt, 17 October 1905, A/27/6.

60. *Ibid.*

61. *Ibid.*

62. See A.W. Southall, 'Padhola: comparative social structure' in Proc. E.A.I.S.R conference, Makerere, January 1957, p. 5; M. Twaddle, 'Politics in Bukedi', Ph.D. dissertation, London University, 1967, Chapter 3.

63. Sadler to Cubitt, 25 July 1905, A/27/6.

64. *Ibid.*

65. Sadler to London, 27 July 1905; copy in A/27/6, ESA.

66. Cubitt, 16 August 1905, A/27/6, ESA.

67. *Ibid.*

68. 22 September 1905, A/27/6, ESA.

69. The view of C.W. Hobley, *Kenya from Chartered Company to Crown Colony* (London 1929), p. 135.

70. Sadler to Cubitt, 2 September 1905, EPMP 210/8 (currently [1992] kept with ESA).

71. Kakungulu, *Diary*, Vol. 2, p. 98.

72. *Ibid.*

73. *Uganda Notes*, August 1905.

74. Ormsby to family, 12 September 1905, Ormsby Papers (OP).

75. Ormsby to family, 30 September 1896, OP; E.B. Haddon, interview at Cambridge, 3 March 1965.

76. Sadler to Ormsby, 11 March 1904, OP.

77. Ormsby to London, 7 June 1904, FO/2/862, PRO.

78. 'Notes on Native administration', pencilled notes in Ormsby's handwriting on inside front cover of J.M. Coote, *Diary*, seen through courtesy of H.B. Thomas; Coote's *Diary* is now at Rhodes House, Oxford.

79. *Ibid.*

80. *Ibid.*

81. J.B. Purvis, *Through Uganda to Mount Elgon* (London 1909), pp. 258–60.

82. See M. Twaddle 'Decentralized violence and collaboration in early colonial Uganda', in eds A. Porter and R. Holland, *Theory and Practice in the History of European Expansion Overseas: Essays in Honour of R.E. Robinson* (London 1988), pp. 71–85.

83. S. Lwanga-Lunyiigo, 'The colonial roots of internal conflict' in ed. K. Rupesinghe,

*Conflict Resolution in Uganda* (Oslo 1989), pp. 26–7; J. Vincent, *Teso in Transformation* (Berkeley 1982), pp. 47, 96.

84. Kakungulu, *Diary*, Vol. 2, p. 85.
85. I am indebted for this information to Professor E. Steinhart.
86. Kakungulu, *Diary*, Vol. 2, p. 94.
87. See H.B. Hansen, *Mission, Church and State in a Colonial Setting: Uganda: 1890–1925* (London 1984), pp. 260–304 for the definitive account.
88. Kakungulu, *Diary*, Vol. 2, p. 99.
89. The divorce was finalized on 3 February 1905 and the second volume of Kakungulu's diaries reproduces Judge Ennis's letter on this, p. 95.
90. Kakungulu, *Diary*, Vol. 2, pp. 100–1.
91. Wamala, 'Obulamu'.
92. Kakungulu, *Diary*, Vol. 2, p. 100.
93. *Ibid.*, pp. 95, 99–100.
94. Ormsby, 30 November 1905, EPMP 210/8; Kakungulu, *Diary*, Vol. 2, p. 108; P. Kagwa, 'Omukwano', p. 84.
95. Ormsby, 30 November 1905, EPMP 210/8.
96. *Ibid.*
97. *Ibid.*
98. Boyle, 10 January 1907, SMP 84/07; Ormsby, 19 February 1907, SMP 279/07, ESA.
99. Boyle, 12 March 1907, SMP 309/07, ESA.
100. T. Kagwa, 'Kakungulu Omuzira Omuwanguzi', Vol. 2, p. 49; Simioni Waswa, 'Kakunguru mu Bukedi' unpublished ms, MUL, para 112.
101. *Ibid.*; D. Musoke, *Ebyafayo bya Bugisu* [cited p. 157], p. 26.
102. Ormsby, 30 November 1905, EPMP 210/8; Cubitt, 18 December 1905, and Boyle, 19 December 1905, A/10/5, ESA.
103. Ormsby, 30 November 1905.
104. *Ibid.*
105. Wilson to Boyle, confidential, 8 January 1906, EPMP 210/8.
106. H.H. Bell, *Glimpses of a Governor's Life* (London, n.d.), p. 92.
107. *Ibid.*
108. *Ibid.*, pp. 96–8.
109. *Ibid.*, pp. 111–14.
110. Boyle, telegram, 27 April 1906, A/10/5, ESA; Kakungulu, *Diary*, Vol. 2, p. 129.
111. Ormsby, 8 May 1906, encl. Boyle, 17 May 1906, SMP 319/06, ESA.
112. Boyle, 17 May 1906.
113. Minute by Bell, 26 May 1906, SMP 319/06.
114. Minute by Tompkins, 8 June 1906, SMP 319/06.
115. Bell, *Glimpses*, p. 127.
116. Bell to London, 29 November 1906, copy in SMP 1760/08, ESA. Writing to a 'Dearest little Auntie' on 25 June 1906, Bell even remarked that 'He could raise an army in an hour, by a single beat of his war drum, and has to be watched rather carefully': Bell Papers (BP), RCS Library, London.
117. Bell, 29 November 1906, (BP), RCS Library, London.
118. 'Ebigambo bya Busoga', statement in Luganda by Kakungulu (1924), encl. with report by J.M. Gray in 1924, SMP 1760/06, ESA; Boyle, telegram. 18 June 1906, EPMP 235/08. Bell also wrote to his aunt on 25 June 1906 that 'Kakunguru also came back from Entebbe with me [to Jinja] in the "Mackinnon". I had made him a happy man, for I had just consented to add 30 square miles to his territory'. BP, RCS Library.
119. Bell, *Glimpses*, p. 127.

# Eight

# Transfer to Busoga
# 1906–13

## 1

Scenically, Busoga resembles Buganda. Flat-topped hills covered by equatorial forest alternate with valleys choked with papyrus reeds in the southern parts of both areas, just as both northern sections are characterized by drier ridges of land divided from one another by seasonal swamps. Bananas also proliferate in southern Busoga as luxuriantly as upon the western slopes of Mount Elgon or along other shores of Lake Victoria. There are close links, too, between the southern dialect of the Lusoga language and the kind of Luganda spoken close to the River Nile. Culturally as well as ecologically, Kakungulu could therefore expect to feel at home.

Politically also he was no stranger. While *Mulondo*, Kakungulu had had many contacts with Busoga. Immediately before becoming *Kimbugwe*, he had also accompanied Captain Williams on the expedition which installed Miro as effective ruler of Kigulu. Immediately after resigning his Kimbugweship, too, he had exercised an informal paramountcy over several Soga principalities from Bugerere. In 1898, as we saw in Chapter 4, he had nearly succeeded in transforming this essentially informal sway into a formal dominance; but manoeuvring within the Ganda chiefly class at the time had prejudiced his success, and his chances in Busoga had been prejudiced still further by the local protectorate agent, on the ground that British power would suffer once any Ganda chief was installed as an intermediary.[1]

In 1906, opposition on the second score existed no longer. William Grant was now retired from protectorate service, and his successor as British sub-commissioner at Jinja had anxieties of another kind. Grant had been preoccupied with establishing British control in a political field in which Ganda chiefs earlier played competing roles with Nyoro leaders

221

as enslavers of the Soga as well as referees of their succession disputes. When Ganda chiefs continued to demand tribute from Busoga in the late 1890s, Grant inevitably viewed them as rivals rather than allies. But in 1900 the situation changed. In that year Ganda chiefs formally abandoned their claims upon Busoga under the Uganda Agreement, in return for greater powers for chiefs within Buganda itself, Nyoro chiefs having been finally defeated in the previous year, with the capture of Kabalega along with Mwanga. The British task in Busoga now changed from control to administration.

This task Grant tackled in two ways: amalgamating the multifarious chieftaincies of pre-colonial Busoga into 14 chiefdoms for purposes of taxation, and establishing a central court of justice at Jinja. But before Grant really had a chance to implement either policy fully, he retired from British protectorate employment in Uganda because of ill-health.[2]

Alexander Boyle had a very different disposition. Grant had started his East African career as an IBEAC hand, Boyle as a protectorate clerk. Grant had become fluent in several Ugandan languages, Boyle still had only a smattering of Swahili. Grant lived with an African wife, Boyle was one of the first British officials with a non-African wife. In early 1903, Grant still regarded Ganda chiefs as potential obstacles to British control of local affairs. At the end of the same year, Boyle was already employing some of them in the task of administering Busoga more efficiently.

One such was Salimu Bwagu, Sadler's interpreter at Mbale. Another was Ali Lwanga. Both were Muslims who had abandoned Buganda during the 1890s upon the entrenchment in power of Christian chiefs there like Apolo Kagwa and Semei Kakungulu. Lwanga had sought refuge in Bula-mogi county, where he was to be remembered for his skill in manufacturing soap and for his popularizing of Swahili foods.[3] Bwagu worked initially as a caravan leader to the East African coast, then as an interpreter for William Grant. But in 1897 his career had imploded. This was because, as the rebellion of Mwanga II in Buganda coalesced with elements of the Sudanese mutiny in Busoga to form a broader rising against British rule, it became clear British policy to exclude Muslims from administrative positions in Busoga.[4] Bwagu was arrested upon suspicion of conspiracy,[5] and Lwanga confined himself to cattle trading now that work interpreting for William Grant was no longer possible.[6] Yet within weeks of taking over from Grant, Boyle was employing Bwagu as an interpreter as well as a tax-collector around Jinja, and Lwanga as a second interpreter in the district office.[7]

Partly this was sheer ignorance of their previous careers by a British official unacquainted with local politics. Partly, it was the politics of deferential persuasion again, played now by Ganda Muslims who remained Ganda as well as Muslim. But, more generally, it was also the work of a British official, whose predecessor had basically solved the problem of colonial control but bequeathed the dilemmas of colonial administration. Now the previous loyalties of local allies were of less concern than their utility. Ultimately Boyle pinned his hopes for a really efficient set of African intermediaries in Busoga upon 'a new generation of Chiefs with ideas more enlightened and minds less besotted in youth with hemp and drink.'[8] But until that elite emerged from the new schools being established by CMS missionaries and their Roman Catholic counterparts throughout the Uganda Protectorate,[9] Boyle was ready to employ anybody who proved efficient. When reviewing his first year at Jinja, Boyle divided the credit for the progress made thus far in Busoga equally between 'the more progressive chiefs' and 'the traders'.[10] The former all happened to be Ganda. The latter were mostly South Asians.

In the last chapter we saw how South Asian traders concentrated around Kakungulu's enclosure at Mbale in increasing numbers after the railway reached Lake Victoria from the East African coast. When Kakungulu moved to Jinja, Mbale was still the largest urban centre in eastern Uganda, serving this railway at one remove. Jinja was not to become a substantial township until several years later, when a further feeder railway would be opened linking Jinja to new cotton-producing areas around Lake Kyoga. Before this happened the leading centres of South Asian settlement in Busoga were Iganga, where some 20 merchants were established as early as 1904, and Kamuli, which accommodated a further 15.[11] From these centres South Asian traders spread throughout Busoga, spending a fortnight here, living for three months there, everywhere creating 'a want among the natives for clothing other than barkcloth'[12] and paying 'a fair price for any marketable produce'.[13] Indeed, sometimes prices seemed too fair for the local British official: 'the price of chillies', remarked Alexander Boyle in April 1905, 'had reached such a high water mark that it was enabling the natives to obtain their tax with a mimimum of labour and in time would probably have done great harm to the cheap labour market on which planters in this province will have to depend' in future.[14] He therefore cut the maximum price of chillies in Busoga arbitrarily by half.[15]

For the administrative as opposed to the economic future of Busoga, Boyle put his faith in Christian missionary education. In 1904 £81 was voted towards the cost of a hostel for Basoga boarders at Mengo High School, Kampala, to which were sent young princes like Nadiope and Oboja, the two subsequent rulers of Bugabula and Kigulu counties.[16] Two years later, another CMS high school was opened in Jinja itself where, upon a diet of Scripture, English grammar, and a daily swim in the River Nile, 26 boys were taught 'of the Saviour, and habits of truthfulness and cleanliness'.[17] Later high schools to educate future chiefs in Busoga were established at Iganga, Kaliro, and Kamuli.[18]

In December 1905, Boyle decided upon the administrative framework within which this future elite would operate. Professor Cohen has discovered 68 principalities in pre-British Busoga, and illustrated many aspects of their corporate life.[19] William Grant reduced this diversity during the 1890s, and Alexander Boyle now proposed an even smaller set of amalgamations:[20]

That there be nine sazas [counties] instead of 14 as formerly, the five sazaships being done away with by being absorbed into the other nine.

| | | | |
|---|---|---|---|
| 1. Miro | [Kigulu county] | Kasaja | to be absorbed into Luba |
| 2. Tabingwa | [Luuka] | Makoba | to be absorbed into Luba |
| 3. Gabula | [Bugabula] | Nyago | to be absorbed into Luba |
| 4. Sebondo | [Bulamogi] | Mkono | to be absorbed into Miro |
| 5. Nanyumba | [Bunyuli] | Kibambi | to be absorbed into |
| 6. Luba | [Bunya] | | Lusoboya. |
| 7. Menia | [Bugweri] | | |
| 8. Musitwa | [Bukooli] | | |
| 9. Lusoboya | [Butembe] | | |

These newly consolidated chiefdoms are shown in the map below. Apart from Busiki, which later became a full county, this division was to be followed for the remainder of the period of British protectorate rule during the twentieth century. Boyle proposed that it should come into operation on 1 April 1906.[21]

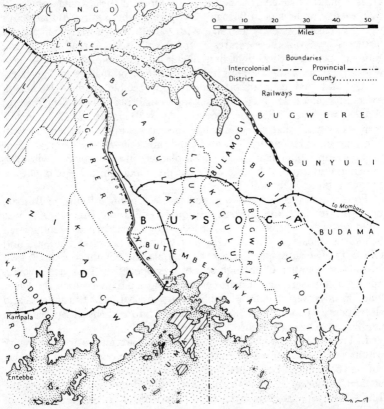

Map 11 *Busoga District.* (From map in M.C. Fallers, *The Eastern Lacustrine Bantu* (1960))

Grant's administrative amalgamations in Busoga were reduced in number by Boyle before Kakungulu became President of the Busoga *Lukiko* later in 1906. It is therefore misleading for Busoga's leading anthropologist to suggest that it was Kakungulu who was principally responsible for 'the amalgamation of the many small kingdoms' of Busoga district into a single integrated structure, and to say that this 'innovation' of Kakungulu's met with 'surprisingly little resistance' from the Soga themselves.[22] Another innovation is accredited to Kakungulu by the same authority with rather more justice. This was the 'adoption of Ganda political units' throughout Grant's and Boyle's newly integrated administrative structure. 'Although he ruled for only eight years, Kakungulu's forcefulness, his deep conviction of the superiority of the Ganda, and the support which he received from the British, served to implant the Ganda system so firmly that Soga have difficulty in recalling earlier conditions.'[23] The same scholar also ascribes to Kakungulu a third crucial administrative change in early colonial Busoga, about which we shall have more to say shortly too – 'the division of each chief's area into his *bwesengeze*, or personal estate, and his *butongole*, or area of official jurisdiction'.[24] Nonetheless, in considerable contrast to Bukedi, the basic British framework for local administration in Busoga had already been decided upon in essentials by British protectorate officials before Kakungulu appeared on the scene.

William Grant had also established a special district court at Jinja. But it did not work properly.[25] Alexander Boyle therefore asked Sydney Ormsby to report upon it in 1905. Ormsby thought it was 'doing excellent work in showing the Chiefs what justice really is', but that its work was 'almost nullified owing to the lack of power in carrying out its judgements'.[26] This diagnosis struck Boyle as unhelpful,[27] as too did Ormsby's suggested remedy: stationing a second British administrator at Jinja in order to cure this 'lack of power' among the Basoga.[28] As it happened, Ormsby was posted to Mbale instead of Jinja, and the Busoga district council and court continued unchanged until Semei Kakungulu became its president.

Boyle liked Kakungulu. However insolent Kakungulu might have appeared to British protectorate officials at Mbale, he was always careful to behave deferentially towards their superiors at Jinja and Entebbe. To Boyle Kakungulu was friendly as well as deferential. 'My present abode', complained Boyle to Entebbe in 1904, 'is in a very precarious state, so much so that Kakunguru implored me to go out of it'.[29] Boyle was also impressed by Kakungulu's encouragement of cash-cropping in Bukedi, just as he was dismayed by the lack of it displayed by Soga chiefs.[30] The presidency of the Busoga district council was a role demanding diligence. It was equally a role which could be presented to Kakungulu as being more influential than it really was because Kakungulu would wear the same 'boosties' as the contemporary kings of Nkore, Toro, and Bunyoro,[31] and he would appear to have comparable status in official photographs.

Retrospectively, Kakungulu's promotion to Busoga seems a remarkably neat decision. In Busoga, British colonial control had been established by

1906, but the new order was proving economically difficult. In Bukedi, the problems were reversed: raising revenue presented fewer difficulties than securing political paramountcy while Kakungulu remained in position there. By moving Kakungulu from Mbale to Jinja, Boyle resolved both problems. But to analyse the transfer principally in these terms, is to confuse effects with causes. When the decision was made, the unattractiveness of Kakungulu's remaining in Bukedi clearly weighed more heavily than the attractiveness of employing him in Busoga. However, Boyle was prepared to take a chance, because Kakungulu was unlikely to cause as much trouble in Busoga as in Bukedi, and personally he liked Kakungulu. At Mbale, Kakungulu was a political nuisance. In Jinja, Kakungulu could be separated from his following and neutralized.

There is a further point. On the British side, these calculations would have been inconceivable if Busoga had not by now been firmly under British control; if its principal chiefly structural components had not already been decided upon; if Luganda had not already become effectively the language of subordinate administration; if Ganda assistants unattached to Kakungulu by either clientage or religion had not already been working with Boyle in Busoga; or if a Ganda-educated successor elite of chiefs had not already started to be trained in CMS high schools. Later suggestions that Kakungulu himself was the author of all these circumstances invert cause and effect. There is another point. *After* Kakungulu resigned his presidency of the Busoga district council, Busoga would be caught up in a sharpening of communal sentiment, to such an extent that Semei Kakungulu would subsequently become a symbolic representation of Ganda cultural aggression, and his years of power in Busoga accredited with more creativity than any other period of his public career.

Empirically, this is absurd. To be sure, Kakungulu did prove administratively creative during his years of service in Busoga, much to the initial pleasure and ultimate embarrassment of the British protectorate authorities who promoted him there. But we must analyse this administrative creativity, not retrospectively through the distortions of subsequent ethnic sentiment refracted in later participant anthropological studies, but contemporaneously through study of what quickly became one of Kakungulu's principal concerns at the time: the politics of survival.

## 2

When Kakungulu went to Bukedi he took several thousand followers with him. When he was transferred to Busoga, he brought less than 100.

> These are the few prominent ones who came with him. Yowasi Mivule, who became his katikiro when he reached Jinja. Temuteo M. Kagwa, Kauta, who was later put in charge of the porters in Jinja township. Musa Damulira, his secretary. Mikaeri Kiwanuka. Altogether there were 60 men.[32]

Mivule was a staunch Protestant who joined Kakungulu when his former patron in Buddu requested him to become a Roman Catholic and he refused.[33] He was also one of Kakungulu's most faithful followers in Bukedi, holding a middle-grade office there immediately before Kakungulu's promotion to Busoga.[34] Temuteo Kagwa was Kakungulu's classificatory nephew in the Lungfish clan of Buganda. Damulira had worked for Kakungulu previously as his private secretary in Bukedi. Mikaeri Kiwanuka was later to become a county chief in eastern Uganda. The names come from a chronicle dictated by Temuteo Kagwa, the only one of Kakungulu's vernacular lives, incidentally, to say anything about his career between 1906 and 1913.

Even this chronicler found it difficult to depict those years in heroic terms. Prowess as a hunter during youth, daring as a warrior in early manhood, brilliance as a general in campaigns against Buvuma and Bunyoro during maturity, and everlasting fame as the conqueror of Bukedi in early middle age – these were themes easily assimilable to the heroic traditions of both oral poetry and the new Christian historiography inaugurated by Apolo Kagwa's *Bakabaka Bebuganda*. But now Kakungulu was a British-employed bureaucrat. His principal tasks were to run a council of uninterested chiefs without a sizeable following of his own to back up his efforts; to dispense justice before an apathetic court; and to encourage sufficient cash crops in order to make British administration in Busoga financially self-supporting – but not so many that the possible future welfare of European planters there might be unduly prejudiced, as the 'great crash' of 1929–33, which was to so prejudice Uganda Protectorate officials against planters and in favour of peasants, still lay a quarter-century ahead.

Besides the character of the job, there were problems with colleagues. Some, as we have noted, were Ganda. A few were fairly wealthy already. Most had alliances with local big men: none were indebted for their positions to Semei Kakungulu. Insofar as they acknowledged any Ganda figure other than themselves, it was Apolo Kagwa. Salim Bwagu was indebted to Kagwa for saving his life during the 1890s in much the same way that Muslims in Bukedi like Yusufu Byakuno had been indebted to Kakungulu.[35] Kagwa was friendly with a Ganda clerk in the district office who sent him confidential reports during Kakungulu's period of office.[36] Kagwa also had influence with young notables from Busoga then being schooled in Buganda, even marrying one of his daughters to the most notable of them all, Nadiope of Bugabula. Soon after settling down as President of the Busoga District Council, Kakungulu must have felt as much counter-balanced by Kagwa there as himself balancing Kagwa in Buganda.

In response, Kakungulu initially played the traditional politics of deferential persuasion. 'Kakungulu killed a leopard. Sent to Mr. Boyle.' 'Kakungulu killed a leopard. Sent to Mr Grant [Thomas, William Grant's brother who became collector at Jinja after William's retirement].' 'Mr Boyle gave an order to the Lukiko that Kakungulu is to be supplied with labourers every month and food every day.' Thus three entries within four days in the *Record of Collector's baraza, Jinja station* for November 1906.[37] The entries were typical.

Some problems also proved easier for Kakungulu to resolve than others. Over-production of saleable produce was one. Within 20 years the population of Busoga had fallen drastically. Sleeping sickness caused most of this decrease, indirectly as well as directly. Since sleeping sickness killed more men than women in Busoga, and because men played crucial roles in subsistence agriculture alongside women, food production suffered much more in Busoga than in Buganda. Siphoning off remaining able-bodied men to work on forced labour projects in order to pay new taxes hardly helped matters. Nor did declaring predatory pigs to be 'protected game'.[38] A year after Kakungulu arrived at Jinja, the rains failed yet again. A famine ensued, following the earlier one of 1898–1901 and the immediately succeeding sleeping sickness epidemic. In the course of this second famine in Busoga, 'many thousands of men, women and children perished'.[39]

Because of the famine, even the modest targets for cash-cropping set by British protectorate officials could not be sustained. For this Kakungulu could not be blamed. It was, in several senses of the phrase, an act of God. Concerning the administration of justice, on the other hand, he was rightly considered to be more accountable to his British superiors.

> In the days before his coming, people were harshly treated in court, and sometimes beaten by askaris. Kakungulu said that any person who thrashed another without reason would be liable to six months' imprisonment. 'People are not to be mishandled before I see them', he said,

reports his chronicler.[40] It was a just compliment. A British protectorate official by no means inclined to pay Kakungulu unnecessarily favourable compliments, admitted that only rarely was there any appeal against the 'weekly baraza presided over by the Mganda chief Kakunguru'. Generally his judgements do indeed appear to have been 'impartial and just'.[41]

Alexander Boyle was even more complimentary. From being a meeting of persons 'from whom it was most difficult to obtain a real opinion' and who 'generally said whatever they believed the Collector wished', the Busoga district council had been transformed into 'a real Council prepared to express the views of the country generally and anxious to make any reforms which they believe to be for the welfare of the district.'[42] Considering his original reasons for transferring Kakungulu to Busoga, this transformation must have struck Boyle as an unsolicited bonus.

One of the reforms concerned Boyle's consolidated chiefdoms. 'The second task', continues Kakungulu's chronicler,

> was to mark the boundaries of the various counties. He decided to set up sub-counties throughout the district; these had not existed before his coming to Busoga. But decisions in all cases were made by the people called *bisoko*. There were no parishes [*miluka*] in Busoga; *bisoko* were the closest equivalents.[43]

The innovation with which Kakungulu is commonly associated in early colonial Busoga, namely the 'adoption of Ganda political units' throughout the newly integrated political structure,[44] therefore does appear to have some substance. But to stress its Ganda character at the expense of its other attributes, is to mislead in several respects.

To start with, Kakungulu did not dictate where boundaries should go. To the extent that he was a free agent, he allowed village leaders to make the crucial decisions. Even his chronicler admits this. As a result, administrative experts subsequently discovered 'perhaps some greater recognition of the traditional element' in the sub-county and parish boundaries of colonial Busoga than in the county divisions which had already been decided upon by British administrators before Kakungulu arrived.[45] Nor does Kakungulu appear to have gone about this work exhibiting any very 'deep conviction of the superiority of the Ganda', as has been alleged subsequently.[46] He was careful not to give Ganda names like *Kago* or *Mugema* to county chiefs in Busoga; 'he did not like them', comments his chronicler [47] – hardly surprisingly, considering the very recent trouble they had caused him at Mbale. However, Kakungulu did acquiesce in the use of Ganda titles for sub-chieftaincies in Busoga, largely because local British officials considered them to be the most suitable names for the new units.[48]

Yet to minimize Kakungulu's role here is almost to fall into a third error: suggesting that verbal change in this sphere was as significant at the time as it was to be perceived subsequently. This is to push back into Soga political consciousness in the 1900s an awareness of Ganda cultural aggression that only emerged at a later date. It is also to ignore the very real stumbling-blocks in administrative remodelling of Soga institutions during Kakungulu's time in Busoga: tasks rather than titles. For 'Kisiki', explains Kakungulu's chronicler,

> was not recognized as a county chief in Busoga then, although he himself was a prominent man and his country was called Busiki. This Kisiki was not an intelligent man. He did not want to attend the district court at Jinja, and only rarely appeared in public: that is why his county was added to Kigulu. But apparently he agreed with this step, since he made no attempt to oppose it.[49]

Political maladroitness apart, the man found the new colonial responsibilities of a chief less congenial than his earlier role as a local notable.

But council duties in Busoga did not fully occupy Kakungulu's energies at Jinja. As in each of his earlier offices, he also engaged in trade. But now it was not slave-catching westwards of Lake Victoria, as during Mutesa I's reign, nor the long-distance adventuring to the East African coast in which several of his counterparts in the Buganda kingdom subsequently engaged.[50] He did still keep ivory collectors and hunters operating in Karamoja as he had done throughout his Bukedi days; one of his ivory-collecting forays from Mbale actually reached into what is nowadays southern Ethiopia during the earlier 1900s.[51] But now most of his extra-conciliar entrepreneurial energies went into the new Asian-dominated retail trade.[52] Together with a Pathan merchant, on 1 December 1906 he opened shop at 2 Lubas Road, Jinja, trading as 'Kakunguru & Co'.[53]

His partner was Mohamed Yusuf, one of the very first South Asian merchants to operate in Jinja township. Unlike most of his companions, Yusuf appears to have been an unscrupulous character. 'General contractors, hide merchants, commission agents' was how Yusuf described his business at Jinja Auction Mart before Kakungulu arrived at Jinja as President of the Busoga Lukiko.[54] 'A notorious stirrer up of strife' and 'a clever plausible rascal', was how British administrators later described him.[55] In 1908 Kakunguru & Co went bankrupt. Yusuf absconded to Bukedi, leaving Kakungulu behind at Jinja to pay the debts. In 1911 Yusuf abandoned Mbale too. 'I am now in the service of Mr A. Alidina Visram and am too far away from Uganda', he was then able to write from Mombasa.[56]

When Kakunguru & Co went bankrupt, Boyle appointed himself receiver and Kakungulu forfeited his protectorate salary for several months. Rumours multiplied in Buganda about illegal cattle sales in Busoga. 'You might mention to Mr Boyle that there are rumours to the effect that Kakunguru recently sold 100 of his cattle in Buganda', minuted Hesketh Bell at Entebbe. 'I should like to know whether that is correct'.[57] The sales turned out to be legal, organized by none less than Zakariya Kisingiri, one of the three Regents ruling Buganda during the minority of Daudi Chwa as well as Kakungulu's classificatory brother in the Lungfish clan.[58]. To raise still more cash, Kakungulu exchanged heifers amongst his remaining cattle for bullocks from what is now western Kenya; sold a house in Jinja to the British Trading Company for another pittance; and received little more from the ubiquitous Alidina Visram in exchange for 1,920 acres of *mailo* land in Buganda.[59] 'It being very undesirable that a native chief of the high rank of the Kakunguru should suffer the degradation of being declared a bankrupt,' he had been allowed to sell the land to Visram, reported Bell in a special despatch to London in January 1909.[60] What Bell did not explain was that those financial difficulties had also been one of his reasons for recommending a £100 pay rise for Kakungulu two months before.

There were also other reasons. The loyalty, intelligence, and energy which Kakungulu displayed as president of the Busoga district council clearly pleased both Bell and Boyle, whose original reasons for removing him from Bukedi had been based more upon fear than hope. Kakungulu was an intelligent man, declared Boyle; 'one of the most able, if not the most able, native' in the whole protectorate, and one 'who never fails to inculcate progressive measures and ideas'. At present Kakungulu's salary was commensurate with the status of a county chief in Buganda. Boyle now suggested that, besides an immediate pay increase to £300 per annum, Kakungulu should be formally 'ranked as an equal of the three Regents of Buganda when the Kabaka resumes his responsibilities.'[61] Politically, Kakungulu had come a long way since coming to Busoga.

Five days' later, Hesketh Bell commemorated the 67th birthday of the British king by holding an agricultural and industrial exhibition at the newly named Coronation Park, Kampala. After his opening speech,

Plate 14. *Kakungulu as President of the Busoga chiefly council, photographed (on the extreme left) at the 1907 exhibition at Kampala with the African kings and chiefs, British governor and officials, and leading Catholic and Protestant missionaries.* (Royal Commonwealth Society, Bell Collection)

Kakungulu and the county chiefs of Busoga advanced in procession to the dais, followed in turn by the kings of Bunyoro, Ankole, Toro and Buganda with their respective chief ministers and suites.[62] According to the surviving written draft of his speech, Bell addressed Kakungulu thus:

> To Kakunguru, and the Chiefs of Busoga.
>
> I wish to express to you my pleasure at seeing you all here today. I congratulate you warmly on the excellent quality of the exhibits which have come from Busoga, and I feel sure that had it not been for the terrible famine which afflicted your country a few months ago, the products of Busoga would have been more worthy of the province. Kakunguru, I congratulate you, in the face of all your compatriots, on the excellent work which you have done in Busoga, and I am glad to think that the Provincial Commissioner has so able and loyal a Chief to help him in the administration of the country.[63]

According to Kakungulu himself, Bell added to these words during translation the further comment that Kakungulu was worthy to become 'President of Busoga' instead of merely president of its district council.[64]

Immediately the exhibition ended, Kakungulu's principal enemy within the Uganda Protectorate's chiefly elite counter-attacked. On the grounds that he was neither a true chief minister nor a proper native king, Apolo Kagwa successfully argued that Kakungulu should be excluded from the official photographs of both Ugandan chief ministers and Ugandan native kings taken after the exhibition.[65] Only in a picture of the whole concourse is Kakungulu therefore included, on the extreme left. Just before the exhibition took place, Kagwa also attempted to get Kakungulu's claim to *mailo* land at Buundo in Kyagwe cancelled through a strategy which moved the British Land Officer at Entebbe to recommend that 'a reprimand from His Excellency to the Regents would not be out of place'.[66] Kakungulu however capped Kagwa by selling the land in dispute to pay the protectorate receiver, albeit at a much reduced price. Several months later, Kakungulu was again complaining about encroachments upon his estates by Apolo Kagwa.[67] Kagwa also had local contacts in Busoga which, as we have suggested already, on occasion he was able to manipulate to Kakungulu's discomfort. To these was now added a much older Ganda propaganda weapon in fresh attire: rumour-mongering through vernacular newspapers.

## 3

When Kakungulu was in Bukedi the only newspapers in Uganda had been English-language ones, apart from those imported from the neighbouring East Africa Protectorate. Soon after arriving in Busoga as president of the district council, *Ebifa mu Buganda* was started under CMS auspices in Buganda, to be followed shortly afterwards by *Munno* printed by the White Fathers.[68] Earlier we saw how effective rumour-mongering had proved during the early 1900s: then its effectiveness had been enhanced by distance from the protectorate capital as well as by a certain jealousy of a wealthy African chief by a more impoverished British administrator.[69] Racial consciousness still prospered amongst British officials in Busoga – as we shall shortly see – but it seems to have been bureaucratic uncertainty about Kakungulu's actual role in the district that now gave rumour-mongering against him increased force.

In November 1908, Alexander Boyle had added a 'status ... considerably greater than that of an omusaza [county chief] in Buganda' to the role he had originally envisaged for Kakungulu in Busoga.[70] He had also recommended a pay increase of £100 and suggested that Kakungulu's position there might be made formally equivalent to that of Apolo Kagwa when Chwa II came of age in Buganda. Seemingly, that equivalence was brought still closer by the treatment accorded to Kakungulu during (if not immediately after) the agricultural and industrial exhibition. But there are promises and promises. In the old Buganda kingdom, oral promises at public audiences were treated seriously: honour was above all a matter of public repute. Under the British protectorate, both inside and outside Buganda, everything important had to be recorded increasingly on paper. In Bukedi, in the early and middle 1900s, this process had not been sufficiently advanced to cause Kakungulu real anxiety. Hayes Sadler had composed a special memorandum when restoring Kakungulu to power there in 1904, but to Kakungulu this piece of paper was politically less important than the great assembly in which it was publicized. Now times had changed significantly. With increased specialization within the British protectorate administration, and increased bureaucratization within its proliferating technical branches (land survey, medicine, printing and veterinary, initially), the shift from an oral-based administrative culture to one established upon secretariat files was almost complete. In fact, 1907 marks the inauguration of separate yearly files in the Entebbe secretariat archives which were to survive until the very end of British rule in Uganda. This being the case, an extempore promise by one British protectorate governor upon some public platform in Kampala was even less binding than a verbal assurance made by a predecessor upon some mountain spur in eastern Uganda.

Apolo Kagwa had good backing on paper for his position in Buganda. Kakungulu did not for his in Busoga. There was no written 'Usoga Agreement' comparable to the Uganda Agreement of 1900. 'The country is considered to have been conquered by us', the protectorate governor was now writing; 'all the land which is not beneficially occupied by natives is to be held as Crown land; and we fortunately find ourselves free from many of the difficulties which hamper the [British protectorate] administration with the kingdom of Buganda'.[71] Unlike Kagwa, Kakungulu had therefore to suffer the indignity of his contract of employment in Busoga being constantly revised.

In essence, Kakungulu's political survival now depended upon his usefulness as an administrative middleman continuing to outweigh his convenience as an ethnic scapegoat for the deficiencies of British protectorate rule. Already there had been one warning light. In April 1907, a

Ganda ferryman had been murdered just north of Busoga and Kakungulu had commented publicly that his countryman would have been still alive if the British official concerned had followed his advice.[72] That particular British official did not appreciate the resultant publicity at protectorate headquarters, and counter-attacked at the first opportunity. This arose when another Ganda chief died in Bugabula, and Kakungulu asked what pension the dead chief's relatives should receive, and what compensation indeed other Ganda chiefs in Busoga might reasonably expect to obtain when finally vacating their posts. In retrospect it seems a not unreasonable query, granted British preference now to progressively introduce a bureaucratic rather than an heroic chiefly culture. Furthermore, as one British administrator at the time remarked, it was a query that was 'bound to arise fairly often as time goes on and the Basoga themselves advance'.[73] However, the British official who had been piqued by Kakungulu's comment on the ferryman's murder thought otherwise. No hard and fast rule should be laid down, this official insisted, and Kakungulu should be reprimanded for suggesting that one should.[74] A mild reprimand was therefore delivered. 'No one who has worked well for the Govt has any reason to doubt that he will be well looked after but everything depends on how they do their work.'[75]

Later there were other warnings. When local tax revenue continued to fall below target, even when the latest famine appeared to be over, it was easier for British officials to blame Kakungulu than to do anything about it themselves. 'In reviewing my time in Busoga', wrote one of them, 'my chief blame falls upon Kakunguru for when I was new in the District & called on him for taxes he assured me that they would be very easily collected in time. I have had to find out for myself that the Basoga are very slow payers.'[76] While Boyle remained at protectorate headquarters, such excuses were seen as such, at least until such time as Kakungulu became embroiled in controversial land claims on the wrong side of the sleeping sickness epidemic in Busoga.[77] But when Boyle left Uganda the situation changed totally.

At first glance, this is the classic dilemma of the appointed chief in British colonial Africa – the man in the middle.[78] But, upon closer inspection, several dissimilarities emerge. Kakungulu's dilemma was now not only that of implementing British policies conflicting with local interests.[79] Kakungulu was an expatriate in Busoga as much as his British masters, in these same British masters' eyes; indeed, as we have already noted, his British overlords specifically promoted him there in order to neutralize any 'local' support he might still have possessed elsewhere in the Uganda Protectorate. Nor was Kakungulu's basic problem now that of reconciling traditional role expectations with bureaucratic norms – 'everyone in the same empirical situation subject to equality of treatment', as Max Weber puts it [80] – for arguably Kakungulu was already more bureaucratic in behaviour than local British officials. In so far as the matter can be categorized outside a straightforward power struggle, Kakungulu's dilemma in early colonial Uganda was that of an ethnic middleman also working as an administrative one. That Kakungulu had by now realized this, is evidenced by his request that Ganda expatriates should receive appropriate compensation upon relinquishing their posts in Busoga. For not only were he and other Ganda persons training local people to take over their jobs, but shortly yet another administrative elite would be emerging from the new missionary high schools to take over from them, too.

Politically, Kakungulu was also somewhat isolated in Busoga as regards his religious allegiance. Protestant Christianity in early colonial Busoga was closely identified with Ganda culture.[81] But it was not the only book-based religion to be followed by Ganda chiefs locally for, as we have already noted, several were fervent Muslims. However, Protestantism suffered in Busoga by having been less closely associated in the popular mind with the defence of traditional liberties than Islam (because of the events of 1897–8), as well as because of the activity of Ganda notables like Bwagu and Lwanga imposing Islam from above. Kakungulu's commitment to Protestant Christianity was undoubtedly less advantageous to him politically in Busoga than it had been either in Bukedi or in Buganda; though, paradoxically, CMS missionaries were now sometimes suspicious of the extent of Kakungulu's personal commitment to any kind of Christianity because of the comparatively large numbers of Muslims frequently to be encountered within his immediate entourage.[82] That was also probably the case during his later days at Mbale, when he must also have disturbed CMS missionaries by so ostentatiously marrying a former Ganda Muslim king's daughter by customary rather than church ritual.[83] But by 1908 at least one CMS missionary was again writing that 'The chief Kakungulu is one of our most sympathetic chiefs and has done more to help us than any other man in the missionary work of the Native Church' and at Mbale he had 'sent to have one of his best houses put into order' for another CMS missionary to move into.[84] Personally, too, his years in Busoga were to be of considerable subsequent spiritual significance in his developing understanding of the Protestant religion. Politically, however, his Protestantism was a diminishing asset.

Besides the diminishing utilities of the Protestant connection, of behaving deferentially, and of walking the administrative tightrope between being sufficiently efficient to retain his post in Busoga and not exposing his immediate British superiors to adverse publicity by being too efficient, Kakungulu had only one other weapon to assist his political survival: the threat of resignation. Unfortunately this too was a weapon of decreasing utility. For, upon his promotion to Busoga, Kakungulu's kingdom in Bukedi quietly collapsed as former followers hastened to bureaucratize chiefly office there, first through acceptance of percentage rebates on taxes collected, then by accepting essentially salaried terms of service from British protectorate officials.[85] As a result, Kakungulu's threats of resignation became more bargaining counters to win political points in Busoga than any serious threat to reduce British power drastically again in Bukedi. Furthermore, Kakungulu's position in Busoga was now so circumscribed by the presence of other Ganda chiefs, and so insecure in view of the imminent return of a local successor elite from school, that even the political points Kakungulu could make now tended to be modest ones. As much as he had ever been in pre-British Buganda, Kakungulu was now dependent upon the favour of his overlord for his continuance in power.

As at the court of Mutesa I, Kakungulu endeavoured to behave in public both deferentially and efficiently. Unfortunately, both endeavours became increasingly ineffectual once Alexander Boyle was replaced as provincial commissioner of the eastern province (as the post of 'sub-commissioner of the central province' was renamed when the British protectorate governor himself was renamed 'governor' in 1907)[86] by a man less amenable to flattery and anyway uninterested in efficiency amongst Africans for its own sake. Further complications would be created by the new government departments concerned with medicine and land – the former would strain Kakungulu's loyalty to British protectorate power in a wholly new way as well as providing his enemies within the wider Ganda chiefly class with further opportunities for rumour-mongering, while the latter would underline still further the elusive character of oral promises made to him earlier by Governor Hesketh Bell.

# 4

Hesketh Bell was a good despatch writer. Before leaving Uganda in 1909, he composed special despatches on cotton production and sleeping sickness in Uganda.[87] Besides impressing his superiors in London, these despatches have established a posthumous reputation. 'One of the most notable governors' in the British colonial empire, writes the historian of the British Colonial Office at this time,[88] 'energetic and courageous'.[89] The reality was more complicated. Bell was not the worst governor of the Uganda Protectorate, but he was not the best. Socially he was better connected with politicians in London than his predecessors, and professionally he was ambitious.[90] His skills were essentially literary: presenting problems advantageously on paper. Politically, he was not especially innovative. Within days of reaching Uganda, his correspondence changes from a stress upon reform to an emphasis on continuity. Only in the health and economic spheres did Bell innovate, sometimes in actuality and catastrophically, sometimes principally in letters to London.

Foreign plantations largely fell into the second category, though at the beginning of his period of office Bell compared himself to Lord Milner ('not so much, they said, in appearance, but in manner, voice and in many other ways')[91] and there were many plans for intervention by capitalist concessionaires connected with South Africa. Very little came of these schemes, apart from a growing polarization within the British protectorate administration between officials – like Bell and Boyle – prepared to see African land rights whittled away for the benefit of European planters or South Asian indentured labourers, and those – like Boyle's successor as provincial commissioner at Jinja, Spire, and Bell's successor as governor, Jackson – not so readily prepared to see Africans deprived of ancestral lands.[92] Concerning cotton production, however, Bell's policy was less at odds with other British officials.

He did not introduce the crop to Uganda. Credit for that must be divided between the CMS missionary who distributed the first substantial supply of cotton seeds in the early 1900s, and the Ganda chiefs like Kakungulu who first forced Ugandans to grow them. But Bell did meet British businesmen who urged that only certain varieties of cotton should be grown in Uganda, and he did subsequently promulgate rules embodying these suggestions which Ganda chiefs again enforced. Only then did Bell compose a self-laudatory despatch.[93] On the basis of this despatch the Colonial Office hoped that Bell would organize cotton production successfully in Northern Nigeria. Unfortunately Bell did not prove successful there and, following an unhappy experience during a railway journey, Bell was demoted to the governorship of Mauritius.[94]

In the same year, the Busoga railway was opened in Uganda. Bell loved railways and persuaded Winston Churchill, during a visit to the protectorate as junior minister at the Colonial Office, to share his enthusiasm:

> I know that it is quite impossible to obtain £2,000,000 of money and I will not vex my soul and waste my influence in struggling over what I cannot get. But I believe the Chioga route, for £600,000 or £700,000, is within our reach, if we only pull together and make a determined fight; and with railway ferries on Chioga and the Victoria there will be no question of breaking bulk at any point between Nile mouth and Mombasa.[95]

But this proved too expensive for the British Treasury, even with Churchill's campaigning. All the Treasury would approve was a loan of £200,000 to pay for track between Lake Victoria and the first navigable section of the River Nile; and it only agreed to this little line because Bell convinced Churchill that it would have 'a greater effect than any other on the development of trade within the Protectorate'. 'Such a line', Bell argued, 'would pay almost from the outset and it would immediately bring a great increase of traffic to the Uganda Railway [from Kisumu to Mombasa].'[96] In fact, it did neither.

To start with, the railway was badly situated. 'To hear people talk of the Jinja-Kakindu railway one would imagine that it was going to introduce the Millenium', complained the Kampala manager of the Uganda Company in 1911, but the benefit drived from it by the Uganda Protectorate was 'totally insignificant'. 'All the districts round by Kumi and Mbale from which so much cotton has been obtained this year will not be helped in the slightest degree, and in numerous cotton districts on this side of the Nile we shall be no better off than we were before.'[97] In fact, the problem of transporting the greater bulk of cotton produced to the Kisumu railhead was solved by a massive increase in human porterage in the short term,[98] and ultimately by the construction of a decent network of feeder roads.[99] But for the moment even existing roads had to be neglected in order to pay for the railway between Jinja and Kakindu. The road from Mbale was bad enough, complained the Uganda Company's Kampala manager ('one strip of between 6 and 8 miles took me four hours to traverse in a rickshaw pushed by four men – what chance would a waggon and oxen have?'), but the one to Kakindu was worse still ('they have to branch off altogether and go through a swamp').[100]

The new Busoga railway also proved expensive to run. Most short railways run at a loss, but this one was especially expensive because of the continuous sudd-cutting required to keep Lake Kyoga navigable as well as to provide access to the very large number of ports around the lake at which steamers had to call in order to collect cotton because of the defective roads behind them. Matters became worse when the water level rose by ten feet, drowning innumerable piers, causeways and sheds; worse still, when World War I led to a depression in world trade. For unforeseeable events Bell should not be blamed. But he as much as anybody was responsible for the extraordinary belief that the short Busoga railway would increase local trade dramatically above levels already made possible by the Kisumu–Mombasa line.[101] The art of development planning, comments one authority, 'lies in avoiding the grandiose investments that the economy cannot afford, whilst not inhibiting economic growth through failing to provide facilities for the growing sectors of the economy.'[102] Regarding the Busoga Railway, Bell scored low marks on both counts.

His policy regarding sleeping sickness was also defective, though here he shared the misapprehension common amongst Europeans at the time that it was a new disease introduced into the East African interior during the Scramble for Africa. Now we know otherwise. Following John Ford's study of *The Role of Trypanosomiases in African Ecology* (1971), we know that it was 'not so much a new disease but new conditions which led to the epidemics'.[103] Before going to Uganda, Bell had been told that sleeping sickness would be his greatest problem.[104] Shortly after reaching Uganda he ordered that the whole lake shore of Lake Victoria should be cleared of people. We know now that the sleeping sickness epidemic had reached its peak in southern Busoga during 1902–3. Thereafter the epidemic declined irregularly throughout the Uganda Protectorate.[105] The worst was therefore over when Bell arrived. But meeting his immediate predecesssor at Mombasa hardly helped him to understand this. 'Old Sadler has got the fear of death in him over the business and fusses round in great excitement', commented his doctor. 'A large proportion of the white inhabitants of Entebbe are quite certain they have S.S. and begin to quake at the first sign of ill health'.[106] This was the setting in which Bell took the most drastic decision of his governorship shortly after reaching Entebbe. 'Not only must the sick be removed from the lake shore but also all the healthy people. The whole of that country must be completely depopulated.'[107]

This drastic decision did have roots in earlier policy. Hodges, the medical officer, favoured segregating sleeping sickness victims at special camps. He had just discovered that *glossina palpalis* – the particular tsetse fly whose bites transmit the causative trypanosomes to human beings –

clustered in undergrowth along the lake shore, and together with local chiefs had cleared wide swathes of land along the Entebbe peninsula of both bush and people and, as a result, the risk of contracting sleeping sickness there soon became quite small.[108] This policy Bell now extended to the whole protectorate — with three crucial changes. First, in place of selective clearance decided upon by local medical officers in collaboration with local chiefs, all land within a two-mile radius of the lake shore was to be evacuated regardless of existing concentrations of people or potential clusters of tsetse flies. Secondly, this belt was to be cleared of people but not of bush. Thirdly, responsibility for clearance was to lie not with medical officers but with protectorate administrators and chiefs assisted by a new British functionary: OCSSAM (Officer-in-Charge Sleeping Sickness Administrative Measures).

The policy was misguided in a number of respects. To start with, it was based upon an 'egregious overestimate'[109] of continuing deaths from sleeping sickness. Secondly, it was implemented at a time when people needed more rather than less land, because of famine and of the increased susceptibility of hungry people in particular to disease. Thirdly, the evacuation zone made little ecological sense. In Buganda, it was several times wider than necessary; in Busoga, it ran through areas already abandoned to bush. 'Sometimes', as a subsequent authority pointed out, 'it is possible for a population to live within a few hundred yards of fly-infected shore without need to come into contact with fly; at other times the lake is the only source of water supply, and it is quite impossible for a population to live within a mile or two of it without coming into contact with fly ... The boundary as proclaimed at two miles from the lake shore was wrong and unreasonable.' Furthermore, the deaths reduced by wholesale evacuation were less than the lives that would probably have been saved by more selective clearances of the sort originally envisaged by Hodges.[110]

That the policy was implemented at all, was a considerable tribute to the loyalty and power of chiefs in both Buganda and Busoga. But it was not a policy that could be implemented without strain to these chiefs. The Busoga railway added considerably to the work load of Semei Kakungulu.[111] OCSSAM struck at the very basis of his life-style, and ultimately at his religious beliefs too.

This is not to suggest that error as regards sleeping sickness lay all on one side. Ganda chiefs were frankly incredulous when informed that *glossina palpalis* was responsible for the scourge.[112] But this incredulity is explicable on other grounds than 'African superstition'.[113] The hysterical attitude of the local British community towards sleeping sickness did not assist objective evaluation of its cause, though undoubtedly it did speed the arrival of a succession of sleeping sickness experts from Europe to enquire into it. *Glossina palpalis* is now known to have survived for generations in the lakes region of Eastern Africa before the British colonial entry, without causing any major epidemic.[114] From the studies of John Ford we now know that the British colonial entry, and its German and Belgian counterparts in what are today Tanzania and Zaire, broke down a whole range of informal ecological controls keeping the scourge at bay during earlier times. 'Like their British neighbours across the Kagera in Ankole', remarked Ford, 'the Germans looked upon themselves as saviours of people sunk in centuries of barbaric misery. Few realized that they were the prime cause of the suffering they were trying to alleviate'.[115] Visiting medical experts changed their minds several times about the cause of sleeping sickness before plumping for *glossina palpalis*.[116] Might they not change their minds again? One of Kakungulu's countrymen in Busoga contributed an article to the new vernacular press, urging Africans to pray that God might reveal a suitable remedy for sleeping sickness to European doctors.[117] Kakungulu himself would later declare publicly that he preferred to leave his trust in God undivided with any medical intermediary, European or African.

In February 1909, OCSSAM reported on Kakungulu. He lived at the end of a small peninsula jutting out into Lake Victoria:

> very narrow, about 500 yds width and about 1000 yds long. It is covered with dense forest, except for a few cleared patches where natives are building houses and planting bananas. The hill itself has been partially cleared on the East and South and has been planted with bananas. On the West and North there is forest reaching to the shore. On both sides of the peninsula there is a small fringe of swamp and papyrus, varying in thickness from about 50 yds to 120 yds. The landing place itself is very little cleared. The swamp and papyrus fringe has numerous small channels leading through it to the lake. I found one dug-out unregistered, about 100 yds to the west of the landing-place, hidden in the swamp. There are many fly in the forest. Several settled on me and Capt. Tufnell, who had accompanied me. The natives living here are obliged to pass through this forest and swamp to fetch water.
>
> On my last visit here I was informed that the Chief Kakunguru was doing the necessary clearing, but very little has now been done, and to make this peninsula and hill absolutely safe there remains an enormous amount to be done, it would probably take, even with a large staff, several months to do. I am informed that Kakunguru is unable to do this owing to financial troubles. This hill is the headquarters of the Saza chief of Busoga, who is often visited by other Chiefs and their followers. His living here constitutes a danger to the whole of Busoga.

OCSSAM recommended that the whole peninsula be evacuated until clearing was complete. 'Several natives whom I saw working had signs of Sleeping Sickness.'[118]

At Entebbe, Alexander Boyle thought OCSSAM's estimate for clearance expenses was excessive.[119] Another official favoured evacuation – 'Altho' it would be very hard on the Kakunguru to move him, yet I consider in the interests of the country and the S.S. scheme he ought to go and that early.'[120] The British medical authorities at Entebbe also considered evacuation to be 'the proper course'.[121] Bell thought otherwise:

> If the Kakunguru be evicted entirely he would have a just claim to heavy compensation.

I consider that he may be allowed to retain possession of the land for the remainder of his lease which, I believe, is only for four years more, on the following conditions:

He is to contribute, either in cash or in men, half the cost of clearing which remains to be done.

He is not to have more than 50 persons living on the land.

Those who live on this peninsula may proceed to and from the mainland, but visits to the peninsula from the mainland are to be restricted as much as possible.

Chiefs and their retinues, who wish to confer with the Kakunguru, are not to go to the peninsula, but are to see him in a Banda or Baraza on the mainland, outside the fly-infected limits, to which Kakunguru will proceed as often as necessary. This place will, in fact, be his office.

As soon as any person, among the 50 who are permitted to reside on the peninsula, show signs of S.S. he is to be sent to the S.S. camp, and Kakunguru will be held responsible for this. If, after a reasonable period of notice, Kakunguru is found to be harbouring on the peninsula any person showing signs of S.S. he will be liable to be ejected from the property without compensation.

It is likely that Kakunguru may ultimately find it too inconvenient to continue to live on this peninsula and will ask for a residence elsewhere.[122]

Two months later, the trick had worked. 'Of his own accord', reported the local British protectorate administrator, 'Kakunguru has vacated this hill pending completion of clearing ... Kakunguru has already done a certain amount of clearing.'[123]

## 5

Upon accepting promotion to Busoga, Kakungulu had asked Boyle for a suitable site upon which to build a house. At the same time he had asked when he should return to Bukedi. 'No, you shall not return there', Boyle had replied. 'You shall always stay here and every European who will be sub-commissioner of this place will find you here.'[124] Though the tenancy Boyle granted on paper was only a temporary one, Kakungulu concluded from these oral remarks that his actual occupation of the site would be lengthy. After all, had not Boyle in company with Bell also promised to provide him with *mailo* land in Busoga to compensate for any diminution that might need to take place in his Mbale estates ?

In October 1906, Kakungulu asked for the freehold. 'Since I started to cut and cleaning this wooded hill Kirinya', he declared to Hesketh Bell,

it looks so well now and a lot of money have been spent by me to do so. It is very troublesome-work, yet which will take a great deal of expenditure from me. I am afraid of having received a written permission issued to me by A.G. Boyle H.M. the Sub-Commissioner which is as follows:-

Permission is granted to S. Kakungulu to build on the wooden hill (its name) Kirinya and at the same time I have warned him that if the

Government require it for any purpose he is liable to be turned out.

Well, sir, according to the above written permission I exactly understand that my money will be spent for nothing but a loss.

I therefore request you, if I have found favour in my lord's sight, to be so very obliged and let your servant bring one of my private miles and be put here on this wooded hill Kirinya.[125]

It was a reasonable request, considering the promises made to Kakungulu upon his transfer to Busoga. It was a clear request, translated into English by his private secretary, and typed. But British officials were embarrassed by it.

The main problem was European housing. As the British protectorate administration of Uganda became entrenched, so its British personnel multiplied. As British numbers grew, British health and prestige became increasingly problematical concerns, in addition to the further anxieties created by sleeping sickness. When providing plots for South Asian traders at Mbale, for example, Boyle was most concerned to select ones 'which will not be between the prevailing winds and the European houses'.[126] Now Kakungulu's housing site at Jinja seemed objectionable for another reason. 'The hill in question is the high wooded hill passed on the right in entering Jinja harbour', minuted Boyle. 'The view from there is the best in Jinja and would be suitable for European houses. I am consequently unable to recommend such land being granted freehold to the Kakunguru.'[127] Bell was more worried by the financial aspect. 'In a few years this hill will probably be valuable property', he minuted further,

> and I cannot agree to the grant of the whole of it, as a freehold. I would, however, be willing, as a special favour, to grant him a freehold of 3 acres, on which his house would stand, and a lease of 7 years of the rest of the ground. He would, however, be required to put up a house worth at least £400, and no buildings must be put up on the leased land.[128]

Boyle was appalled. Though valuing Kakungulu's advice on property as a friend, he did not desire him as a neighbour on Kirinya hill; 'he would overlook all the houses'. Boyle therefore wrote another minute. Kakungulu should be allowed 'the 10 acres mentioned by His Excellency the Commissioner for so long a time as the native administration remains in Jinja' – and that, he now thought, should not be so long as he had suggested previously.[129] Bell agreed, and therefore only offered Kakungulu 'a lease for seven years at a nominal rent'. Allied to this grant was the request that Kakungulu should clear Kirinya hill of heavy vegetation, but no more was said about the necessity of building an African stately home there.[130] It was with evident relief that British protectorate officials now noted that 'at present the Kakunguru has only built a mud and wattle house, on which he has put an iron roof.'[131]

Kakungulu appears to have accepted the situation without further written comment. With the few followers he had been allowed to bring from Mbale, and the hundred or so labourers supplied monthly by the

Plate 15. *The ruins of Kakungulu's house overlooking Jinja harbour on the edge of Lake Victoria, photographed in 1970. Its position – also overlooking British colonial officials' residences – led to Kakungulu's removal from it (see pages 242–47).* (Author's photographs)

Busoga district council, he set about clearing Kirinya hill. It proved a difficult task.

In February 1909, British sleeping sickness inspectors visited Kirinya hill. As we have seen, the southern and eastern shores they found fairly clear of vegetation by this time, but on the north and west forest reached down to the lake shore. Concerned as they were at the incompleteness of the clearing, they were still more disturbed by the number of Kakungulu's followers with evidence of the disease. One examination revealed '8 out of 15' of his followers suffering from it. 'Finally an examination was made of nearly 100 of Kakunguru's people, and 70% were found to suffer from sleeping sickness.'[132]

In the new Ganda vernacular press, European dismay at these findings became intense disapproval. The various health checks on Kakungulu's followers at Jinja were written up in *Ebifa mu Buganda* in a way which suggested that Kakungulu himself had behaved in an uncooperative manner towards British medical procedures.[133] In the light of Kakungulu's subsequent opposition to Western medicine, it is tempting to detect early opposition to it here. But whether this was so is impossible to say. Independent supporting evidence is lacking, and the data supplied by the *Ebifa* correspondent were, to say, the least, ambiguous. Besides increasing the number of sufferers above OCSSAM's estimates, even in the *Ebifa* account British officials were reported as exhibiting more concern at Kakungulu's lack of punctuality in sending retainers for medical examination than any lack of sympathy by him for health checks as such. Such absence of punctuality is of course explicable in several ways. One is defective communication between European doctor and African chief; another is resistance within Kakungulu's following to procedures considered misconceived; and yet another is reluctance by Kakungulu himself to push workers already doing an unrewarding task on Kirinya hill still further. All that can be said for certain now about the *Ebifa* report is that it was composed by a local ally of Apolo Kagwa in the Jinja district office, and that its publication in the heart of Buganda did Semei Kakungulu little good at British protectorate headquarters. In *Ebifa* OCSSAM's statistics were upped by ten per cent. Orally those figures would have been increased to a very considerable extent further by the time news of them reached the protectorate governor's verandah.

'Although the Europeans have not yet found the medicine that cures sleeping sickness, at least they have discovered what causes it. All readers should therefore pray that God might enable the Europeans to discover the medicine for sleeping sickness.'[134] Earlier we alluded to this exhortation with which the *Ebifa* article ended, and implied that subsequently it would provide Kakungulu with food for thought. These thoughts would acquire further urgency when British veterinary doctors proved as fallible in Uganda initially as the medical officers dealing with human beings. 'The Veterinary Dept is causing consternation in Busoga by injecting cattle. Practically all such cattle die.'[135] But, before his thoughts on European medicine matured, Kakungulu had more immediate challenges to face as a result of OCSSAM's examination of his followers. One was Hesketh Bell's trick to get him and his followers off Kirinya hill without compensation. Another was the demand which soon arose among his followers as a consequence that Kakungulu should resign his presidency of the Busoga district council and return with them to Mbale.

Such pressure was hardly new. On earlier occasions when friction with British protectorate officials reached a peak, and the continuance of Semei Kakungulu as a loyal ally of such officials held diminishing attractions, there had been pressure from within his clientage for Kakungulu to withdraw cooperation. In 1895 and 1902, we saw how among other things he capitulated to such pressure on occasions when his clientage was sufficiently large for resignation to be accepted by British officials only as a matter of some concern. Now his clientage was not large enough to worry British protectorate officials very much. However, it was still large enough for them to worry about it medically, and to grant Kakungulu a temporary tenancy on another hill near Jinja on which his followers might settle with their families.[136]

At the end of the month, Kakungulu asked for the freehold of the new site. Probably realizing that his position was somewhat precarious in view of the adverse publicity aroused by OCSSAM, he did not ask for a new *mailo* grant but for acquisition by transfer: 4 square miles from his Mbale estate and 2 from his *mailo* lands in Buganda to be surrendered in return for 6 at the new site. Again the request was clearly expressed in English, and this time did not concern an area where British families might fear an African chief overlooking their gardens. Bell responded to it by deciding to harass Kakungulu off Kirinya hill without compensation, and sending the new application off for more careful consideration by Lands and Surveys.

The proposals for Kirinya were conveyed to Kakungulu less than three weeks before Bell left Uganda on final leave.[137] For some months Lands and Surveys then sat upon Kakungulu's application for land at Batambogwe. On 23 August, Kakungulu took the matter into his own hands and purchased Batambogwe hill and surrounding land from a Soga notable 'for ever for one thousand years' in return for 3,500 rupees, handing over 64 cows immediately in part payment.[138] Whatever the British protectorate authorities might do (or not do) on paper, the Soga notable knew who his superior was in face-to-face relations. Lands and Surveys continued to consider the matter. In December 1909 it gave its opinion. To exchange *mailo* lands in Bukedi for non-*mailo* ones in Busoga would be uneconomical: to mix ones in Buganda with ones in Busoga would be unethical.[139] Nonetheless, after further heartsearching at Entebbe, it was agreed to allow Kakungulu to acquire one square mile on Batambogwe hill. Kakungulu was told to consider himself fortunate to get even this. 'His Excellency wishes it to be clearly explained to Kakunguru that he is in this matter receiving exceptional treatment, and that this must be the end of exchange of land' – as far as Kakungulu was concerned.[140]

Now Kakungulu brought his purchase of Batambogwe and the surrounding area during the interval into the relevant British minute papers. With disarming frankness he revealed everything to Frederick Spire, Colvile's valet who had now become Boyle's successor as provincial commissioner at Jinja:

Dear Sir,
I have the honour to inform you that when I left Mbale to come here my people were very sorry to leave their food. And also when they left Kirinya they burst into tears and myself was sorry and they asked me to tell the Government to give me permission to go back to Mbale. When I saw that the Government would not let me go back there I settled with Kyebambe to sell me a mutalla called Batambogwe and he agreed to sell it to me. This is the reason why I bought this mutalla for my people were afraid to sow their seed or plant everything. But since I bought this mutalla I was afraid to tell you, for I knew that I owe the Government many Rupees and other people whose things were wasted by Mohamed Josef, and that you would ask me where I got the money. I was waiting to pay all the debts, and after paying I would tell you. But now I am telling you these things which you have asked me about Batambogwe therefore I want to let you know this reason.

Yours faithfully,
S. Kakungulu
President.
Jinja
23.2.10[141]

Spire sympathized. He offered 95 acres of unoccupied land at Batambogwe 'in lieu of compensation for losses incurred by removal from Kirinya', as Lands and Surveys now suggested. Kakungulu refused this offer. Spire therefore recommended protectorate acceptance of the *status quo*: that the offer of 95 acres as a freehold grant had been refused, and that Kakungulu should 'retain possession' of the whole area unofficially acquired from Kyebambe.[142] It was a sensible solution, but it was quickly undermined by inter-departmental squabbling between old hands and new bureaucrats in the British protectorate administration at Entebbe, and still further complicated by additional flurries of paper within Lands and Surveys.

Though disapproving of Kakungulu's tastes in housing ('the style and dimensions of which are far beyond the reasonable requirements of a man in his station'), Spire was impressed by his honesty. Nor could Spire have approved of how Bell had arranged for Kakungulu's removal from Kirinya hill, still less of how Boyle now ordered Spire himself to implement the removal. Boyle argued that he had not given Kakungulu Kirinya; that to allow Kakungulu to keep the Batambogwe area would make nonsense of British protectorate law on bankruptcy; and it would also make it more difficult to resist demands from Soga chiefs for quasi-freehold tenures similar to the *mailo* lands already enjoyed by their Ganda counterparts under the terms of the 1900 Agreement.[143] The second argument was the only reasonable one. The third was clearly illogical – the freehold gift of

95 acres would have been the awkward precedent, not land administered on more customary terms – though probably Spire would have considered it yet another attempt by the opposing British protectorate faction at Entebbe further to whittle away African land rights and make such lands more accessible to future European planters. But the first argument was clearly a lie. Spire might not have known about promises made privately to Kakungulu by Bell and Boyle on *mailo* transfers, nor about requests that Kakungulu should construct a stately home in order to protect future European property values; but he did have Salim Bwagu and Ali Lwanga to verify what Boyle had actually said in public assembly.[144]

Kakungulu was telling the truth. The situation soon deadlocked. Boyle was blocked by Spire, Spire by Lands and Surveys. Kakungulu repeated his position several times: 95 acres were insufficient to compensate for monies spent on clearing Kirinya hill, but if no compensation was forthcoming he wanted to acquire a substantial estate on Batambogwe hill by transfer.[145] In the meantime, he was careful to ensure that the Busoga district council approved of his actual residence there, if not the British protectorate administration.[146] But it was not until Kakungulu finally retired from the presidency of this institution in 1913 that he would finally acquire a protectorate title to 545 acres for the 'fine 2-storey house [being] built on the top of the hill [at] really a charming spot looking clear over a wooded plain broken by arms of the Lake & islands beyond', specially surveyed by the recently appointed British protectorate surveyor, H.B. Thomas.[147]

# 6

For Kakungulu, residence at Batambogwe provided refuge from the tensions of protectorate politics. To British officials, his house-building there seemed evidence of something else. 'In these projects', wrote H.B. Thomas subsequently,

> Kakunguru was ministering to his now all-pervading passion for personal aggrandisement, and the governance of Busoga only claimed his attention so far as it seemed to offer a field in which to carve out for himself a new kingdom. His special duties of tutelage of the Basoga chiefs were more and more neglected, and at length the government decided that his usefulness in Busoga was exhausted. In truth there was now no place for him in the complex of modern administrative machinery which was now taking shape around him.

This was the new British protectorate stereotype of Kakungulu. Perhaps it originated with the district commissioner accompanying Thomas on his survey of Batambogwe hill, perhaps elsewhere.[148] But, whatever its origins, the stereotype summed up what the young professionals now joining the British administration of Uganda thought about Kakungulu. He was an old-fashioned warlord. He spent too much time on unnecessary house-building, too little on advisory work. He was out of place in a modern government.

Like other stereotypes, this one distorted the truth but had an element of truth in it. Kakungulu did build substantial residences on Kirinya and Batambogwe hills to indulge 'out-moded' ambitions as he had done earlier at Mbale, Budaka and Mpumudde. The 'all-pervading passion for personal aggrandisement' was no new phenomenon but the continuance of an older quest for honour. But the character of Kakungulu's residences in Busoga had been also influenced, as we have seen, by British policy. He survived as president of the Busoga district council for seven years by successfully adapting himself to several changes in British policy. In fact, his basic error lay in behaving *too* bureaucratically, for he lost his job as president of the Busoga district council not when he lost interest in doing it efficiently, but when he protested that the job had been downgraded.

How this happened deserves attention. In April 1909, two new officials arrived at Jinja: Isemonger, to be district commissioner of Busoga, and Spire to be provincial commissioner of the eastern province.[149] To begin with, both treated Kakungulu as he was treated by Soga – as 'president of Busoga'. In a report submitted on 20 May, and which Spire forwarded to Entebbe without comment, Isemonger said as much: 'Busoga is divided into 10 counties, each of which has its chief and sub-chiefs, over all of whom is the Mganda chief Kakunguru.'[150] Boyle disagreed. 'No. Kakunguru is only president of the Lukiko.'[151]

This was more than a quibble. Just before his transfer to Entebbe, Boyle had suggested that Kakungulu's position in Busoga should be upgraded further. OCSSAM's survey in February 1909 sabotaged that recommendation at source. Not only did it provide Kakungulu's enemies within the Ganda chiefly class with new opportunities for rumour-mongering in newspapers as well as by word of mouth; it destroyed Boyle's basic confidence in him. A financially bankrupt African ally was bad enough when a penny-pinching policy had to be implemented out of allies' own pockets; one seemingly out of sympathy with British policy itself on matters of life and death like sleeping sickness regulations, was far worse. Before February 1909, Boyle had been embarrassed by Kakungulu's house-building plans as well as by his bankruptcy; after the OCSSAM survey he appeared to be appalled by every aspect of the man. Hesketh Bell had said certain things orally at the agricultural and industrial exhibition. Kakungulu had also received a pay rise to £300. But nothing about any further promotion had actually been mentioned in correspondence with London. Boyle's present quibble was therefore more than a quibble: it was a paper quibble.

Only when paper quibbles between British protectorate officials clashed could their African allies play off one official against another. This was not such an occasion. Boyle's successor at Jinja was only too glad to co-operate with him in down-grading Kakungulu's status. Indeed, shortly he would go further. On 13 July 1909, Kakungulu was absent from the Busoga district council because of sickness and he sent his *katikiro*, Yowasi Mivule, to preside in his place. But Mivule was not allowed to occupy the chair. Instead another Ganda chief suggested that the most senior chief present should preside. This suggestion came from the person deputising for Ali Lwanga. Lwanga was caretaking Luuka county at this time, while its titular head attended Balangira School, Kamuli, and would have been the most senior chief present. It is not known whether Salim Bwagu was also present; if so, he would have been the only possible competitor with Lwanga's deputy for the honour. However, lengthy discussion ensued under the DC's guidance. Eventually a majority of those present agreed that, henceforth, the chairmanship of council meetings should rotate among all county chiefs in Busoga on a monthly basis,[152] a decision which Spire immediately ratified.[153]

Effectively, the rotating chairmanship reduced Kakungulu's role in the affairs of the district council from executive to advisory level. If that was not demotion enough, Spire reduced it still further by rewriting the role of the district council itself shortly afterwards:

> This body of natives is purely advisory to the Government for administration of native affairs under the direction of the District Commissioner.
>
> The Government has chosen Kakunguru to be its head and no member appointed can be dismissed except with the sanction of the Provincial Commissioner. In the same way no member becomes such unless and until he is approved by the Government. The Lukiko may suggest a member but the Government may appoint another.
>
> Fines, fees, market dues etc. which are brought into the Lukiko Fund are not to be drawn upon except with the signature of the Provincial Commissioner. All expenditure vouchers must be certified as correct by the District Commissioner before the Provincial Commissioner is asked to sign.[154]

Before Spire's arrival, Kakungulu had transformed this assembly from a collection of yes-men into 'a real Council'. Now Spire was returning it to its earlier role.

Why did Spire do this? Dilatoriness over British sleeping sickness policy undoubtedly accounted for Kakungulu's first demotion. But not the second one. To explain that, we must look further at colonial Busoga as well as at its new provincial commissioner.

In the Uganda Protectorate throughout the 1900s Busoga occupied an ambiguous position. It was classifiable both among the centralized states to the south and west of the River Nile, and among the decentralized polities to the north and east of it. William Grant had treated Busoga within the second framework, Alexander Boyle within the first. Grant had in effect turned himself into the paramount chief of Busoga, installing amenable allies in each subordinate position. Boyle acted differently. More concerned with improving administration than with sustaining control, he employed Ganda chiefs in crucial intermediary roles and encouraged Kakungulu to raise the Busoga district council to a position approximating more to that of the Mengo Lukiko within the Buganda kingdom. When Spire arrived, this trend was reversed.

It is tempting to interpret Spire's behaviour here as a response to Busoga's administrative ambiguity, accentuated by previous service as a protectorate official amongst the 'stateless societies' of northern and eastern Uganda – parts of which are now in southern Sudan and western Kenya too – strengthened still further by his social need as a former valet to Colonel Colvile to exercise dominance, and to be seen to exercise it, over Semei Kakungulu. But policy considerations were also important. The headless African multitude created by excessive European interference with traditional life, was a spectre already starting to disturb British colonial officials throughout Africa. Spire was not alone in feeling that unrestricted economic development from outside – of the sort envisaged by Boyle and Bell – was politically unwise as well as financially unnecessary once a British protectorate or colony came within sight of balancing its books. Busoga was now 'taking off' as regards cotton production.[155] Nor was Spire the only British official in Uganda to believe that the 'modern' functions of African local government should be separated from the 'traditional' ones, and that both should be closely controlled by British officials rather than by African chiefs. Though his precise balance of reasons for downgrading Kakungulu's position as council president may elude us, it is clear that Spire was influenced by general policy considerations as well as by more personal imperatives.

Nonetheless, Kakungulu was still administratively useful to Spire after this double demotion. Kakungulu could be blamed when insufficient taxes were forwarded to Entebbe, as already noted.[156] As long as Kirinya hill remained overgrown, Kakungulu rather than the British protectorate administration could take responsibility for this too.[157] Besides continuing utility as an administrative scapegoat, Kakungulu could still be used whenever necessary as administrative middleman. The administrative side of the Busoga district council was being deliberately run down. But there was still the extension to the new railway line to be built and this required a labour force of between 3,000 and 4,000 men, excluding permanent plate-laying and unloading gangs.[158] Supervision of this labour force was devolved upon Kakungulu,[159] and in carrying out this task he doubtless displayed the same talents for organization that had so impressed Colvile during the Bunyoro campaign of 1893–4. In the book he published about that campaign, Colvile gave Kakungulu due praise.[160] When the Jinja–Kakindu railway was opened on 1 January, 1912, Spire did not thank Kakungulu at all for his contribution. It was 'the Basoga' who were praised for building the new railway.[161]

Unsurprisingly, Kakungulu then requested permission to resign his administrative position in Busoga for a second time. But now he was even weaker tactically than he had been at the time of his earlier request to return to Bukedi: his personal following had since been still further depleted. Most British protectorate officials still opposed his return to Bukedi. Kakungulu's managerial talents were needed for further railway construction – the Busoga railway was now being extended from Kakindu to Namasagali – and it was thought that Kakungulu might still be able to resurrect his former following and cause 'trouble' once he returned to Bukedi.[162] Kakungulu was therefore required to remain in Busoga. He therefore made the best of his position: managing railway labour with his customary skill, and playing local rivals off one against another with equal competence.

Soon the resultant chiefly in-fighting in Busoga became exceedingly complex. To older rivals like Ali Lwanga and Salim Bwagu, and younger ones like Ismairi Katende (Apolo Kagwa's confidant in the Busoga district office), were now added the younger Soga notables just starting to return from school. Probably Katende still caused Kakungulu most difficulty. His position as interpreter to Isemonger gained most in influence from Kakungulu's lessening powers as council president. It may also have been Katende who suggested to Isemonger that Kakungulu's absences from council sessions and residence at Batambogwe were evidences of administrative laxity. It was certainly Katende who translated and sent on Isemonger's orders to Kakungulu with greater forcefulness than diplomacy.[163]

Kakungulu counter-attacked in two ways. First, on several of the occasions when the Busoga district council constituted itself as a court of law, Kakungulu drew attention to Katende's misdeeds.[164] He also attempted to play Katende off tactically against Nadiope of Bugabula, who was now Apolo Kagwa's son-in-law. Conflict here reached a peak over tax collection in Jinja township. Katende claimed this fell within his sphere, Nadiope that it lay within his jurisdiction. Kakungulu helped the dispute along by comparing Busoga with Buganda:

> He said that in Buganda there is one township for *bazungu* [white people] and one for the Kabaka, and both of these were ruled over by the county chief *Kago*. The township of the *bazungu* at Entebbe was also ruled by the county chief *Mugema*. 'I want to do the same here: a man of Nadiope should rule this township as well'.
>
> Then *Bwana* [Isemonger] told him that what you say happens in Buganda does not necessarily happen here.
>
> Then I knelt down and pleaded like this: 'My lord, I know myself that since long ago the township of Jinja has not been under county jurisdiction. Its autonomy is confirmed by its tax receipts. These are brought from Entebbe with "Jinja" written upon them, while all county tickets have their respective county names marked on them. If "Budiope" had been written I would have known that I was in the domain of Nadiope'.

The reporter was Ismairi Katende; his report contained in a confidential letter to Apolo Kagwa.[165]

The DC's (or possibly PC's) words on this occasion must have preyed further on Kakungulu's mind. In October 1912 Kakungulu evidently could again stand the strain no longer. Spire and Isemonger had just appointed yet another chairman of the Busoga district council without consulting him. Kakungulu protested. Katende again summarized the outcome for Apolo Kagwa:

All the chiefs had assembled except Kakungulu. He had not been attending the Lukiko for a whole month because he was very angry because Semu had been given command without consultation. About this he was furious and wrote a letter to Bwana Spire full of serious accusations like '*Bwana*, you know that I am the one who was put in Busoga just as if I was their king' and 'There is nothing the *bazungu* can do here without consulting me or gaining my permision, just as the *bazungu* in Buganda can do nothing without the knowledge of the Lukiko of Mengo' and 'You, Spire, you do not acknowledge my true status: that is why you do such despising things'...

*Bwana* said that the words of this letter seem to imply that the protectorate government is subordinate to this council. 'No, protectorate government rules lukiko here and Bwana Makubwa is very angry to see words that abuse like this; it is very shameful. The Lukiko of Buganda has power because it has its kabaka. Note that there is no Kabaka in Busoga, only the protectorate official who rules over it as though he were Kabaka. If a person does wrong he is driven away without referring to the lukiko: the lukiko is only here to help us in some things.' But his words were very angry and cannot all be reported in a letter.

Kakungulu was 'a terrible man', concluded Katende. 'Perhaps he has been bewitched by the female Muhima as the proverb says !'[166]

It was unnecessary to go to proverbs to explain Kakungulu's behaviour. Kakungulu had lost his temper. But each of his statements to Spire concerned the role that Bell and Boyle had originally persuaded him to accept in Busoga. Since then that role had been considerably downgraded. Kakungulu was not therefore giving expression to any particularly new passion for personal aggrandisement at this time, but to an honourably older one. Tactically, too, there was reason for Kakungulu to lose his temper now. At best, he might regain something of his former status as leader of 'a real Council'. At worst, he would get what he had already been refused twice: permission to resign his administrative office in Busoga.

The worst did not happen immediately. All that emerged directly from the council meeting at which his letter was discussed, bad feeling aside, was clarification of difference between the Buganda and Busoga situations as perceived by British protectorate officials. This had been glossed over when Kakungulu accepted office in Busoga in 1906, and had bedevilled his career ever since. Now Kakungulu played his last political card. He denounced Spire to the new protectorate governor.

Kakungulu's chronicler summarizes events:

After a tour of Busoga the PC and Kakungulu arrived in Busia which was then under Busoga district. At Busia the PC calculated all the money he had spent on chicken, vegetable, eggs and his servants' food. The PC then asked Kakungulu how much he had spent. Kakungulu replied that all his food had been donated to him. When the PC heard this he lost his temper and said 'How can a big man like you eat the peasants' food without paying for it?' Kakungulu commented: 'The chiefs agreed to give me food here. Have you seen anyone accusing me before you of stealing their food? I cannot buy food in this country: I am not just a stranger like you'. The PC then said: 'I do not like travelling with you any longer' and Kakungulu too said 'Neither do I want to travel or work with you: I will go back to my land in Bukedi'. Immediately Kakungulu packed up his things and returned to Batambogwe, leaving Bwana Spire to continue with the safari.

When the President arrived at Jinja he wrote to the Governor 'I do not want to work with Spire because he despises me' and the PC wrote the same adding that if the Government still needed Kakungulu 'I will leave him the Eastern Province and go back to Europe'. The Governor invited them both to discuss the matter, and after failing to make them agree allowed Kakungulu to return to his Mbale estate and become county chief of Mbale. This happened in 1913.[167]

Though the story clearly lost no colour in the telling, it retains the ring of truth. Indeed, the official letter which Spire eventually wrote demanding Kakungulu's resignation partly corroborates it by remarking that 'During the Governor's recent visit to Jinja Kakungulu complained to His Excellency that I hurt his dignity nearly two years ago while on tour with His Excellency ...' But Spire's burden now was a more personal one:

> Kakunguru is not really clever, far from it, he is extremely obstinate and wildly and childishly ambitious ever craving for the impossible in the form of a Kabakaship. He has an extraordinary craze for house-building far beyond his station ... I have no doubt Kakunguru merely brought the matter [of food supplies in Samia] forward as a means of attracting attention to himself. His enormous conceipt [sic] has led him into many difficulties during the past 20 years.

Kakungulu should now be forced to resign. 'In view of the progress of Busoga and the forthcoming return of several young Basoga Sazas from the High Schools, I think the sooner Kakungulu is disposed of the better.'[168]

The political wheel had now turned full circle for Kakungulu. At the court of Mutesa I he acquired office as an elephant hunter through technical competence (*magezi*), though he soon discovered that to retain office required attention to the classic Ganda arts of flattery (*okufugibwa*) and denunciation (*kuloopa*) as well as fighting bravely on the battlefield and doing his job as an ivory culler efficiently. During Mwanga II's reign British commissioners progressively displaced the Ganda king as the principal manager of scarce resources in Buganda. Through success in war, the Protestant religion, and his ability to attract and retain a sizeable following, Kakungulu had climbed steadily up the ladder of honour. Finding his way ahead in Buganda blocked by Apolo Kagwa, he built up alternative positions in the interstices of British rule elsewhere, first in Bugerere, then massively in Lango, Teso, Bukedi and Bugisu. His promotion to Busoga was a deliberate attempt to encapsulate him within the Uganda Protectorate on British terms, and to deal bureaucratically with what by now appeared an excessively embarrassing side of Kakungulu's pursuit of honour. To start with, the terms of transfer to Busoga were generous. At the close of Kakungulu's time there, they were more restrictive. Furthermore, with his status in Busoga downgraded and his following to a considerable extent dispersed, Kakungulu was now as dependent upon the British protectorate governor for his fate as he had ever been upon a Ganda king. And the British protectorate governor was now Frederick Jackson.

### 7

Frederick Jackson assumed office in April 1911. He had been away in the neighbouring East Africa Protectorate for nearly a decade, and was distressed at what had happened during his absence. One development which distressed him was the 'system, now in vogue, of administering certain districts in the Northern and Eastern Provinces through the agency of Baganda.'[169] This is not the place to describe in detail how Ganda agents came to be employed as administrative intermediaries in many parts of the Uganda Protectorate after Kakungulu's transfer to Busoga; here it must suffice to say that they had not only multiplied further within each of the areas formerly controlled by Semei Kakungulu in eastern Uganda, but were already spreading widely elsewhere. They had proliferated in Teso, increased in Bugisu, reestablished themselves in Padhola, consolidated their positions in Bugwere, Bunyole and Pallisa, and were now returning to Lango, the scene of Kakungulu's earlier and least success. Soon they would be entering Kigezi too.[170]

In February 1911 a junior British official in Lango, who happened to be the nephew of a British cabinet minister,[171] complained to his immediate superior about the matter. 'The state of affairs as it exists would be incredible if it were not a fact', wrote J.O. Haldane. Ganda agents in Lango were by now paid small salaries but their followers still received nothing from the protectorate administration. 'We accept their certainly useful services upon the *openly unspoken but officially gainsaid* understanding that we concede them the right to live by underhand methods of plunder so long as they employ it discreetly and don't *oblige* us to scrutinize their conduct.' Neither in theory nor in practice did this system do British protectorate administration any credit.[172]

Many of these criticisms were just. With Kakungulu's transfer to Busoga in 1906 and the intensified British demands for tax in eastern Uganda thereafter, many Ganda agents in Bukedi became straightforward marauders. There were the inevitable incidents, but Hesketh Bell managed to hush most of them up. Judicial enquiries were rigged and punitive expeditions disguised as police manoeuvres now that they could no longer be blamed simply upon Baganda. Missionaries protested, contrasting current atrocities with the comparative peacefulness of Kakungulu's earlier regime.[173] But it was to no avail; as Bishop Tucker commented, it was like arguing with a brick wall.[174] When Jackson returned to Uganda as governor, he found Haldane's protest at Entebbe together with supporting statistics. He was horrified. He declared the Ganda agents would have to go. As it happened, Ganda agents would prove more difficult to remove than the new protectorate governor envisaged, some of them remaining in power for another 30 years. But Jackson was not to know that in April 1913.

'He should have been retired earlier, and the members of the [Busoga] Lukiko given a fair chance of showing what they could do without him', minuted Jackson in commentary upon Spire's letter of denunciation:

> In the past the Basoga chiefs have been treated in a manner that is, perhaps, as well to draw a veil over. They were up to 10 years ago independent 'Kabakalets', but in an arbitrary manner they were downgraded to the position of Saza Chiefs, and hereditary succession is all that is left to them; and in order to retain the remnant of their rights and 'Kitibwa' [honour] they are now educating their sons at Budo school and elsewhere, in order to fit them for their future responsibilities.[175]

Jackson too had his code of honour, but as far as Africans were concerned it was one closer to Rider Haggard than the European middle ages.[176] It was a matter of noble birth rather than reckless renown in armed combat; reckless courage was clearly now a matter more for non-Africans than Africans in British African protectorates. However, Jackson does appear to have tried to reconcile differences between Kakungulu and Spire at a special meeting in April 1913, as Kakungulu's chronicler relates.[177] Some Britishers in Busoga, too, feared that Kakungulu could still not be dismissed from office without the likelihood of rebellion erupting.[178] But when Kakungulu resigned from the presidency of the Busoga district council in June 1913 with dignity rather than recrimination, it was clear that British fears on this score had been misplaced. 'K thanks the Govt & exhorts the Lukiko. The Lukiko thanks K for his work'.[179] All that Spire now needed to do, was to compose a mildly defamatory despatch.

Spire overplayed his hand. Not content simply with Kakungulu's resignation, Spire wanted all remembrance of the man removed from Busoga: 'it would be better if there were no Native Court in Jinja, that the post of President of the Lukiko be abolished, and that appeals from the County Court should be held by Administrative Officers when on tour.'[180] But that was to go too far. The shift from an oral to a paper-based political system enabled British protectorate administrators to disregard verbal promises made by Sir Henry Hesketh Bell and Sir Harry Johnston. But printed laws were another matter. Though Spire had downgraded the administrative powers of the Busoga district council in 1909, its judicial role had been strengthened in the same year by the Native Courts Ordinance applying to the whole protectorate.[181] To accept Spire's proposal to abolish its judicial functions now, commented the protectorate's Acting Chief Justice, would be contrary to both 'equity and general expediency'. It would make nonsense of the legal structure of the Uganda Protectorate.[182]

There was also the editorial in the Church Missionary Society's newspaper *Uganda Notes* to be considered:

> We heard with mingled feelings of the resignation of Semei Kakungulu from his office as President of Busoga. He has undoubtedly done a great

work, and is a man of quite exceptional ability, with the faults and qualities of a strong man. If his retirement may be taken as an indication on the part of the Government that his work is done, and that the Basoga are now sufficiently advanced to undertake their own government without external help from the Baganda, we are thankful for it. But on the face of it the removal of Kakungulu leaves Busoga in a difficult position. They have no king, as have Buganda or Bunyoro; they have no centre of native government apart from the native council, where the nine *Saza* chiefs meet on equal terms. And it would be difficult to find any really progressive country which has no common head: the whole tendency of modern government is towards unification.[183]

Spire back-pedalled. At no time had he desired the legal functions of the Busoga district council to be abolished, the protectorate's Chief Justice now reported him as saying. Spire's sole object was 'to secure the abolition of the office of a permanent President of that body'.[184] This proposal was duly approved, Jackson signing a special proclamation reconstituting the principal court of Busoga as 'a committee of any seven or more members of the Lukiko, presided over at each sitting by such member of the Court as may be elected by it to be President for such sitting'. The same proclamation also formally abolished the office of 'President of the Lukiko of Busoga'.[185]

Later a demand arose within Busoga for the office to be revived. In 1919 Ezekieri Wako, one of the first Soga to be educated at a CMS high school, was appointed chairman of the Busoga district council with the title *Isebantu Kyabazinga*. Undoubtedly this appointment owed much to the enhanced ethnic feeling which emerged among the mission-school elite of Busoga district immmediately after the First World War.[186] But clearly it owed something to Semei Kakungulu too.

Therein lay Kakungulu's principal claim to administrative and political creativity in colonial Busoga. Not determining its administrative shape – the crucial decisions there had been taken before he arrived as president of its district council, and afterwards Kakungulu was only important in influencing the shape of intra-chiefdom boundaries. Not introducing Ganda political culture singlehandedly into Busoga district. Not imposing any particular land settlement there – Soga chiefs agitated for *mailo* lands to be granted to them both before and after his presidency in Busoga, and Kakungulu was only one among several influences where other tenures were concerned. The Busoga railway was certainly in part a monument to his administrative talent, but it would be unjust to saddle Kakungulu with principal responsibility for building this particular track. His main creative contribution to Soga colonial politics was to turn the particular position he held in Busoga into a desirable political prize, at least so long as British protectorate rule lasted in Uganda. Spire might downgrade it, he might even abolish it. But Soga chiefs and intellectuals would agitate to resurrect it later, as they still do today – and they did, and do, this at least partly because of what Semei Kakungulu had made of the position between 1906 and 1913.

# *Notes*

1. Earlier pioneering studies of Busoga include: D.W. Cohen, *Womunafu's Bunafu* (Princeton 1977); L.A. Fallers, *Bantu Bureaucracy: a Study of Integration and Conflict in the Political Institutions of an East African People* (Cambridge 1956); D.M. Mudoola, 'Chiefs and political action: the case of Busoga, 1900–1962', Ph.D. dissertation, Makerere University, 1974; P.F.B. Nayenga, 'An economic history of the lacustrine states of Busoga, Uganda, 1750–1939', Ph.D. dissertation, University of Michigan, 1976); and T. Tuma, *Building a Ugandan Church: African Participation in Church Growth and Expansion in Busoga 1891–1940* (Nairobi 1980).
2. See above, p. 197.
3. A.B.K. Kasozi, 'Islam in Busoga', unpublished paper, Makerere University, 1970; M. Wright, *Buganda in the Heroic Age* (Nairobi, 1971) p. 185.
4. Johnston to Tucker, 1 December 1900, copy in A/23, ESA.
5. D.A. Low, 'The British and Uganda', D.Phil. thesis, Oxford 1957, p. 496.
6. Boyle to Entebbe, March 1906 [no day given], A 10/5, ESA.
7. *Ibid.* Also Boyle to same, 7 July 1904, A 10/4, ESA.
8. Boyle to Entebbe, 26 February 1906, A 10/5, ESA.
9. T. Watson, 'A history of church missionary high schools in Uganda 1900–1914: the education of a Protestant elite', Ph.D. dissertation, University of East Africa, 1968. RC secondary schools await their historian, though there is some discussion in O.W. Furley, 'Education and the chiefs in East Africa in the inter-war period', *Transafrican Journal of History* 1 (1971), pp. 60–81; H.P. Gale, *Uganda and the Mill Hill Fathers* (London 1959); and R. Heremans, *L'Education dans les missions des Peres Blancs en Afrique centrale 1879–1914* (Brussels 1983), pp. 297–313.
10. Boyle to Entebbe, 16 January 1905, A 10/5, ESA.
11. Boyle to Sadler, 31 August 1904, A 10/4/, ESA.
12. Boyle to Entebbe, 27 October 1904, A 10/4/, ESA.
13. Boyle to Entebbe, 16 January 1905, A 10/4/, ESA.
14. Boyle to Entebbe, 15 April 1905, A 10/4/, ESA.
15. Memo by Boyle, 11 April 1904, A 10/4/, ESA.
16. Lansdowne to Entebbe, 10 June 1904, 27 August 1904, A 22, ESA.
17. J.E.M. Hannington, annual letter for 1907, CMS Library, London.
18. See Watson, 'Church missionary high schools'.
19. D.W. Cohen, *The Historical Tradition of Busoga: Mukama and Kintu* (Oxford 1972), pp. 15–16.
20. Boyle to Entebbe, 22 December 1905, A 10/5, ESA.
21. *Ibid.*
22. L.A. Fallers, 'The Soga', in ed. A.I. Richards, *East African Chiefs* (London 1960), pp. 82, 84.
23. *Ibid.*, p. 84.
24. *Ibid.*, p. 85.
25. Sadler to London, 27 February 1904, FO 856, PRO.
26. Ormsby to Jinja, 2 February 1905, A 10/4, ESA.
27. Boyle to Entebbe, 27 February 1905, A 10/4, ESA.
28. Ormsby, 2 February 1905.
29. Boyle to Sadler, 23 July 1904, A 10/4, ESA.
30. Minute by Boyle on Busoga monthy report for January 1905, undated, A 10/4, ESA.
31. Minutes by Tompkins, 12 July 1906, and Bell, 10 October 1906, SMP 704/06, ESA.
32. Paulo Kagwa, 'Kakungulu Omuzira wa Uganda', p. 75.
33. Salimu Mbogo, interview at Kachumbala, Teso, 31 May 1964.
34. *Ibid.*
35. Byakuno had been linked to Kakungulu by a blood-brotherhood relationship, though oral sources differ over whether it was a direct one or secondary (through Byakuno's father, Tebukoza; see above, p. 22). Byakuno fought on the Sudanese side at the siege of Bukaleba in 1897–8 and would have been shot by the British but for Kakungulu's mediation. See Kasozi, 'Islam in Busoga' for Bwagu.

36. See below, notes 164 and 165. The man worked earlier for Kakungulu as a secretary at Budaka (Kakungulu, *Diary*, Vol 2, p. 54).
37. Lukiko Order Book (LOB), entries for 22, 24 and 26 November 1906; consulted at Eastern regional office, Mbale.
38. A.R. Tucker, 7 September 1909, in *Report of the Committee on Emigration from India to the Crown Colonies and Protectorates*, PP, Cd 5194, Vol. 3, p. 154. See also B.W. Langlands, 'The population geography of Busoga district', occasional paper 40, Geography Department, Makerere University, 1971.
39. Tucker, *ibid.*
40. P. Kagwa, 'Omuzira', pp. 76–7.
41. T. Grant to Jinja, 12 May 1908, SMP 966/08, ESA.
42. Boyle to Entebbe, 23 October 1907, SMP 1564/07, ESA.
43. P. Kagwa, 'Omuzira', p. 77.
44. Fallers, 'Soga', p. 84.
45. Lord Hailey, *Native Administration in the British African Territories* (London 1950) Vol. 1, p. 26.
46. Fallers, 'Soga', p. 84.
47. P. Kagwa, 'Omuzira', p. 77.
48. LOB, entries for 10 and 30 April 1907.
49. P. Kagwa, 'Omuzira', p. 78.
50. See A.T. Matson, 'Baganda merchant venturers', *Uganda Journal* 32 (1968), pp. 1–15, and J.A. Rowe, 'Mika Sematimba', *Uganda Journal* 28 (1964), pp. 195–6.
51. DC Nimule to DC Mbale, telegram 31 March 1911, MA, mentions one Juma bin Salim working on Kakungulu's gun licence for this purpose. Kakungulu to Boyle, 15 June 1904, encl. Boyle to Entebbe, A/24, ESA, also reports that he despatched an ivory-collecting expedition northeastwards from Mbale in 1903 and that this expedition reached as far as Mani Mani beyond Lake Rudolph.
52. See further my survey of 'East African Asians through a hundred years' in eds C. Clarke, C. Peach and S. Vertovec, *South Asians Overseas* (Cambridge 1990), pp. 149–63.
53. Minute by Land Officer (LO), 5 January 1910, SMP 958/9, ESA.
54. Boyle to Entebbe, 17 July 1904, enclosing 'Yoosef' to Jinja, 14 July 1904, A10/4, ESA.
55. Spire to Chief Secretary (CS), 19 April 1910, enclosing Pellew Wright to Spire, 14 April 1910, C/40/1910, ESA.
56. Statement by M. Yusuf, 27 January 1911, C/95/1910, ESA.
57. Minute by Bell, 12 September 1908, SMP 1474/08, ESA.
58. Boyle, telegram, 15 September 1908, SMP 1474/08, ESA.
59. Tuffnell to Entebbe, 5 January 1909, SMP 1474/08, ESA.
60. Bell to London, 25 January 1909, copy, A 39/11/09, ESA.
61. Boyle to Entebbe, 4 November 1908, SMP 1760/08, ESA.
62. 'Official Report, the Uganda Agricultural and Industrial Exhibition', *Uganda Official Gazette*, 15 November 1908; reproduced in *Uganda Notes*, November 1908.
63. SMP 1823/08, ESA.
64. This was Kakungulu's subsequent recollection in 'Ebigambo bye Busoga', encl. with J.M. Gray to Entebbe in SMP 1760/08, but not forwarded to London with the main report.
65. Dimbwe, interview at Nkoma, Mbale, 24 July 1964.
66. Allen to CS, 28 November 1908, SMP 1909/08, ESA.
67. Isemonger to Jinja, 13 September 1909, EPMP 148/8, ESA.
68. G.P. McGregor, *King's College, Budo: the First Sixty Years* (Nairobi 1967), pp. 21–2; J.A. Rowe, 'Myth, memoir and moral admonition: Luganda historical writing 1893–1969', *Uganda Journal* 33 (1969), pp. 217–18.
69. See above, pp. 144, 168.
70. Boyle to Entebbe, 4 November 1908, SMP 1760/08, ESA.
71. Bell to London, 11 November 1908, SMP 1760/08, ESA.
72. Cooper to Entebbe, 2 May 1907, SMP 549/07, ESA.
73. Cooper to Grant, 13 August 1907, SMP 113/07, ESA.
74. Grant to Entebbe, 25 August 1907, SMP 113/07, ESA.
75. Boyle to Jinja, 23 September 1907, SMP 113/07, ESA.

76. Isemonger to Jinja, 4 February 1910, encl. Spire to Entebbe, 8 February 1910, SMP 1069/08, ESA.
77. Boyle to Isemonger, undated but clearly mid-February 1910, SMP 1069/08, ESA.
78. See W.J.M. MacKenzie, *Politics and Social Science* (Harmondsworth 1967), p. 181; M. Gluckman and J.A. Barnes, 'The village headman in British Central Africa', *Africa* 19 (1949); L.A. Fallers, 'The predicament of the modern African chief', *American Anthropologist* 57 (1955), pp. 290–305.
79. *Ibid.*
80. *The Theory of Social and Economic Organization*, trans. T. Parsons (New York 1947), p. 340.
81. T. Tuma, *Building an African Church* (Nairobi 1980), pp. 56–7.
82. 'The Mohammedan question', *Uganda Notes*, August 1906.
83. See above, p. 211
84. J. Roscoe to CMS, 28 July 1908, G3A7/1908b, CMS archives.
85. See M. Twaddle, 'Politics in Bukedi', Ph.D. dissertation, University of London, 1967, pp. 232–76, for further details.
86. H.B. Thomas and R. Scott, *Uganda* (London 1935), p. 65.
87. H.H. Bell, *Report on the Introduction and Establishment of the Cotton Industry of the Uganda Protectorate*, 14 September 1909, PP, Cd 4910, 1909; and *Report on the Measures Adopted for the Suppression of Sleeping Sickness in Uganda*, 17 November 1909, Cd 4990, 1910.
88. R. Hyam, *Elgin and Churchill at the Colonial Office 1905–1908* (London 1968), p. 478.
89. *Ibid.*, p. 357.
90. This is clear from the Bell Papers (BP) at the Royal Commonwealth Society, London; other diaries deposited with the British Library, are closed until next century.
91. Diary entry for 10 June 1906, reporting visit to Entebbe by Sydney Goldman; and letter to 'Dearest little Auntie', 25 June 1905: copies in BP.
92. T. Taylor, 'The establishment of a European plantation sector within the emerging political economy of Uganda, 1902–1919', *International Journal of African Historical Studies* 19 (1986), pp. 52–4.
93. See C. Ehrlich in eds V. Harlow and E.M. Chilver, *History of East Africa* (Oxford 1965), Vol. 2, pp. 403–6 and 'The marketing of cotton in Uganda 1900–1950', Ph.D. dissertation, University of London, 1958, pp. 55–89, as well as Bell, *Report on the Measures*.
94. Travelling on the Orient Express, he was left at one stop in his pyjamas after the train had moved on to another station.
95. Churchill to Bell, 1 January 1908, SMP/C/47/10, ESA.
96. Bell to Churchill, 24 January 1908, copy, SMP/C/47/10, ESA.
97. G.W. Hogg to Entebbe, 26 May 1911, SMP 362/08, ESA.
98. M.F. Hill, *Permanent Way: The Story of the Kenya and Uganda Railway* (Nairobi 1947), p. 327.
99. E.K. Hawkins, *Roads and Road Transport in an Underdeveloped Country: a Case Study of Uganda* (London 1962).
100. Hogg to Entebbe, 26 May 1908, SMP 362/08, ESA.
101. There was also the inequitable financing of the Busoga railway and associated marine: as a charge to the Uganda Protectorate rather than the Uganda Railway, without a fair share of freight or customs revenue. See Hill, *Permanent Way*, pp. 320–1, 340–1, 357–8.
102. Hawkins, *Roads and Road Transport*, p. 27.
103. As Maryinez Lyons summarizes Ford's arguments in 'Sleeping sickness in the history of the Northeast Congo (Zaire)', *Canadian Journal of African Studies* 19 (1985), p. 628.
104. Bell, *Glimpses of a Governor's Life* (London n.d.), p. 98.
105. B.W. Langlands, 'The sleeping sickness epidemic of Uganda 1900–1920: a study in historical geography', occasional paper 1, Geography Department, Makerere University, 1967; W.D. Foster, *The Early History of Scientific Medicine in Uganda* (Kampala 1970), pp. 93–107.
106. Quoted by Foster, *The Early History*, p. 104.
107. Bell, 4 September 1906; reproduced *Glimpses*, p. 135.
108. Foster, *The Early History*, p. 105; Bell, 12 May 1906, reproduced *Glimpses*, p. 118.

109. W.F. Fiske, *A History of Sleeping Sickness and Reclamation in Uganda* (Entebbe 1927, restricted official circulation), p. 11.
110. *Ibid.*
111. Ernest Haddon, a junior official during part of Kakungulu's time in Busoga; interview at his Cambridge home, 3 March 1965.
112. Langlands, 'The sleeping sickness epidemic', p. 5.
113. Thus H.G. Soff, 'Sleeping sickness in the Lake Victoria region of British East Africa, 1900–1915', *African Historical Studies* 2 (1969), p. 258.
114. Langlands, 'The sleeping sickness epidemic', p. 5.
115. John Ford, *The Role of Trypanosomiases in African Ecology* (Oxford 1971), p. 143.
116. See Foster, *The Early History*, pp. 93–100 for a good summary. Fiske, *History of Sleeping Sickness*, p. 12, also noted that 'The natives were surprisingly well informed concerning the conclusions reached at Mpumu laboratory, but they respectfully declined to give credence to these conclusions'.
117. Ismairi Katende, 'Jinja, Busoga', *Ebifa mu Buganda*, March 1909, p. 8.
118. Wyndham to Entebbe, 3 February 1909, SMP 190/09, ESA.
119. Minute by Boyle, 8 March 1909, SMP 190/09, ESA.
120. Minute by Tompkins, 23 March 1909, SMP 190/09, ESA.
121. PMO, 22 March 1909, SMP 190/09, ESA.
122. Bell, 10 April 1909, SMP 190/09, ESA.
123. Spire to Entebbe, 12 June 1909, SMP 190/09, ESA.
124. 'Ebigambo bye Busoga', see note 64.
125. Kakungulu to Bell, 8 October 1906, SMP 1085/06, ESA.
126. Boyle to Entebbe, 18 August 1904, A 10/4, ESA
127. Same to same, 15 October 1906, SMP 1085/06, ESA.
128. Minute by Bell, 19 October 1906, SMP 1085/06, ESA.
129. Boyle to Entebbe, 29 October 1906, SMP 1085/06, ESA.
130. Minute by Tompkins, 13 November 1906, SMP 1085/06, ESA.
131. *Ibid.*
132. Goodliffe to PMO, encl. Hodges to CS, 25 February 1909, SMP 190/9, ESA.
133. Ismairi Katende, 'Jinja, Busoga', *Ebifa mu Buganda*, March 1909, pp. 4–8.
134. LOB, 23 July 1912.
135. Kakungulu to Boyle, 30 March 1909, EPMP 100/9, ESA.
136. *Ibid.*
137. Minute by Bell, 10 April 1909; Spire to Entebbe, 12 June 1909; both SMP 190/9, ESA.
138. Agreement by Kyebambe, 23 August 1909, EPMP 100/9, ESA.
139. Minute by Allen, 20 December 1909, EPMP 100/9, ESA.
140. LO to PC Jinja, 4 February 1910, EPMP 100/9, ESA.
141. EPMP 100/9, ESA.
142. Spire to LO, 28 February 1910, EPMP 100/9, ESA.
143. On Soga chiefs' demands, see P.F.B. Nayenga, 'Chiefs and the "land question" in Busoga'.
144. Here Spire's support for Soga chiefs' demands probably prompted him to support Kakungulu's land claims against the danger of white planters' encroachment.
145. Spire to LO, 30 March 1910; Kakungulu to Spire, n.d. and 10 May 1910, EPMP 100/9, ESA.
146. LOB, 16 March 1909.
147. H.B. Thomas to parents, 10 June 1913, H.B. Thomas Papers, Royal Commonwealth Society Library, London.
148. H.B. Thomas in *Uganda Journal* 6 (1939), p. 135. The principal source for this view was probably P.W. Perryman, 'History of Kakunguru', 30 June 1920, SMP/C/29/06, paras 10 and 11.
149. *Uganda Official Gazette*, 1 April 1909, p. 71, and 15 April 1909, p. 83.
150. Isemonger to Jinja, 20 May 1909, encl. Spire to Entebbe, 24 May 1909, SMP 925/09, ESA.
151. Boyle, inscribed on Isemonger, *ibid.*, inscription undated.
152. LOB, 13 July 1909; Isemonger to Spire, 12 August 1909, encl. Spire to Entebbe, 18

August 1909, SMP 319/9, ESA.
153. Spire, *ibid.*
154. 'Notes on the functions of the Lukiko of Busoga', glued to LOB flyleaf.
155. See P.F.B. Nayenga, 'Commercial cotton growing in Busoga District, Uganda, 1905–1923', *African Economic History* 10 (1981), pp. 175–95.
156. Spire to Entebbe, 8 February 1910, SMP 1069/08, ESA.
157. LOB, 23 November 1909.
158. *Uganda Notes*, September 1911.
159. Ernest Haddon, interview, 3 March 1965.
160. H. Colvile, *The Land of the Nile Springs* (London 1895), p. 80.
161. LOB, 2 January 1912.
162. Coote to Spire, 5 April 1911, copy in SMP 1760/08, ESA; E.B. Haddon and H.B. Thomas, personal communications.
163. E.g. entries in LOB for 15 February 1910 and 11 March 1911.
164. First regarding a lady called Buwogo (LOB, 15 September 1909), then an unmarried niece of one of Kakungulu's personal retainers (LOB, 20 April 1910), finally in connection with Kuliemu (LOB, 17, 18 and 30 May 1912).
165. Katende to Kagwa, 12 September 1912, Kagwa Papers, CD/55, MUL. I am indebted to John Rowe for this reference.
166. Katende to Kagwa, 30 [no month] 1912, copy at pp. 74–5 in letterbook in Kagwa Papers at Makerere; I owe this reference to John Rowe, too.
167. P. Kagwa, 'Omuzira', p. 78.
168. Spire to Entebbe, 16 August 1913, SMP 1760/08, ESA.
169. Jackson to London, 14 July 1911; copy in A 39/18/1911, ESA.
170. A.D. Roberts, 'The sub-imperialism of the Baganda', *Journal of African History* 3 (1962), pp. 435–50, is the pioneering account. See also J. Tosh, *Clan Leaders and Colonial Chiefs in Lango* (Oxford 1978), Chapters 5 and 6. See also Twaddle, 'Politics in Bukedi', pp. 232–61.
171. As noted by Bell to his aunt, 22 June 1908, BP.
172. J.O. Haldane to Knowles, 6 February 1911, SMP 519/09, ESA.
173. Tucker to CMS, 9 August 1907, G3A7/1907b, CMS archives. See further my 'Segmentary violence and political change in early colonial Uganda', *Proceedings of the East African Universities' Social Science Conference*, Nairobi, December 1969.
174. Tucker, *ibid.*
175. Minute by Jackson, 30 July 1913, SMP 1760/08, ESA.
176. Not only was Rider Haggard acquainted with Jackson's family in Britain, but Jackson himself probably featured in at least one of his romances of Africa.
177. LOB entries for 1 and 4 April 1913 confirm the chronicler's account.
178. E.B. Haddon and H.B. Thomas, personal communications.
179. LOB, 3 June 1913.
180. Spire to Entebbe, 13 May 1913, SMP 1760/08, ESA.
181. Ordinance 15 of 1909, Uganda Protectorate. See H.F. Morris, 'Two early surveys of native courts in Uganda', *Journal of African Law* 11 (1967), pp. 159–74, and H.F. Morris and J.S. Read, *Uganda: the Development of its Laws and Constitution* (London 1966), pp. 39–43.
182. Acting Chief Justice to CS, 11 September 1913, SMP 1760/08, ESA.
183. *Uganda Notes*, August 1913. The editorial was unsigned.
184. Chief Justice to CS, Entebbe, 22 December 1913, SMP 1760/08, ESA.
185. *Uganda Official Gazette*, 15 January 1914.
186. W.F. Nabwiso-Bulima, 'The evolution of the Kyabazingaship of Busoga', *Uganda Journal* 31 (1967), pp. 93–4.

# Nine

# Withdrawal to Gangama
# 1913–20

### 1

Three waterfalls tumble down the Nkokonjeru escarpment which rises nearly three thousand feet behind Mbale township. In front of it stretch the Namatala swamp and the plains of Bukedi and Teso. The site is a picturesque one, controlling the tiny strip of land separating the foothills of Mount Elgon from the upper reaches of the Lake Kyoga drainage-system. But in 1913 Mbale was an unhealthy place. Plague was endemic in the African and Asian quarters, malaria rampant in the British residential area. Before Kakungulu had been transferred to Busoga, Sydney Ormsby had bemoaned its feverish climate. When Kakungulu gave up the presidency of the Busoga district council, Ormsby was dead of blackwater fever and his successors compiling monthly lists of other Europeans' deaths. The nearness of the Nkokonjeru escarpment seemed to increase the miniscule British community's concerns about its health. 'It had an oppressive atmosphere very trying to the nerves.'[1]

Economically, Mbale was in difficulty. Hesketh Bell had calculated that the political costs of keeping Karamoja open to traders operating out of the Uganda Protectorate, in terms of metropolitan unpopularity, would outweigh the economic benefits once affrays resumed between ivory traders and local peoples. He had therefore prohibited access to the area from Mbale. Only when this closure led to a general economic depression throughout eastern Uganda was Karamoja again reopened to trade.[2] However, with cash-cropping in cotton within sight of rendering the Uganda Protectorate independent finally of British grants-in-aid, Bell's successors did not bother unduly about other kinds of economic development. Seemingly resentful that Swahilis, Somalis and South Asians should have prospered where his own expedition to Karamoja in 1889–90 had failed so dismally, and eager to suppress yet another 'abuse' which seemingly had taken root during his 10-year absence in the neighbouring

East Africa Protectorate, Frederick Jackson stopped the ivory trade with Mbale completely.[3]

The effect upon Mbale was immediate. Besides the finance, equipment and marketing facilities built up at Mbale by successive ivory-collecting caravans, the Karamoja trade had stimulated further exchanges of cows, donkeys and even ostriches, amongst Karamojong peoples, and in turn generated further trade at Mbale itself. 'A legacy of debts is about all that remains of what used to be a profitable and flourishing business,' lamented the Mbale District Commissioner in April 1911.[4] Most traders from the East African coast had scattered elsewhere. British Indian merchants who stayed on were uncertain about their futures. For years they had co-operated with British protectorate officials in marketing *simsim, chiroko,* groundnuts and beeswax, but their fattest profits had always come from the Karamoja trade in ivory and cattle. Now that trade was over. Cash for other projects was in short supply. To make matters worse for the Mbale merchants, many other traders from the Gujarat region of western India were migrating into the East African interior immediately before the First World War, and seemingly diverting much of their earlier retail trade to a diversity of smaller towns. The future of Mbale seemed bleak.[5]

Cotton provided some financial respite shortly before the First World War. Three multinational companies sent representatives to live at Mbale, but nobody knew how long they would stay.[6] Any further increase in the cotton trade seemed more likely to assist smaller towns like Tororo or Nagongera than a larger one like Mbale.[7] The port of Bugondo on Lake Kyoga appeared more likely to be advantaged as a regional centre by the new railway from Jinja than would Mbale, more than forty miles away from it. Ginneries were being built at Bugondo, and that other hallmark of colonial modernity had also appeared there: urban crime.[8] To be sure, another ten years would show how groundless was the belief that Bugondo could replace Mbale as the economic capital of eastern Uganda. Another decade would also show how ephemeral was the threat to Mbale's future posed by localized diversifications in retail trade. After the First World War, a mushrooming network of motor roads and a railway extension through Mbale itself towards northern and northwestern areas of the Uganda Protectorate again emphasized its strategic importance astride that tiny strip of land separating the Nkokonjeru escarpment from the Namatala swamp.

But this is to jump ahead. When Kakungulu returned from Busoga in June 1913, most people at Mbale were pessimistic. The African quarter was a small fraction of the size it had been during the Karamoja trade and rent by factional fights for what scarce resources remained. One faction was composed of Kamba, Nyamwezi and Kikuyu tribesmen from what are nowadays Kenya and Tanzania. Another was formed by Somalis and Swahilis.[9] Relations between Europeans and South Asians on the whole were more amicable. But British officials were already complaining about living within a stone's throw of the South Asian bazaar and the 'Swahili village' because of the dangers both supposedly posed to their health.[10]

In the interests of European hygiene, Kakungulu's house at Mbale had been razed to the ground during his service in Busoga.[11] However, his estate outside the township remained the peri-urban area that it is still today. The special tax of two rupees which Kakungulu had been allowed to continue levying upon families on the estate during his absence in Busoga, had acted as a break upon further settlement, but it was not clear in June 1913 how long this additional tax would continue.[12] The estate's boundaries were still contested by Kakungulu.[13] It was therefore with some apprehension that local British protectorate officials watched him again settle down as chief of Mbale county, a position he had retained throughout his service in Busoga.

Interest focussed especially upon how Kakungulu would react to the political changes that had taken place around Mbale since 1906. The most fundamental change had been the collapse of his earlier kingdom. Before Kakungulu had departed for Busoga, Ormsby had attracted many of the most competent administrators amongst Kakungulu's followers into direct protectorate service as agents remunerated through tax rebates. Immediately Kakungulu himself left for Busoga, the rest of his kingdom collapsed. Rituals ended, kingship titles were discontinued.[14] What Grant and Jackson had failed to achieve through dismissal in 1902, Boyle had succeeded in doing by promoting Kakungulu to Busoga four years' later. But now that position too had ended. Now British protectorate officials had to deal, not only with Kakungulu's opposition to *pax Britannica* over administrative and land tenure questions, but his opposition to *pox Britannica* too.

*Pax* and *pox* were interconnected.[15] Cash-cropping in cotton for overseas markets had been, and was still, encouraged by British protectorate officials, along with roads, rapid urbanization, railways, population movements involving traders from South Asia as well as soldiers from the other side of the Indian Ocean, other parts of Africa, and Europe too; and all this toing and froing increased the dangers of disease. John Ford has emphasized the importance of two sets of events in particular in breaking down earlier ecological controls upon the spread of diseases – 'the rinderpest panzootic, which wiped out cattle and wildlife [which Frederick Lugard had first encountered during his march westwards through Nkore in 1891],[16] and smallpox which, together with famine, reduced the human population [as during the closing stages of the Ganda succession war immediately preceding Lugard's entry, and in the course of the Ganda-British grand army's progress through Bunyoro in 1893–4]. These two sets of events ... upset the ecological controls which had long contained the threat of trypanosomiasis.' Indeed, 'a host of ecologically ignorant authoritarian measures, many of them intended to control tsetse' which were introduced by European imperialists made things actually much worse and led to the further expansion of tsetse fly belts.[17]

In Busoga, as we saw in the last chapter, Kakungulu fell victim economically and politically to the advance of trypanosomiasis. At Mbale, his attitudes towards sickness and misfortune of all kinds would repay the British protectorate authorities abundantly in kind through opposition to their medical policies as well as his continuing lack of a 'proper sense of the authority of District Officers, or indeed of the Provincial Commissioner'.[18] In 1920 Kakungulu complained to his friend (and former CMS missionary), John Roscoe, that he had 'had to endure much annoyance' from British officials in Uganda, 'from continual variations in policy'. 'Promises have been made and withdrawn, and he has been moved from one locality to another as chief, though he has always managed to retain one part of his possesions at Mbale, where he rules over miles of country inhabited by the Bagesu.'[19] 'The Bagesu' were what brought Roscoe to Mount Elgon, as part of the Mackie anthropological expedition.[20] But he could hardly avoid commenting upon what was additionally worrying British officials about Kakungulu: his membership of an anti-medicine movement.

This cult, reported Roscoe, appeared to be 'a mixture of Judaism, Christianity, and Christian Science'.[21] In the particular version of it to which Kakungulu himself adhered, Judaism seemed especially influential. But prominent in it too was that 'strong objection to medical men and their medicines and treatment' shared by all members of the new faith.

## 2

Long before the religion of Malaki was formed, Ganda Protestants were divided in their support for doctors and medicine. 'One of my first recollections on reaching this country at the end of 1890', Archdeacon Baskerville recalled in 1914, 'is going with the late Mr Pilkington to see the Mugema [Joswa Kate, administrative chief of Busiro county] who was suffering from a large abcess on the leg, our object being to induce him to put some medicine in it.' Not only did he refuse, but soon afterwards Kate and others started writing letters 'saying that they objected to taking medicine and that doing so was contrary to the Bible and that doctors were emissaries of Satan.' More seriously, 'almost a month ago we were informed that a certain teacher holding a Senior Certificate from the Diocesan Council by name Malaki Musajakawa at Kitala [also situated in the Busiro county of Buganda] had been appointed pastor of this anti-doctor body and had *actually begun baptising people*.' Since that had happened, 'the movement has proceeded by leaps and bounds'.[22]

It had indeed. As early as October 1914 protectorate police reports put its baptized membership in Buganda at around 10,000 with 'Police and "boys", Cooks and Bakope [peasant cultivators] ... all joining the new sect' in great numbers as well as chiefs led by Joswa Kate. During 1915 'many thousands of Baganda and others' were baptized in Buganda alone by Malaki Musajakawa.[23] By 1921 the estimated baptized membership of the new faith exceeded 90,000 in Buganda, the comparable figure for Bukedi, then an area of probably at least equivalent total population, being unknown. But already Malakite recruitment had begun to lose momentum in Buganda, though it continued to sustain modest membership gains in Bukedi probably into the late 1920s.[24]

In Buganda, employment opportunities increased markedly in the early twentieth century with the possession of a baptismal certificate. This was one consequence of the 'Christian revolution' which had reshaped the kingdom during the last two decades of the nineteenth century. Structurally, the main beneficiaries of this reconstruction were Buganda's administrative chiefs. Not only was their corporate distinctiveness carefully defined for the first time, but their powers over clan leaders, and the complex of king's officials radiating out from the palace compound, increased enormously. In the process recruitment to chiefly office in Buganda became a routinized matter of religious affiliation, segmented along denominational lines.[25] The possession of a Christian name was also useful in non-chiefly occupations. 'An unbaptised person is often subject to ridicule,' noted a European missionary in 1915, 'and not to have a Christian name is to be ranked with illiterates, all education as yet being in Christian hands.'[26]

On the eve of the First World War, the region around Mbale was administered by British officials through a system of appointive chiefs reconstituted from Kakungulu's earlier kingdom. As in Buganda, appointment to chiefship was closely tied to religious allegiances and the preparation time required for church membership growing in length. Preaching in Westminster Abbey in January 1914, the Anglican bishop of Uganda declared that 'Every candidate for baptism, unless too old to learn or too blind to see, must first learn to read the Bible for himself. Every baptised member of the Church must possess his own New Testament.'[27] Clearly, immediate baptism upon a straightforward confession of faith increased both the attractiveness and the ease of becoming a Christian. But in Bukedi baptismal candidates tended to be ethnically as well as economically structured. 'There is a marked movement towards Christianity in the district', it was reported in 1919; 'the number of Baganda who have entered the country in large numbers as administrators and teachers has great weight with the local people, and a desire to "become as Baganda" was sometimes being given as the reason for asking for baptism.'[28] Needless to say, Malakite missionaries offering easier baptism than the CMS benefitted to a correspondingly greater extent from these ambitions, though numerically to nothing like the extent of their successes in Buganda.[29]

Nevertheless, the very first converts to the new faith in Bukedi were not illiterate local people, but literates. For the most part these were clerks, traders and chiefs, and people who had recently retired there. One such was Samwiri Tekiwagala, who had been a baptized Protestant when he first came to Bukedi with Semei Kakungulu in 1899, but by 1914 was living in retirement there as a fairly wealthy small farmer and cattle-keeper. He was one of the very first people around Mbale to respond to Kakungulu's call to join the religion of Malaki:

> This religion started in Buganda. It was started by Mugema Kate and Malaki Musajakawa, who was a Protestant first. Then Malaki left the Protestants and started the new religion with Mugema. It was called the religion of Malaki, but it was really the religion of God.

266

Plate 16. *The author with a leader of the Abamalaki movement in Uganda, who relates at pages 266–8 Kakungulu's reasons for opposing vaccination and other western medical practices.* (Author's photograph)

The cause of the religion was that we saw the Europeans who brought us the Bible were not doing what it said, though they told us to do what it said.

The Europeans disregarded the real Sabbath on which God rested: they chose to observe another day which is not commanded in the Bible. For when God had sent his son Jesus and he was buried, his mother and followers did not visit his tomb because it was the Sabbath. They came to see him the next day because they feared to come on the Sabbath, the real Sabbath, and when they came the day after the Sabbath, he had risen. But the Europeans observed this day as the Sabbath, instead of the real Sabbath as the Sabbath.

Today you can see all these hospitals which the Europeans have built, and do you think these are commanded in the Bible? They are not. How many people who go there are cured of their illnesses? Only sick people go there, and they go there to die. Moreoever, when the Europeans first came to Buganda, they told us to burn our pagan shrines and to stop our witchcraft. What is a European hospital but a pagan shrine [*essabo*]? Also, when you go to Makerere, near there you will find a place [presumably meaning the Uganda Museum] where the Europeans took our things of witchcraft and they keep many things there just as in a very large shrine. Why do they do these things? The missionaries also collected things from shrines. Are these things commanded in the Bible which they gave us to obey?

The actual person who brought the religion of Malaki to this part was Kakungulu. He was once going to Jinja when he found a doctor there who told him that if he wanted to go to Kampala he would have to be inoculated first. Kakungulu refused. The doctor told him that if he were not inoculated he would not be able to go to Kampala, because every-body was being inoculated. Kakungulu refused again, and said he was going back to Mbale. And when he came back to Mbale, he started the religion of Malaki here. He built a church at his house immediately and announced publicly that he had joined the people of Malaki.

Then we began to observe the religion of Malaki in this part, and many Baganda joined it. We believed it to be the religion of God who can do all things [*Katonda omu ainza byonna*], the religion of the God who does not need to use medicines which are not mentioned in the Bible. We wanted to leave our local doctors [*basawo*], our spirit possesion cults [*emmandwa*], and our drugs [*eddagala*]; and, unlike the Europeans, we wanted to obey the Bible completely.[30]

Clearly emphasized in Tekiwagala's text are several motivations. The recruiting role of Kakungulu, and the distaste for Western medicines which failed to provide effective cures, are both emphasized, as also are those suspicions of 'the Europeans' so characteristic of the time. But what is most clearly revealed is the Biblical dynamic in recruitment to the new faith, the desire 'to obey the Bible completely' as far as the literate converts were concerned.

The frequent correlation between publication of the Christian Bible in African vernacular languages and the incidence of independent Christian movements amongst African peoples in the modern world is now well established.[31] The peoples and cultures of Buganda and Bukedi were no exception. Immediately the Bible was published in Luganda, CMS mission-aries quarrelled with their converts over marriage. 'I can trace a decided falling back from the time we introduced the whole of the Bible into the land,' confessed John Roscoe. 'They found that men such as the Patriarchs and the Old Test. Saints had a plurality of wives ... and concluded that we were setting a much more difficult standard than was necessary or warranted from the Bible.'[32] If Old Testament saints were allowed several hundred wives, why were Ganda Protestants restricted to only one?

As far as the new faith was concerned, even more serious differences concerned the treatment of sickness and the initiation of believers. Sickness was more serious because the Bible spoke more clearly upon it than upon marriage, condemning in several parts of the Old Testament recourse to doctors or healers (*basawo*, in Pilkington's translation). The demands of Scripture also coincided with inadequacies in contemporary European medicine. 'Nothing could induce Mugema to believe that because Doctors cannot cure some diseases they cannot do any good', remarked one protectorate official in November 1914. 'He believed that the power to heal rested with God alone'.[33] Kakungulu was saying the same by 1914.

Christian initiation was also a serious matter because parts of the Christian Bible itself provided strong justification for immediate baptism. 'Malaki and Mugema assert that their teaching is founded on St Mark XVI.16 and St Matthew XXVIII.19', reported a British official. 'They assert that when people are baptised Malaki asks them only if they believe in God and the resurrection of Christ. If they say yes they are baptised and are exhorted to go out and preach the Gospel and follow the teachings of Christ and the example set by his life'.[34] In other words, Christian baptism was conditional upon faith, not the increasingly lengthy and expensive education provided by CMS missionaries in the new high schools and elsewhere. Scripturally, the religion of Malaki appeared irrefutable to its most literate converts.

Quite why this was so deserves comment. To a large extent, it was a question of Biblical consistency with the perceived facts of life, especially regarding the treatment (or rather non-treatment) of African sicknesses in an era of epidemics mystifying Europeans as well as Africans. But it was not just a consequence of consistency. It was also a result of literacy. Literacy changes several of the ways in which religious beliefs may be held. To start with, religion becomes more rigid once its teachings are preserved in the permanent forms that literacy makes possible. It becomes still more rigid when spiritual authority itself resides in a written Word of God, as it was in so many churches of the Protestant tradition at the time the new faith emerged. However, already there were rumblings of discontent among more conservative CMS missionaries in Uganda about the textual criticism of the Christian Bible taught at King's College, Budo, in the tradition of nineteenth-century continental European scholarship.[35] Older Christian chiefs at the royal capital of Buganda were also discomforted at more intrusive criticisms of their sexual behaviour by younger, more evangelical CMS missionaries.[36] In such situations Biblical teaching tends to become important in itself, and schism a possibility wherever obedience to it conflicts with wisdom deriving from other sources.

At the start of 1914 Kakungulu was also much affected by the death of his chiefly deputy at Mbale, Esitasio Nkambo. Nkambo, a 'tall, fine looking man, with the beautifully courteous manners of the Baganda of his class' as one British protectorate official subsequently described him,[37] was the only one of Kakungulu's county chiefs from the kingdom of Bukedi not to desert him by now for direct protectorate employment. In his final illness, Nkambo refused to take drugs offered by local CMS personnel.[38] In a letter to Apolo Kagwa shortly before Nkambo's death, Kakungulu wrote 'we do not know whether he will die for it is only God who knows'.[39] In May 1914, Kakungulu also corresponded with Joswa Kate, increasing the likelihood that his opposition to Western medicine too had been germinating for some time, prompted not only by earlier embarrassments over sleeping sickness clearances in Busoga and the burning of his Mbale home because of plague, but by prolonged personal study of the Luganda Bible too.[40] The occasion for Kakungulu's formal break with CMS teaching, however, was a dispute over plague inoculation in August 1914.

Paulo Zinabala accompanied Kakungulu on his journey to attend the coming-of-age celebrations of *Kabaka* Daudi Chwa in Buganda and later wrote up an account of the incident in the minutebook of the Malakite congregation at Mbale.[41] According to this source, when Kakungulu arrived at Jinja and asked for the customary permission to proceed across the River Nile, he was ordered to uncover his arm by a European there so that he might be inoculated. Kakungulu refused, saying he did not take medicine. An Indian orderly then grabbed his arm forcibly. Kakungulu's companions in turn grabbed the Indian and 'we started struggling and some medicine bottles broke'. The Indian orderly asked African askaris standing nearby to seize Kakungulu. They refused. Subsequently the European in charge of inoculation told Kakungulu to see the Jinja DC. The DC told Kakungulu to find the protectorate doctor. When he was finally found burning corpses of plague victims elsewhere in Jinja, the doctor told Kakungulu that he would not be allowed to cross into Buganda without a certificate of inoculation. Kakungulu repeated that he did not wish to be inoculated: 'The medicine has no power, only God has that.' According to Zinabala, the doctor then said 'many things'. Finally he told Kakungulu that, if he still refused inoculation, he should return to Bukedi. This Kakungulu did, arriving back at Mbale on 6 August. Kakungulu immediately separated from the Anglican congregation there, opening a separate church on his private estate on 1 November 1914.[42]

At the end of 1914, Archdeacon Baskerville suggested that all religious teachers in Uganda should be registered.[43] This suggestion was passed on to protectorate headquarters at Entebbe with the PC's approval. This was because, now that 'Mugema's doctrine of "Christian Science"' had been 'mixed up by Mulaki in his interpretation of the Bible with regard to reading for Baptism ... mischievous consequences may ensue.'[44]

## 3

At Entebbe the chief secretary considered registration 'a good thing', because new religious movements should be discouraged as tending 'to unsettle the people'.[45] Wallis, acting governor during one of Jackson's absences, did not agree. There had been 'some little friction' over treatment for venereal diseases at the new Mulago hospital in Kampala. Semei Kakungulu had also 'preferred to return home rather than be inoculated from plague' at Jinja. But in both cases there was a clear 'personal aspect' and thus far there had not been 'any serious opposition to vaccination or to medical administrative measures for the good of the community'. In Wallis's view, the appeal of the new sect lay in two areas. First, there was the appeal of Old Testament marital customs to 'a certain easygoing section of the Native Anglican Church', especially ones 'with a smattering of education'. Secondly, the new religion was a reaction against recent moralistic overkill by Protestant as well as Catholic missionaries. As a result 'men of responsible standing' had been obliged 'either to leave their respective Churches or to dismiss the additional wives, who afterwards swelled the number of native prostitutes'. By comparison, Wallis considered the 'Christian Science teaching' to be a secondary consideration likely to die out in due course. Anyway, the new religion was a problem for missionaries, not government officials. Officials should not interfere, 'unless the public safety or health is endangered'.[46]

Behind Wallis's reluctance to interfere lay a desire by many British officials to distance themselves from Christian missionaries. Not only were there reservations about earlier agreeing to the CMS desire to impose upon the African peoples of the whole protectorate monogamous marriage, customary if not Christian in character.[47] Protectorate officials were also acutely aware of pursuing lower standards of sexual morality for themselves than those currently demanded of Ganda Christians.[48] In addition, the economic support for Christianity created during the 1890s (and formalized, like so much else, through the Uganda Agreement of 1900) was coming under attack. Tenants on church lands, both Catholic and Protestant, were required to work under virtually feudal conditions. Self-support, like sexual morality, could clearly be carried too far by Christian missionaries. Admittedly, the British protectorate in Uganda was dependent upon missionary societies providing the high schools required to equip the new chiefly elite to replace their first set of allies, but in other matters protectorate administrators now wanted to distance themselves as much as possible from the missionaries.[49]

Baskerville's request for restriction by registration was therefore rejected. Instead, the principle of religious liberty enshrined in the Brussels General Act of 1890 was again underlined, together with neutrality regarding denominational allegiances provided that protectorate laws were not disobeyed. Secondly, the use of forced labour for any church or school building was in future to be constrained. In Lango, this policy was pursued so energetically by J.H. Driberg that he himself had to be constrained.[50] For how ultimately could Christian missionary societies be expected to provide schooling for future chiefs if protectorate officials were too unfriendly towards them? Nevertheless, both British administrators and African chiefs had to deal with the Malakites as best they could within a general tightening up of British official benevolence towards all religious organizations.

Bishop Willis thought the Acting Governor wrong to regard the CMS campaign on monogamy as a cause of the new movement. 'The Chiefs, such as Mugema, who are supporting the movement are conspicuously moral. Those who join it are not, so far as I can learn, baptised Christians but pure heathen.'[51] The PC Buganda thought Malaki Musajakawa should be warned that he might be prosecuted under clause 24 of the law against venereal disease.[52] But Wallis vetoed this suggestion too: 'Persecution will only fan [the movement] into flame.'[53] In January 1915 he pointed out that in Cape Colony, 'some five or six years ago', the administration had been disturbed when a section of 'the well-known Lovedale Mission broke away and started a Native Church of its own'. But officials decided to ignore the breakaway group, and now 'little is heard' of it. 'In Nyasaland shortly before I left (1910) there was a similar movement', but this had 'since died out'. Such movements were best left to mission churches to deal with. Colonial governments should not interfere. To arrange for the registration of religious teachers, as Anglican archdeacon and bishop currently demanded, 'savours of persecution, the onus being placed on the Government'.[54] The ruling chiefs of Buganda admittedly took a different line, and already the PC Buganda was experiencing difficulty in constraining chiefly persecution of Malakites there.[55] This was before the Chilembwe rising of 1915 in Nyasaland would put a very different perspective upon the comparative dangers of religious independency in southern Africa.[56] Frederick Jackson, now returned to his governorship, therefore took Wallis's (pre-Chilembwe rising) advice and wrote to Bishop Willis suggesting that ridicule rather than repression was the best way to deal with the new religion:

> It appears to me that so long as you issue cards proving baptism into the Native Anglican Church the mere assumption of a Christian name by Pagans will not raise them in the social scale as they may hope, but will only stamp them followers of silly, misguided, obstinate old men like Mugema & Kakanguru & Malaki who have practically reverted to Paganism.[57]

## 4

How correct was Jackson in assuming that Kakungulu had 'practically reverted to Paganism'?

In his study of *Witchcraft, Oracles and Magic among the Azande* peoples of the Anglo-Egyptian Sudan, the anthropologist Evans-Pritchard remarked upon the differences between their views and scientific or even common sense views. 'Common sense observes only some of the links in a chain of causation. Science observes all, or many more, of the links. In this place we need not define scientific notions more clearly because Azande have none, or very few, according to where we draw the line between common sense and science.'[58] 'Witches, as Azande conceive them' cannot therefore exist, but ideas about witchcraft played a part 'in every activity of Zande life' and provided 'a natural philosophy by which the relations between men and unfortunate events are explained and a ready and stereotyped means of reacting to such events.'[59] More recently, Gwyn Prins has stressed 'that whereas in scientifically oriented cultures, the concentric physiological, social and cosmological spheres of existence are sharply drawn and discrete so that activity in one need have no implication in others, in traditional societies the spheres are acutely interactive', and as many more aspects of society appear to be involved in supporting 'the accepted image of understanding and control in that environmemnt' in such societies, their 'core concepts' also seem to be both 'more pervasive' and of 'greater importance for social definition than in scientifically oriented society'. Thus Prins argues that 'the history of the primary colonial encounter in Bulozi', in the west of what is nowadays Zambia, 'was essentially the history of how the Lozi defended the core areas in the perception of their world which were in this case entangled with certain aspects of Lozi kingship.'[60]

In Buganda, too, the physiological, social and cosmological spheres of existence were overlapping in pre-British times, though here what both Prins and Vansina call 'the debility of our reconstructions' of the pre-European period make it impossible to be very precise about the extent of this overlapping.[61] But in one crucial respect Buganda differed from both Bulozi and Zande country during the first years of the European colonial encounter. For, as Ham Mukasa put it in his account of meeting the Lozi king in London just before Edward VII's coronation in 1902: 'he was not a Christian, and he did as he liked'.[62] Unlike Bulozi, Buganda was already ruled by Christian chiefs at the time of the British colonial takeover and, unlike Lewanika, Daudi Chwa was unable to do as he liked in questions of core culture. However, once the Christian Bible had been translated into Luganda, some Ganda Christians quickly discovered Biblical support for the idea of an arbitrary and all-powerful Supreme Being who punished just and unjust alike through medical catastrophes such as plague, small-pox, and sleeping sickness.

In pre-British times, Katonda had not been a deity of much importance. 'His work of creation being ended,' writes Dr Pirouet, 'he had slipped into virtual oblivion, and impinged but little on people's lives. It was Christian missionaries who developed this particular *lubaale* into the Sustainer as well as the Creator' of all living things.[63] But the cosmological setting in which this happened appears to have been a very fluid one, in which it was difficult to distinguish between existing religious specialists, the new scientific medical doctors introduced by the Europeans, and indeed Europeans themselves.

At the close of the nineteenth century, remarked Sir Albert Cook, 'every white man was looked upon as a *musawo*, or doctor'.[64] Mutesa I had been treated by Speke, the first European to visit Buganda, for a sore finger; and by Felkin, one of the earliest CMS missionaries, for his gonorrhea.[65] The traditionalist religious reaction towards the end of *Kabaka* Mutesa's life was closely linked with his greater devotion to the shrines and spirit mediums of Ganda gods, after which he vacillated between the various forms of Christianity, Islam and Ganda traditional religion then current in his kingdom. *Basawo* traditionally charged fees, as too did Alexander Mackay in order to keep down the numbers pestering him for drugs – a bunch of bananas from the poor, a goat 'if the patient is rich and the case some tedious matter'.[66] But there were no long-term CMS (nor, indeed, any other) medical missionaries working in Buganda until Cook arrived in 1897 and opened Mengo hospital in 1900. Cook was an energetic and conscientious doctor, as his surviving medical notes on patients indicate; in 1905 Burroughs Welcome donated a dispensary to Mengo, and in 1910 it became the first hospital in East Africa to have an X-ray machine. Cook was careful to perform operations with African witnesses in order to establish their scientific character. But as all operations were preceded by prayer, and there were numerous services at Mengo at other times, Cook resembled earlier *basawo* in mingling surgery with ritual and incantation.[67]

Cook was a successful surgeon, but so too were earlier *basawo* in Buganda. According to T.P. Fletcher, because of 'the cruelties practised by the rulers and others in power, the services of medicine men were always in great demand'. They were 'the most powerful body in the whole country' and 'an extremely wealthy one too'. Besides surgery, *basawo* performed exorcisms and prepared drugs, worked magic when required, and could manipulate fetishes. They were pivotal people in a society which struck Fletcher from the old men he interviewed at the start of this century as having been not especially religious, but one in which Baganda 'worshipped or sought to appease [a] shifting and shadowy multitude of unknown or unseen powers or influences making for evil rather than for good.'[68] In religion, as in other spheres of life, it was sensible to be respectful to those with power or influence.

After Evans-Pritchard's portrayal of the Azande it became customary for scholars to consider many an African tribe before European imperialist penetration as 'a wonderfully integrated but brittle social mechanism'.[69] But more recently anthropologists of Africa have had second, and third, thoughts. In Buganda T.F. Fletcher considered that 'the old regime appeared to have lost power with the death of Mukasa, the Katikiro in the latter days of Mutesa and the early days of Mwanga', while subsequently the 'constant upheavals that took place in conjunction with the slow leaven at work of the Christian religion caused religious matters of a purely indigenous nature to fall into decay.'[70] But, fifty years later, Rigby and Lule argue that 'with its removal from the public and political sphere, Kiganda religion has become [possibly] *more* important to the average individual, especially in the towns.' This is because 'Science does not necessarily eliminate religious, or 'magical' belief. In crisis, most human beings appeal to forces other than those in the realms of science, and Kampala townsmen are no exception.'[71] From Rigby and Lule's account, Ganda religion appears both resilient and heterogeneous. In this respect it is like many other parts of tropical Africa. For, as Feierman points out, we must note how people employ multiple therapies and explanations of misfortune,[72] and, as Last argues, what they 'don't want to know' too.[73]

From these perspectives, Western medicine was not an enormous success as far as Semei Kakungulu's generation was concerned. To start with, British officials recruited doctors to look after their own health and that of their Sudanese and Indian troops.[74] There was only a handful of protectorate doctors and, even when they had time, ignorance of local languages reduced their usefulness in treating Africans in the newly established government hospitals. So too did the multiple character of most Africans' medical problems. For, as a subsequent handbook of Uganda reported, every African patient being treated for venereal disease under protectorate auspices 'is a latent or active subject of malaria, and harbours one or more varieties of helminths. From 50 to 80 per cent have or have had syphilis or yaws or both, and it is probable that the same is true of gonorrhea, while leprosy, spirilium fever, and dysentery, among other diseases, are far from rare'. All the diseases which 'had attained serious proportions' in Uganda, the handbook considered to be 'social diseases which will pass and come under control with the improvement of the social, moral, and sanitary conditions of the people, as plague and leprosy have passed from England'.[75] But this was written in 1935, when the importance of eradicating mosquitoes from urban areas was realized; when the role of cotton-seed as rat-attracting material was understood; and when the desirability of improving African urban housing in order to eliminate TB was appreciated.[76] Earlier official handbooks had largely ignored African health problems, as too had most protectorate doctors. 'It is practically impossible to treat a native satisfactorily except when he is under strict surveillance in a hospital and the knowledge of this fact is a reason why many medical Officers take so little interest in their work,' one PMO had written shortly before Kakungulu became a Malakite.[77]

That so many victims of sleeping sickness placed in camps soon died in those very same camps; that so many victims of venereal disease treated at Mulago hospital in Kampala, subsequently suffered serious relapses; and that so many cattle vaccinated, died shortly afterwards – these things did not raise the prestige of British government doctors and vets in the eyes of Ugandan Africans. Prins remarks that in Bulozi hospital treatment in the first years of the European colonial encounter was overwhelmingly of a 'low intensity' kind – 'specific categories where Western medicine was conspicuously powerful: malaria, conjunctivitis, some peripheral venereal diseases, diarrhoea, wounds. But medical reports echoed a constant refrain about the puny scale of effort against the mass of visible disease – syphilis, eye ailments, leprosy, smallpox.'[78] However, in Bulozi there was no great ecological catastrophe such as the sleeping sickness epidemic which so dramatically reduced the populations of the Lake Victoria littoral and further underlined the difference between low intensity situations, in which European doctors were often helpful, and those 'sicknesses of God' regarding which Europeans appeared, for the time being at least, every bit as powerless as Africans.

Here therefore a question arises. How far was Kakungulu's response to the sleeping sickness epidemic, and his recruitment to the religion of Malaki, influenced by 'blocking mechanisms' which Prins has typified as characteristic of African 'core culture' during the early colonial period ?[79]

Here the minutebook of the Malakite sect at Mbale for the mid-1910s shows how one small segment of Britain's newly subjugated African empire fought back intellectually against intrusive and multiple misfortune. Not in desperation, because some previously close-knit and fragile consensual society had just fallen apart, or was just about to; but because its customs seemed no more unacceptable in Biblical terms than newly imported British ones.

Take, for example, the question of polygynous marriage, of which the Church Missionary Society disapproved, and against which British protectorate officials had been persuaded by them to legislate:

This is how the marriage of one wife was introduced in Europe in the Christian religion. In the past the Europeans used to marry a number of wives just according to individual choice. But as European men increased in knowledge so too did the European women. The women claimed equal status with the men and asked for their own *lukiko* [society or council]. After some time the men agreed and gave them their own *lukiko*. Then, after they had received their *lukiko*, they agreed among themselves that they were no longer interested in marriage of many wives to a single man. 'We want every women to stay with one husband and to share a single house.' They continued to say 'We have no worries in one home with one wife' because it appears that they also had trouble with prostitutes as we do here in Buganda with our Baganda wives today. It is said that after their discussions the women took their proposals to the *lukiko* of the men and it was agreed that a law regarding marriage should be made along these lines. Then, afterwards, the one-wife marriage became observed in Christianity as well.

These things were told me by an old Englishman and I would not doubt the truth of his words.

S. Kakungulu

This note appears in the minutebook for 1 December 1915. Its account of European sexuality is tendentious and inaccurate, but no more tendentious and inaccurate than many views of African sexuality held by Englishmen at that time.[80] In January 1916, following correspondence with Malakites in Buganda, it was agreed formally that 'The law of one wife was never made by God [*Katonda*]' and the wedding ceremony in the CMS prayerbook was set out 'according to the customs of the Europeans and not according to the instructions of the Bible'.[81]

Medical doctors were objected to by Kakungulu's co-religionists at Mbale in similar terms. As they were not recommended, indeed sometimes forbidden, in the Bible, they should be dealt with like adulterers: punished and shunned. Their medicines should be treated as one's Muslim brother-in-law treated meat from a non-Muslim butcher: not brought anywhere near one's house.[82] Only behaviour positively advocated in the Christian Bible, or not prohibited in it and customary in local usage, should be adopted by true followers of God.

It was the same with the name of God's son. This had been the subject of considerable discussion by European missionaries throughout East Africa. 'Isa Masiya' had been used by the CMS in Uganda, 'Yesu Kristo' by Roman Catholics there as well as by Anglican missionaries elsewhere in East Africa.[83] On 3 December 1915, the Mbale Malakites agreed to use 'Yesu Kristo' because that was the word used in the Luganda version of the Bible. 'Isa Masiya' seemed to be neither an English nor a Luganda expression. 'How can we take then something we know nothing of?'

Kakungulu's opposition to spirit mediums had changed considerably in character since plundering their shrines during the early days of *Kabaka* Mwanga. Kakungulu's approach to both behaviour and therapy was now Biblical. Where the Bible was neutral on local custom, or difficult to understand, Kakungulu did what appeared most congenial to him in the light of wider Biblical teaching about the one true God. His opposition to missionary medicine and protectorate vaccination was therefore not just the action of a silly, obstinate and misguided old man. To be sure, there was misguidedness arising from Pilkington's use of the word *musawo* for witchdoctor in the Old Testament despite its employment already for modern medical practitioner in the Uganda Protectorate. To be sure, there was cantankerousness in Kakungulu's adoption of the new religion so soon after his enforced retirement from Busoga. To be sure, there was obstinacy and pique after the incident over inoculation at Jinja in August 1914. It would also be a mistake to ignore entirely Kakungulu's continuing quarrel with Apolo Kagwa,[84] as Kagwa was a most active supporter of the new protectorate regulations on plague, venereal disease, and the like.[85] But Kakungulu's basic objection to CMS evangelists and missionaries supporting medicine at the same time as preaching discipleship of the one true God, was basically Biblical. Here it was CMS teaching itself which appeared to him to have practically reverted to paganism, though at least one 'blocking mechanism' in Ganda traditional culture does seem to have also influenced his thinking here.

This was the inevitability, unpredictability, yet essential unnaturalness of death. 'Death is like taxation: it is inescapable', 'Death does not kill in one way only', 'Death does not announce its arrival' run several Ganda proverbs (*Olumbe musolo: teruddukwa, Olumbe sirutta bumu, Olumbe terulaga nnaku*).[86] In a section of the East African interior still limited to hoe technology, many 'sicknesses of man' continued to multiply misfortunes in peasant families. In Busoga there had been terrible calamities caused by trypanosomiasis during Kakungulu's service there. Now at Mbale further fatalities were caused by a second 'disease of God': plague.[87] The earliest Christian missionaries in Buganda had reported that death was never considered a natural event.[88] When researching attitudes towards sickness in a suburb of Kampala nearly a hundred years later, Southall and Gutkind discovered that still 'Death is rarely thought about as a natural event, even if it results from an accident'.[89] It was surely this particular 'blocking mechanism' which reinforced Kakungulu's Biblical beliefs when the new Mbale DC told Kakungulu to enforce health measures.

According to Kakungulu, Isemonger said:

All the European nations and all the nations of Asia and Africa all know the Doctor [who dispenses] medicine. Wherever you go you will meet with doctors, for they guard the whole earth on account of their wisdom from any disease which kills people ... Also did not God order the doctors to acquire wisdom and to discover medicine so that they might cure people from evil disease, smallpox and plague. Well now, do you see doctors healing cows?
Then S. Kakungùlu replied:-
'You, do you see them recovering?'
Isemonger replied:– 'No, but some are cured.'
Again S. Kakungulu answered, 'Are there not cows which do not get any medicine which recover.'

277

He replied, 'They recover'.

Again S. Kakungulu asked, 'Sir, the people of the King [George V], these nations you mention who have doctors, do not many die? Isemonger replied, 'They die'.

Again S. Kakungulu asked 'Have not these doctors much wisdom? Those who follow the wisdom of medicine, do they not die ?' Isemonger answered 'They die'.

Again S. Kakungulu asked 'Sir, what is it that kills the Kings and the doctors, those who have so great wisdom ... God killed them.'

S. Kakungulu said 'Why did not the doctors refuse these people to die?'

Mr Isemonger replied:- 'Let us stop this discussion about religious matters. Let us do our work about earthly affairs.'[90]

Thereafter, British protectorate policy in Uganda was to leave Kakungulu alone as much as possible, even making Mbale county a *de facto* quarantine zone in which inoculation policies pursued elsewhere were simply not enforced. This policy was especially favoured by the Oxford and Cambridge graduates now rising within the British administration; by men like A.H. Cox and P.W. Perryman, subsequently to become Resident of Buganda and Chief Secretary at Entebbe respectively.

Unfortunately the policy had one crucial defect: it did not deal with Kakungulu's cattle outside Mbale county. For, as a prominent person emanating from one of the smaller pastoralist kingdoms in the East African interior, Kakungulu was well aware of the desirability of keeping cattle and crops in more than one ecological zone in order to 'spread the risk', as it were, regarding famine and other unexpected calamities, like the massive clearances of both people and cattle ordered by the British protectorate administration to counter the sleeping sickness epidemic. Many of Kakungulu's cattle therefore turned up from time to time in parts of Busoga and Buganda where he had estates dating back beyond 1900. British administrators might look the other way when Apolo Kagwa appropriated one of these estates in Buganda, while successive British officials at Jinja might try to return his lands in Busoga to communal ownership. But what would happen to Kakungulu's cows inoculated against tsetse fly or pleuro-pneumonia in such areas? To whom did they belong once Kakungulu disowned them as 'rendered unclean' by inoculation? Eventually, to the acute embarrassment of British protectorate officials at Entebbe, a special Ordinance on Straying Cattle had to be drafted during the early 1920s and be sent to London for approval. When this happened, the metropolitan authorities had to be told officially and fully about the religion of Malaki, and a tentative defence made of protectorate officials' reluctance to impose health regulations universally. Most embarrassingly of all, the protectorate authorities at Entebbe had to explain why a Silver Medal for Chiefs had been recommended for presentation in 1921 to the very person for whom the special Ordinance on Straying Cattle had to be passed. Fortunately for British officials in Uganda, their superiors in Britain do not appear to have realized the full extent of their embarrassments with Semei Kakungulu.[91]

Plate 17. *Kakungulu photographed in 1919 or 1920. The two Europeans with him are Archdeacon Baskerville (left) and the Reverend Mathers, both CMS missionaries.* (By courtesy of Ibrahim Ndaula of Mbale)

In another respect, too, British officials were lucky with Kakungulu in 1917, this time not even realizing how lucky they were. This was when Kakungulu wanted to exchange lands from his estates in Buganda and at Mbale for a much bigger set of estates in Busoga.[92] Perryman, then DC Mbale, was happy to support the application. Kakungulu's estate at Mbale had become 'an embarrassment ... for many reasons which I need not specify' and there was 'practically no room for expansion [as regards urban development] except in the direction of Kakungulu's land.'[93] Spire, still PC Jinja, vetoed the proposal; partly because he considered 'Mbale has had its day', partly because the request had originated with Kakungulu and therefore was automatically suspect.[94] British officials in Busoga also opposed Kakungulu acquiring another 2 or 3 miles of private estate in their district because of growing distaste for 'landlordism' and increasing respect for Soga traditional religion: Batambogwe was the home of a Soga spirit god and Kakungulu in their view should shortly have to relinquish what land he had there already.[95] In fact, Kakungulu did not; basically because he possessed a validated certificate for Batambogwe. But the Land Officer, remembering earlier awkwardnesses when his Mbale estate's boundaries had been fixed, feared further difficulties and recommended instead that the *status quo* should be undisturbed.[96] So the suggested transfers were not made.

Thereby the British administration of Uganda unwittingly escaped any problems that might have arisen from Kakungulu building up further support in Busoga for his anti-medicine movement, because that was why he wanted additional land there. Instead Kakungulu stayed at Mbale, moving his principal residence further up in the western foothills of Mount Elgon to Gangama. It was there that he started a second separatist sect, initially known as the 'community of Jews who trust in the Lord' (*Kibina kya Bayudaya absesiga Katonda*).[97]

## 5

Kakungulu's adoption of the new religion, remarked his relative in the Lungfish clan of Buganda, Salimu Mbogo,[98] was both a social and a private matter. Kakungulu was deeply distressed at losing so many of his earlier followers when British officials took over his kingdom in Bukedi and used 'Baganda Agents' to administer it. He was also, Mbogo commented, spiritually unstable. He had contemplated becoming a Muslim at the close of 1888, after the expulsion of many Christians from the Buganda kingdom and before he himself fought energetically yet again on the Christians' behalf. Just before Kakungulu left Bukedi for Jinja nearly twenty years' later, Mbogo claimed that he very nearly became a Muslim again. This was around the time he married Kalema's daughter Dimbwe in 1905.[99] Dimbwe herself claimed that on the contrary Kakungulu remained a 'strong Protestant' throughout, and financed the building of at least one church during his stay in Busoga.[100] But such patronage was characteristic of the first generation of Christian chiefs from Buganda and, remarked Mbogo (though as a good Muslim he disclaimed any intimate knowledge of it), Kakungulu's establishment of the Bayudaya community was the typical act of a spiritually restless man who was changing his religious views right up to the very end of his earthly life.[101]

But why was Kakungulu's final faith *Jewish*?

Characteristic of early CMS preaching in Uganda, as of Evangelical Anglican preaching in Britain in the late nineteenth century, was the appropriation of ancient Judaism. As Henry Nevinson recalled:

> This strictly Biblical education produced among those who, like myself, belong to the last century, the peculiar illusion that both the promises and the threatenings of the Jewish lawgivers and prophets were specially designed for ourselves by a foreseeing Power. We never doubted that we English Evangelicals were the Chosen People, and when every Sunday evening, we sang the *Magnificat*, 'As he promised to our forefathers, Abraham and his seed for ever,' we gave no thought to the Jews; and when soon afterwards, we sang in the *Nunc Dimittis* 'To be a light to lighten the Gentiles, and to be the glory of thy people Israel,' we meant that Missionary Societies would spread the light of the Gospel to negroes, Chinese and Indians, while God's English people retained the glory.[102]

Besides this displacement of consciousness, the political, environmental, and cosmological factors we have noted, and the personal factors and 'insults' to which we must shortly turn, there are a number of earlier personal influences, both direct and indirect, of which we should also be aware.

First there was O'Flaherty, a CMS missionary who stressed at the Ganda court that 'Jesus Christ was a Jew ... [and] we Europeans did not follow one of our race, we looked for the truth where it was to be found, and we found it among the Jews.' [103] Possibly because of this emphasis, Robert Walker noted during the 1890s that 'the customs & manners of the Jews' were of 'the greatest interest' in Buganda. So too were 'The distances places were from one another & all matters of history & commerce'.[104] Then, after meeting Kakungulu and his followers at Mbale in 1904, J. J. Willis proclaimed that:

> In the economy of Missions in this part of Africa the Baganda are called upon to play a part not dissimilar to that played by the Jews in the first age of Christianity. Wherever the apostles went in their missionary travels they found Jews, men of their own race and language, possessing and acknowledging the same Scriptures, and animated by the same faith and hope.[105]

Surviving relatives and followers stressed Kakungulu's continuing admiration of the courage of Peter and Paul in confronting the power of the Roman Empire.[106] However, when asked how this admiration translated into practice, one follower revealed that Kakungulu retained respect for the Roman Empire too. This was indicated by his naming one group of followers in Bukedi the *kitongole kitalyana*, after 'the Italian band' led by the Roman centurion mentioned in the Book of Acts: 'a devout man, and one that feared God with all his house, which gave much alms to the people'.[107] Cornelius had been one of the earliest followers of the true faith, but he was not necessarily a Jew.

What was the true faith now ? Kakungulu too was a devout man and a giver of alms to the people. Before 1914 he had supported many CMS-trained evangelists in Bukedi. After 1914 he was the religion of Malaki's most generous supporter in eastern Uganda. Pastors and teachers paid by him were sent to work at many centres in what later became Bugisu, Bukedi, Busoga, Lango, and Teso districts. In January 1915 a church council was set up at Mbale. This was to counter suggestions that the religion of Malaki would wither away locally once Kakungulu died or withdrew his patronage. This council was initially less concerned about marriage than its counterpart in Buganda; the sabbath on a Saturday rather than a Sunday was its first substantial subject of discussion, followed by rituals for prayer (with upturned hands, unlike Malakite practice in Buganda, as also was the new custom of holding weddings only at night) and debates about the rightness or otherwise of eating meat from animals inoculated by government veterinary officials.[108] In 1916 a new calendar with 30 days to the month was agreed by the Mbale Malakites. This was worked out by Kakungulu from the Book of Exodus. Kakungulu also published in this year his first booklet of texts, hymns and exhortations: it was printed at his expense by the Uganda Printing and Publishing Company in Kampala.[109] In 1917 the Mbale Malakites received a letter from their co-religionists in Buganda stating that Kate had acquired a printing press of his own for 330 rupees from Budo; the letter was dated in the English manner rather than in Kakungulu's Jewish fashion.[110] At the same time Joswa Kate wrote to Kakungulu pointing out that, as it was clearly desirable to print a common Malakite servicebook, they should not keep on changing customs and beliefs but agree on a common front.[111] It was not advice which Kakungulu would follow.

In 1918 Kakungulu suggested to the other members of the Mbale church council that, instead of celebrating Christ's death in a common communion service, everybody should break bread in their own homes. Initially this was not a popular suggestion. Other council members argued that not only was this a major change but it was one likely to bring them into disrepute with CMS-connected Christians who would say 'You break bread at beer parties'.[112] Eventually the Mbale Malakite council, with Kakungulu listed as attending in his capacity as titular head, agreed to celebrate the breaking of bread three times a year: on the day of Christ's death, on the following Sabbath (or Saturday), and on the day of Christ's resurrection (Sunday) too.[113] This was clearly a compromise between the Christianity of CMS teaching and practice (barely an annual communion, Bishop Tucker had complained during Crabtree's time)[114] and the religion portrayed in the Old Testament and some parts of the New Testament. It was not a compromise that could long survive Kakungulu's introduction of circumcision.

This was in 1919, and involved several of Kakungulu's newly born children as well as those of a number of his followers;[115] Kakungulu himself had been circumcised some time before.[116] Sulemani Mutaise spoke for those Malakites at Mbale who opposed circumcision as not practised even in later New Testament days.[117] Kakungulu responded by suggesting separation between himself and the opponents of circumcision and meeting for prayer only with those circumcised in his own home.[118] A few weeks later, Kakungulu had second thoughts, stating that only one person (meaning Mutaise) had caused the separation. Instead he suggested that the community should come together again as if nothing had happened. However, as the compiler of the minutebook makes clear at this stage, it was not possible to behave as if nothing had happened. For the moment, a single community survived: some in it supported circumcision, some did not. But it was not a situation that could last very long. However Malakite morale at Mbale was temporarily strengthened by discovery of a recent CMS annual report which compared their religion in Uganda to teaching called Christian Science outside Africa ('we were very glad that the Gospel was to spread in Europe, and that there is a certain religion there too which does not take medicine but trusts in God alone').[119]

In January 1920 the division reemerged. Kakungulu now told local Malakites that it was no longer a matter of circumcised and uncircumcised factions surviving within the same religion. He himself was now no longer a member of the religion of Malaki.

Earlier Kakungulu had been discomforted by attacks on circumcision from Buganda, presumably from Malakites there. Some said that he had only persuaded certain of his followers to be circumcised by force, others by promises of material benefit, some critics even said that his support for circumcision made him into a Muslim. Kakungulu admitted that he considered these criticisms and attacks hurtful. Nonetheless, he hoped that the split between circumcised and uncircumcised Malakites at Mbale would not prove complete; it should be treated, he remarked, more like the differences between Roman Catholic Christians associated with Rubaga and Nsambya cathedrals in Buganda than with the original Malakite secession from fellowship with CMS-associated Christians at Mbale.[120] Kakungulu also promised to support Malakites who disagreed with him over circumcision, in dealings with the British protectorate authorities over their common opposition to doctors, medicine, and the inoculation of people and cattle.[121] However, his critics over circumcision in the Malakite church council at Mbale told him plainly that they could not understand why he was now dividing congregations in eastern Uganda over this issue. It would be better to seek advice from Buganda before any irrevocable decisions were made about a practice which had surely been replaced by baptism in the New Testament. 'We are Gentiles in nature but Jews in spirit, and our circumcision should be in spirit too', these critics of Kakungulu in the Mbale Malakite council now argued.[122]

But it was to no avail. Yekoasi Kaweke, Kakungulu's *katikiro* at Gangama, told the Malakites that they could no longer expect to receive any portion of Kakungulu's tithed income. Kakungulu confirmed that the split was complete. Why had he separated from the religion of Malaki? 'Because of your insults, that is why I have separated completely from you and stay with those who want to be circumcised: and we will be known as the

Jews.'[123] It was not a very convincing explanation, commented the compiler of this section of the Mbale Malakite minutebook. The insults were made by mere boys, not by elders of the religion of Malaki itself. What is the real reason for your separation from us? 'There is no other reason than your insults,' was Kakungulu's recorded reply.[124]

Arye Oded, an Israeli diplomat in Uganda during the 1960s, visited the Bayudaya community near Mbale and taught them 'many things', according to Kakungulu's successor as the community's leader at the time.[125] Oded considered that Kakungulu's conversion to the Malakite faith was caused by his being 'bitterly disappointed' at his treatment by the British authorities, while his subsequent formation of the Bayudaya community was principally the result of his closer reading of the Old Testament. Oded notes that in 1922 Kakungulu published another 'book of rules and prayers'. 'The contents of the book show clearly how far Kakungulu had moved away from Christianity towards Judaism. His book, ninety pages long, is actually a guide to the Jewish religion and a handbook for teachers of the community. In it Kakungulu continually demanded complete faith in the Old Testament and all its commandments.' However, Oded admits that 'although he declared himself a Jew', Kakungulu 'still believed at that time in the New Testament and in Jesus Christ. His book of prayers and rules contains many verses and sections from the New Testament.' Kakungulu's further movement towards Judaism, if not yet his 'complete conversion' to it, was principally attributable to his starting 'to study and meditate on the Old Testament for long periods'.[126]

Admittedly, there were few other publications in Luganda that Kakungulu could have studied and meditated upon at this time. A British protectorate official considered that it was 'clearly an unwholesome & undesirable state of affairs' in Uganda that 'an educated youth has practically nothing to read except the Bible'.[127] The PC's conference in 1923 recommended that more 'suitable books' should be translated into Luganda at protectorate expense in the interests of more general enlightenment. Among those mentioned were 'Kipling's Jungle Books, Just so stories and History of England for boys, and the expurgated edition of the Arabian Nights'.[128] But these translations would arrive too late to influence Kakungulu's way of thinking.

Anyway 'insults', by his own admission, were important in the creation of the Bayudaya community in addition to further reflection. Initially, as we have noted, Kakungulu regarded emerging differences between Bamalaki and Bayudaya as comparable to the contrast between Roman Catholics attending the Rubaga and Nsambya cathedrals patronized by the White Fathers and Mill Hill Missions respectively; as a difference, in Kakungulu's own words, of preaching rather than ritual.[129] Perhaps this is a model of religious pluralism to be taken seriously in accounting for Kakungulu's further break with the religion of Malaki.

Immediately before Captain Lugard marched into the Buganda kingdom thirty years before, Ganda Muslims had been surprised by the sudden segmentation of Ganda Christians into separate Roman Catholic and

Protestant politico-religious groupings. In the 1890s, a CMS missionary remarked on the possibility of Ganda Protestants fighting amongst themselves as well as against the Catholics, so strong were fissiparous tendencies and insults between chiefs at that time.[130] Christian missionaries have been accused of causing mayhem between their respective clusters of converts in Buganda from time to time, but their role in the local politics of Buganda in the late nineteenth century was at most indirect. The missionaries' principal political importance lay in preventing a weak Ganda king from reasserting his authority over their converts by breaking up subordinate groupings made vulnerable by personal animosities. How had they done this? By stressing Anglican belief, Archdeacon Walker had remarked, as a 'ground of agreement' between Protestants rather than as a springboard for conflict directly with Roman Catholics.[131] If Roman Catholic missionaries in Buganda had not acted with similar resolution, the Catholics of Rubaga and Nsambya might likewise have been fighting one another before the nineteenth century was out.

But now that century was almost twenty years astern. Archdeacon Walker had been succeeded by Archdeacon Baskerville, and the religion of Malaki had no European missionary helpers. Though Winston Churchill had lauded the administrative convenience for the British Empire of many Ganda becoming Bible-readers and literates in a single generation,[132] British officials at Mbale saw the inconveniences of this intellectual transformation. In particular, they regretted Kakungulu's bombarding them with texts.

'I told him clearly that the Government did not discuss religion', reported Isemonger to Spire after failing to persuade Kakungulu to accept the latest protectorate health regulations in September 1915. 'His version appears to be somewhat similar to a bible class [in which] we all held bibles in our hands ready to turn up chapter and verse.'[133] Subsequent DCs fared no better. Other Ganda chiefs and clerks at Mbale felt that Kakungulu's Bible-thumping was bringing them into disrepute. 'He has undoubtedly become a partial religious maniac', commented the provincial commissioner in 1923, 'and the responsible Baganda in Bukedi are distinctly upset at Kakunguru's present attitude which they say is lowering the prestige of the Baganda and their name for loyalty to the Government.'[134] The politics of *okufugibwa* were now operating against Kakungulu. In the absence of a sympathetic foreign missionary to assist in holding the new denomination in Uganda together, there was little chance that Kakungulu's suggestion that differences between the circumcisers and non-circumcisers at Mbale should be treated as comparable to those differentiating Roman Catholics associated with Rubaga and Nsambya would be treated seriously.

Christian Science has survived organizationally in North America and Europe, remarks Bryan Wilson, because its 'doctrine and social practice' had been 'definitively laid down by Mrs Eddy', its founder, and because its 'Board of Directors operates essentially as a body of managers, not as prophets or inspired leaders'.[135] The religion of Malaki was organized differently. Kate and Kakungulu, its two principal chiefly supporters, both had (as the Mbale minutebook of meetings and correspondence indicates) equality of esteem with Malaki Musajakawa. Doctrinally, too, it was different. According to Mrs Eddy's *Science and Health* (1875), suffering and death were the effects of 'false thinking'; in reality they did not exist.[136] This was not what either Kate or Kakungulu understood the Bible to teach. To them, suffering and death did exist along with matter itself; if they had ever finally agreed upon a common confession of faith, it would probably have been called, not *Science and Health* but *Bible and Health*. In fact, Kate and Kakungulu never did agree upon a common confession because, intellectually, they also suffered from that other fault of fundamentalists: 'when there are no modernists from which to withdraw, fundamentalists compensate by withdrawing from one another'.[137] There were also the 'insults'.

The suggestion that some adherents of the new religion in eastern Uganda adopted Kakungulu's view on circumcision because of material incentives, or personal pressure, was probably hurtful to Kakungulu because it was in part true. Malakite recruitment, as we saw earlier, was multi-faceted and involved many people not previously within Kakungulu's clientage. Recruitment to the Bayudaya community came almost exclusively from what remained of that following, both around Mbale and on his estates in Busoga, where tenants who followed Kakungulu's religious preferences enjoyed rent rebates and exemption from certain labour services.[138]

By 1918 the religion of Malaki had become a considerable burden to Kakungulu. Membership was declining apart from Busoga, where Kakungulu attempted (unsuccessfully, as we have seen) to add to his estates by exchanging lands already owned by him in both Buganda and Bukedi. The British protectorate authorities in eastern Uganda were now acting increasingly harshly towards Malakite requests for church sites and for exemptions of Malakite teachers from forced labour projects.[139] Kakungulu was also now charging local Malakite teachers for his first pamphlet of Biblical quotations and exhortations.[140]

Increasing ethnic consciousness accentuated other difficulties. As we have noted already, Sulemani Mutaise was about to irritate Kakungulu by the vigour of his Biblical counter-attack against the introduction of circumcision, and in later years Mutaise would be a stalwart supporter of the Young Bagwere Association's campaign against excessive numbers of Ganda clerks and chiefs working in eastern Uganda;[141] new ethnic tensions, in other words, were starting to be articulated. On Kakungulu's estate around Mbale, there was little ethnic sentiment apart from the intrusive Ganda one, with which subsequent 'imagined communities'[142] would be compared. Indeed, from one point of view, Kakungulu's creation of the Bayudaya community at Gangama can be considered an attempt to create a new kind of community in the peri-urban setting of early colonial Mbale, and itself a new form of tribalism.[143] From another, it can be viewed as an attempt to create a clientage to replace the one which, as Salimu

Mbogo remarked, British protectorate officials destroyed by transferring him to Busoga.

There were indeed 'many things', as the compiler of the Mbale Malakite minutebook remarked,[144] behind Kakungulu's formation of yet another independent religious movement in addition to intensive Bible study. Another consideration was the love affair between the wife he married so expensively at Mbale in 1905, princess Dimbwe, and his brother Sedulaka Kyesirikidde. Dismissed on Boyle's instructions in 1904, Sedulaka had worked as an adviser to the incoming generation of missionary-educated chiefs at Budaka between 1905 and 1914, and from 1917 to 1919 he was sub-county chief at Mbale.[145] Kakungulu brought a formal charge of adultery against his brother in 1918 and separated formally from Dimbwe shortly afterwards.[146] He then married several new wives. When children were born to these wives, questions arose regarding their initiation and naming. Kakungulu resolved these questions by having them circumcised as members of the new community along with a number of his personal followers.

Yet another matter was Kakungulu's decision in the same year to repudiate his membership of the Lungfish (Mamba) clan of Buganda. The issue had arisen earlier in the 1910s, when members of the Heart or Mutima clan in Buganda had written to Sir Apolo Kagwa requesting that Kakungulu's name should not be included in the history of the Mamba clan then being completed in Kagwa's house;[147] however Kakungulu's name and reputed ancestry were included in the history of the Lungfish clan of Buganda published a few years later.[148] Now, possibly partly because of his estrangement from his younger brother Sedulaka, who still considered himself to be a member of the Lungfish clan of Buganda, Kakungulu 'spread about a manifesto declaring that his father was not, as previously supposed, a Mukoki peasant, but was really a reigning prince of the Baziba in ex-German territory who visited his mother in Koki.'[149]

None of these actions increased Kakungulu's popularity within the ruling circle of chiefs in Buganda. The Mamba clan was still the largest single descent group there. Dimbwe, reported P.W. Perryman, was also 'a half-sister of the Kabaka and this accusation has caused Kakunguru to be extremely unpopular in higher circles in Buganda.'[150]

But unpopularity cut two ways. In Buganda, whose county chiefs had visited Bukedi during 1917 and commented adversely that Kakungulu's following at Gangama 'including his Katikiro, sub-chiefs, etc, consists of nobodies – uneducated men of peasant origin',[151] Kakungulu might be less highly regarded. At Gangama, however, any suggestion that the dispute over circumcision should be referred for comment to Buganda was unlikely to be regarded favourably by Kakungulu. On the contrary, as his reputation in Buganda plummeted following his divorce from Dimbwe and his repudiation of the Mamba clan, and it became clear that 'The natives in his "sphere of influence" [at Mbale] are the overflow from neighbouring and more crowded counties … of several tribes, and have no sense of loyalty to their titular chief',[152] Kakungulu's commitment to the Bayudaya community grew stronger and stronger.

Perryman remarked that Kakungulu was 'not dangerous'.

He has the will, but not the power, to be so. He is ageing rapidly. He is not exactly an asset to Bukedi, but if he is treated with tact by the District officers concerned, in view of his past services which were undoubtedly valuable, I do not think he is likely to cause open trouble.[153]

This was written before Kakungulu asked the protectorate authorities for permission to travel to Britain to protest in person about his grievances.[154]

# *Notes*

1. A.H. Cox, personal communication; J.R.P. Postlethwaite, *I Look Back* (London 1947), p. 31. It was a universal complaint among early British officials.
2. Ormsby to Kampala, 24 February 1908, Bell, minutes of 13 March 1908 and 17 April 1908, SMP 1667/07, ESA.
3. Jackson to CO, 4 July 1911, SMP 1667/07, and minute of 13 February 1913, SMP 3022/10, ESA.
4. Petition by Mbale traders, 13 May 1913, MMP 58/13, MA.
5. MDAR 1912–13 by A.H.Watson, 11 April 1913, MA.
6. *Ibid.*
7. *Ibid.*
8. *Ibid.*
9. Spire to CS, 13 May 1913, SMP 3022/10, ESA.
10. W.J. Simpson, 'Report on sanitary conditions in the East Africa Protectorate, Uganda and Zanzibar', 2 July 1914, SMP 4186/10, ESA; B.R. Ram, interview.
11. Ibrahim Ndaula, personal communication.
12. This is clear from correspondence in SMP 1760/08 and EPMP 6/13.
13. *Ibid.*
14. See my London Ph.D. thesis, 'Politics in Bukedi', pp. 234–5.
15. See L. Doyal and I. Pennell, ' "Pox Britannica": health, wealth and underdevelopment', *Race and Class* 18 (1976), pp. 155–72.
16. See above, p. 77.
17. John Ford, *The Role of Trypanosomiases in African Ecology* (Oxford 1971).
18. A.H. Watson to P.W. Cooper, 5 May 1914, EPMP 6/13, ESA.
19. J. Roscoe, *The Soul of Central Africa* (London 1922), p. 243.
20. J. Roscoe, *The Bagesu and Other Tribes of the Uganda Protectorate* (Cambridge 1924). See also S. Heald, *Controlling Anger: the Sociology of Gisu Violence* (Manchester 1989), p. 30.
21. Roscoe, *Soul*, pp. 262–3.
22. Baskerville to Knowles, 18 November 1914, Abamalaki file, Namirembe Archives, Kampala.
23. MacKenzie to Knowles, 10 November 1914, encl. Knowles to Entebbe, 11 November 1914, SMP 4219, ESA; *Uganda Notes*, January 1916, p. 9.
24. The 1921 Uganda census gives an estimate of 91,740 Malakites for Buganda. For Bukedi I have relied upon Yokana Toto, oral text recorded at his home at Kimalaki village, Bugwere, on 23 November 1968 and PCEP to Entebbe, 20 May 1930, S/5, ESA.
25. See above, pp. 152, 166, for earlier discussions of this cleavage.
26. *CMS Gazette*, March 1915, p. 81.
27. J.R. Roe, *A History of the British and Foreign Bible Society* (London 1965), p. 182, note 2.
28. *Proceedings of CMS 1918–19*, p. 49.
29. Yokana Toto (see note 24).

30. Oral text recorded at his home at Nkoma village, Bugisu on 20 August 1965.
31. D. Barrett, *Schism and Renewal in Africa* (Nairobi 1968), p. 105.
32. Roscoe to Baylis, 20 April 1907, G3A7/1907a, CMS archives.
33. Mackenzie, 17 November 1914, SMP 4219, ESA.
34. *Ibid.*
35. Cook to Baylis, 4 December 1911, G3A7/ 1911b; Walker to Baylis, 13 January 1912, encl. ETs of H.W. Duta to Walker of 1 January 1912 and 20 January 1912 which protest against Weatherhead's teaching at Budo leading to students saying other CMS missionaries had been misleading them, G3A7/1912a, CMS archives.
36. See *Uganda Notes*, July 1913, p. 70.
37. A.H. Cox, personal communication.
38. Mbale Malakite Minutebook (MMB), 1 January 1914. Nkambo died 18 February 1914.
39. Kakungulu to Apolo Kagwa, 13 February 1914, CF14, Kagwa Papers, MUL.
40. Joswa Kate to Kakungulu, 27 & 30 May 1914, copies in Reuben Musoke Papers, MUL.
41. 'Ekitabo ekya Lukiko lwe Nyumba ya Katonda Omu Ainza Byona' (MMB), seen by courtesy of Yokana Toto.
42. *Ibid.* In fact it is the first entry in the minutebook.
43. Baskerville to Knowles, 18 November 1914, Namirembe archives.
44. Knowles to Entebbe, 4 November 1914, SMP 3219, ESA.
45. Jarvis to Governor, 6 November 1914, SMP 4219, ESA.
46. Wallis, 11 November 1914, SMP 4219, ESA.
47. See Holger Bernt Hansen, *Mission, Church and State in a Colonial Setting: Uganda 1890–1925* (London 1984), Chapter 16 for a full discussion.
48. Many British protectorate officials had African mistresses; Boyle had been one of the first to bring out a British wife.
49. Hansen, *Mission, Church and State,* for the best account.
50. J. Tosh, *Clan Leaders and Colonial Chiefs in Lango* (Oxford 1978), p. 195.
51. Willis to Knowles, 6 November 1914, SMP 4219, ESA.
52. Knowles to Entebbe, 18 November 1914, SMP 4219, ESA.
53. Wallis, 21 November 1914, SMP 4219, ESA.
54. *Ibid.*, 8 January 1915, SMP 4219, ESA.
55. Katikiro to Sekibobo, 2 January 1915, Kabaka's circular to chiefs on Abamalaki, 8 February 1915, copies in Abamalaki file, Namirembe archives, Kampala.
56. G. Shepperson and T. Price, *Independent African: John Chilembwe and the Origins, Setting and Significance of the Nyasaland Native Rising of 1915* (Edinburgh 1958) is the classic account.
57. Jackson to Willis, 16 January 1915, Abamalaki file, Namirembe archives.
58. E.E. Evans-Pritchard, *Witchcraft, Oracles and Magic among the Azande* (Oxford 1937), p. 12.
59. *Ibid.*, p. 63.
60. G. Prins, 'Disease at the crossroads: towards a history of therapeutics in Bulozi since 1876', *Social Science and Medicine* 13B (1979), p. 287.
61. *Ibid.*, p. 285, citing J. Vansina, *The Children of Woot* (Madison 1978), p. 209.
62. Ham Mukasa, *With Uganda's Katikiro in England* (London 1904), p. 150.
63. M.L. Pirouet, 'Traditional religion and Christianity in Buganda and Acoli', seminar paper, Centre for African Studies, SOAS, 8 March 1973, p. 3.
64. A. Cook, *Uganda Memories* (Kampala 1945), p. 50.
65. D.L. Zeller, 'The establishment of western medicine in Buganda', Ph.D. dissertation, Columbia University, 1971, p. 61; C.T. Wilson and R.W. Felkin, *Uganda and the Egyptian Soudan* (London 1882), Vol. 2, pp. 9–10.
66. Zeller, 'The establishment', quoting Mackay, 22 January1882, reproduced in *CMI*, 1883, p. 536.
67. K. Timpson, 'Patients and nurse at Mengo', *Mercy and Truth* 3 (1899), pp. 288–90; Zeller, 'The establishment', pp. 98–111, has a good discussion of Cook and Mengo Hospital.
68. Fletcher to Manley, 17 November 1923, G3A7/1923/115, CMS archives.
69. Margery Perham, *Colonial Reckoning* (London 1961), p. 115. See A. Kuper, *Anthropology and Anthropogists* (London 1983).
70. Fletcher to Manley, 17 November 1923, G3A7/1923/115, CMS archives.
71. P. Rigby and F. Lule, 'Continuity and change in Kiganda religion' in *Town and Country*

in *Central and Eastern Africa* (London 1975), pp. 213–27.

72. S. Feierman, 'Change in African therapeutic systems', *Social Science and Medicine* 13B (1979), p. 279.
73. M. Last, 'The importance of knowing about not knowing', *Social Science and Medicine* 15B (1981), p. 387
74. Zeller, 'The establishment', p. 157.
75. H.B. Thomas and R. Scott, *Uganda* (London 1935), pp. 303–8.
76. *Ibid.*, pp. 309–11.
77. Moffat, 12 August 1992, MUL.
78. G. Prins, 'Disease at the crossroads', p. 294.
79. *Ibid.*, p. 298.
80. See Megan Vaughan, *Curing their Ills: Colonial Power and African Illness,* (Cambridge and Oxford 1991), p. 133.
81. Mbale Malakite minutebook, 19 December 1915.
82. Kakungulu, pamphlet of *c.*1916 in Ndaula Papers, Nkoma, Mbale.
83. See G.K.A. Bell, *Randall Davidson* (London 1935), Vol. 1, pp. 563–6.
84. For example, Kakungulu to Kagwa, 13 February 1914, CF14 in the Apolo Kagwa Papers in MUL, where he criticizes Kagwa for preventing one of his letters reaching Daudi Chwa.
85. See Zeller, 'The establishment', *passim*; also above, pp. 232, 244.
86. F. Walzer, *Luganda Proverbs* (Berlin 1982), proverbs 3979, 3980 & 3982.
87. Thomas and Scott, *Uganda* (1935), p. 309.
88. J. Cussac, *L'Apôtre de l'Ouganda: Le Père Lourdel* (Paris 1944), p. 73; Roscoe, *Baganda*, p. 98.
89. A. Southall and P. Gutkind, *Townsmen in the Making* (Kampala 1957), p. 111.
90. Isemonger to Spire, 11 November 1915, quoting English translation by A.H. Cox of Kakungulu to Isemonger, 14 September 1915.
91. The Silver Medal was awarded in 1921 (*Ebifa mu Buganda*, August 1921, p. 173), and the Straying of Animals Ordinance published in the *Uganda Government Gazette* on 30 December 1922: it was defended in Acting Governor Jarvis to Colonial Office, 10 January 1923 (copy in SMP 7634, ESA).
92. Perryman to Jinja, 2 December 1917, EPMP, ESA.
93. *Ibid.*
94. Spire to Land Office, 19 December 1917, EPMP, ESA.
95. DC Jinja to PCEP, 11 December 1917, EPMP, ESA.
96. LO to PCEP, 10 December 1917, EPMP, ESA.
97. Kakungulu to DC Mbale, 11 October 1922, quoting English translation by Cox in Mbale archives, MMP 928.
98. Salimu Mbogo, interview at his home at Amusi, Teso.
99. *Ibid.*
100. Princess Dimbwe, interview at Ibrahim Ndaula's home.
101. S. Mbogo, interview.
102. H.W. Nevinson, *Fire of Life* (London 1935), p. 432.
103. Reported by A. Mackay, 12 October 1881; repr. *CMI*, August 1882, p. 489.
104. R. Walker, 9 July 1895, WP.
105. *Uganda Notes*, November 1904, pp. 159–60.
106. Kezironi Zake, Princess Dimbwe, interviews
107. K. Zake, 20 June 1964. The reference is to Acts 10:1. The English translation is from the Authorised Version.
108. Mbale Minutebook (MMB), esp. pp. 453, 61, 87 and 90.
109. MMB, p. 96.
110. MMB, p. 117: Kate to Kakungulu, 8 August 1917.
111. *Ibid.*
112. MMB, p. 127.
113. MMB, p. 138.
114. See above, p. 204.
115. MMB, pp. 142–3.
116. Possibly during the 1880s, at a date not noted in any surviving chronicle; possibly just

before he became President of the Busoga chiefly council in 1906, according to his relative Salimu Mbogo. However, Princess Dimbwe, his 'ring' wife at that time, specifically denied that he had ever been a Muslim.

117. MMB, p. 142.
118. MMB, p. 143.
119. MMB, p. 146: this was the *CMS Proceedings* for 1914–15.
120. Minutes of 29 January 1920 meeting.
121. Minutes of 22–23 December 1920 meeting.
122. *Ibid.*
123. *Ibid.*
124. *Ibid.*
125. Zakayo Mumbya, interview, 13 September 1965.
126. A. Oded, 'The Bayudaya of Uganda: a portrait of an African Jewish Community', *Journal of Religion in Africa* 6 (1974), pp. 173, 167–86.
127. E.L. Scott to CS, 30 July 1923, SMP 7919, ESA.
128. Minutes of PC's conference, 18 July 1923, SMP 7919, ESA.
129. *Ibid.*
130. See above, p. 110.
131. *CMI*, September 1892, pp. 682–3. See Hansen, *Mission, Church and State*, for a magisterial discussion; my 'The emergence of politico-religious groupings in late nineteenth century Buganda', *Journal of African History* 29 (1988), pp. 81–92 for some further notes.
132. W.S. Churchill, *My African Journey* (London 1908), Chapter 5.
133. Isemonger, 11 November 1915, SMP 4219, ESA.
134. Guy Eden to CS, 1 May 1923, SMP 1760/08, ESA.
135. Bryan R. Wilson, *Religion in Secular Society* (Harmondsworth 1969), p. 214.
136. See F.L. Cross, *Oxford Dictionary of the Christian Church* (1958), p. 276.
137. E. J. Carnell in eds M. Halverson and A. Cohen, *A Handbook of Christian Theology* (London 1970), p. 147.
138. H.B. Thomas, personal communication.
139. This is a constant theme in the Mbale Malakites' Minutebook, and for Teso is reflected in J. Vincent, *Teso in Transformation* (Berkeley 1982), pp. 244–7.
140. *Ibid.*
141. For this connection, see my ' "Tribalism" in Eastern Uganda' in ed. P.H. Gulliver, *Tradition and Transition in East Africa: Studies of the Tribal Factor in the Modern Era* (London 1969).
142. B. Anderson, *Imagined Communities: Reflections on the Origin and Spread of Nationalism* (London 1983).
143. I owe this insight to Christine Obbo.
144. MMB, p. 143 (written by Paulo Zinabala).
145. For S. Kyesirikidde's earlier career, see above pp. 20–1, 142, 163–4, 212. At the time of the affair he was sub-county chief at Mbale.
146. Gray, 'Kakunguru in Bukedi', p. 32; P.W. Perryman, 'History of Kakunguru', SMP/C/209/06.
147. Abayanja to Apolo Kagwa, 26 March 1912, CD/143, Kagwa Papers, MUL; 'Abayanja' is one of the names used by members of the Mutima clan according to M.B. Nsimbi, *Amanya Amaganda* (Kampala 1956), p. 266.
148. E.M. Buligwanga, *Ekitabo Ekitageza Ekika kya Mamba* (Mengo 1916).
149. Perryman, 'History of Kakunguru'.
150. *Ibid.*
151. *Ibid.*
152. *Ibid.*
153. *Ibid.*
154. Kakungulu to Governor, Uganda Protectorate, 17 September 1924, SMP 1760/08, ESA.

# Ten

# Counting Costs
# 1920–8

## 1

Kakungulu's disenchantment with British rule came to a head in a dispute over land for Makerere College. His estate there dated from the days of *Kabaka* Mwanga.[1] Initially Kakungulu offered to sell it for 350 rupees an acre – the price at which Apolo Kagwa was currently selling his *mailo* land at Kampala – or to exchange 10 acres of it at Kampala for 100 acres nearer Gangama.[2] The British authorities preferred the second suggestion but could not agree where the 100 acres should be granted. Areas adjoining Kakungulu's estate at Mbale seemed unattractive for the very reason that Kakungulu found them attractive: they were densely settled.[3] An area adjoining his property at Batambogwe proved objectionable for religious as well as demographic reasons: 'the principle Spirit Hill of Busoga is included in Kakungulu's land there, a fact which irritates the Basoga very considerably.'[4] Protectorate administrators therefore appealed to Kakungulu's presumed ethnic sentiment. 'His Excellency states that Kakunguru should be informed of the Kabaka's generosity in agreeing to lease, rent free for 99 years, some 42 acres' at Makerere, 'the Kabaka having realized that this is a work that will bring advantage and benefit to the natives.'[5] The appeal failed. 'He says that Chwa will naturally want to help his own people, but as regards himself he is no longer a Muganda.'[6] Protectorate officials next hinted at compulsory purchase, either under the Uganda Agreement of 1900 or through the more cumbersome application of the Indian Land Acquisition Act.[7] Go ahead, Kakungulu replied, though he did have another suggestion. However, when the Mbale DC discovered that this suggestion, too, involved a densely populated area in the western foothills of Mount Elgon, he lost his temper: 'you called me a fool and insulted me very much indeed. And you called my religion of the Jews a bad one and also *a lying one* and then you drove me away saying "Leave my presence",' complained Kakungulu.[8]

This was not treatment Kakungulu was prepared to suffer. The land on Mount Elgon was really already his by right of conquest. In August 1922 he approached Ernest Haddon, now acting commissioner for the eastern province but in 1906 a junior official at Jinja:

*This is the following matter how I conquered Bukedi –*
I, B.S. Kakungulu captured Bukedi district [beginning] in 1895 my soldiers who came with me number 1246 and they had with their followers 4321 men in all totalling 5567 armed with 1246 guns. The cost to feed and look after them was £421500 and the cost of the arms and ammunition were £652300 ...

If suitable land was unavailable by exchange, Kakungulu would accept compensation in cash.[9]

Haddon felt that 'if a promise has been given it should be kept'.[10] The Assistant Secretary for Native Affairs at Entebbe thought otherwise. 'Most of his letter is nonsense. His occupation of Bukedi was a big freebooting expedition in which he & his followers enriched themselves – the suggestion of heavy out-of-pocket expenditure is absurd.'[11] The Land Officer at Entebbe agreed that there was little point in arguing with Kakungulu. 'At the same time were I in his place I should feel as he does; he thinks he has a right to all the land.'[12] After a search through the secretariat archives, Kakungulu was told that he already had all the land to which he had freehold title; Hayes Sadler had granted him leasehold rights to an additional 20 miles of land adjoining his Mbale estate 'for grazing and agricultural purposes', but leasehold should not be confused with freehold tenure; his pension from Busoga was higher than the one awarded to Stanislas Mugwanya, the former Regent of Buganda; Kakungulu should consider himself 'treated generously'.[13]

A copy of this statement was 'read over' to Kakungulu at Mbale in December 1922.[14] Kakungulu told the DC that he 'understood' it.[15] What he did not tell the Mbale DC was that earlier in 1922 Kabalega, the deposed king of Bunyoro, had also written to him. Kabalega was shortly returning from exile in the Seychelles and again asked Kakungulu to look after his children. 'Look after them properly, telling them what big people do – because they are still young and do not understand the days of the Europeans.' However, as in the Luganda version of Kabalega's letter the word used for 'days' was *naku*, and *naku* may also be translated into English as 'sorrows', the second half of his sentence was ambiguous; it also meant 'because they are still young and do not yet realize the sorrows caused by the Europeans.'[16] It was a nuance which Kakungulu must have appreciated poignantly.

In 1924 Kakungulu presented an expanded version of his petition to the British protectorate authorities. In it he listed not only his outstanding land claims but the costs of his conquests in northern and eastern Uganda: £1,156,440.[17] In a ledger commenced in 1920, Kakungulu provided the British magistrate at Mbale commissioned to enquire further into his case, with a breakdown of the wealth with which he had paid for his conquests:

October 5 1889 Kabaka Mwanga deputed me to fight Kalema and drive him out of his capital at Lunguja Rubaga. I raided the Arab camp and took away many tusks of which I received 537 (ivory frasilas).

The Kabaka gave me the chiefship of Mulondo where there were many elephants. I had many hunters. Of the ivory I received 2450 (ivory frasilas).

As regards cattle I first of all had many because Kabaka Mwanga sent me on the following wars – Sese, Buvuma, & Bunyoro. Until I came from Bugerere I had 13280 cattle of which I sold 8623. I also in these places raided the cattle of the Mukama (sc of Bunyoro), in Ganyi (Lango) at Lagonyi, the war at Kitosi, Ukererwe, Kabalasi, and Kavirondo.

Of copper bracelets (masinga) I received 1190
Of loads of cowries I received 252095
Of copper ornaments I received 2362500
Of hoes I received 4283670
In Bugerere I received ivory of 184
When I was Kimbugwe I had hunters who hunted elephants & I received 346.
The number of cloths and goats is unknown to me ...

Kakungulu states he expended all the property above received in buying arms and ammunition for his expeditions since 1895. He has no other documents to prove his claims except the above ledger.[18]

The magistrate had little difficulty in rubbishing Kakungulu's ledger. Besides being time-barred there was 'no real evidence' in it; it was based mostly on oral hearsay. On the other hand, there was documentary evidence for guns and money having been supplied by the British protectorate authorities in his support during the 1890s and 1900s.[19] Jarvis, acting Governor at Entebbe, agreed. Kakungulu's financial demands were 'fantastic'. The offer of kingship by Sir Harry Johnston was unfortunate, to be sure, but it could be regarded 'as having been rescinded as soon as it was made' upon Kakungulu's removal from office in 1902. If it had been honoured at the time, it would have been necessary to dishonour it later. 'The British Administration could not have permanently accepted an arrangement by which hundreds of thousands of natives of different tribes were to be handed over to a small alien ruling class' of other Africans.[20]

This was a theme to which the Mbale magistrate who investigated Kakungulu's claims in 1924, returned forty years later in an article in the *Uganda Journal*:

He and his followers behaved with all the arrogance of *herrenvolker* in the lands into which they managed to make their way. Crabtree's comment upon the fact that, with few exceptions, neither Kakunguru nor his followers took any real trouble to acquire the languages of those countries is evidence of only one of the many short-comings of Kakunguru and his followers, which disqualified them from being regarded as leaders of alien races amongst whom their lot was cast. There is no doubt that, thanks in no small measure to his superiority in weapons, Kakunguru became a successful *conquistador*, but it seems clear that both he and his followers lacked the qualifications and ability to set up a permanent kingdom in Bukedi.

Gray was appalled by Kakungulu's arrogance. 'He presented his many claims in a dignified manner as though he were in fact a king, demanding what was his right. With his tall, stately figure and his long beard, he certainly looked the part.' However, in Gray's view, 'the legendary Kakunguru was in no small measure the creation of Semei Lwakirenzi Kakungulu himself.'[21]

## 2

How just was this view? John Milner Gray, author of histories of The Gambia and Zanzibar and numerous articles on Uganda, was an unqualified believer in the benefits of British rule abroad. Behind his portrait of Kakungulu as an adventurer who only conquered Lango, Teso, and other parts of eastern Uganda for his own benefit, and who principally succeeded in this endeavour because of guns and ammunition supplied by the British protectorate authorities, lay the premiss that the occupants of these areas would have benefitted by having British DCs as their initial protectorate overlords. That premiss is hardly confirmed by the atrocities which occurred in areas north and east of the River Nile under direct British control *after* Kakungulu became president of the Busoga district council.[22] But, more critically, direct British administration of all the societies incorporated within the Uganda Protectorate at the end of the nineteenth and the start of the twentieth centuries was simply not an option on offer.

It was crucial during the European scramble for African colonial territory to establish an imperialist 'presence' within the various 'spheres of influence' as speedily as possible, and to do so at the lowest possible expense to European taxpayers. Almost everywhere in tropical Africa this meant doing deals with locally powerful groups.[23] In Uganda, British officials entered one such 'sphere' through a kingdom engaged in civil war and promptly attempted to play one faction in it against another. Eventually, British officials were forced to rely upon one particular faction for support: the Protestant Anglican grouping to which Semei Kakungulu belonged. With British assistance, this faction extended its power and influence both inside and outside Buganda. Under the Uganda Agreement of 1900 it was transformed into a landed aristocracy together with allies from remnants of earlier Roman Catholic and Muslim politico-religious groupings. By the 1920s the influence of this aristocracy within Buganda was under threat from a cash-cropping peasantry buying up land from the more improvident and unfortunate landlords, and by missionary high schools providing richer peasants' children with other avenues for advancement. Outside Buganda, Ganda chiefs were increasingly replaced by 'local people'. Kakungulu had certainly benefitted from British assistance during the 1890s and 1900s. But British officials undoubtedly benefitted materially from his aid too.

This the British surveyor of Kakungulu's estate at Batambogwe had admitted privately to his family:

> I could not help noticing his fatherly way with all his people. I should think he is a born leader & one whom his men look instinctively up to. It is a great pity that the Govt find it impossible to work with him for these big chiefs have an influence with the people which we can never hope to attain; in fact we live by bluff and did the chiefs refuse to help us – well! we could just hold the big stations but the development of the rest of the country would be impossible.[24]

In fact, it was possible for the protectorate government of Uganda to survive by replacing Kakungulu and other chiefs of his generation with a more subservient set of mission-schooled subordinates. But to whose advantage? Landlordism continued. When Kakungulu died, his estates were passed on to his sons.

> The grant formed part of the recognition for notable services accorded by an impoverished government at a time when native wealth and power were only capable of satisfaction in terms of land, which at the same time was almost the only commodity which the protectorate government then possessed. The promise of this grant was made known when Mbale was on the frontier of a turbulent, inaccessible and little-known district and had not yet been selected as a government station; when the establishment of a pseudo-feudal chieftainship by an alien native was looked upon as eminently fitting; when Kakunguru's place in the administrative machine was still indeterminable; and long before attention had been focussed on the disadvantages of native land-lordism.[25]

But, after Kakungulu's death, the same surveyor considered that part of his estate should be purchased for the wider community. 'We do not for a moment suggest that the Government should confiscate any portion of the reward which, it may be freely admitted, Kakungulu richly deserved. But we do suggest that the time has come when some portion of that reward should be commuted from land to money.'[26] It never was, because the British protectorate administration of Uganda never had enough money to spare.[27]

Wealth, one British official remarked, was not something which Kakungulu himself was interested in for its own sake.[28] His conquest of Bukedi was an adventure in an older, heroic mould. His followers were given rifles and ammunition, but not maxim guns; and guns were still used in tactics designed essentially for spearmen.[29] Kakungulu prohibited his followers from employing their weapons to accumulate the older kind of wealth, slaves, when he realized that these were objectionable to British officials, though existing slaves were retained unless ransomed or rescued by Christian missionaries.[30] But only towards the end of his life did Kakungulu fully appreciate the importance of money as the wealth of the new age.

'Money is prestige', the anthropologist Audrey Richards was told in the rural areas of Northern Rhodesia during the 1930s when the services of others, claimed earlier on other grounds, could now only be bought for cash.[31] Money was important enough in Uganda by the 1920s for Kakungulu to calculate his claims against the British protectorate in a special ledger, but not of overwhelming significance if its receipt contravened what he now considered to be God's will.

Shortage of cash was a constant constraint upon British policy in Uganda. Even when revenue from the cash-cropping peasantry finally freed it from imperial grants-in-aid during the First World War, the protectorate government continued to govern on the cheap. Missionary organizations continued to provide primary and secondary education, with the protectorate providing minimal education at tertiary level until the Second World War.[32] Chiefs recruited on 'merit coupled with education',[33] administered peasant societies whose pre-British cults were treated respectfully by British officials.

It is difficult to say how far this respect was dictated by desire to legitimate British overrule in customary terms, how far it was a reflex by officials now dependent upon Ugandan peasant revenues for payment of their salaries, how far it was inspired by a more idealistic egalitarianism and communalism opposed to grosser aspects of the slow but seemingly relentless capitalist penetration of the African interior at this time. In the present state of research, it is impossible to say. It is also at present difficult to say how far Uganda in the interwar era resembled nearby Northern Rhodesia and Nyasaland, where 'co-operation between ritual healers and customary rulers point to a kind of deep structure of customary authority' forming a 'grid' with which British colonial officials had to come to terms as much as more modern popular movements.[34] However, it should be clear from this study that in Uganda, as in British Central Africa, British officials did not have enough money or power to create a really modern state. 'Quite the contrary, it calls to mind medieval forerunners, in which the Church ... worked hand in glove with the state, bearing part of the cost, and ... law and administration formed part of the crazy quilt of local particularity.'[35]

Part of the particularity of Uganda concerned, and still concerns, its fragmentation between kingly and non-kingly societies. Here the surveyor of Kakungulu's final land claims (H.B.Thomas), if not the magistrate (Gray), considered that it was his political misfortune to have been born 50 years too late.[36] Nowadays, too, we realize that interrelationships between biological descent and a common culture are both complex and controversial. But in the late nineteenth and early twentieth centuries it was assumed by British officials in Uganda that culture *was* biology. An 'alien native' like Kakungulu was therefore an unacceptable king to them, particularly after the First World War when the protectorate administration was financially self-sufficient. Kakungulu no longer considered himself to be a Muganda by the 1920s. In colonial Uganda, as in early medieval Europe, 'The inhabitants of an area are likely to develop a common culture, particularly if they are governed as a unity, and they will then tend to breed with each other more than with outsiders.' However, in this matter 'the facts of biological descent in the distant past are probably less important than is the creation or maintenance of political solidarity in the present.'[37] Songs surviving from Kakungulu's kingdom in Bukedi indicate considerable intermarriage with local peoples during the 1900s, while his personal chronicler records his frustration at it being dismantled at the very moment it was becoming known as Bukungulu.[38] In retrospect, Bukungulu seems to have been not essentially dissimilar in mode of formation from earlier kingdoms in the interlacustrine region of East Africa.

## 3

Bukungulu failed amongst other reasons because, unlike Kahaya in the more westerly kingdom of Toro, Kakungulu was not in British eyes a prince. He was a monarch both made and unmade by themselves. It is tempting to interpret Kakungulu's repudiation of the Mamba clan in favour of the Babito of Koki as a belated attempt to acquire princely legitimacy for political reasons as well as a response to his wife Dimbwe's affair with his younger brother Sedulaka. But, as remarked at the start of this study, a number of Kakungulu's contemporaries were fathered by individuals other than those publicly acknowledged as such for most of their lives.[39] Martin Southwold, too, sees clanship disputes as evidence that life at Ganda village level is not so different from life in neighbouring societies in Uganda speaking comparable Bantu dialects but lacking kingship.[40] Kinship, not kingship, is the crucial issue. Kakungulu's repudiation of the Mamba clan in 1918 can therefore be interpreted as plausibly in terms of village factionalism as of high politics. The issue is patently one on which the outsider must remain agnostic. What is indisputable about it, however, is that it marked yet further evidence that Kakungulu no longer considered himself to be a Muganda.

That was what Kakungulu had remarked when the British authorities had tried to play upon ethnic patriotism in order to persuade him to part with land for Makerere College free of charge. Subsequently British officials sought compulsory purchase of Kakungulu's estate on Makerere hill through application of the Indian Act. Kakungulu fought this attempt to reduce further the value of his landholdings bitterly through the protectorate courts. In 1926 the case came to the High Court at Entebbe. Kakungulu had personally agreed a price of 100,000 shillings for the land with the Mbale DC. The protectorate authorities now repudiated this agreement and argued for a lower price by compulsory purchase. A key role was now played by the Mbale DC's interpreter, Kakembo. He told the High Court that Kakungulu had in fact earlier accepted that higher authority might vary the price he had negotiated with the Mbale DC. That destroyed the essence of Kakungulu's arguments, which had been based upon the sanctity of his agreement with the Mbale DC. Possibly Kakungulu might have fared better with a rather different argument in court, the Ganda newspaper *Matalisi* speculated. But it was 'terrible' (*kitalo*) for any landowner to be awarded only Shs 28,000 in compensation for such expensive land, the newspaper continued; particularly as Kakungulu's tenants would receive almost as much compensation from the protectorate authorities for displacement as Kakungulu himself.[41]

Subsequently, the 'Makerere land case' became important symbolically in the development of anti-British sentiment in Buganda, much as Kakungulu's final dismissal as Mbale county chief in 1923 had been paraded through the vernacular press as an earlier example of arbitrary British protectorate behaviour.[42] The ruling chiefs of Buganda thought otherwise. They were extremely nervous of Kakungulu and others who opposed the new health regulations, in case they brought Buganda into disrepute with Britain and led to withdrawal of the limited privileges enjoyed under the terms of the 1900 Agreement.[43] The British protectorate authorities did not need to worry excessively when the British colonial secretary wrote stating formally that Kakungulu's grievances were not real ones.[44] Kakungulu had indeed spent immense portions of his wealth in the British imperial interest, but they were not kinds of wealth quantifiable in current British coinage.

His religion, too, remained an embarrassment for the British protectorate authorities, as white Jews employed as mechanics, railway and water engineers and the like in the new protectorate towns chanced upon the Christian Jewish community near Mbale and told Kakungulu more about orthodox Judaism. As a result Kakungulu dropped many remaining Christian customs during the last two or three years of his life. According to Zakayo Mumbya, a man called Yusufu (Joseph, in English) was 'the first real European Jew who saw Kakungulu' at Kampala during the hearing of his Makerere land case.[45] 'It was Yusufu who told us that it was not right for real Jews to break bread like the Christians. So we stopped this custom. We also stopped the washing of feet when he came to us. We called ourselves the followers of Moses and followed those parts of the Holy Bible which he wrote.' Yusufu gave the Bayudaya of Gangama a Jewish Bible ('a big book which contained only the Old Testament'), but as it was written in Hebrew they could not use it. Yusufu probably also tried to teach Kakungulu how to kill a chicken correctly at the time of the Makerere land case. But, as Zakayo remarked, 'Kakungulu did not like his method, so we never adopted it as part of our religion'. A year later, just a few months before Kakungulu died, another European Jew whom Kakungulu had encountered during the Makerere land case visited Gangama. He 'told us that we should follow Moses completely; and after he came we stopped baptism and just followed circumcision.'[46] Nonetheless, though brought closer to international Jewry as a result of visits by European Jews, the Bayudaya community of Kakungulu's last years remained a mixture of both Christianity and Judaism, with faith in Christ remaining prominent in Kakungulu's beliefs.[47]

The increasing shift towards internationally recognized standards of Jewish practice amongst the Bayudaya at Gangama, before and after Kakungulu's death, paralleled the growing global respectability of another

Plate 18. *Members of the Bayudaya ('Jewish') community of Mbale, founded by Semei Kakungulu and photographed shortly before Idi Amin's persecution of 'all Zionist forces in Uganda'. Zakayo Mumbya (see p. 299) is fifth from the right, Samusoni Mugombe (see p. 304 note 47) third from left.* (Author's photograph)

separatist Christian movement in colonial Buganda: the Christian Ortho-dox Church of Reuben Spartas. This, after a brief flirtation with Garveyite congregations in southern Africa, went into communion with the Orthodox see of Constantinople and sent Ganda priests for training in Greece.[48] The Bayudaya of Gangama have still to send their first rabbi for training in Israel, Idi Amin's break with Israel and subsequent campaign against Zionist influence in Uganda preventing the first qualified candidate from taking up rabbinical studies there.[49] Otherwise the Bayudaya of Gangama, like the Orthodox Christians of Buganda, continue to reveal that mixture of intellectual independence and çoncern for ecclesiastical order which would appear to result both from study of the Luganda Bible by the first generation of literates in their country, and to be yet another reflection of 'core culture'.

The Bayudaya community of eastern Uganda never opposed British protectorate rule during Kakungulu's lifetime. That, at any rate, was the view of Bayudaya themselves in the 1960s:

What sorts of things did Kakungulu preach to you about?

He always preached to us about the same things: the commandments of God and the prophets.

Did he ever preach about politics (*bufuzi*)?

He had become disillusioned with politics, as he told us himself. He told us to seek first the kingdom of God and to forget about the things of earth and its rulers.

Did Kakungulu ever criticize Europeans in his sermons?

Never. He welcomed European Jews who came to visit him. He told us that the most important thing was for us to practise the true religion of the Bible, and not to accept what the missionaries had taught us without discernment.[50]

On 24 November 1928 Kakungulu died, most probably of pneumonia.[51] He was unattended by any doctor. A few days later he was given an official funeral. Ham Mukasa gave the eulogy, underlining the importance of his work for British imperialism in his earlier years, but not saying much about later ones. The Christian fighter who first came to fame in the kingdom of Buganda as 'the man who defeated the Muslims' had died a Jew in another part of the Uganda Protectorate.[52] Some government askaris were present at the funeral, and they fired a volley in Kakungulu's honour and memory. But there were not many askaris, and Ham Mukasa was too tactful to say why. The reminiscences of Yona Wajja, recorded by a Ganda policeman at Mbale and published in serial form in *Munno* newspaper, are less discreet, mentioning amongst other things Kakungulu's tendency in his very last years to refuse to move off the road whenever a British protectorate official's vehicle came along.[53] It was also Wajja who sat upon my verandah in Mbale municipality thirty-five years later and told me that Kakungulu's was a story that should be told.

'The reward of the warrior is honour', Jasper Griffin notes in a study of Homer and ancient Greece, 'but the demands of individual honour will often conflict with those of the community'.[54] During his lifetime, Kakungulu's quest for honour conflicted with the demands of a number of communities, both ones already existing and ones progressively 'imagined' as his career unfolded. In the very disturbed conditions immediately before, during, and after the British imposition of a protectorate, new groupings of a politico-religious kind crystallized and the translation of the Christian Bible into Luganda ultimately led Kakungulu to revise his ideas about the Christian God's honour and glory too. During the same generation a slave-based mode of production was undermined and replaced by cash-cropping lords and peasants in a colonial state, owning property on quasi-freehold terms in some parts of it, and enjoying 'customary tenures' in others. Ethnic divisions emerged mirroring these socio-political transformations and building them up further upon the complex mosaic of cultural symbols highlighted by the conquests of Kakungulu and his contemporaries.

Conflict continues today over these matters. *Weekly Topic* newspaper denounces Kakungulu as 'a mercenary of the British, a thief and a traitorous man',[55] while another contemporary Ugandan writer attacks him for betraying Buganda by hunting *Kabaka* Mwanga 'like a wild beast'.[56] Controversy shows no sign of ending where Semei Kakungulu and the creation of Uganda are concerned. History is here the continuation of conflict by other means.

Apolo Kagwa, Kakungulu's great rival, fell out finally with British protectorate officials over beer-permits at Mengo–Kampala. Opposition to his long tenure of the Chief ministership of the Buganda kingdom had been building up from King Daudi Chwa and the new missionary-educated chiefs since the early 1920s, and British administrators exploited this opposition deftly.[57] In August 1926 Kagwa was forced to retire, and within six months he was dead.[58] His funeral was much grander than Kakungulu's. Many British administrators attended it, together with 'an immense gathering' of between six and seven thousand Africans. A choir from Budo School, which Kagwa had supported so generously, sang his favourite hymn. A leading CMS missionary gave the sermon. In it he described Apolo Kagwa as 'a great and far-seeing African statesman' and exhorted the vast congregation to continue supporting western medical and veterinary practices.[59] Posthumously, however, Kakungulu's career has attracted greater public attention in Uganda than Kagwa's. This is surely because, whereas Apolo Kagwa's energies were concentrated so largely upon Buganda, Kakungulu's directly affected other areas of the protectorate where popular values were frequently so different from those then dominant in Buganda. On the eve of independence from Britain in 1962, a committee of newly empowered politicians expressed regret that the turbulent area of Karamoja in the extreme north-eastern corner of Uganda 'did not come into contact with Kakungulu's "civilising" influence which did so much to subdue and settle the other tribes . . . and to establish close administration so essential to maintenance of law and order'.[60] Nonetheless, the people of Budaka still refused to allow the plaque commemorating his achievements in this realm to be attached to its plinth.

# Notes

1. 'He bought the estate from Mwanga and Apolo Kagwa sent a Muganda who measured out boundaries. Kakunguru states that there was no question of his purchasing any particular number of acres; he bought a piece of land without numerical reference to its size and this Muganda "fundi" delineated it': Cox to PCEP, 31 October 1921, EPMP 148/8, ESA.
2. DC Bukedi to PCEP, 13 December 1920, EPMP 6/13/112, ESA.
3. Cox to PCEP, 8 June 1921, file 928/40, Mbale District Commissioner's Archives (MA).
4. PCEP to Land Officer, Entebbe, 9 April 1921, file 928/40, MA.
5. LO to PCEP, 5 May 1921, file 928/40, MA.
6. Cox to PCEP, 25 June 1921, file 928/40, MA.
7. PCEP to Land Officer, 9 April 1921, copy, MA.
8. Files 928/40–2 in the Mbale Archives are full of such suggestions.
9. Kakungulu to Governor of Uganda, encl. Haddon to ASNA, 10 October 1922, SMP 1760/08, ESA.
10. *Ibid.*
11. Scott, 24 October 1922, SMP 1760/08, ESA.

12. LO, 28 October 1922, SMP 1760/08, ESA.
13. Acting CS to PCEP, 6 November 1922, copy, SMP 1760/08, ESA.
14. Minute by A.C.W., 4 December 1922, on Acting CS, 6 November 1923 (copy also in SMP 1760/08, ESA), 928/42, MA.
15. *Ibid.*
16. John Kabalega to B.S. Kakungulu, 15 March 1922, copy with Kibuga manuscript; seen by courtesy of Ibrahim Ndaula of Nkoma, Mbale. For their part, British officials were worried lest Kabalega and his sons proved 'dangerous' upon their return, and Kabalega stayed in a house of Kakungulu at Jinja rather than live immediately again in Bunyoro (PCEP to ASNA, 1 December 1922, SMP 77/21a, Jinja District Archives). A letter of 6 August 1923 from Kakungulu in the Mbale Archives ('Native Affairs: Mbale Township') indicates that he did help Kabalega financially with several of his children's education. Kabalega died at Jinja in that year.
17. Kakungulu to Governor of Uganda, 17 September 1924. Copies of this petition and enclosures are to be found in PRO/CO/536/135; SMP 1760/08 in the Entebbe Secretariat Archives; and, most fully, among the Gray Papers in the RCS Library, London.
18. 'Kakungulu's claims', notes in J.M. Gray's handwriting in RCS.
19. Gray to CS, Uganda, 26 December 1924, copy, RCS.
20. Jarvis to London, 3 April 1925, CO/536/135, PRO.
21. J.M. Gray, 'Kakunguru in Bukedi', *Uganda Journal* 27 (1963), pp. 54, 31.
22. See M. Twaddle, 'Decentralized violence and collaboration in early colonial Uganda', in eds A. Porter and R. Holland, *Theory and Practice in the History of European Expansion Overseas: Essays in Honour of Ronald Robinson* (London 1988), pp. 71–85; 'Politics in Bukedi', Ph.D. dissertation, University of London, 1967), Chapters 9 & 10.
23. See J. Lonsdale, 'The European scramble and conquest in African history' in eds R. Oliver and G.N. Sanderson, *Cambridge History of Africa* (Cambridge 1985), Vol. 6, pp. 682–766; and ed. M.Twaddle, *Imperialism, the State and the Third World* (London 1992), pp. 1–22.
24. H.B. Thomas to father, 24 June 1913, H.B. Thomas Papers, box 1, RCS Library.
25. HBT to CS, draft enclosure with HBT to PCEP, 18 June 1929.
26. *Ibid.*
27. Increasing costs of land at Mbale made the matter still more difficult: 'in 1931 the whole estate was valued at . . . just under £1 an acre while in 1947 the Registered Proprietor values it at £20 an acre', G.M. Gibson to CS, 15 May 1947, file on 'Kakunguru's Estate' at Lands and Surveys Office, Mbale.
28. Perryman, 'History', p. 7, in SMP/2/29/06, ESA.
29. See above pp. 48, 150.
30. This was clear by the time he reached Bugerere; in Bukedi, followers caught seizing slaves were handed back to the peoples affected for punishment.
31. A.I. Richards, *Land, Labour and Diet in Northern Rhodesia* (London 1939), p. 220.
32. O.W. Furley and T. Watson, *A History of Education in East Africa* (New York 1978), pp. 95–118, 186–208.
33. L.P. Mair, *An African People in the Twentieth Century* (London 1934), p. 198.
34. K.E. Fields, *Revival and Rebellion in Colonial Central Africa* (Princeton 1985), p. 260.
35. *Ibid.*, p. 274.
36. H.B. Thomas, '*Capax imperii* – the story of Semei Kakunguru', *Uganda Journal* 6 (1939), p. 136.
37. S. Reynolds, *Kingdoms and Communities in Western Europe 900–1300* (Oxford 1984), p. 284.
38. E. Kibuga, *History* [unpublished ms in possession of Ibrahim Ndaula of Mbale], p. 23.
39. See above, p. 16.
40. This is an argument of his Cambridge Ph.D. thesis, based on fieldwork during the 1950s.
41. 'Omusango gwa Kakungulu', *Matalisi*, 17 November 1926 [copy in MUL]. Summaries of civil case 127 of 1926, B.S. Kakungulu v. Attorney-General of Uganda, are in SMP 8586/77, ESA, LOMP 3160/14 at Lands & Surveys, Mbale, and SMP 1760/08, ESA. See also Jarvis to London, 21 April 1926, copy in SMP 1760/08, ESA.
42. 'Ebigambo bya Owekitibwa Gavuna byeyogera nga agoba B.S. Kakungulu mu Saza

lye Mbale', *Munyonyozi*; undated cutting in Miti Papers, box 1, MUL.
43. M. Twaddle, 'The religion of Malaki revisited', Social Science Conference, Makerere, 1968–9; much of the relevant correspondence is in SMP 4219, ESA.
44. CO to Entebbe, 15 June 1925, and Entebbe to Kakungulu, 24 July 1925; copies in SMP 1760/08, ESA.
45. Zakayo Mumbya, interview, 13 September 1965. This took place at an open session of the Bayudaya community in the synagogue at Gangama, with sect members intervening from time to time.
46. *Ibid.*
47. This is my impression and was the testimony of Samusoni Mugombe, who became Mumbya's rival for leadership of the Bayudaya community. After Kakungulu's death the Bayudaya community divided into those wishing to retain a toehold within Christianity, and those wanting to break ties with Christianity completely. Arye Oded, an Israeli diplomat in Uganda during the 1960s, persuaded the community to reunite and later published 'The Bayudaya of Uganda', *Journal of Religion in Africa* 6 (1974), pp. 167–86.
48. See F.B. Welbourn, *East African Rebels* (London 1961), pp. 77–102.
49. I last visited the Bayudaya near Mbale in 1986, after Idi Amin had forced them to break contacts with Israel but before any ties had been reestablished again with Israel.
50. Zakayo Mumbya, 13 September 1965.
51. PCEP to CS, 28 November 1928, SMP 1760/08, ESA; *Uganda Herald*, 30 November 1928.
52. Ham Mukasa, 27 November 1928; *Ebifa mu Buganda*, pp. 45–8.
53. Yona Wajja's memoirs were serialized in *Munno* as 'Ebyafayo bya Omugenzi Omwami Simei Lwakirenzi Kakungulu' in 1932–4; the fullest surviving set is at the White Fathers' archives in Rome.
54. J. Griffin, *Homer* (Oxford 1980), p.43.
55. Quoted by Apolo Nsibambi, p. 229 in ed. K. Rupesinghe, *Conflict Resolution in Uganda* (Oslo, London and Athens, Ohio, 1989).
56. S. Lwanga-Lunyïigo, in *ibid.*, p.26.
57. M. Twaddle, 'The Bakungu chiefs of Buganda under British colonial rule, 1900–1930', *Journal of African History*, 10 (1969), p. 315.
58. K. Ingham, *The Making of Modern Uganda* (London 1958), p. 168. Kagwa's protest to the British government is reprinted in part in D. A. Low, *The Mind of Buganda* (London, 1971), pp. 70–3.
59. *Uganda News*, 4 March 1927.
60. *Report of the Karamoja Security Committee under the Chairmanship of B.K. Bataringaya* (Entebbe: Government Printer, 1961), p. 7.

# Index

Amin, Idi, 7

Ansorge, British official, 107, 112-13, 114

Arabs, fighting with Muslims in Buganda (1889), 53; burnt alive, 55

armies, Ganda, 13-14, 97; Nyoro, 95; Kagungulu's in Bukedi, 151-4

Ashe, Robert, CMS missionary, 78-9, 90, 107, 110

Asian traders, 223, 229-30, 262-3

atrocities, against K's family in Koki, 43; against Muslims in Buganda, 55; against Roman Catholics there, 72, against Iteso people, 142

*baddu* (slaves), 119

Bagisu, Bagishu, Bageso, *see* Gisu

Bahaya chiefdoms, 37

*bairu* (agriculturalists or grain-eaters) in Nkore, 42, 51

Bajja battle, 44-5, 48, 59

*bakafiri*, 'pagans', 47

*bakopi* (free cultivators, peasants), 60

*bakungu* (county chiefs or 'big men'), 9-10, 33-4, 37

Balimwogerako, praise name for K, 91, Ganda fort, 154-5

*balubaale* (gods), 6-9

*balyabulo* (grain eaters), 51-5

*balyangege* (fish eaters), 51

bananas, food of Baganda, 8; none in Ketosh country, 116; plenty on Mount Elgon, 139, at Mbale, 183-4

*banubi* (Nubians, or Sudanese soldiers recruited by Lugard), 71-2, 101

Banyala, people of Bugerere, 121-2, 152

baptism, of K, 80; Malakite views, 266-9, 270-2, 283, 285

*barusura* (musketeers of Bunyoro), 95-6

*basawo* (healers, medical doctors), 268, 273-4

Baskerville, Revd G.K., 117, 265, 270-1, 285, 279

*bataka* (clan leaders), 10-11, 133 (hence *butaka*, family-owned land)

Batambogwe hill (Busoga), 245-8, 280, 296

*batongole* (specialist administrative chiefs), 11, 28, 33-4, 37-8, 59, 125, 225

battles, Bajja, 44-5, 48, 59; Bukaleba, 124-5; Bunkabira, 52-3; Bulwanyi, 82; Lungujja, 50-5; Matale, 43-4, 48, 52; Mawuki, 44-5, 48; Mengo, 110; Ndese, 44; Nsambya, 78-9

Bavuma islanders of Lake Victoria, expedition against, 88-91

*Bayudaya* (Jews), 280-8, 292, 299-301

*Bazungu* (Europeans), 201

beer drinking, CMS more tolerant regarding, 80; Kakungulu attacks excess in Bukedi, 201; Malakite reservations, 282

Bell, Hesketh, British Commissioner and governor, 213-7, 230-1, 236-41, 262

Berkeley, Ernest, British Cmr, 120-1

Berlin conference on Africa, 75

Bernt Hansen, Holger, ix, 86, 131, 219

Bijabiira, man of K, 142, 197, 211

Bina, Yairo, man of K, beaten by Apolo Kagwa, 114-5, 197

Bismarck, German Chancellor, 69-70

Bitege, Leubeni, man of K, 141-2, 164, 199

Bito clan of Koki, 15-18, 287, 298

blood-brotherhood ceremonies, 6, 27, 33, 41

Boyle, Alexander, 198-201, 293-4, 214-6, 222-8, 240-1

Brussels General Act, 73, 271

Buckley, Revd T.R., CMS missionary, 166, 176, 180

Budaka, viii, 161-8, 301

Budo school, printing press sold to Kate, 282, and Apolo Kagwa, 302

*bufuzi* (administration), 162, (politics), 300-1

Buganda, kingdom, growth of, 1, 29, 102

Bugerere awarded to K, 105, 117-26

Bukedi, 14, 138-9, 265; K's kingdom there called Bukungulu, 298

Bulingugwe island, 45-51, 56, 58, 72

Bulwanyi, battle, 82

Bunkabira, battle of (1889), 52-3

Bunyaga, Ganda chief, 6, 11, 20; shelters K, 43

Bunyoro, kingdom, 1-4, 41, 60, 95-102; *see also*

# Index

pastoralist lifestyles, 1, 20, 278
Paulo Kibi, informant, 7, 17
pawns, 151
pax Britannica, 264
peasantry, creation of, 101-2; food free to K,
    252; sicknesses of, 277; buyers of mailo land
    in Buganda, 295; rescues UP from debt to
    Britain, 292, 301
Peel, J., 25
peoples of Uganda: Ganda, 5-15; Gwere, 148-9;
    Iteso, 142, 202; Jopadhola, 160, 205-9; Koki,
    1-7; Kumam, 119; Langi, 119-41; Soga,
    221-56; see also Gisu
Perham, Margery, 102
Perryman, P.W., British official, 278, 280, 288
Peters, Carl, 69-70, 73-5
Pilkington, George, CMS missionary, on battle,
    of Mengo, 72-3, 97, 123, 125, 265
Pirouet, L., 273
plague, 269-70, 277
plundering expeditions, role of in Buganda, 1, 4,
    13-14, 47
politico-religious groupings, 295, 301; during
    Buvuma campaign, 94; after Muslim
    rebellion of 1893, 94; effect on katikiroship,
    108, 173-4; compared with religion of
    Malaki and Bayudaya, 284-5; see also
    Catholicism, factionalism, Islam and
    Protestantism
polygyny, 80
Portal, Sir G., British commr, 83-4, 93, 96
pox Britannica, 264
praise poetry and songs, 78, 111-12, 161; see also
    Kakungulu's names
predatory pigs, 228
Prins, G., 272-3
prostitutes, 276
Protestantism, 23, in Busoga, 235, 253, 269; see
    also politico-religious groupings
Purvis, Revd J.B., CMS missionary, 186, 205,
    209-10, 211

Queen Mother (Namasole), 11, 33
Queen Sister (Lubuga), 11; K marries, 105-7
Queen Victoria, compared to Caesar, 104

railways, 223, 237-8, 250-1
Rakai, 5
Ranger, T., 218
reading, 284; see also literacy
rebellions – imaginary against Britain, by
    Mudiima, 112-3, actually by Mwanga II,
    123, by Nubian/Sudanese soldiers, 124-6,
    possibly by K, 113, 182-3; actually by
    Jopadhola in 1905, 205-9
Richards, Audrey, 297
Rigby, P., and Fred Lule, 274
rinderpest, 1, 264
Robinson, Ronald and Gallagher, John, x, 68,
    148
Rumbold, Captain, British soldier, 147
religion, traditional in Buganda, 8-9, in Busoga,
    280, 292; British respect for, 297; see also
    Bayudaya, Catholicism, factionalism, Islam,
    Malaki, Protestantism and Spartas
revolution, Christian or Muslim, 152, 266; see
    also class struggle and monetization
Roscoe, J., CMS missionary and anthropologist,
    94, 113, 265, 268
Rowe, J., ix, translations quoted and

forthcoming, 61n22
Rubaga as well as Cathedral at Ganda capital,
    166
rumours, 39, 230, 232-3, 236, 248

sabbath, Malakite view of, 267, 282
Sanderson, G.N., viii, 68, 83-4
Scramble for Africa, nature of, 295
Sebowa, Alexis, chief and and RC leader, 45,
    78-9, 81; parentage, 16
Sebwato, Nikodemo, 41, 43, 45, 49, 58, 79, 92;
    threat to Apolo Kagwa's position, 110-1
Sebwato, Mulisi, 81-2, 127-8
Sedulaka Kyesirikidde, brother of K, 6, 23, 287
Sekibobo (county chief of Kyagwe), 122
Selim Bey, Nubian leader, 91-2
Semakokiro, king of Buganda, 33-4
Semfuma, Tomasi, 79, 124
Semukasa, Tomasi, 79-80, 124
Semuwemba, father (disputed), of K, 4-6, 15, 42
Serwanga, brother of K, 42-3
Sese (or Sesse) islands in Lake Victoria, 54-7,
    882
sicknesses, of man and God, 275; Malakite view
    of, 268; Biblical perspectives, 273
slavery, 1-7, 12-13, 14, 19, 20, 28, 34-5, 59-60;
    during Buvuma campaign, 90-1, 93, 95;
    Protestant chiefs' decl. against, 100-2; none
    seized in Bugerere, 119; in Koki, 1, 43;
    territory granted in place of by British, 102;
    'our wealth' (Zimbe), 91, 122, 151, 174, 179,
    296
sleeping sickness, 238, 264, 275
smallpox, 264; in Ganda army (1894), 94, 100
Soga chief replaced by K, 88; chiefs v. K in
    Busoga (1898), 126-7
Soga people, 221-56
Southall, Aidan, and Gutkind, Peter, 277
Southwold, Martin, 6
Spartas, Reuben, Orthodox Church of, 299-300
spear warfare, in Nkore and Zululand, 42
Speke, British explorer, 66
Spire, Frederick, valet and water transport
    officer, 96; administrator, 246, 248-53, 255-6
spirit medium (emmandwa omw'emmandwa), 6, 276
Stanley, H.M. 66-8
Steinhart, Ed, 42, 97-9
Stokes, Charles (or Charlie), trader, 44, 74
Sudanese troops and Muslim rebellion (1893),
    91-2; v. Bunyoro (1893-4), 97, 114; v.
    Ketosh (1895), 115-16; themselves rebel
    (1897), 124; medical care, 274; see also
    banubi
Supreme Being, 273
Swahili language, 26, 200

Tarrant, British official, 145, 147
tax revenue, reason for joining K, 174, 167, 171,
    174, 177, 202, 234; K supposedly obstructs
    at Budaka, 180; a cause of the Jopadhola
    rising of 1905, 205
Tebukoza, 4; Sekibobo, 22-3, 27, 40-1, 45
Tekiwagala, Samwiri, man of K and Malakite
    leader, 121-2, 159, 164-5, 266-8
Ternan, Trevor, British official and soldier, 122,
    138
Thomas, H.B., surveyor, 247, 296-7
Tompkins, British official, 214
Toro, kingdom reestablished in 1891, 96
tribalism, Bayudaya, community as form of, 228;